The Contours of Masculine Desire

THE CONTOURS
OF MASCULINE DESIRE

Romanticism and the Rise of Women's Poetry

MARLON B. ROSS

New York   Oxford
OXFORD UNIVERSITY PRESS
1989

Oxford University Press

Oxford New York Toronto
Delhi Bombay Calcutta Madras Karachi
Petaling Jaya Singapore Hong Kong Tokyo
Nairobi Dar es Salaam Cape Town
Melbourne Auckland

and associated companies in
Berlin Ibadan

Published by Oxford University Press, Inc.,
200 Madison Avenue, New York, New York 10016

Oxford is a registered trademark of Oxford University Press

Library of Congress Cataloging-in-Publication Data
Ross, Marlon Bryan, 1956–
The contours of masculine desire :
romanticism and the rise of women's poetry / Marlon B. Ross.
p. cm. Bibliography: p. Includes index. ISBN 0-19-505791-0
1. Romanticism. 2. Poetry—Women authors—History and criticism.
3. Desire in literature. 4. Feminist literary criticism.
I. Title. PN603.R67 1989 809'.9145—dc20 89-9436 CIP

9 8 7 6 5 4 3 2 1

Printed in the United States of America
on acid-free paper

For my Parents

Acknowledgments

The idea for this book was born in the classroom, and so it is appropriate that I thank all of those students, graduate and undergraduate, who, through their refreshing curiosity, helped to sustain my interest in this project. Since this is a book that views intellectual influence as a fortuitous phenomenon to be embraced, it is also appropriate that I thank James K. Chandler, who, first as a teacher and now as a friend, has been more than generous with his time, energy, knowledge, and support, and who, in both his conversation and his criticism, has always more to teach than I can possibly learn. I would also like to express my gratitude to all those colleagues, former and present, who have always been willing to listen and respond in good faith. I am especially grateful to Stacey Olster, who took time out of her busy summer schedule to read the first chapter, who helped me to tighten my sprawling prose, and who helps me keep everything in perspective through her good sense and good humor. Alan Nadel read an early version of the first chapter; he and Michael Yetman talked with me about this project when it was still an inchoate idea in my head. A true friend in need, Alvin Snider volunteered, before I could gather the audacity to ask him, to wade through the whole manuscript for its final revision. By offering insights that could have come only from his unusual breadth and depth of learning, he nudged me closer to the historicist conception of the project toward which I originally aspired.

A summer grant from the Research Foundation of The State University at Stony Brook provided crucial financial support and time when they were most needed. Indiana University Press permitted me to reprint as a part of Chapter 1 my article from *Romanticism and Feminism,* a timely collection of essays edited by Anne K. Mellor.

Although these and many others have motivated, encouraged, supported, and shared in my desire to write this book, only I, of course, and the limits of my knowledge, can be responsible for the limitations revealed in the contours of my discourse.

Contents

The Contours of Masculine Desire

Introduction:
The Premises of Desire

Romanticism is not simply a historical period that includes any writer publishing work between two arbitrary dates; it is—or it has become—a complex of values and beliefs, a set of structural, thematic, and generic tendencies, an approach to the world with its own assumptions and aims. It has become an ideology, with all the self-contradictory diversity entailed in ideological patterning. As critics have pointed out, romantic poets write from a position and a perspective that it would be impossible for a woman living during the time to take. This is not just because of the cultural stereotypes of gender roles during the period—though such roles are crucial determinants[1]—but also because romanticism is historically a masculine phenomenon. Romantic poeticizing is not just what women cannot do because they are not expected to; it is also what some men do in order to reconfirm their capacity to influence the world in ways sociohistorically determined as masculine. Even though women begin to write publicly and to be known by the reading public as writers during what we have come to call the romantic period, critics have not charted their influence in the "high" poetic genres for which that period has become critically acclaimed. This does not mean that women had no palpable or traceable literary influence on poetry during the early nineteenth century. Indeed, one of the crucial insights that feminist criticism has taught us is to question the *absence* of women as active subjects in any phenomenon, for that reputed absence may be an effect of the fear of their actual presence. Historians have always acknowledged that there were women poets writing in the early nineteenth century, but we have purged the real and pervasive presence of these women either by categorizing them as extremely minor romantics or by considering them so uninfluential that they need only be mentioned or, in most cases, not mentioned at all.

The canon of romantics remains wholly male at a time when rediscovered women writers are finding more or less comfortable homes in many other periods and genres. Although Dorothy Wordsworth and Mary Shelley are occasionally considered female romantic writers, their inclusion in the romantic canon proves extremely problematic. If one of romanticism's definitive characteristics is the self-conscious search for poetic identity, how can Wordsworth, who tended not to conceive of herself as a poet, be considered a "romantic"?[2] Dorothy's journal entries are rarely rewritten as poems—the way we see William rewriting his and her entries or Percy Shelley rewriting his; her journal insights are rarely offered to the public and are seldom transformed into the poetic conventions considered at the time to be the highest and most honorable kind of elocution. Mary Shelley's writing, besides being in "prose" (the "lower" form of expression), dissents with romanticism, and Mary's loving devotion to the editing of Percy's poems displays a confidence in his work that she does not seem to have in her own.[3] The comparison of these two women is instructive. Dorothy certainly does not receive the kind of encouragement from William that Mary receives from Percy; however, in both cases the women are overshadowed (and overshadow themselves) by the men they see as poetic geniuses, and in both cases the woman intertwines admiration for the poet's genius with devotion and love supposedly not predicated on genius alone. It is impossible to disentangle the woman's literary and intellectual modesty from the specific emotions each feels for her beloved. Both women must sense to what extent these men need a loving other, and an other whose interest is constituted more by a capacity to listen than a tendency to converse, whose concern is defined more as devotion than as friendly rivalry, as difference rather than sameness. It is no mistake that these women are written into the men's poems as extensions of themselves (Dorothy in "Tintern Abbey" and Mary in the Dedication to the *Revolt of Islam,* for instance), but when these men need conversants and rivals, they turn to their fellow poets, not the women they are closest to (as William turns to Coleridge in *The Prelude* and Percy turns to Byron in *Julian and Maddalo*). Even when the female herself is a writer, she is seen as creative in a different sense, in a way that can be felt as less threatening to the male poet. Because her gender "naturally" places her in a different arena, he can de-emphasize any competitive urge between them and instead appropriate her difference as a source of inspiration and as leverage for his will to write. The male–female relation predicated by society and nature, as the poet understands such, is one of complementarity rather than contestation, so that if women must be seen as competing at all for poetic mastery, they are seen as competing with other women in their own arena, not with men. Romanticist critics have taken this logic a step farther. By considering these two female writers as supreme representatives of the feminine arena of romanticism, we promote the idea that romanticism is the standard according to which all poets must be judged; we reconfirm the assumption that women necessarily compete in a different (complementary) arena while simultaneously we make their sphere a mirror image (an obverse imitation) of the original masculine sphere. Women writers of the period inevitably become partial dissenters—like parishioners who are dissatisfied with the local church but do not have the resources to set up their own, or in attempting to set up their own, discover that the local church is actually universal and inescapable.

Our critical acceptance of Dorothy Wordsworth and Mary Shelley as female (minor) representatives of romanticism is troubling not just because their relation to romanticism as an ideology is extremely problematic, but also because they represent women who are extremely timid about their own authorship. I would suggest that their interjection in the romantic canon is more a result of their kin relation to male romantics than a result of their "romantic" tendencies. We certainly need to understand the influence of these women on romanticism, but as long as such feminine influence is limited to wives and sisters who write hesitantly, or who write under the glaring eyes of self–professed great men, that influence will always be viewed as secondary and marginal at best. Critics will be able to say that Wordsworth is actually more important for what she nurtures in her "greater" brother than what she is unable to nurture in herself. Like the romantics, who make women (and the world) an extension of themselves, romanticist critics have made women writers of the period an extension of male romanticism. Such reasoning also makes it easier to ignore the pervasive, fertile, and powerful influence of women poets during the "romantic" period, allowing us to keep intact the idea that romanticism can serve to describe the whole period by equating the male romantic poets with all the literature of the time. Dorothy Wordsworth and Mary Shelley become tokens within the romantic canon, excusing us from confronting the reality of one of the most important literary phenomena of British literary history, the rise of women's poetry toward the end of the eighteenth century. Furthermore, it prevents us from considering the ideological limits of romanticism in history and thus keeps us from establishing some critical and historical continuity between contemporaneous romantic and nonromantic writers, and some critical and historical distance between ourselves and romantic ideology. There is, however, an alternative way to view women writers of the time, a way that allows us to understand the female writers as subjects in their own right, a way that begins to trace the full range and depth of feminine influence while not marrying women writers to their male counterparts.

This alternative entails the two projects intertwined within this study: 1) We must seek to place romanticism within history, rather than taking it as definitive of history. We have to ask how the romantics fit within a larger historical, literary, and cultural context, and we have to begin to flesh out the other crucial literary strains that were competing with and joining with "romanticism" during the period. In this study, I have approached this project by showing how other literary traditions within the same period help to make romanticism what it becomes. I think it is especially important to examine the tradition of feminine poetry that emerges during the period, not as a minor tradition feebly mirroring romanticism, but as a real force in its own right shaping romanticism as it shapes itself. 2) This means that we must move outside of romantic ideology—not an easy task, since we have inherited the premises of that ideology as the basis for our own critical establishment. In order to understand the early nineteenth-century tradition of feminine poetry, we must stop thinking as belated romantics, and try to think ourselves into other traditions, now obscure and alien to us. The difficulty of this project is indicated by the fact that we do not even have a literary term for this important movement, the rise of feminine poetry. We do not have a term for the group of women writing during the nineteenth century who see themselves, and are seen by their contemporaries as a new literary breed. As we recover their place in history, we must be sure not to examine them in isolation. Too wary of wedding them erroneously to the romantic movement, we may stray too far in the other direction and forget their complex interrelations with romantic discourse. We must get "inside" romantic ideology. We must see how that ideology is shaped from "external" influences, one of the most important being the feminine poets. We must get "inside" the ideology of these feminine poets. We must see how their ideology is shaped by the sway of romanticism and its eventual canonization. I hope that this quadruple focus creates a dialectic that is fruitful both for history and literary analysis.[4]

The female poets who publish so successfully in the early nineteenth century necessarily wrestle with similar conflicts as their male counterparts, but their gender is so crucial a factor in their cultural and literary experience that it alters the effect of shared social conditions and turns these writers into a distinct class, with its own ideological patterning, rather than merely a species of the overarching class of romantic poets. As we shall see, the writers and readers of the time are extremely conscious of this new class of poets, and they are forced to cope with the concept of the *male* poet not as a universal, but as a particularity. They, too, tend to see the woman poet as a deviation, a special case, but the pressure of present circumstances discourages them from simply attaching this new breed of writers to their male predecessors as an extension. The recovery of these feminine voices, then, is also a way of *localizing* romanticism, demonstrating its real limits in history by examining its *limited* influence on individuals who lived within its purview.

In their now classic study *The Madwoman in the Attic,* Gilbert and Gubar point out the appropriateness of Harold Bloom's gendered poetics for the patriarchal nature of the Western literary tradition. They examine the various ways in which Western writers have used the "metaphor of literary paternity" and how this patriarchal conception of writing has reduced women "to *mere* properties, to characters and images imprisoned in male texts because generated solely . . . by male expectations and designs" (12). In her excellent study *Women Writers and Poetic Identity* (which appeared a year after *Madwoman*), Margaret Homans demonstrates how three female poets (Dorothy Wordsworth, Emily Brontë, and Emily Dickinson), confronted with a hegemonic masculine tradition, attempt to write within that tradition while reshaping it for the feminine voice. Coincidentally making an argument similar to Gilbert and Gubar's, Homans points out, speaking specifically about the masculinist romantic tradition, how "the powerful self is inextricable from the use of efficacious language, since the powerful self is so often the poet, or a poet. He constructs the strong self from his own strong language" (33). Both studies lay fertile ground for a reexamination of the historical manifestations of self–imaging in literature as well as how such self–imaging has been based on the gendered socialization of poets. Building on these studies, we must flesh out the myriad ways in which the poetic vocation has been sociohistorically defined as distinctively masculine and how such definition historically has affected not only women's attempts to speak within the context of an alienating tradition but also men's attempts to speak a universal and holistic language in the context of a gendered tradition that alienates them, as well, from the whole.

In order to situate romanticism within history, we must go beneath it to the invisible machinery of desire that fuels its efficiently operating ideology. Because it is impossible to re-create a historical moment or to generalize about the production of desire without relying on some tenable but unprovable premises (not the least of which is the idea that a historical moment can be critically reconstructed), I want to examine briefly those premises that ground my discourse by attempting to delineate their function and significance without trying to prove their veracity. Throughout this study, I employ four crucial terms that may need some definition beforehand: desire, ideology, masculine, and feminine. Although I shall provide stipulative definitions here, all of these terms should be viewed as local, applying to the specific period of history under examination. And though the terms themselves are necessarily problematically general and generally contested, as I use them in the study, they should acquire increasing semantic precision. In a sense, this study is an attempt to define the terms by analyzing how they operate in the literary processes of one particular sociohistorical moment. Nonetheless, I feel obliged to provide some preliminary all-purpose hooks to hang these terms on, and in so doing simultaneously to characterize the major premises that have enabled me to link these terms in a single objective.

In *Anti-Oedipus,* Gilles Deleuze and Félix Guattari attempt to give "desire" a historical face: "We maintain that the social field is immediately invested by desire, that it is the historically determined product of desire, and that libido has no need of any mediation or sublimation, any psychic operation, any transformation, in order to invade and invest the productive forces and the relations of production. *There is only desire and the social, and nothing else"* (*Anti-Oepidus: Capitalism and Schizophrenia* 29). Although I find Deleuze and Guattari helpful as a starting point, my use of the term "desire" diverges quickly from theirs. They are interested primarily in offering a Marxist critique of established psychoanalytical theory and practice by redefining the relation between the desiring unconscious—both individual and collective—and social production (doing work, making money, keeping records, acquiring commodities, consuming ideas, writing literature, etc.). I am interested in understanding how desire—both conscious and unconscious—shapes the literary production of early nineteenth-century Britain. There are two premises and one question, however, that I would like to borrow from Deleuze and Guattari. The first premise is that "desire produces reality" (30). The second premise is that the reality produced by desire is "historically determined," which means that desire itself is defined by historical process. The question is, "how, in the subject who desires, desire can be made to desire its own repression" (105).

The desire I refer to is the energy that drives all human activity. It has neither object nor origin, for it is the engine of pure process, the motion of pure temporality. In accordance with physical laws, energy expends itself. Desire moves inexorably towards death, not as an objective or destination, but merely as the end of itself. "For desire desires death also, because the full body of death is its motor, just as it desires life, because the organs of life are the *working machine*" (Deleuze and Guattari 8). Apparently, this is the course of individual desire: energy that *seems* to engender itself within the individual psyche and then to exhaust itself in death. But if we consider desire as also the collective energy of communal human activity, then we can say that it has no origin—except in the unspecifiable beginning of human existence—and no end—unless in the potential self-destruction of humanity itself. When I mimic Deleuze and Guattari's claim that desire produces reality, I mean that human beings have created the world according to the dictates of their collective desire. Our energy forces us to produce interminably, but the energy itself is neutral: it cannot determine the aim or rationale or justification for production; such aims, rationales, justifications are stalling devices, maneuvers resorted to in attempting to cope with the fear of the directionless energy of life. Desire itself is the momentum of uncontrollable movement; it is change, or more specifically the motor of historical process. Just as energy cannot expend itself without producing an effect of its own expending (without *production* of some sort), so desire produces its effect, its residue, in human activity. Reality is the inclusive name for this residue, but we must also consider the network of tangible and intangible products that constitutes and enables the production of reality: civilization, power, work, love, sex, money, guns, books, poems. All of these things (reality) are not simply residue, however; they are also the fuel that resupplies desire and enables its continued momentum—otherwise desire would expend itself in communal death. In terms of the individual psyche, this residue or desideratum gives the human being objects and objectives not supplied directly by desire itself. This production of productivity gives the individual something to desire, something to do and some things to do it with. In terms of collective desire, desideratum gives humanity a realm and a reason for its ceaseless action. In other words, in order for desire to reproduce itself and sustain its momentum, it must produce its opposite, counterdesire, the continuous attempt to produce products that will satiate and thus halt the desiring process. Instead of halting desire, these products fuel an endless cycle of reproductivity. I produce a book to halt my desire, but the book instead reproduces my desire—not only in that it incorporates my desire but also in that once the book is finished, I must replace it with another object in the hope of stilling desire; not only in that the book is merely a temporary object of desire, but also in that it reproduces desire in others, who must read, or criticize, or rewrite my book.

If it is true that desire produces reality, it is also true that reality, as the product of desire, reproduces desire, as a product of itself. Unconscious desire spawns the conscious desiring that enables civilization. Unconscious desire creates in me a conscious desire to write without diminishing unconscious desire itself, so that they each move within the movement of the other, often as though they are correspondent breezes, to borrow from Wordsworth. This premise is important because it indicates (as we shall see in Chapter 2) how the romantic poet's unconscious desire produces his conscious desire to write, and how the conscious desire produces poetry, a product containing the traces of both desires, conscious and unconscious. Because it is pure energy, desire itself is everchanging, but the productivity of its products is necessarily stabilizing. Desire produces reality (the productivity and products of civilization), which tries to stabilize desire, to give it a habitation and a name, but instead reality simply manages to reproduce conscious desire, the desire to stabilize desire—the desire to complete a job, to love one who returns love, to write a perfect poem. So instead of having to contend only with its unconscious desire (boundless, aimless, sourceless, undifferentiated), humanity also has to contend wih the desire to halt desire (to find an origin, an object, or an end that will suffice).

The (re)production of desire comes under the rubric ideology. Ideology is the attempt to control desire, the attempt to stabilize the energetic process of interminable change. If desire is temporal, ideology is spatial. It is the magnetic field in which desire runs its course. Or more precisely, it is the magnetic force that binds reality together for the individual and for humanity. As a magnetic force, ideology is largely invisible and seems to work miracles. It enables us to see the world as a comprehensible whole. It enables us to view our productivity as meaningful design, and it causes us to arrange reality as though it has already arranged itself. Ideology is the repression of undirected movement, the ordination of historical process. It attempts to substitute visionary stasis—territory to be conquered—for incessant change. In other words, it is the desire to get beyond desire, to step outside of history. We shall see in Chapter 1 that this urge is strong in romantic poetry, and helps to explain the way the romantics conceptualize their literary production.

Desire and ideology are contentious foes, but this does not mean that they cannot work in tandem. Because desire gives birth to counterdesire, it also parents ideology, the desire to stop desiring. But ideology only manages to fashion desire, to direct it toward a certain end, to give it discernable contours, to make it partly conscious. As ideology shapes desire, desire inevitably subverts ideology, for that unconscious movement of desire that cannot be contained by ideology comes back to haunt ideology, pushing ideology along into and in history. Desire produces ideology, ideology reproduces desire, desire shapes ideology, ideology reshapes desire in an endless spiraling dialectic that can never achieve synthesis. As Deleuze and Guattari argue, desire is intrinsically revolutionary: "desire does not threaten a society because it is a desire to sleep with the mother, but because it is revolutionary. . . . Desire does not 'want' revolution, it is revolutionary in its own right, as though involuntarily, by wanting what it wants" (116). What desire wants, of course, is its own energetic fulfillment, a history unbound by ideology. By this reasoning, ideology is counterrevolutionary, even when it attempts to be radically anarchic. Wordsworth and Shelley must contend with this reality. As we shall see in Chapter 2, Wordsworth, in an earnest quest for the origin of desire, glimpses anarchy in the form of the French Revolution and the London carnival, and retreats into the folds of blessed ideology. Ideology is always there waiting to embrace him, but it is a different thing to desire ideology consciously, to adore it, and to slumber in its arms unawares. Wordsworth's sole project becomes to ordain desire, to order it and sanctify it by suppressing its blasphemous directionlessness. I call the ideology that results from this project *self-possession,* a crucial element of the larger ideology of romanticism itself. In Chapter 4, we shall see why Shelley becomes disillusioned with self-possessing ideology, and how, in attempting to reclaim the revolutionary tendency of desire, he revises Wordsworth.

Although ideology operates as though it is a seamless field of force, fiercely organizing all production in its reach by patterning desire itself, it is actually a seamed field, sewn together by a variety of factors, the most important of which is history itself. Ideology enforces a pattern on an aggregate of conflicting productions, but without entirely patching up the conflicts inherent in human productivity. Although ideology pretends to be a closed system in an attempt to do its organizing work as efficiently as possible, it is actually an open system. Or more precisely, it is an open system that is always attempting to close itself. It attempts to oust from its purview every aspect of itself that threatens the perfect symmetry of its operation. But it is the friction of its own magnetism that keeps ideology vital and that disables its self-closing. Ideology is necessarily fissured, self-contradictory, uneven, and sometimes weakest where it appears strongest. We see this immediately in Chapter 1, as we examine how the romantic ideology of the strong poet develops out of fear of the feminine. But in attempting to assure their own sociopolitical strength by casting out and smoothing over the feminine, romantic poets only manage to repress the feminine, which returns with the full force of desire in many forms. Their romantic ideology promises an escape from the pressures of change in history—suppressing the sites of market publishing and women's writing—but unconscious desire seeps through the fissures of their ideological patterns and moves them through the current of historical change.

This brings us to the second premise. The reality that desire produces is history itself, rather than some transcendent existence beyond history or some immanent existence inside the individuals who act within history. There is a continuity within history that allows us to reach back to past existence, but the reaching itself is a historical act, and falls under the sway of ideology and into the movement of desire.[5] Although I appeal to individual psyches in this study, I take these psyches more as the individualized manifestations of historical processes than as the fully conscious agents of ideological patterning and historical change. I attempt to discriminate whenever possible between individuals as conscious agents of action and reaction, and individuals as unconscious manifestations of change; of course, many times the distinction is too fine to be of service and is not always relevant in any case. But such a distinction becomes crucial in Chapters 6–8 especially, where we are dealing with women writers who must make conscious and unconscious decisions about their careers based on the climate of change. Does Felicia Hemans unconsciously "decide" to present herself as a feminine poet in the same way that Wordsworth and Byron are compelled by unconscious desire to promote a masculine self-image? I think the situation is different for her, that as an individual put in a situation of making change rather than, like Wordsworth and Byron, primarily forestalling change, Hemans's desire becomes more self-conscious, more the matter of a conscious dilemma than of an unconscious reflex reaction. This does not mean that Hemans in every situation is working more self-consciously, only that in regard to this particular sociohistorical relation between gender and poetic career she must be more fully conscious in order to act at all. Ideology whispers to Wordsworth that he must be masculine in various subtle ways that take the form of assumption; it screams to Hemans that if she is to write poetry and succeed she must *not* be masculine; she must find ways to be feminine while engaging in an activity that is marked by ideology as masculine.

I do not want to suggest that masculine desire precedes feminine desire in some metaphysical, ahistorical sense, only that in the historical moment we are examining masculine poetry precedes feminine poetry. "Masculine" and "feminine" are sociohistorical labels—though very complex ones—for ideological tendencies. Whereas desire, in its ever-changing, energetic movement to fulfill itself, tends to obliterate distinctions and boundaries, ideology encourages categories based on convenient, but often arbitrary differences. For it is only through the production of interrelated parts that a whole can seem to be assembled. All that we can know is historicized desire, desire reproduced by human productivity, desire reshaped by the categories of ideology (such as genre, gender, social class, or political faction). This is why Wordsworth's search for the origin of desire within himself is deluded, why Shelley's search for the end of communal desire is doomed to failure. Rather than returning to or leaping toward some undifferentiated, uncategorized desire, they only discover discrete particularities of desire, mutilated by their own histories, by the ideologies that fashion history.

This is also why rivalry and influence become crucial for the male romantics. Desirous of self-possession, of an ideology that owes nothing to any source outside the desiring self, they discover themselves caught in tropes of repetition. The fear of repetition is so overwhelming to the romantics because repetition stresses the disorderliness of desire, the static nature of ideology. Because desire is the essence of energetic change, it is also the essence of aimless, uncontrollable repetition. Romantic ideology, in order to assert the purposeful nature of self-possessing desire, attempts to reject the repetitious nature of desire. The romantics come to believe that even when the poet has no control over his desire, his desire is subject to some transcendent control that gives it an origin and an end within himself—enabling him to progress. In other words, he can still be in control of his destiny, of his poetic production, even when he loses possession of his desire, if only his destiny has a higher source of control. Wordsworth believes this, and Coleridge tries to believe it. The romantic poet fears most that his destiny may come to be controlled by another, that he will be forced to *repeat* another's desire, that his desire will not be the source of its own influence and progression. As we shall see in

Chapter 3, Coleridge is the supreme case of a poet influenced almost to the volume of silence. And in the final chapters, we come to see how and why women writers, though also trapped within a web of entangled desire and ideology, do not fear the kind of influence that almost silences Coleridge.

If desire is indeed revolutionary, why does it reproduce itself in such a reactionary way? How does desire come to authorize its own repression? Or to put the question again in Deleuze and Guattari's language: " 'Why do men fight *for* their servitude as stubbornly as though it were their salvation?' How can people possibly reach the point of shouting: 'More taxes! Less bread!' " (29). How does the female poet come to desire the feminine sphere in which the male desires to lock her? Why does she not instead revolutionize poetry by desiring whatever desire wants? Such questions can only return us to history, to the fact that desire is always historicized and hemmed in by ideology. Even as women poets begin publicly to record their own experience for the first time in history, they do so under the shadow of masculine ideology. Even as these women perform the revolutionary act of articulating feminine desire, they do so partly as the historicized objects of masculine desire. Desire may be revolutionary in merely wanting what it wants, but desire is never divorced from sentient human beings who fear the tremor of desire always working within them. Human beings never want merely what desire wants, and they rarely, if ever, embrace the revolution that the potential of unleashed desire portends.[6]

One objective of this study, then, is to trace the dialectic between desire and ideology in men's and women's writing in the early nineteenth century. Focusing on Wordsworth and Byron, Chapter 1 demonstrates how romantic ideology rises from the fear of uncontrolled change and unregulated desire, especially the fear of emasculation implied by the emergence of influential literary women, the consolidation of an unruly, self-willed reading public, and the increasing cultural influence of the utilitarian professions. Resorting to the myth of the masculine poet's unrivaled power over culture, the romantic plants the seeds for his own self-canonization, for his victory over popular women poets. Chapter 2 concentrates on Wordsworth and Pope in order to study how the romantic conception of poetic desire differs from the conception of poetry-writing dominant in the early eighteenth century. This chapter also prepares us for understanding why the first women poets prefer some aspects of Augustan ideology to that of their male romantic contemporaries. Chapters 3, 4, and 5 examine how romantic poets cope psychologically and poetically with the desire *not* to be influenced, believing that strength grows from desire that fathers itself. Focusing on Wordsworth's influence on Coleridge, Chapter 3 demonstrates how Coleridge combats that influence by exploiting conventionally feminine poses, but without embracing the marginal status implied by the feminine. In Chapter 4, I consider how Percy Shelley begins to redefine masculine romantic desire, as a result of his relation to Mary Wollstonecraft and Mary Shelley. I analyze how both Percy and Mary Shelley, unlike Coleridge, attempt to embrace feminine influence as a way of saving their culture from self-possessing rivalry. In Chapter 5, I examine how

Keats, at first disposed to feminine influence, feels compelled to stage a self-conscious rite of poetic passage away from feminized desire and into poetic manhood. Asking how cultural rituals of maturation affect the concept of poetic development, I also examine how Mary Tighe, who influences Keats, conceptualizes poetic maturity differently from Keats.

By including an analysis of Tighe's poetry, Chapter 5 serves as a transition from masculine desire regulated by romantic ideology to the emergence of the female poet. In Chapter 6, I chart the rise of a uniquely feminine poetics out of the specific historical circumstances of eighteenth-century British culture. Moving from the female Augustan scribbler, represented by Lady Mary Wortley Montagu, to the bluestocking poet, represented by Hannah More, from the bluestocking to the sentimental poetess, represented by Anna Barbauld, Chapter 6 begins to explore how these pioneering women enable the acceptance of female poetry-writing by making it an extension of the traditional feminine role, while also helping to place self-restricting limits on feminine writing, limits with which their poetic daughters must contend. Chapter 7 further analyzes these limits by concentrating on the reception of Felicia Hemans by both male and female writers. How does the politics of taste during this period dovetail with the politics of gender? How is it that a poet like Hemans, so respected in the nineteenth century, can be obliterated so entirely from literary history, covered over by romantic ideology? Having distanced ourselves from romantic desire by reconstructing the masculinity of its ideological enterprise, perhaps we can examine the female contemporaries of the romantics with less literary baggage. Chapter 8 discusses the work of what I call the *affectional* poets, represented by Hemans, Joanna Baillie, and Letitia Elizabeth Landon. These later women poets benefit from female Augustans, bluestockings, and sentimental poetesses, and in their attempt to record more fully feminine desire, they design an ideology of their own. In this final chapter, we see the consequences of history at work in the affectional poets, linking them to romantic ideology, but more importantly also linking them to their foremothers, to their female and domesticated male readers, and to one another in ways not experienced before in British literature. Their desire is not new, for women have always desired in the corridor of history, but it is newly expressed in a public form that wins them new accolades, as it brings them new traumas.

There is never a new beginning for desire, just a new direction within history. And such is necessarily the case for my own desire in writing this study. Though I do not discuss the particular contours of desire that have engendered this particular production, or the particular ideological field that enables me personally to view romanticism and masculine desire as one whole picture, I hope that my designs are never far from the surface. My argument is not so much for a new canon of literature, as for a more radical, noncanonical approach to how we think about literature and its history.[7] I want to suggest that our business should not be the perpetuation of static canons, but instead the perpetuation of critical curiosity, so that we and our students will always be as open to reading new poets in new ways as we are to re-reading familiar ones in old ways. Recognizing that writing history is always a process of partly arbitrary selection, I do *not* desire simply to set up yet another canon, consisting of these specific women writers on whom I have chosen to focus in this study. I strongly believe, however, that *not* to include, in our conferences and journals, in our critical books and anthologies, in our undergraduate and graduate courses and seminars, the actual historical phenomenon that such writers represent, means that we fail both as historians and critics, both as keepers of our cultural past and as molders of cultures yet to come. And more broadly, I believe that even though we must accept the limits that ideology in general places on our desire, this does not mean that we must also accept the limitations of those specific ideologies that divide our desire into specious categories for the purposes of domination and conquest. By driving recurrent desire in a new direction, by exploiting the history that we cannot escape, perhaps we can more easily embrace the desire that makes change and that subverts the stasis of ideology.

1

Romantic Quest and Conquest: Troping Masculine Power in the Crisis of the Poetic Calling

> Possessions have I that are solely mine,
> Something within, which yet is shared by none—
> Not even the nearest to me and most dear—
> Something which power and effort may impart.
> I would impart it; I would spread it wide,
> Immortal in the world which is to come.
> (Wordsworth, *Home at Grasmere* 686–691)

When Tom Moore sets out to compose his memoir of Lord Byron in 1828, he takes up the question of what makes a man into a poet. Considering Byron's scandal-plagued career, it is not surprising that Moore feels compelled to justify the man's mode of life in relation to his poetic greatness. But even if Byron had led a life like Wordsworth's, less prone to public controversy, Moore probably still would have addressed the question of the making of a poet. During the years between 1790 and 1830, poets, critics, and readers all invested tremendous intellectual energy into defining the make-up and status of the poet. In addition to the famous inquiries conducted in prefaces and defences, treatises and reviews, letters and poems by all the well-known romantic writers, numerous others, many whose names are now forgotten, attempted to answer the question, often while attempting to judge the merit of those romantic poets we now consider great. Indeed, this obsession with defining the poet's nature is so endemic to the time, so much more intense within this period than in any other, that we could consider it one of the most distinguishing attributes which qualifies this slot of time to be marked as a literary period. Moore's readers, then, would not be surprised by his interest in the question, although they might have been somewhat startled by the answer that he gives.

Attempting to justify Byron's waywardness and unhappiness in marriage, Moore sets forth the idea that domestic life and poetic genius are entirely incompatible. "The truth is, I fear, that rarely, if ever, have men of the higher order of genius shown themselves fitted for the calm affections and comforts that form the cement of domestic life. . . . [T]he same qualities which enable them to command admiration are also those that too often incapacitate them from conciliating love" (Moore's *Works of Lord Byron* 3: 125). At the heart of Moore's conception of poetic genius is more than a mere rationalization of Byron's unorthodox mode of life. Like so much literary discourse of the time, Moore's memoir is genuinely concerned with defining the role and status of the poet. Writing toward the end of the romantic period, Moore states unequivocally what is often a submerged premise in the works of the romantic poets:

It is, indeed, in the very nature and essence of genius to be for ever occupied intensely with Self, as the great centre and source of its strength. . . .

To this power of self-concentration, by which alone all the other powers of genius are made available, there is, of course, no such disturbing and fatal enemy as those sympathies and affections that draw the mind out actively towards others; and, accordingly, it will be found that, among those who have felt within themselves a call to immortality, the greater number have, by a sort of instinct, kept aloof from such ties, and, instead of the softer duties and rewards of being amiable, reserved themselves for the high, hazardous chances of being great. In looking back through the lives of the most illustrious poets—the class of intellect in which the characteristic features of genius are, perhaps, most strongly marked,— we shall find that, with scarcely one exception, from Homer down to Lord Byron, they have been, in their several degrees, restless and solitary spirits, with minds wrapped up, like silk-worms, in their own tasks, either strangers, or rebels to domestic ties, and bearing about with them a deposit for posterity in their souls, to the jealous watching and enriching of which almost all other thoughts and considerations have been sacrificed. (3: 127–128)

No wonder Moore expresses misgivings when Byron decides to marry Annabella Milbanke. During the depressed and directionless years between 1812 and 1814, after he has achieved unprecedented fame as a poet but before he has decided that his fate is to wander in exile from his kind, Byron, afraid of being tempted into a totally ambitionless, dissolute life, begins to consider marriage as a stabilizing force. "A wife would be my salvation," he says (2: 310). Acknowledging that he, too, is concerned about "attaching Byron to virtue," Moore nevertheless suggests that in looking to the "result, I should have seen, not without trembling," that the happiness of the innocent woman chosen for this sacrifice would be "risked in the experiment" (2: 341). Because a poet must be willing to take risks, to pursue the "high, hazardous chances of being great," rather than being tied down by "softer duties and rewards," Byron's decision to marry endangers not only the virtuous woman who would save him from waywardness but also the poet who would be great.

However delightful, therefore, may be the spectacle of a man of genius tamed and domesticated in society, taking docilely upon him the yoke of the social ties, and enlightening without disturbing the sphere in which he moves, we must nevertheless, in the midst of our admiration, bear in mind that it is not thus smoothly or amiably immortality has been ever struggled for, or won. (3: 129)

Although this concept—the poet as one who is outside or above society—has become so familiar that it is a cliché, it is a new idea in nineteenth-century Britain, one nurtured by a small group of male writers whom we now call the romantics. At the time that Moore is writing, however, his conception of the poet is still controversial, with both William Wordsworth and Felicia Hemans, for quite different reasons, raising objections to the idea that domesticity stifles poetic genius.

Ironically, Moore's conception of the poet grows from ground cultivated by Wordsworth himself. It is Wordsworth who, through his poetic practice, celebrates what Moore calls "the very nature and essence of genius . . . for ever occupied intensely with Self, as the great centre and source of its strength." When Moore pits domesticity against poetry, when he locates poetic desire within the "Self," when he views poetry as a grand manly calling, he is simply explicating and extending the logic hidden within the romantic conception of the poet. Like the other romantics, Moore does not want to single out poets, even as he makes them the torchbearers of supreme strength and genius. "In reviewing the great names of philosophy and science," he writes, "we shall find that all who have most distinguished themselves in those walks have, at least, virtually admitted their own unfitness for the marriage tie by remaining in celibacy;—Newton, Gassendi, Galileo, Descartes, Bayle, Locke, Leibnitz, Boyle, Hume, and a long list of other illustrious sages, having all led single lives" (3: 134). Why does the marriage "tie" become a "yoke" (3: 135) in Moore's argument?

When Thomas Love Peacock argues in his 1820 essay "The Four Ages of Poetry" that social progress has become the province of science rather than poetry, he is implicitly referring to the domestication of poetry. Peacock's essay is the mirror image of Moore's memoir. The premises of both are based in the central tenets of romantic ideology, but whereas Moore unintentionally reduces the romantic conception of the poet almost to absurdity by taking these premises, with utter earnestness, to their logical conclusion, Peacock intentionally reduces this conception to absolute absurdity by exaggerating the conclusions that could be drawn from those premises. Peacock may intend to be ironic, but he nonetheless pours salt on a wound that has long been irritable to romantic writers. In suggesting that the history of poetry is a progress, beginning with the theft of material power from kings and ending with the theft of intellectual power from the masses, Peacock comes too close for comfort to the romantic version of poetry's progress, while stressing every issue that the romantics would repress. In his satire, Peacock parodies a strategy characteristic of romantic discourse when he searches out the origin of the poetic vocation. At the same time, Peacock parodies the kind of philosophical discourse, practiced by Locke and Rousseau, which searches for historical and political truth by returning to man's origin in a state of nature; Peacock, however, hearkens back to Hobbes's more cynical version of man's origin in a state of war, a version that contradicts the romantics' more nostalgic view of "man's" origin:

The natural desire of every man to engross to himself as much power and property as he can acquire by any of the means which might makes right, is accompanied by the no less natural desire of making known to as many people as possible the extent to which he has been a winner in this universal game. The successful warrior becomes a chief; the successful chief becomes a king: his next want is an organ to disseminate the fame of his achievements and the extent of his possessions; and this organ he finds in a bard, who is always ready to celebrate the strength of his arm, being first duly inspired by that of his liquor. This is the origin of poetry, which, like all other trades, takes its rise in the demand for the commodity, and flourishes in proportion to the extent of the market. ("Four Ages of Poetry," reprinted in *Shelley's Critical Prose* 159)

With his characteristic wit, Peacock literalizes, and thus deflates, the guiding metaphors that romantic writers use to claim their cultural power. The origin of the poet becomes directly connected to the origin of the warrior and the king, as the poet becomes literally a propagandist on the king's payroll; more impressively, it becomes associated with the origin of "power and property," as the poet becomes the means through which possessions can be extended in space and time. Drunk on the power (and the liquor) of the tyrant he serves, the poet, like the king, is no better than a beggar or a thief. "In these days [of early barbaric society], the only three trades flourishing (besides that of priest, which flourishes always) are those of king, thief, and beggar: the beggar being, for the most part, a king deject, and the thief a king expectant" (159). Suggesting that the beggar is really a thief in disguise (waiting " a convenient opportunity to prove his claim"), Peacock implicitly suggests that these first poets are actually worse than beggars (failed kings awaiting the proper time to steal again) or thieves (aspiring kings), because poets are merely the "organs" of kings, stealing from kings what kings have stolen from others. Poets, Peacock writes, "are observing and thinking, while others are robbing and fighting: and though their object be nothing more than to secure a share of the spoil, yet they accomplish this end by intellectual, not by physical power. . . . A skilful display of the little knowledge they have gains them credit for the possession of much more which they have not" (160). By making others believe that thinking and observing (both, of course, activities crucial to Wordsworthian poetics) constitute real work (Wordsworthian "effort") and supercede the physical work of robbing and fighting, the poet is able to commit a sort of mental theft to the second order, taking possessions that are solely his and spreading his rule wide and long, without physical exertion.

The question is one of *productivity* in society. In Peacock's satire, the poet's claim that his *labor* contributes to the social good is dubious, since poetry is a kind of false, parasitic activity. Peacock's language repeatedly brings attention to poetry's real source of power, which has nothing to do with productivity. Poetry, in its origin, is a trade, and "like all other trades," relies on "the demand for the commodity . . . in proportion to the extent of the market." This is not something that romantics want to hear, much less to admit. Peacock anachronistically pushes the capitalist function of poetry-making back to its origin, making economic exchange an intrinsic grounding reason for the existence of poetic endeavor. As we shall see, the marketing of poetry, in the eyes of the romantics, is an extrinsic phenomenon that plagues poetry in its latter days and robs poetry of its genuine merit and use in society. According to Peacock, however, poetry is a form of economic exchange no different from any other trade *except* that what poets sell is a false commodity that can be used for no real purpose; thus, like the capitalist speculators who have become so common in early nineteenth-century England, poets are able to get something for nothing. The poet becomes one who seeks "to impose [his deception] on the common readers of poetry, over whose understandings the poet of this class [contemporary poets of the age of brass] possesses that commanding advantage, which, in all circumstances and conditions of life, a man who knows something, however little, always possesses over one who knows nothing" (169–170). Rather than producing useful goods or a common good, the poet thrives on others' ignorance and on his own success in hiding his theft.

The progress of poetry is actually an infinite regress of illusion, for not only is poetry theft to the second order (using intellect to steal influence from those who steal possessions through physical strength); it is also theft multiplied upon itself (poets stealing from previous poets stealing from previous poets):

Thus the empire of thought is withdrawn from poetry, as the empire of facts had been before. In respect of the latter, the poet of the age of iron celebrates the achievements of his contemporaries; the poet of the age of gold celebrates the heroes of the age of iron; the poet of the age of silver re-casts the poems of the age of gold: we may here see how very slight a ray of historical truth is sufficient to dissipate all the illusions of poetry. (164)

As poetry feasts upon itself, it consumes itself until it loses its capacity to deceive, and so it must attempt to replenish and re-empower its own original myth of power. "Then comes the age of brass, which, by rejecting the polish and the learning of the age of silver, and taking a retrograde stride to the barbarisms and crude traditions of the age of iron, professes to return to nature and revive the age of gold. This is the second childhood of poetry" (165). Peacock sees his own age as a second childhood "in which the puling sentimentality of the present time is grafted on the misrepresented ruggedness of the past" (169). As Peacock traces his satirical history of poetry, he, like the romantics, sees it as a history of bold action degenerating into sterile refinement that spirals into reclaimed vigor.

We must keep Peacock's parody in mind as we examine the romantic writers' "straight" version of poetry's progress, for the parody, in the explicitness of what it ridicules, makes it clear exactly what the romantics have at stake. How can poets "stamp . . . their power and utility on the real business of life" (170) if they are merely refined thieves disguised as rugged prophets of power? But even if poetry is "not useful, it may be said it is highly ornamental, and deserves to be cultivated for the pleasure it yields. Even if this be granted, it does not follow that a writer of poetry in the present state of society is not a waster of his own time, and a robber of that of others" (170). By refusing to grant the "ornamental" nature of poetry, the romantics also hope to forestall that regress into illusion whereby poetry becomes the wasteland of "harmony, which is language on the rack of Procrustes; sentiment, which is canting egotism in the mask of refined feeling; passion, which is the commotion of a weak and selfish mind; pathos, which is the whining of an unmanly spirit; and sublimity, which is the inflation of an empty head" (171). In appealing to each attribute that the male poets of his time exploit to signal their influence (harmony, sentiment, passion, pathos, sublimity), Peacock allows us to see both how ridiculous these self-aggrandizing poets can appear to their contemporaries and how tenuous are the achievements of romantic poets in their own time, even in 1820, supposedly the apex of the romantic era.

Percy Shelley's militant response to Peacock's jocular essay indicates how seriously the romantic poets in general take this matter of the poet's marginality in society. When Shelley talks about the power of poetry, he immediately also talks about the greatness of the men who write the poetry, one issue spilling over into the other. And though he acknowledges that a poet may sometimes sink to the level of ordinary, dull existence during the course of a long life, he insists that during composition, in his poetic moments, the poet must be a greatly extraordinary man. Shelley walks along a double edge. He wants to grant the poet power within his culture, a potent voice of the people as supreme legislator, but at the same time he cherishes the poet's outsider status, the poet as Satanic voice or daredevil. Moore also walks this double edge when he glorifies Byron's outsider status as a sign of the poet's greatness within culture.

By denying the role of domesticity in a poet's life, Moore hopes to bolster the strength of the poet within culture. He hopes both to assert that poetry is a true manly enterprise and to repress the function of the "feminine" in poetry's progress, to diminish the reality of a "profession" that has become increasingly domesticated, an activity that seemingly has been taken over by blushing maidens, timid spinsters, and busy matrons reading poetry and even writing it in the comfort of their homes, rather than by courageous warring men on the figurative fields of battle. In contrast, by 1830, when Moore starts publishing his memoir, William Wordsworth has long been domesticated, not only in that he has become known as the poet of domestic affections, but also in that he has been writing his poems under the umbrage of the secure domicile that he celebrates in his poetry. It would seem, then, that Wordsworth might prove the perfect foil to Byron, the perfect example of how the poet has been tamed and emasculated under the guise of civilizing progress and domesticity. Whereas Byron sneers at the women who court him, divorces the one who marries and attempts to tame him, and eventually exiles himself from his native land and the whole herd of humanity, all in order to prove his mesmerizing power over the very ones who can never understand him, Wordsworth settles down with sister, wife, home, country, and God, after a brief flirtation with revolutionary France. As we shall see, however, Byron, the wicked and worldly womanizer, and Wordsworth, the stern and virtuous patriarch, are but opposite sides of the same coin.

When James Currie writes a memoir of Robert Burns that Wordsworth thinks might jeopardize the late poet's reputation, Wordsworth composes a defence of Burns, a defence, like Shelley's and Moore's, that assumes a direct correlation between the life a man leads and the poetry he writes (see "A Letter to a Friend of Robert Burns" in *William Wordsworth: Selected Prose* 414–430). Somehow Wordsworth has to find a way of discounting Burns's scandalized and unhappy domestic life while retaining his faith in the correspondence between a poet's character as a man and his genius as a poet. Wordsworth, however, takes the opposite tack from Moore. Rather than claiming that a poet by nature cannot be happy when domesticated because poetic genius requires the manly risk of worldly adventure and self-introspection, Wordsworth claims that human flaws that would ruin the domestic life of an ordinary man are purged and conciliated by the poetic endeavor of an extraordinary man. Burns, he says, "was a man who preached from the text of his own errors; and whose wisdom, beautiful as a flower that might have risen from seed sown from above, was in fact a scion from the root of personal suffering" (425). The true genius turns the personal suffering of a particular domestic situation into the universal knowledge that enables the poet to rule both his suffering and his domestic environment:

The poet, penetrating the unsightly and disgusting surfaces of things, has unveiled with exquisite skill the finer ties of imagination and feeling, that often bind these beings to practices productive of so much unhappiness to themselves, and to those whom it is their duty to cherish;—and, as far as he puts the reader into possession of this intelligent sympathy, he qualifies him for exercising a salutary influence over the minds of those who are thus deplorably enslaved.

Not less successfully does Burns avail himself of his own character and situation in society, to construct out of them a poetic self,—introduced as a dramatic personage—for the purpose of inspiriting his incidents, diversifying his pictures, recommending his opinions, and giving point to his sentiments. (424)

Wordsworth, thinking explicitly of Burns and implicitly of Coleridge, writes the lines, "We Poets in our youth begin in gladness; / But thereof come in the end despondency and madness." In "Resolution and Independence," the poem from which these lines are taken, Wordsworth is anxious to assert that poets do not have to end in madness, to become social outcasts, in order to be great, but rather that their greatness depends on their capacity to rule their passions, achieving independence through resolution and vice versa. For Wordsworth, the domesticated poet is only weak if he is mastered—by emotion, by chaos, by domestic trials, by political strife, by men in other vocations, by the reading public, by past poets, or by poets to come. Conversely, to the extent that he masters the domestic situation in which he finds himself, he is strong and worthy of serving as a founding patriarch of and above culture, despite any salient flaws that may mar his character as a mere man living within that culture.

All of these writers—Wordsworth and Byron, Moore and Peacock—in different ways are caught in the forcefield of romantic ideology. It is an ideology born of the history that made it, but whose aim has been to suppress its own making. By this, I mean that romanticism grows out of the peculiar historical situation of Britain at the end of the eighteenth century: a situation in which the power of poetry, representing all forms of *belles lettres,* is being questioned on so many fronts that poets are forced self-consciously to redefine the meaning of poetry and its relation to those who write and read it. The consolidation of a market-based publishing industry; the liberalization of forms of governance; the democratization of social life; the education of increasingly larger segments of the population; the emergence of a new class of industrialists, bureaucrats, and scientists who are gaining power to influence the direction and shape of culture in palpably utilitarian ways; and the rise of women as the nurturers of literary discourse—all of these forces combine at the end of the eighteenth century to challenge the idea that poets are the most powerful legislators of culture. The irony is that this idea itself is created as a part of romantic ideology in order to keep at bay these changes. The romantic poets come to believe, and to convince their descendants in the literary establishment, that the greatness of a poet has no direct relation to the reading public who either buys or does not buy his work; that poets' influence in politics and history may not be palpable but is nonetheless more real than the influence of utilitarians who engineer, oversee, and operate the machinery of society; and that great poetry can be written only by powerful men capable of reaching grand visionary heights. It is an ideology that sheds its own birth in a domesticating present by claiming an origin in itself, in the poet's own empowering desire to write. This is why the romantic poet is compelled to say: "Possessions have I that are solely mine, / Something within, which yet is shared by none— / Not even the nearest to me and most dear— / Something which power and effort may impart."

When Wordsworth, referring to his poem on the growth of a poet's mind, recognizes that his project is "a thing unprecedented in Literary history that a man should talk so much about himself,"[1] he is bringing attention to the anxious self-consciousness that pervades all romantic poetry, to the persistent effort of the romantic poet to find in his own voice an aboriginal self that re-creates the world and that emblematizes the capacity for seizing meaning in the world. And of course Wordsworth is right. We cannot imagine any poet before him or his time writing a poem about the coming to being of the poetic self. Romantic poets are driven to a quest for self-creation and self-comprehension that is unprecedented in literary history. When Harold Bloom, identifying the cause of this quest for poetic self-possession as cultural belatedness, claims that "[a]s poetry has become more subjective, the shadow cast by the precursors has become more dominant," he also is underscoring the precariousness of the poet's status in relation to his world since the end of the eighteenth century (*Anxiety of Influence* 11). Bloom, himself a romantic as well as a romanticist, tends to read all poetry from the position of the romantic self-crisis and develops a poetics of influence based on the accurate insight that "self-appropriation involves the immense anxieties of indebtedness" (5). In other words, the self can be established only in relation to other things on which it depends for its self-definition. In "The Internalization of Quest-Romance," the seminal essay that fathers *The Anxiety of Influence,* Bloom focuses on the paradoxical nature of romantic self-questing, as he points out that the romantic poet moves farther and farther within, in an attempt to find the source of the self, in an attempt to embrace all that is without (see *Romanticism and Consciousness* 3–24). The poet's relation to the world, much like his relation to his literary fathers, is fraught with anxiety, because the apparent externality of that world threatens the necessary myth that he fathers vision by fathering himself. Anything within the purview of that world is also a potential vehicle as well as a threat, for every external pressure, though it stresses the limits of selfhood and the impossibility of self-creation, can be exploited to move the poet and his audience toward the myth of self-possession. Solipsistically magical, the "self" can transform any external object into an aspect of itself while pretending to deny the externality of that object; it can envision and contain the infinite world by peering into the finite self, appearing to liberate the self from its own borders, appearing to capture the world for itself, appearing to father the world.

This myth of *self-possession*[2] enables the historical resituation of the poet, allows him to adapt psychologically, philosophically, and pragmatically to historical forces that are beyond his control as a human being but that nurture the myth of self-control as the primary means for *containing* those forces (limiting their influence while accepting their inevitability). The self-questing of the romantic poet enacts the attempt to re-establish a relation with—a hold on—the world, a relation that is predetermined by the nature of the historical changes that envelope and transform the poetic vocation itself. By focusing on the two poets who would seem to be most dissimilar in the romantic canon, Wordsworth and Byron, this chapter examines how the romantics resort to masculine metaphors of power, not only because they are socialized and indoctrinated into a masculinist tradition, but also (and tautologically) because these metaphors allow them to reassert the power of a vocation that is on the verge of losing whatever influence it had within and over that tradition. In examining how these poets exploit masculine metaphors of power, however, we must also consider the specific historical phenomena that these metaphors attempt to repress, particularly the unprecedented way in which women writers are beginning to make their influence felt in late eighteenth-century literary discourse.

1

Both male and female writers are extremely sensitive to the radical changes that are being experienced by all social groups during the early nineteenth century. Overwhelmed by changes that are highly visible and deeply visceral, these writers fear that humanity has lost control of its own destiny.

Whether it is Edmund Burke alarmed by the whirlwind of revolution on streets too close to home, or William Wordsworth frightened by the contradiction between mechanized work and anarchic carnival on London streets, or Felicia Hemans dismayed by the swarm of faceless admirers who intrude into the privacy of her sitting room, the image of the monstrous mob conjures up visions too terrible even for the most talented writers to articulate. This fear of losing control within both public and private life, this sense of public alarm impinging into the deepest core of private experience, induces a feeling of vulnerability, a terror of being helpless amidst the crowd, of being crowded in and invaded even in moments of solitude.[3] Sensing the loosening of the feudal and rural ties that bind each individual to a familiar unit and that secure an impression of personal belonging, the individual begins to feel the pressures of an estranged self. As Charles J. Rzepka points out, the homeland becomes a place of homeless wanderers who can no longer be at home because they have been thrown into the territory of an intensified self-consciousness:

Greater social mobility, mass urbanization, the disappearance of sumptuary laws, all had the general effect of making England an island of strangers. It became increasingly difficult for the self to find a recognizable place in English society, harder to tell if what others saw was the true self, or if the self was being compromised, made false, taken away from its "owner" by more fluid and less dependable categories of public identification. (*Self as Mind* 23)

Simultaneous mass estrangement and self-intensification result in the conflicting desires for solitude, an escape from the monstrous mob, and for self-forgetfulness, an escape from the intensified consciousness of self. Byron's *Childe Harold's Pilgrimage* best articulates this conflict, as the poet feverishly seeks relief from the mob only to repopulate his solitude with crowds from the haunting past of humanity, and as he seeks self-forgetfulness ironically by estranging himself further from the madding crowd. Byron also best articulates the helpless vulnerability, the incapacity for action, that threatens an estranged self overwhelmed by the pressures of unpredictable change. Being estranged only intensifies the feeling of weakness; viewing the mob of strangers only intensifies the sense of lost control. Since Byronic homelessness can mean succumbing to the disease of helpless inaction, no wonder Wordsworth returns compulsively to "spots of time" that reaffirm the security of home; no wonder he composes so many homeless wanderers who magically create a sense of home within the solitude of self. Unimpressed with the heroism of self-conscious inactivity, Wordsworth attempts to transform suffering into a form of manly action. Nevertheless, his suffering heroes, including himself, are but the obverse of Byron's. Mired in circumstances that seem beyond their control, cut off from a common humanity, the romantics must find sources of strength within the self, and must find ways of making the sole self a sufficient focus of heroic action in a world enlarged and complicated by massive change.

As a world of strangers brings intensified self-identity into being, it also immediately threatens to overwhelm that identity, to reabsorb it into the overpowering mass. Even while equivocating between self-annihilation (negative capability) and self-aggrandizement (the egotistical sublime), the romantic poet recognizes that the only match for an overwhelming mass is a poetics of mythic self-possession. Although the poet may have no visible effect on his confused society, he has, according to romantic ideology, an unrivaled effect on the desire that fuels social productivity. The poet is strong because of the power of his desire regulated by poetic production.

Bloom's "strong" poet is a useful epithet because it identifies so clearly the assumptions undergirding romantic and much postromantic poetry, and because it indicates how that conception is rooted in premises of masculine potency. Even before the reign of romantic ideology, poetry is considered a contest in which men can test their powers, but for the romantics this masculine contest accrues profound and intense meaning with consequences that are seen as universal and momentous. It becomes chivalric jousting transformed to meet the conditions of a social system in which power manifests itself no longer in physical strength but in the strength of various kinds of cognitive and metaphorical exchanges. It becomes the means through which desire can be stabilized while at the same time intensified and empowered.

According to the romantic notion which we have already seen Peacock mock, as political power becomes progressively derived not from the combined strength of individual men in combat but from a complex of mental operations (military strategy, technical inventiveness, parliamentary deliberation, propaganda, etc.), the individual or society that devises ways of establishing and sustaining mental influence becomes the strongest and rules the world. Just as economic power becomes determined primarily by abstract transactions of capital rather than by the immediacy of agricultural and mercantile bartering, so sociopolitical power becomes metonymic and abstract, the province of literacy (broadly defined) and intellect. The American and French Revolutions have graphically shown the romantics how secular ideologies and propaganda can controvert preordained physical realities, have shown how the ideas of individual men can be stronger than the actual strength of the most powerful imperial armies. In this sense, romanticism is not so much a reaction against the Enlightenment spirit, but a culmination of it. More than any poets before them, the romantics believe that power is the province of *ideas*—whether the knowledge is scientific, historical, political, philosophical or narrowly technological. And they also believe that to govern these ideas—to wrestle them into an organic whole that seems to make sense in universal terms—is to govern the world itself. In other words, they discover the power of ideology to reshape historicized desire.

In this very real sense the romantics, some of them unwittingly, help to prepare England for its imperial destiny. They help teach the English to universalize the experience of "I," a self-conscious task for Wordsworth, whose massive philosophical poem *The Recluse* sets out to organize the universe by celebrating the universal validity of parochial English values. Wordsworth, Blake, Coleridge, Southey, Shelley, all start their literary careers as propagandists, as men concerned with self-consciously propagating certain ideologies through their poetry in the hope of transforming political reality, while Byron, as a member of the House of Lords, seriously considers a career in politics. And why not? If the idea is the source of power, why cannot poets, who deal in the interchange of ideas, join in the contest for power? Indeed, since poets practice the skills of inspiring allegiance to what is otherwise unreal (in being figurative and fictional) and making concrete and familiar what is otherwise abstract and alien, they have perhaps the best chance of accruing power. And since they need not rule directly, but only by proxy, they need not display the official signs of power to be strong.

The romantics believe that on their individual visions and on the visions of all strong poets depends not just the fate of a party or nation, but the fate of humanity itself, the capacity for humanity to envision is own fate. The romantic poet, then, bestows upon himself the mantle of the medieval romance quester not only because he writes internalized romances but also, and more importantly, because he has taken the virile role of the chivalric savior. On his exploits—now intellectualized and metonymic, based on individual vision that operates always in forms of displacement from the social whole—civilization itself depends. Medieval peasants and ladies are replaced with the lower classes, orphans, beggars, widows, idiots, virgins, and those particular women in the poets' lives who inspire them to greater heights of self-possession. And like the knight, the romantic poet proves the strength of his vision, his right to defend and protect, through masculine rivalry, through competition with other men who also claim to be strong enough to sustain the whole and protect the weak with singlehanded might.

Conveniently, the romantic poet is able to retain his masculine identity as romance quester as he also identifies subliminally with two new masculine roles (even as he self-consciously counters them) that become significant in the early nineteenth century: the scientist and the industrial capitalist. This process indicates the continuity of gender identity through changing economic-historical phases (a sort of masculine prototype that evolves with the changes themselves), and it gauges the heavy pressure on men who desire power to identify with the prototype in order to feel and become empowered. The scientist searches for laws that he takes to be natural and universal, and, as inventor, he originates powerful ways of applying those laws to transform the material conditions of society. The male poet wants to claim the same powers: mastery over nature, originality, and capacity to transform the material conditions of society through his poetic inventions. The romantic poet, however, wants to claim even greater powers of mastery over the world. Limited by the limitations of material cause and effect, the scientist can effect material change only. The romantic claims that his power is limited only by his own capacity for self-possession. Since his materials derive from the human spirit or soul, from powerful feelings and deep thoughts, his power is more universal, higher, and profounder, and it can influence not only the spiritual realm but also the actual material conditions which owe their existence to that higher realm.[4]

The industrial capitalist competes with the scientist to become the new strong man, and his province becomes the new economic terrain of fierce international competition, speculation, and unlimited growth. He, like the romantic poet (or vice versa), believes that power derives from self-creation, that the stability of the whole relies on the capacity for individual self-regulation (since there are yet few governmental regulations on this new kind of enterprise). He also views his individual desire as the focus of manly conquest in that the laws of supply and demand are manipulated by the dictates of his own private desire. Like the romantic poet, he sees his task as the regulation of public desire without diminishing it, since that desire is the source of his power over that public. He must not only regulate the unruly desire of a laissez-faire market but also refuel, harness, and direct the unpredictable energy of a massive labor force. The competitive market in which he is forced to prove his power represents a risk of contamination for the poet. The poet claims that his capital is the element of pure vision, unlike the crude and corrupting alloy of money through which the capitalist seizes his empire. The market of readers in reality, however, serves as a constant reminder to the romantic poet, as Peacock demonstrates, that his power is actually, like the capitalist's, impure, for it is dependent on the desire of an estranged mass.[5]

As the contest moves from the court and the patronage of gentlemen to the publishing house and the market of the common reader, the poet's success becomes literally more dependent on the power of self-possession, the potency of his individual vision, his ability to captivate and rule a diverse, saturated and fickle public, and part of his power will depend on the newness and originality of his readerly appeal. As long as his productivity is defined by its dependency on an aristocratic class, his project is more or less traditional and customary, a matter of representing the strength of his discourse by displaying its continuity with poetic tradition and displaying its allegiance to the party of his patron. To stray too far from his literary inheritance would symbolize a threat to the validity of his patron's inherited authority and would in turn threaten his own means of support. To bring too much attention to his own individuality would demean that relation and the honor bestowed upon him as an inheritor of the literary-political tradition and as a citizen with a specifiable and immediately identifiable place in the literary-political hierarchy.

Unlike the patronized poet, however, who represents social stability and the collective consciousness already preordained through his identification with those who actually rule, the romantic poet seeks to stabilize his readership through his own individual power and to become a representative of collective consciousness by gaining the allegiance of an ever-widening audience. His rule is metonymic in a different sense: it is indirect in relation to the actual structures of governance, but it is directly related to his creative power over those who must be ruled. He need not have any relationship with those in power in order to be a celebrated poet, and in fact lower social rank and familial obscurity can be sufficient cause for his celebrity as it stresses the myth of the great poet's unmediated condition, his "natural" talent and origi-

nality, his virile power of self-creation and self-possession. Although he may
be a fierce ideologue, the romantic poet refuses to see himself as a political
partisan, for that would reduce his vision to the ephemeral politics of the
faction, the party, and the nation. He claims that his vision transcends party
politics and social hierarchies, and even the literary conventions that grow out
of such politics and hierarchies, but simultaneously he does not want to give
up the capacity to chart the fate of the worldly empires he supposedly transcends.

However we assess his new role, whether in relation to an estranged
mass, to his reading audience, to his economic status, to his vision, to his
fellow poets, to his self-image, to his literary inheritance, or to his sociopolitical function, the romantic poet is thrown back upon his power of self-
possession, a power that is repeatedly willed in the poetry by both overt and
subliminal appeals to the virility and masculinity of his creative project, and
a power repeatedly reconfirmed through his specific relations with the feminine in his poetry and his life.

2

When Byron attacks his fellow poets in *English Bards and Scotch Reviewers,* he returns again and again to a handful of interrelated complaints
leveled against each poet: the readerly appeal to women and the lower
classes; the wild, common, and pathetic (in the nineteenth-century sense)
subject matter; the softness (one of his favorite descriptive terms in the
poem) of the poet's persona; the bastardization of literary conventions; and
the process of market publishing that opens the poetic vocation to anyone
self-confident enough to consider himself (or herself even) a poet. Most of
his complaints are capsulized in the following lines, which sketch a caricature
of the man who later becomes his close friend and biographer, Thomas
Moore:

> Who in soft guise, surrounded by a choir
> Of virgins melting, not to Vesta's fire,
> With sparkling eyes, and cheek by passion flush'd,
> Strikes his wild lyre, whilst listening dames are hush'd?
> 'Tis Little! young Catullus of his day,
> As sweet, but as immortal, in his lay!
>   (*Poetical Works* 283–287)

As Byron castigates the "soft guise" of Moore, he is also criticizing the poet's
aim, the female audience. Repeatedly Byron reminds us that women have become a primary audience for poetry and always he targets that audience as
representative of the detriment done to poetry in his own age. The poet who
writes primarily for women feminizes the whole poetic process. With this
feminized audience in mind, the poet must steer a difficult course between
stirring the audience to facile passion and tracing "chaste descriptions on thy
page, / To please the females of our modest age" (271–272). Byron's por-

trait of Bowles is even more damning. He pictures him "still whimpering through three-score of years," the "great oracle of tender souls." Whether Bowles writes of the "fall of empires, or a yellow leaf," his poetry is contaminated by sympathy's "soft idea" and he, like Moore, achieves popularity through this feminized appeal:

> All love thy strain, but children like it best.
> 'Tis thine, with gentle Little's moral song,
> To soothe the mania of the amorous throng!
> With thee our nursery damsels shed their tears,
> Ere miss as yet completes her infant years.
>
> (342–346)

Byron's "gentle" here is ironic, for he is claiming that poetry has replaced its true gentility with a gentleness that derives from a sort of childish sentiment. Taking seriously their role as maternal nurturers and exploiting that role as a justification for writing poetry, many women writers composed works explicitly aimed at the young. Byron's attack, then, is not only aimed at the "nursery damsels" and the infant "miss" who would constitute a market for the new children's literature; he is also attacking the tremendous influence of this market on all poetry. Even grown men begin to write for the damsels and their children; even grown men begin to write like matrons. In Byron's complaint we can hear the same tone that suffuses Peacock's ridicule, when he says of the contemporary poets of the age of brass: "[B]ut for the maturity of mind to make a serious business of the playthings of its childhood, is as absurd as for a full-grown man to rub his gums with coral, and cry to be charmed to sleep by the jingle of silver bells" ("Four Ages of Poetry" 171).

Part of Byron's complaint is the sheer popularity of poetry—its appeal to so many and from so many classes and occupations, the female and the child serving repeatedly to indicate how low the craft has sunk. Just as the poet and the audience have become soft, so have the subject matter and the poetic forms. "The simple Wordsworth, framer of a lay / As soft as evening" (237–238) and "gentle Coleridge," "[t]he bard who soars to elegise an ass" (262) are two of the major culprits. This feminized process causes otherwise skillful male poets, such as Scott, to trivialize their talents and encourages common men to aspire to gentleness by way of the poetic vocation.

> When some brisk youth, the tenant of a stall,
> Employs a pen less pointed than his awl,
> Leaves his snug shop, forsakes his store of shoes,
> St. Crispin quits, and cobbles for the muse,
> Heavens! how the vulgar stare! how crowds applaud!
> How ladies read, and literati laud!
>
> (765–770)

The marketing or commodification of poetry inevitably results in the vulgarization and feminization of literature, so that the very basis of taste is eroded by crowds that applaud and ladies who read. Byron's manly Popian satire represents not only an attempt to vilify his "soft" fellow poets but also an attempt to demonstrate his own patrilineal descent from the line of Dryden and Pope.

The parodies Byron sketches of Moore and Bowles, however, could well be used against Byron himself. No poet masters the art of emotional manipulation better than he, none exploits the combination of pathos, wildness, and passion more successfully to gain the applause of crowds and the readership of ladies. Byron's conscious desire to be a certain kind of poet is fissured by the unconscious desire to dramatize his own vulnerability. And his desire is so splintered, even in a poem like *English Bards,* which purports to establish a firm satirical voice, that it is often difficult to sift out conscious praise from unconscious envy, conscious ridicule from an unconscious desire to emulate. How seriously should we take his ridicule of Moore, a poet whom he elsewhere praises? Is Byron creating a mythic distance between himself and his contemporaries by composing a fictional satirical persona who can deflect potential criticism from the real Byron, who is actually close to Moore? Is Byron's satire a form of psychic defense as much as a form of literary attack?

With the publication of *English Bards,* Byron positions himself against his first volume of poems *Hours of Idleness.* It is this first volume that provokes some contemporary critics to ridicule Byron, and tit for tat provokes Byron's wholesale ridicule of contemporary writers in *English Bards.* As Jerome McGann has pointed out, one of the most important influences on *Hours of Idleness* is Moore's *Poetical Works of the Late Thomas Little, Esq.,* which Byron knew "by heart." "He was attracted to the poetry," McGann writes, "not only because of the elusive tone that was its characteristic note— a subtle mixture of humor and sentimentality . . . —but also because of the 'personal' appeal that the poetry made" (*Fiery Dust* 10). What Byron learns from Moore, according to McGann, is how to propagandize a poetic personality. "The poetry does not reveal Byron the man, but the poetic personality into which he mythologized himself in his work" (25). The split in consciousness that McGann identifies in *Hours of Idleness* is unintentionally ironic, considering how hard Byron works to dramatize a definable poetic personality for his audience. But that split is inescapable, for it reveals Byron's futile attempt to control both his own desire and the unpredictable market for which he writes. When he writes *Hours of Idleness,* he is more trusting both in the innocence of his desire and in the goodwill of his readers to accept his self-dramatization as a noble, spirited, congenial, playful, half-serious, melancholic, self-teasing, ambitious young man. But this self-dramatization backfires, for rather than attracting the sympathy of his readers, it attracts their ridicule. Having dramatized the vulnerability of his poetic personality, having disarmed himself before his readers, he makes the real poet within the fictional dramatization vulnerable as well. So when he strikes back in *English Bards,* he attacks not only the critics who have become his foes but also the writers who were once his models, the Moores whom he once (and still) desires to become. He attacks the earlier poetic self-dramatization that has made him so vulnerable to his own desire and to the whims of the

public. He arms himself by attempting to displace self-dramatizing vulnerability with a hardened indignation, for he has begun to realize that if he is
to become the hero of his drama, he must protect his Achilles's heel.

This "progression" involves a rite of passage into manhood, a claim to
masculine self-possession, which we shall see Keats also enacting, though in a
different manner. Self-deluded into thinking that *Hours of Idleness* would
establish his claims to his estate literally, to his future fame, to his heroic
ambition, to his rightful place in the patriarchy, Byron is awakened to the
harsh reality of manly combat in a world where many claim to be strong but
few succeed. In *Byron and his Fictions,* Peter Manning lucidly demonstrates
how crucial is the tension between unmanly vulnerability and manly self-
control in the making of Byron's poetic personality. He shows how distressing
incidents in Byron's life are transformed into the self-dramatizing fictions of
his poetry. "Accounts of Byron's behavior at the funeral [of his mother]
reveal a significant pattern," Manning writes. "[H]is struggle to repress any
outward sign of the emotions that gripped him suggests that he too construed
them as 'weakness' unbefitting his ideal of manliness. The feelings that were
thus denied immediate release were transformed into the compelling motivation of his major poetry" (34). What Byron learns is how to manipulate his
emotions without falling prey to them, how to excite his readers' desire while
attempting to regulate his own.

Byron self-consciously avoids becoming the kind of effeminate poet that
he is ridiculing in the caricatures of *English Bards.* Instead, he cultivates the
image of a literary womanizer, a poet who lives for the experience of emotion,
not for the emotion of experience, a poet who can simultaneously make the
cheek flush with passion and the lips form a smirk of derision (as he does
especially well with Don Juan's various love affairs). Byron's ambivalence
only deepens as he matures as a poet: although he writes for the vulgarized
and feminized market, he never forsakes the image of writing for his own
boyish enjoyment, of writing for some self-generating desire for play and
mastery. No matter how many copies of his tales are possessed by "the females of our modest age," Byron himself cannot be possessed. Whether it is
Harold, Napoleon, Cain, the narrator of *Don Juan,* Prometheus, or Manfred
who tests the limits of selfhood, Byron always celebrates his own protean
self-possession by making himself a masquerading hero of his own tale. He
somehow manages to combine the self-involved questing of romanticism with
the self-abnegating satire of the Augustans, and he somehow manages to
write lays of wild passion, self-pity, and amorous sentiment without "softening" his masculine guise.

Even as Byron matures and gains more self-confidence as a writer, even
as he gains critical notoriety and accrues the largest audience of his time, he
is careful to avoid softness. As a poet and as a man, he identifies softness with
vulnerability, vulnerability with earnest feeling, and earnest feeling with
weakness. Any display of emotional effusion in his poetry must be given a
feminine cause or undercut with masculine derision or both. At the beginning

of *Childe Harold's Pilgrimage,* for instance, as other men aboard the ship are overcome with grief in their leavetaking, Harold remains philosophically and emotionally resolute, even as he is touched by his comrades' deep feelings.

> The sails were fill'd, and fair the light winds blew,
> As glad to waft him from his native home;
> And fast the white rocks faded from his view,
> And soon were lost in circumambient foam:
> And then, it may be, of his wish to roam
> Repented he, but in his bosom slept
> The silent thought, nor from his lips did come
> One word of wail, whilst others sate and wept,
> And to the reckless gales unmanly moaning kept.
>   (Canto 1 stanza 12)

Instead of giving way to "unmanly moaning," Harold transforms his vulnerable feeling into verbal art and artifice: "He seized his harp, which he at times could string, / And strike, albeit with untaught melody, / When deem'd he no strange ear was listening" (stanza 13). Harold refuses even to vent emotion through the artifice of song unless he is assured of "no strange ear." And yet we know, for the narrator has informed us, that Harold is "sick at heart." " 'Tis said, at times the sullen tear would start, / But Pride congeal'd the drop within his ee" (stanza 6). Although Harold is occasionally the object of Byron's satire, serving to shield Byron from himself and from his audience, Byron refuses to allow even his satirical object the luxury of emotional laxity (see Canto 1, stanza 8, for instance). Harold may not be able fully to control his grief, but nonetheless it is fully *his* grief, which he refuses to make the cause of his own vulnerable emasculation. The heroic self-sufficiency in the midst of total vulnerability to his own uncontrollable desire makes Harold all the more heroic, and through transference makes Byron all the more "not that open, artless soul" who becomes the victim of feminine passion—that is, victimizable passiveness. The artlessness of emotion itself is ironically a kind of indictment. Unlike the jejune Byron of *Hours of Idleness,* the Haroldian Byron realizes that he needs the artifice of art not just to express himself, but more so to protect himself from himself. The more he gains control over the technique of his art, the more Byron can give the appearance of having control over unpredictable desire and therefore over the readers whom he desires to conquer.

It is the softness of domesticity that melts the armor of Harold's comrades aboard ship. As they remember the women and children that they leave behind unprotected, they, ironically embarking on manly adventure, internalize the feminine in order to take it with them. As we shall see, for Felicia Hemans, this in itself becomes a courageous and necessary act of survival in an estranging world, an act that only the women who are left behind and supposedly unprotected can teach. For Byron, however, it is simply a sign of weakness, which, even if it cannot be purged, must not be expressed. When, at the beginning of Canto 3, the narrator himself is moved by a similar leavetaking, Byron is compelled to justify the power of emotional outburst experienced by the Byron within the text by displacing the outburst onto his daughter. As his feeling is categorized as paternal concern, Ada becomes the focus of our emotional "excess"; Ada becomes the source of vulnerability, rather than the father himself. Likewise, when Don Juan is overcome by a similar leavetaking from his beloved Julia, the narrator undercuts Juan's emotional display with locker-room satire. Juan's lovesickness is exchanged for seasickness. Juan, the lusty youth capable of cuckolding a much older man, becomes an unseasoned and untravelled boy, overwhelmed by the first lurch of the sea and the first lurch of the heart. Juan's tender feeling is literally defeminized as the natural harshness of the ocean's waves displaces the "naturally" seductive softening effect of Julia's farewell words.

That Byron's contemporaries were extremely conscious of the implications of his pose can be seen from Moore's defence of the poet. The very same incidents that the twentieth-century critic Peter Manning uses to demonstrate how Byron transforms repressed unmanly feeling into the expressions of commanding art, Moore uses to assert Byron's manly virtue and the virtuous manliness of poetic genius in general. In discussing Byron's response to his mother's death, Moore anticipates his readers' response that Byron may be seen as unfeeling and self-absorbed; Moore attempts to create a balance, showing that Byron has strong feeling but is strong enough to suppress it when it threatens to overwhelm him. Moore narrates the incident of Byron's maid discovering him in tears at the bedside of his dead mother. Then he tells how on the morning of the funeral, Byron refuses to attend the burial and instead orders his page Rushton to take his morning exercise of sparring with him. "He was silent and abstracted all the time, and, as if from an effort to get the better of his feelings, threw more violence, Rushton thought, into his blows than was his habit." According to Moore, "superficial observers," seeing a "degree of eccentricity and indecorum" in Byron's behavior "might well bring the sensibility of his nature into question" (2: 34).

It is exactly the sensibility of the poet's nature that Moore wants to exonerate. Suggesting that Byron's fitful, moody temperament might at least in part be attributed to "his early collisions with maternal caprice and violence" (2: 35), Moore clearly sets up Byron as heroic for being able to endure a mother who, in her more thoughtless moments, could be cruel (as when she reportedly ridicules the boy's club foot). More importantly, Moore capitalizes on these hardships and flaws as necessary, though not sufficient, for the making of poetic genius: "If, to be able to depict powerfully the painful emotions, it is necessary first to have experienced them, or, in other words, if, for the poet to be great, the man must suffer, Lord Byron, it must be owned, paid early this dear price of mastery" (2: 37). Just as Byron's difficult relationship with his mother drives him into the risk-taking solitude necessary for poetic greatness, so Byron's eccentric behavior signals an extraordinary man mastering his unusual circumstances by rising to greatness.

Ironically, however, instead of purging the domestic influence which supposedly prevents full poetic development, Moore only manages to stress the pervasiveness of the feminine in the making of a poet by unwittingly em-

phasizing the crucial cause and effect of maternal affection—or its absence—
on the aspiring young poet. On the one hand, Moore is responding to women
writers like Felicia Hemans and Joanna Baillie, who, as we shall see, find
Byron's poetic pose extremely problematic exactly because of the way it
manipulates what they see as the sanctity of affection. On the other hand,
Moore is also responding to a male poet like Wordsworth, who, though in
consonance with Byron in many ways, also represents a threat to the idea
that poetic genius is incompatible with domesticity. Significantly, toward the
very beginning of Moore's memoir he makes a point of arguing *against*
Wordsworth's notion that the origin of the great poet's genius is found in
nature. "The light which the poet sees around the forms of nature is not so
much in the objects themselves as in the eye that contemplates them;" Moore
writes, not realizing that Wordsworth would probably agree fully, "and
Imagination must first be able to lend a glory to such scenes, before she can
derive inspiration *from* them" (1: 22–23). By arguing for the priority of
imagination over nature, Moore is actually arguing for the manly self-
possession of the poet's desire. "[I]mpressions of natural scenery," he says,
"no more *make* the poet than—to apply an illustration of Byron's own—the
honey can be said to make the bee that treasures it" (1: 23). By eradicating
"natural scenery," which is often associated with the domestic scene, Moore
again attempts to free poetic genius from the yoke of feminine domesticity.

   Wordsworth, in a very different way from Byron and his advocate
Moore, is involved in the same kind of pursuit, an attempt to bring the
"feminine" vulnerability of emotion into the realm of "masculine" power.[6]
Although Byron's stories always involve his own self-questing, he never disarms himself, never makes himself vulnerable to his public by revealing the
bard as a naked hero, the way he, in *English Bards,* suggests Wordsworth
does:

> So close on each pathetic part he dwells,
> And each adventure so sublimely tells,
> That all who view the 'idiot in his glory'
> Conceive the bard the hero of the story.
> (Byron's *Poetical Works* 251–254)

Wordsworth not only talks more about himself than any previous poet; he
does so without acknowledging the ritual masks honored by all poets before
his time. Wordsworth claims that the aboriginal self can be empowered only
through honest self-inspection and sincere disrobing of the self to readers.
He presents himself as self-confident that the naked self is in fact the most
virile and natural expression of creative power. I am not suggesting, however,
that Wordsworth's project of discovering and disrobing the aboriginal self
can actually be achieved. What Wordsworth does achieve is a similacrum of
the disrobed self. Wordsworth's *persona* of a poet empowered by nature and
unveiled by his own quest for self-transcendence is itself a mask, but a mask
that he holds onto with such consistency and earnestness that it *apparently*
becomes, even to him, the real naked self. If Wordsworth were to strip the

mask away (an unthinkable act), he would risk not only poetic disempowerment but also poetic suicide. If his persona "be but a vain belief," then his powerful flow of emotion, his strength of vision, is meaningless.

If one of Byron's favorite castigating adjectives is "soft," Wordsworth's favorite laudatory term is "power." For him poetry is defined by a quest for poetic self-identity that is mirrored by the quest for manhood. No poet before him associates the achievement of poetic identity so closely with the passage to masculine maturity. Poems as varied as *The Prelude, The Ruined Cottage, The White Doe of Rylestone,* "Tintern Abbey," the Lucy lyrics, and *The Recluse* all ally the quest for masculine self-possession with the gaining of poetic identity. Even in "Tintern Abbey" where his immediate audience is presumably Dorothy, his objective remains the same.[7] The man who realizes himself is the one who achieves a powerful inner vision that embraces all who come in contact with him, or it is the man who is capable of enforcing such a vision on others. Like the numerous young men in his poems who learn either from the immediate experience of nature or from an older man who has imbibed the power of nature, the poet transforms the seemingly passive feeling of inner life within the self into the outward action of achieved manhood.

Wordsworth's repeated claim of returning to the ordinary language of men in a state of nature must be viewed not only in terms of its duplicitous tendency to elevate the language of the common classes and to celebrate the primordial power of natural experience. It must also be viewed in terms of the image of the poet that Wordsworth is attempting to promote. When Wordsworth says that a poet is a man speaking to men, we should not take the gendered locution lightly. He concocts a history of the poet that makes him a sort of first man, the natural man who is compelled to write from his direct experience in a life of action. In the Appendix to the 1802 Preface to *Lyrical Ballads,* he writes:

The earliest poets of all nations generally wrote from passion excited by real events; they wrote naturally, and as men: feeling powerfully as they did, their language was daring, and figurative. In succeeding times, Poets, and Men ambitious of the fame of Poets, perceiving the influence of such language, and desirous of producing the same effect without being animated by the same passion, set themselves to a mechanical adoption of these figures of speech, and made use of them, sometimes with propriety, but much more frequently applied them to feelings and thoughts with which they had no natural connection whatsoever. A language was thus insensibly produced, differing materially from the real language of men in *any situation.* (*Selected Prose* 302–303, Wordsworth's emphasis)

The origin of poetry in the active life of "real events" stresses the power and influence of the poetic vocation. Ambitious men attempt to achieve the fame of these first poets by mimicking their influential language. The movement from "real events" to "poetic diction," a kind of "progress of refinement" (304) is as well a process of degeneration or corruption, and is perhaps one of the sources for and targets of Peacock's satire; Wordsworth's task is to return the language, and by extension the feeling and thought, to its aboriginal source in the real events, to embolden the language and re-empower the influence of the poet. Just beneath—though not far—Wordsworth's prose lies an ideal of the natural man of action, if not the noble savage, whose daring conquest of the wilderness is naturally expressed in "daring" figures of speech. This is what Wordsworth calls "the language of extraordinary occasions" (303), and although he never specifies these occasions, I think we can imagine the kinds of daring events his earliest poets would be engaged in and record, notably the hunt, the battle, the winning of a woman's love, the conquest.

What remains a submerged but governing paradigm of the poetic vocation in the Preface and its Appendix becomes blatant in the "Essay, Supplementary to the Preface of 1815." Like Byron, Wordsworth here attempts to identify the qualities of great poetry by categorizing and criticizing contemporary readers of poetry, an indication once again of the romantic poet's distress with market-based readership. He begins the essay by noting the effect of poetry on the young of both sexes:

With the young of both sexes, Poetry is, like love, a passion; but, for much the greater part of those who have been proud of its power over their minds, a necessity soon arises of breaking the pleasing bondage; or it relaxes of itself;—the thoughts being occupied in domestic cares, or the time engrossed by business. (*Selected Prose* 387)

The adolescent interest in poetry is emotional, both in that it evokes immediate, noncontemplative, unregulated responses (unlike the response of those who are mature, who have "thought long and deeply") and in that it is all-consuming and undifferentiated desire. This obsession, not dissimilar from the self-indulgent obsession of pubescent love, must, like that love, be broken away from as the young move into responsible adulthood, into domestic cares (for women?) and into business (for men?). Like Byron, then, Wordsworth is implicitly concerned with separating his mature poetry from the sentimental poetry written by ladies for the applause of nursery damsels and children. As Wordsworth acknowledges the necessity (and therefore the social good) of breaking this passionate bond with poetry, he nonetheless wants to assert another kind of passion for poetry appropriate for men, another kind of powerful feeling that is neither thoughtless nor undifferentiated. In order to salvage the influence of poetry during the phase of social responsibility, he must discriminate between vulnerable juvenile emotion and powerful emotion recollected and regulated by the "philosophic mind." Otherwise, readers, like Peacock, will begin to confuse Wordsworth's poetry of powerful emotion with the unregulated passion of children and lesser sentimental poets.

Byron makes a gesture similar to Wordsworth's when he bids adieu to "childish joys" in "To Romance." As Byron leaves romance's "votive train of girls and boys," however, he wants to claim that he is moving beyond the domain of emotion, beyond unregulated emotional experience, to an experience in which emotion is always subordinated to the sobering sway of reality. Byron emphasizes the disjunction between naive subjection to feeling and sophisticated awareness of the limits of feeling, an awareness that is the source of wit. (And as we shall see later, wit belongs to the province of men and is sometimes seen as off limits to women.) The romance votive "turns aside from real woe, / To steep in dew thy [romance's] gaudy shrine" (*Poetical Works* 39–40) The subjection to emotion, characteristic of romance, leads to "deceit," "affectation," and "sickly Sensibility," that is, to self-deceit (thinking that we can fully trust our feelings), as well as to a loss of sense of proportion concerning the significance of our feeling to others and to the indifferent world.[8] As Byron acknowledges, " 'tis hard to quit the dreams / [w]hich haunt the unsuspicious soul" (9–10), but in order for Byron to mature as a man and as a poet, he must break away from this adolescent self-indulgence:

> I break the fetters of my youth;
> No more I tread they mystic round,
> But leave thy realms for those of Truth.
> (6–8)

Unlike Wordsworth, Byron wants totally to disassociate himself from poetry derived from domestic emotion because such poetry inevitably creates a "Fond fool," who loves "a sparkling eye," rather than a hardened worldly realist. Whereas Byron seeks to escape domestication in order to master it, Wordsworth seeks to master domestication by inhabiting it, transforming it, and thus ruling it.

In his Supplementary essay, Wordsworth proceeds to categorize the kinds of readers that result from the breaking of this original passionate ("passion" being another of his favorite terms) bondage.[9] Poetry, in each of these categories, becomes trivialized, its power diminished, and its "occasional" (meaning both infrequent and unserious) readers incapable of judging great poetry. Whether these readers resort to poetry as a "fashionable pleasure," as a "consolation," or as a "study" in old age, they misapprehend and abuse its function. Wordsworth is interested here in establishing the idea that popularity is no sign of lasting power, stressing the productivity of poetry by making an implicit analogy to labor and industry: he has "not laboured in vain," he says, "that the products of [his] industry will endure" (408). Like Byron, he recognizes the massive power that rests in the reading decisions of the public, but his appeal to that power is uneasy and duplicitous. With one hand he grants readers the power they must definitely hold over his poetic fate, yet with the other hand he reinvests the poet himself with full power to determine the influence and endurance of his vision. It is not the "Public," he says, but the "People" that "preserve" great poetry. The difference between the two, however, is less forthcoming. It would seem to be primarily that the People are as divinely inspired as the Poet himself, "their intellect and their wisdom" being neither of "transitory" nor of "local" origin; whereas the Public consists of the "clamour of that small though loud portion of the community, ever governed by factitious influence, which, under the name of the Public, passes itself, upon the unthinking, for the People"

(413). Who are the "unthinking" if not the very People who with time become the "voice that issues from this Spirit"? If we push his logic far enough, we see that the People are actually those who have a power akin to the Poet's, and that their decision endures, quite simply, because the "Deity" has ordained it in the same way that the Poet's power partakes of the "Vision and the Faculty divine" (413). As Rzepka suggests, "Wordsworth is uncomfortable with the idea of an audience completely beyond his power to manipulate outside the boundaries of his persona" (69).

As Wordsworth describes the poetic vocation, we see as well its basis in his assumptions about masculine self-possession, manhood, and male conquest:

If there be one conclusion more forcibly pressed upon us than another by the review which has been given of the fortunes and fate of poetical Works, it is this,—that every author, as far as he is great and at the same time *original,* has had the task of *creating* the taste by which he is to be enjoyed: so has it been, so will it continue to be. . . . The predecessors of an original Genius of a high order will have smoothed the way for all that he has in common with them;—and much he will have in common; but, for what is peculiarly his own, he will be called upon to clear and often to shape his own road:—he will be in the condition of Hannibal among the Alps. (408, Wordsworth's emphases)

Wordsworth begins by remembering the participation of both sexes in the reading of poetry, but he ends by repressing the feminine presence in the poetic transaction. His world of poetry quickly becomes, unconsciously but purposively, a world of aggressive desire and conquest. The association of the great and original poet with the Alps is neither arbitrary nor singular; it is a romantic commonplace with a masculinist rationale. The condition of Hannibal among the Alps is the condition of the man who singlehandedly conquers the world, makes a road for others to follow, but makes them lesser men in following, and makes other and greater roads more difficult to create. It is the poet as man of action, as masculine quester, as ruler of visionary empires. The association of poetry with juvenile love, with puerile emotion, has been scrapped for a more virile association that subsumes the vulnerability of emotion as an active and "profound" power. The wise reader becomes a little Hannibal, who dares to read with an originality that cooperates with the poet's own. Just as the poet aims at transmuting the raw power of passion into daring and influential language, the reader's lesser mission becomes achieving the capacity to read that daring and original language.

Passion, it must be observed, is derived from a word which signifies *suffering;* but the connection which suffering has with effort, with exertion, and *action,* is immediate and inseparable. How strikingly is this property of human nature exhibited by the fact, that, in popular language, to be in a passion, is to be angry!—But,

> "Anger in hasty *words* or *blows*
> Itself discharges on its foes."

To be moved, then, by a passion, is to be excited, often to external, and always to internal, effort; whether for the continuance and strengthening of the passion, or for its suppression. (409–410, Wordsworth's emphases)

As opposed to a feminine poet like Hemans, Wordsworth is anxious to discriminate between the passion that is the intense suffering of a victim's passivity and the passion that is the suffering of exertion, indignation, violent aggression, and conquest. He cannot purge the former meaning from the latter, but he can attempt to subordinate the former to the latter in the hope of being able to exploit both meanings without being vulnerable to the former. Wordsworth himself stresses the relation between "words" and "blows," between seemingly passive inner feeling and external active conquest. Poetic language is no less potent than the actual physical strength of the warrior.

The notion that a life devoted to writing tends to emasculate men may have been nothing new, but it must have exerted intensified pressure on male writers once women had become so overtly influential as readers and writers. In an 1812 entry of his journal, Byron, articulating the pressure not to write, also shows how this pressure is connected to the fear of emasculation and the anxiety of being judged by the public. He begins by making a pyramid with the greatest poet of his time at the peak (W. Scott) and moving down to "The Many" at the base of the pyramid. "I have ranked the names upon my triangle more upon what I believe popular opinion," he writes, "than any decided opinion of my own" (Moore's *Works of Lord Byron* 2: 276). Like the difference between Wordsworth's Public and People, however, this distinction seems dubious, considering that what sparks the chain of thought which leads to the pyramid is his own assessment of Scott. After noting that he owes Scott a letter, he writes: "I regret to hear from others that he has lately been unfortunate in pecuniary involvements. He is undoubtedly the Monarch of Parnassus, and the most *English* of bards. I should place Rogers next in the living list, [etc.]" (2: 275). Byron's journal, though ostensibly written for himself, is obviously intended for posterity; in completing the list, he feels future generations looking over his shoulder, and quickly attributes the ordering to "popular opinion" rather than to his own judgment. From the pyramid his mind moves to a report that he will be attacked in the *Quarterly Review* and the assertion that "I can sincerely say that I am not very much alive *now* to criticism" (2: 276). And the entry ends with the following comment:

I do think the preference of *writers* to *agents*—the mighty stir made about scribbling and scribes, by themselves and others—a sign of effeminacy, degeneracy, and weakness. Who would write, who had any thing better to do? 'Action—action—action'—said Demosthenes: 'Actions—actions,' I say, and not writing,—least of all, rhyme. Look at the querulous and monotonous lives of the 'genus;'—except Cervantes, Tasso, Dante, Ariosto, Kleist (who were brave and active citizens), Aeschylus, Sophocles, and some other of the antiques also—what a worthless, idle brood it is! (2: 277, Byron's emphases)

Without the light humor of Peacock, Byron's point is the same. To make words into blows seems to Byron, at this early age, impossible. Later, Byron will attempt to reclaim the agency of writing by writing into poetry the agency of his "brave and active" life, for a life of writing divorced from actual manly adventure, for him, is no better than a life of writing wed to domestic calm.

Aware of the importance of real agency to Byron's poetic pose, Moore stresses this quality again and again in the memoir. He celebrates Byron's athletic prowess, all the more impressive because of the poet's club foot, and proudly points out that, as a boy, Byron had visions of greatness as a chieftain, hero, and warrior (1: 139). Objecting to D'Israeli's idea that "a youthful genius" tends to have a "disinclination to athletic sports and exercises," Moore puts forward a long list of poets who engaged well in war, "the most turbulent of exercises," and other sports (see the footnote 1: 63–64). It is not enough to be athletic, however; Byron must also roam. Moore speaks of "the stirring and healthful influences of [Byron's] roving life" (2: 10), just as he lauds Byron's "love of solitude" as a necessary ingredient for poetic greatness (2: 4 and 144).

3

While Byron literally goes forth on Wordsworth's solitary quest, feeling the need to make real blows in the world in order for his words to be credible, Wordsworth remains snugly at home, claiming that the impact of his words derives ironically from the metaphoricity of his blows. Able to strike his blow inward as well as outward, the poet—unlike the scientist, the industrialist, or the conqueror—can wed the internal conquest of spiritual possession to the external conquest of material possessions. And as Wordsworth so frequently points out, the poet's conquest is universal, for its realm is the "widening . . . sphere of human sensibility," which allows it to establish its reign over all human beings.

Genius is the introduction of a new element into the intellectual universe: or, if that be not allowed, it is the application of powers to objects on which they had not before been exercised, or the employment of them in such a manner as to produce effects hitherto unknown. What is all this but an advance, or a conquest, made by the soul of the poet? (Essay, Supplementary 410)

Like the conqueror, his "new mission" is "to extend [the] kingdom" (411), but not simply an external kingdom of things, of territory and people, but also the internal kingdom of ideas and feelings.

As Wordsworth re-empowers the poetic vocation and capitalizes on its capacity to cultivate the province of feeling for the manly action of conquest, he also stresses poetry's alliance with science, the discipline that seems to threaten it most. "The appropriate business of poetry," Wordsworth claims in an aside, "is as permanent as pure science" (388). It is in the Preface to *Lyrical Ballads,* however, that we get his most lucid claims for the priority of poetry over science. Science, he suggests, is mediated, local, simply a personal acquisition and limited knowledge, whereas poetry is immediate, universal, and comprehensive knowledge:

The knowledge both of the Poet and the Man of science is pleasure; but the knowledge of the one cleaves to us as a necessary part of our existence, our natural and unalienable inheritance; the other is a personal and individual acquisition, slow to come to us, and by no habitual and direct sympathy connecting us with our fellow-beings. The Man of science seeks truth as a remote and unknown benefactor; he cherishes and loves it in his solitude: the Poet, singing a song in which all human beings join with him, rejoices in the presence of truth as our visible friend and hourly companion. Poetry is the breath and finer spirit of all knowledge; it is the impassioned expression which is in the countenance of all Science. (292)

On the verge of science's ascendency, Wordsworth (and the other romantics) reasserts poetry's more universal and potent capacity, suggesting that it is the poet who leads the way, not the scientist, that it is the poet who serves as the source of authority, not the scientist. And once again his assertion is expressed in a metaphor of masculine conquest, of empire building, that suggests a spiritual Hannibal conquering Alps both of the soul and of the physical world:

In spite of difference of soil and climate, of language and manners, of laws and customs: in spite of things silently gone out of mind, and things violently destroyed; the Poet binds together by passion and knowledge the vast empire of human society, as it is spread over the whole earth, and over all time. The objects of the Poet's thoughts are every where; though the eyes and senses of man are, it is true, his favourite guides, yet he will follow wheresoever he can find an atmosphere of sensation in which to move his wings. Poetry is the first and last of all knowledge—it is as immortal as the heart of man. (292)

The poet comes before the scientist and also after. "If the labours of Men of science should ever create any material revolution, direct or indirect, in our condition, and in the impressions which we habitually receive," Wordsworth states, "the Poet will sleep then no more than at present; he will be ready to follow the steps of the Man of science, not only in those general indirect effects, but he will be at his side, carrying sensation into the midst of the objects of the science itself" (292). Wordsworth is anxious to move the realm of sensation—the poet's inner expanse—into the realm of the "manifestly and palpably material." Even when poets follow—or move alongside—scientists in the revolutions of human history, they are the actual conquerors and rulers of the universe, for without their "divine spirit" the "transfiguration" cannot be achieved. What is only implicit in Wordsworth, but what Shelley in his *Defence of Poetry,* following Wordsworth's lead, makes explicit, is the poet's function of regulating humanity's ability to master the material world. Since the "creative faculty" is "the basis of all knowledge," it "creates new materials for knowledge and power and pleasure . . . and engenders in the mind a desire to reproduce and arrange them" (*Political Writings* 190–191). According to Shelley, if people do not heed this creative faculty, if they blindly follow the scientist without heeding the poet, only catastrophe can result: "The cultivation of those sciences which have enlarged the limits of the empire of man over the external world has, for want of the poetical faculty, proportionally circumscribed those of the internal world; and man, having enslaved the elements, remains himself a slave" (190).

Typically, Byron expresses his competitive urge against scientists and industrialists with the weapon of disdainful exclusion, rather than the kind of inclusion by absorption that we see in Wordsworth and Shelley. In the first canto of *Don Juan* (stanzas 128–133), the narrator's attention is diverted away from the "first and passionate love" of Juan and Julia to the new phenomenon of making and marketing scientific inventions. As usual, there is logic in this train of thought, though at first the divergence may seem merely a diversion. What associates first love with scientific and capitalistic inventiveness is the tree of knowledge, which is the efficient cause of both:

> But sweeter still than this, than these, than all
>   Is first and passionate love. It stands alone,
> Like Adam's recollection of his fall.
>   The tree of knowledge has been plucked; all's known,
> And life yields nothing further to recall
>   Worthy of this ambrosial sin, so shown
> No doubt in fable as the unforgiven
> Fire which Prometheus filched for us from heaven.
>
> Man's a strange animal and makes strange use
>   Of his own nature and the various arts,
> And likes particularly to produce
>   Some new experiment to show his parts.
> This is the age of oddities let loose,
>   Where different talents find their different marts.
> You'd best begin with truth, and when you've lost your
> Labour, there's a sure market for imposture.
>   (Canto 1, stanzas 127–128)

Just as first love must be accompanied by a recollection of the fall, so must human inventiveness. Just as first love reveals the unconscious desire to regain paradise, so with human inventiveness, and both are doomed to fail, for both unleash as much distress (if not more) upon the world as that initial eating of the tree of knowledge. As the Titan who brought light to earth, Prometheus is the appropriate associative transition to "the age of oddities let loose." Prometheus brings the spirit of science and industry to humanity only to bring with it the experience of mindless tyranny. And just as the Promethean fire must always recall the Jupiterian vulture that eats at Prometheus's liver, human productivity—whether it is capitalist, scientific, or poetic—binds humanity to a tyrannical mountain of its own invention. We may begin in seeking a science of truth, but we inevitably end in the "market of imposture."

As much as our desire forces us to make love, it spurs us to make and market our inventions. Both are forms of knowledge in which we risk ourselves in the hope of fulfilling and refining human desire, but both, instead, propagate more desire. Juan's lusty love for Julia only intensifies his lust and love for Julia, or for Haidee, or for whomever replaces the other as the product of Juan's otherwise aimless desire. Likewise, new inventions only intensify the desire to acquire and consume, to invent and market. "What wondrous new machines have late been spinning! / I said the smallpox has gone out of late; / Perhaps it may be followed by the great" (stanza 130). The smallpox vaccination may look like progress, but it is merely a byproduct of an interminable cycle of disease and cure, new disease and new cure. Although the

scientists and capitalists want to conceive of themselves as great men bringing progress a step at a time to an ever-improved culture, Byron is extremely
cynical, to say the least:

> This is the patent age of new inventions
>   For killing bodies and for saving souls,
> All propagated with the best intentions.
>   Sir Humphry Davy's lantern, by which coals
> Are safely mined for in the mode he mentions,
>   Timbuctoo travels, voyages to the poles
> Are ways to benefit mankind, as true
> Perhaps as shooting them at Waterloo.
>   (stanza 132)

The implicit equation of saving souls with killing bodies, the equation of spiritual conquest with warfare, pinpoints the ludicrous tragedy of human aspirations for progress. Perhaps also implicit in Byron's satire is the paradox that
Shelley points out with his more characteristic earnestness. All of these inventions may give humanity the semblance of having enslaved the elements,
but humanity itself remains enslaved by its own acquisitive desire, by its own
inability to control itself, to root out tyranny from a supposedly enlightened
culture. Science can save human souls no more than the market can satiate
human desire.

Appropriately, Byron's digression concludes with the goal gained and
then undercut:

> 'Tis pity though in this sublime world that
>   Pleasure's a sin and sometimes sin's a pleasure.
> Few mortals know what end they would be at,
>   But whether glory, power or love or treasure,
> The path is through perplexing ways, and when
> The goal is gained, we die you know—and then?
>   (stanza 133)

The only pleasure available is the systematically unsystematic sin of erring, of
digression, for moving "through perplexing ways" toward "what end they
would be at" is a form of self-deception. Glory, power, love, and treasure are
all lumped together as end-products that are really themselves only deceptive
byproducts on the way to death. Through this satirical critique of "the patent
age of new inventions," Byron offers a parallel commentary to Wordsworth's
and Shelley's.

Although he does not explicitly include poetic conquest with the other
forms of self-deluding productivity, we would be remiss not to consider the
relationship. Does Byron implicitly exclude the poem he is writing from this
self-deceptive cycle of market enterprise and inventiveness? Through its intentional pleasurable sinning, through its refusal to engage in the deception
of origins and ends, objects and objectives, *Don Juan* could be read as a cure
for this disease—in which case, like Wordsworth and Shelley, Byron views
poetry as capable of superceding the scientific and industrial vocations. But

such a reading is problematic. *Don Juan* partakes of the cycle as much as any other product of human desire, trapping the reader in a process of acquisition and consumption, getting and spending, as surely as scientific or capitalist enterprise. In the basest sense, Byron composes the poem as though it is endless as much because such a ploy allows him to fill his pockets ceaselessly with the income from each new installment as because philosophically he is opposed to the myth of beginnings and ends. He writes the poem for a greedy market of readers who want always more, the more they are given. If anything, *Don Juan* is the perfect paradigm of the futility of attempting to transcend the cycle of desiring productivity, for the poet's self-consciousness of the cycle itself intensifies the irony without slowing the cyclic process.

By turning to *Childe Harold's Pilgrimage* and the significance of the sublime, we can see Byron in a less droll mood, more earnestly attempting to empower and glorify the poetic vocation by associating it with acts of physical conquest. Climbing mountains is the activity that perfectly embodies the poet's charge of self quest and world conquest. Testing the power and limits of self, it stresses the solitude of self-questing and pits the self against nature's power. The height of the mountain represents both the everspiraling ascent of imagination and the everpresent threat of falling, the loss of self-identity, the reabsorption into nature's overriding power. It is from mountains that prophets proclaim their truths; for the poet-prophet the mountain symbolizes the necessary solitude of the leaders of men and the necessary stance of truth, its transcendence, its elusiveness, and its immense might. It is another metaphor of masculine potency, which through association, reinvests the poetic vocation with power and influence.

In the Napoleonic passage of Canto 3 of *Childe Harold's Pilgrimage,* we can see clearly the relation between the poet's quest for self-possession and the conqueror's quest for world possession, each turning into the other with dizzying rapidity.

> [T]here is a fire
> And motion of the soul which will not dwell
> In its own narrow being, but aspire
> Beyond the fitting medium of desire;
> And, but once kindled, quenchless evermore,
> Preys upon high adventure, nor can tire
> Of aught but rest; a fever at the core,
> Fatal to him who bears, to all who ever bore.
>   (Canto 3, stanza 42)

This "lust to shine or rule" is a contagion shared by "Conquerors and Kings, / Founders of sects and systems, to whom add / Sophists, Bards, Statesmen" (stanza 43). Byron's cynical irony disallows the kind of optimism that characterizes Blake's, Coleridge's, Wordsworth's, and Shelley's view of the poet as conqueror, but it does not diminish his need to identify with the conqueror. Byron reminds us that "[h]e who ascends to mountain-tops, shall find / the loftiest peaks most wrapt in clouds and snow" (stanza 45); the solitude of self-possession can be damning and the "reward" of the "summits" "[e]nvied, yet how unenviable!" For Byron the quest for self-possession must inevitably become a mad and aimless masquerade and the empires gained in conquest must become "[a] wider space, an ornamented grave" (stanza 48).

When Byron points out that power, even the power of imagination bridled by the self-possessing poet, breeds only contagion, madness, "keen contest and destruction," and ends, like all things, in death, he is subverting the very basis of poetic self-questing. By suggesting that the power of the soul's empire leads to the same outcome as the power of worldly empires, he calls into question the aim of the quest for self-possession and the wisdom of poetic conquest. Nevertheless, since poets and conquerors are driven by desire that is intensified the more it is quenched, Byron has no choice but to climb the Alps and look down, like Napoleon or Hannibal, at the folly he has conquered. "The clouds above me to the white Alps tend," he says, "And I must pierce them, and survey whate'er / May be permitted" (stanza 109). So it is not surprising that Moore also wants to connect the poet to Napoleon: Byron "was, in short, as much the child and representative of the Revolution, in poesy, as another great man of the age, Napoleon, was in statesmanship and warfare" (2: 132).

In the end, Byron's mask, his identity as a poet, is so tied to the quest for heroic self-possession and visionary conquest that he is unable to end the quest or take off the mask. What enables him to continue questing and conquering, despite the fact that the quest is aimless and the conquest folly, is the presence of the feminine—the prospect of feminine nature, the promise of feminine love, the need to protect feminine purity. Byron turns to "Maternal Nature," to Augusta Leigh, to Julia, to Julie, and to Ada, the only eternally pure presences in his aimless quest. In Byron this feminine presence paradoxically is both the nurturer of the desire that impels the quest and the only escape from "a contentious world, striving where none are strong" (stanza 69):

> Is it not better, then, to be alone,
> And love Earth only for its earthly sake?
> By the blue rushing of the arrowy Rhone,
> Or the pure bosom of its nursing lake,
> Which feeds it as a mother who doth make
> A fair but froward infant her own care,
> Kissing its cries away as these awake;—
> Is it not better thus our lives to wear,
> Than join the crushing crowd, doom'd to inflict or bear?
> (stanza 71)

The feminine consoles his "sorrow," his need to "act and suffer," and encourages him to "remount at last / [w]ith a fresh pinion" (stanza 73).[10] This feminine salvation, however, is itself only temporary, unstable, and perhaps even self-deluding. It does not protect him from the world of masculine competition any more than it snatches him from death. It simply provides him a shelter from which to review and preview the contested territory toward which he must return perpetually to do combat.

Byron borrows the idea of maternal nature as consolation to the quest-weary from Wordsworth via Shelley. Of course, in Wordsworth nature as nurturing mother plays an even more crucial role. For him Mother Nature not only consoles; she is also the primary force in constructing the identity of the poet and fostering the passage of the poet into active manhood.[11] She can, therefore, also be construed as a primary threat to the myth of self-possession. We must be careful not to confuse nature's capacity to bear forth and nurture with that self-justifying power which nature merely serves. Whether we locate that power in the aboriginal self within the self that the strong poet attempts to possess or in some transcendent force above and behind nature that gives meaning to natural signs, it is the alpha and omega of the poetic quest for Wordsworth; it engenders desire and it ever holds out the promise of fulfilled desire, of the fully possessed self, of unmediated and unlimited vision, of the world conquered by the might of self-engendering imagination.

The poem in which Wordsworth talks so much about himself, *The Prelude,* is a quest story, a story that traces one man's search for a self, for a position from which to view the self, and for a position from which to grasp the world once the self is possessed. It is a story that must end in conquest, in a world envisioned and claimed, if the validity of the quest itself is to be ensured. With Coleridge helping to establish the ever-widening borders of the poet's own identity and with the feminine presence of nature exciting his desire and urging him toward self-possession, Wordsworth, after some initial self-doubt, moves confidently toward the "honourable toil" of "manhood now mature" (Book 1, lines 624–625).

Predictably, a climactic moment of the quest (if not the climax itself) occurs as a conquest in the Alps. Ironically, Wordsworth's moment of conquest is constituted not by a vision of the Alps themselves, not by nature's verification of his self-possessed identity, but by a *failure* of such vision. Wordsworth's conquest comes not at the peak—where the mountains would offer him a view of the world he is to claim—but in the descent. The poet stresses here that the power that allows for conquest is beyond or above nature, is situated on some mysterious plane that not even nature's highest mountain can reach. The conquest is all the more miraculous in occurring in the descent, the phase of falling, rather than at Napoleonic heights.

The moment of being powerfully lost, which seizes Wordsworth when the actual vision of having traversed the Alps fails him, is transformed into a moment of re-vision. Through imagination he is able to fulfill the promise of conquest, and furthermore he is able to do so apparently without the troublesome mediation of maternal nature:

> Imagination—here the Power so called
> Through sad incompetence of human speech,
> That awful Power rose from the mind's abyss
> Like an unfathered vapour that enwraps,
> At once, some lonely traveller. I was lost;
> Halted without an effort to break through;

> But to my conscious soul I now can say—
> "I recognize thy glory:" in such strength
> Of usurpation, when the light of sense
> Goes out, but with a flash that has revealed
> The invisible world, doth greatness make abode.
>
> (Book 6, lines 592–602)

Imagination's "strength of usurpation" is greater than the "light of sense" on which any natural vision would depend. The Power that moves Wordsworth toward his poetic identity, which moves him toward his masculine maturity, and which enables him to envision his own world, is a power beyond even nature's ultimate control.

When Wordsworth compares imagination to an "unfathered vapour," he brings attention to its source of authority, or more precisely to the lack of such authority. He does not use the word "unmothered," a word conceptually awkward (and psychologically troubling) from the masculinist romantic perspective but linquistically feasible, because he is not so much referring here to the birth as to the final cause that ordains and justifies existence itself. (Likewise, "unparented" would not work for him in the passage because it brings to mind mere progenitorship rather than justification for existence.) Wordsworth is saying that imagination, or what he more accurately identifies as infinitude and desire, ordains itself, is its own justification, is its own source of authority and originates itself. Wordsworth's allusion to Genesis (the vapour and the abyss) helps to establish the idea that desire gives birth to the human (from the male vantage point) world of perception and value in the same way that God gives birth to the universe and its hierarchies, not as a mother who bears her child from an impregnated seed, but as a father who inseminates existence from nothingness. Mothering implies for Wordsworth bearing forth and sustaining life, giving birth and giving sustenance, an activity that he places secondarily both in terms of temporality and value. In Wordsworth's scheme, mothering merely enacts and nourishes what has already been ordained by motherless fathering. By making imagination father itself, and by unmothering the originating act of fathering, Wordsworth, following Judeo-Christian tradition, manages, in this climactic moment of his quest poem, to defeminize the conquest that has been made possible through the good auspices of feminine nature.[12]

The conquest is the quest itself, a never-ending movement toward fulfilled vision and self-comprehension, an ever intensifying desire for what is desired. It is the optimistic side of Byron's aimless masquerade and foolish conquest:

> Our destiny, our being's heart and home,
> Is with infinitude, and only there;
> With hope it is, hope that can never die,
> Effort, and expectation, and desire,
> And something evermore about to be.
>
> (Book 6, lines 604–608)

As Wordsworth bares his soul to Coleridge, to us, he hopes to convince us that what is within the deepest self, when earnestly searched out, can be unmasked, that the kernel of self-engendering feeling at the heart of self is not weak and undirected but the regeneration of primal strength. Its constitution is not the vulnerability of aimless, undifferentiated, and uncontrollable desire, but the strength of usurpation, the capacity for total vision and unmediated truth, "[t]he types and symbols of Eternity, / [o]f first, and last, and midst, and without end" (Book 6, lines 639–640).

Wordsworth contrasts the mountain-climbing episode of Book 6 with the ultimate sublime experience in the final book of his poem, the ascent of Mount Snowdon. He repeats the images used in the less successful ascent in Book 6, but reunifies all elements as a metonymy of his all-embracing and all-harmonizing vision. Thus, nature, having been purged, is restored, but in a place subordinate to the vision of the poetic mind. Therefore, Wordsworth returns to the image of darkness and light, vapors and brooding, but this time he indicates how at the very moment of his physical *ascent* also miraculously occurs his visionary *assent,* nature working in tandem with mind, nature working for the sake of mind.

> And I, as chanced, the foremost of the band;
> When at my feet the ground appeared to brighten,
> And with a step or two seemed brighter still;
> Nor was time given to ask or learn the cause,
> For instantly a light upon the turf
> Fell like a flash, and lo! as I looked up,
> The Moon hung naked in a firmament
> Of azure without cloud, and at my feet
> Rested a silent sea of hoary mist.
> A hundred hills their dusky backs upheaved
> All over this still ocean; and beyond,
> Far, far beyond, the solid vapours stretched,
> In headlands, tongues, and promontory shapes,
> Into the main Atlantic, that appeared
> To dwindle, and give up his majesty,
> Usurped upon far as the sight could reach.
>   (Book 14, lines 34–49)

Replicating the language of the earlier mountain experience, Wordsworth also reproduces his earlier usurpation without having to discount entirely the presence of nature's nurturing role. Despite his offhand "as chanced," it is no coincidence that he is the "foremost" quester, for his leadership is a sign of his conquering vision, of his ordination of himself. By using Biblical language, such as "lo!," he accentuates his divine role. It is also no coincidence that at the very moment of his achieved ascent, the light breaks across the landscape in full splendor, emblematizing the correspondence between nature's light and his own visionary brightness.

When we come to the end of Wordsworth's quest poem, then, we come to its beginning, to Wordsworth's beginning as a poet and as a man. As we come to know his vision, we are conquered by it, unless we are stronger than he. For Wordsworth, this, of course, need not be an inimical conquest; it takes on, rather, the qualities of a benign (and divine) reign, as indicated by the final lines of his poem:

> Prophets of Nature, we to them will speak
> A lasting inspiration, sanctified
> By reason, blest by faith: what we have loved,
> Others will love, and we will teach them how;
> Instruct them how the mind of man becomes
> A thousand times more beautiful than the earth
> On which he dwells, above this frame of things
> (Which, 'mid all revolution in the hopes
> And fears of men, doth still remain unchanged)
> In beauty exalted, as it is itself
> Of quality and fabric more divine.
>
> (Book 14, lines 444–454)

Wordsworth's earnest optimism and his uncritical self-confidence hinder him from questioning the implications of the idea that poetic identity is constituted by masculine self-questing and visionary conquest. His vision after *The Prelude* is even more hemmed in by the complacency of masculine self-possession and even more tyrannized by an imperial, sometimes even dictatorial, voice. Unlike Byron or Shelley, he never questions how the romantic poetic identity sustains sexual and political hierarchies; how it limits the poet's capacity for sympathy; how it limits readers' capacity for possessing themselves and sharing the experience of vision or how it discourages "the exertion of a co-operating *power* in the mind of the Reader" (Essay, Supplementary 409, Wordsworth's emphasis). Wordsworth seems most comfortable in the role when he is *most* conscious of its sociopolitical implications. Both Byron and Shelley, however, are able to see and to offer a critique of such a vision, because they are so sympathetic and prone to it and so conscious of its limitations in their literary father, Wordsworth. But not even the second generation of romantics, who are much more attuned to the implications of these masculinist metaphors of power, are able to sever their poetic identity from those metaphors. It indicates how culturally entrenched is the feeling that influence must express itself in terms of self-identity, possession, and conquest. It indicates how ingrained is the feeling that power must be defined through distinctions of gender. Poetry motivated and shaped by the desire for self-possession, determined by the poet's aggressive relation to his fellows and the world, is not *intrinsically* masculine, but it is *sociohistorically* masculine. Quest and conquest, too, though able to be appropriated by women, are historically the means through which men have appropriated power for themselves and over women. The romantic desire to articulate visions that can speak for the whole, in the end, is betrayed by the poets' need to adopt a masculine posture in order to fulfill that desire, a posture made to seem natural and universal by suppressing its own vital relation to the politics of gender.

4

Coming down from the heights where romantic poets would have us remain, we confront the reality of early nineteenth-century poetry, a reality
starkly different from the one claimed by masculine metaphors of ever-widening
poetic power. The real situation for Wordsworth includes a literary establishment (publishing houses, the reading public, and numerous popular literary
periodicals) that is extremely ambivalent about his claim to be a poet, much
more to be a great poet. The following statement, from a review of his 1807
Poems, is notable as much for what it gives Wordsworth as for what it
denies him:

Mr. W. doubtless possesses a reflecting mind, and a feeling heart; but nature seems
to have bestowed on him little of the fancy of a poet, and a foolish theory deters
him from displaying even that little. In addition to this, he appears to us to starve
his mind in solitude.—Hence the undue importance he attaches to trivial incidents—hence the mysterious kind of view that he takes of human nature and human life—and hence, finally, the unfortunate habit he has acquired of attaching
exquisite emotions to objects which excite none in any other human breast.

Although the review praises rather begrudgingly two attributes, "a reflecting
mind, and a feeling heart," which Wordsworth himself values, it also brings
attention to the kind of vulnerability that must always accompany these attributes. And the review asserts Wordsworth's failure in the agenda that matters most to him: the project of persuading his readers to accept his vision of
the "mysterious kind of view that he takes of human nature and human life."
What the reviewer condemns in Wordsworth are the very attributes that we
have seen Wordsworth claim as signs of his power. Wordsworth's assertion
that he will teach others how to feel and think by reflecting on his own solitary mind excited by natural objects is held up for scorn in this review.

According to Wordsworth, the point is *not* that he can reflect and feel—
all poets during his time claimed these essential capacities. Rather, the point
is that he can transform vulnerable feelings and seemingly feeble words into
actions and blows that forcefully shape and direct his culture. The reviewer
keeps asunder his feeling and its reflection, his mind and its observed objects,
whereas Wordsworth bases the whole of his poetics on his unique capacity to
marry "exquisite emotions" and seemingly trivial objects to the "philosophic
mind." While accepting Wordsworth's power of self-possession, but denying
its validity and value, and while denying Wordsworth's claim to ever-widening
vision, this reviewer does not even grant—no, more precisely *nature* does not
grant—Wordsworth the "fancy" required of a poet. "When a man endeavours
to make his reader enter into an association that exists in his own mind between daffodils waving in the wind, and laughter—or to teach him to see
something very fine in the fancy of crowning a little rock with snow-drops; he
fails, and is sure to fail." Has the reviewer trivialized and domesticated his
subjects, or does Wordsworth really fail to rule his domestic province of flowers and feelings through a grand universalizing vision? Although Wordsworth

might have been able partially to dismiss such reviews for being retrogressive, relying on outmoded and inadequate eighteenth-century standards, it would be difficult for him to dismiss them totally. Is this reviewer a voice of the pernicious Public, who are unknowing, or of the prophetic People, who determine poetic immortality?

Actually, it is the voice of Lucy Aikin (1781–1864), one of the real flesh-and-blood women who fuels Byron's anxieties in *English Bards and Scotch Reviewers,* writing for the *Annual Review.*[13] Although Aikin is twenty-seven when this review appears, she begins contributing to periodicals at the precocious age of seventeen. Two years after this review, her ambitious poem *Epistles on Women* is published. Aikin belongs to the second wave of publicly influential women poets, a generation who not only read and boldly criticize the work of male writers, but also boldly proclaim their own rights to a poetic vocation. The second-generation woman of letters is not only more visible than her predecessors, but also much more successful in the marketplace of periodicals and publishing houses, where writers' fates are determined. The sheer numerousness of such women and their actual influence as readers, reviewers, and poets could not help but bring attention to not only the changing status of women in British society, but also the changing status of poetry. For, as we shall see, women's emergence as poets signals as much poetry's own increasing marginality among bidders for social power as it does women's changing relation to cultural politics. To gauge the actual psychic adjustment that a poet like Wordsworth must have experienced in knowing that it was likely that a young woman might pass judgment on his poetic production is, of course, impossible. But, as we have begun to see, the aftereffects of this psychic adjustment are palpable in his poetry and in his conceptualization of the poetic vocation.

Not only have women become self-confident critics by the beginning of the century; they also constitute a sizeable part of the literary market, identifiable and extremely influential *as a group.* Some of the periodicals founded during the period, such as *Le Beau Monde,* or, *Literary and Fashionable Magazine, La Belle Assemblee;* or, *Bell's Court and Fashionable Magazine, British Ladies Magazine,* and *Lady's Monthly Museum,* cater expressly to this new market. The establishment of these magazines makes explicit the connection between fashion and *belles lettres,* between poetry and the new reading public, between poetic success and lady readers, a connection that romantic metaphors of self-possessing power are anxious to repress. That a large number of his potential readers are ladies who view literature in such fashion-laden terms can only frustrate Wordsworth's desire to see his audience as an army of lesser Hannibals, who read his poetry in order to understand how to go about their immense duty of shaping and directing culture.

When Wordsworth's 1807 volume *Poems* is reviewed in *Le Beau Monde,* the reviewer is even more explicit than Aikin about Wordsworth's failure to deploy domestic emotion for the sake of larger cultural empowerment. In *Lyrical Ballads,* the reviewer notes, "Mr. Wordsworth . . . gave considerable testimony of strong feeling and poetic powers, although like a histerical schoolgirl he had a knack of feeling about subjects with which feeling had no proper concern" (*Romantics Reviewed* Part A 40). By pointing out that "feeling and nature" are "much in use with the philosophical and *simple* poets, among whom Mr. Wordsworth is ambitious to be enrolled," the reviewer also manages to question the poet's claim to originality. Since Wordsworth's topics are neither "great" nor "universally interesting," his appeal to "our general sympathy" must go unheeded. Like Byron, and many other reviewers of the time, this critic, even though writing for a lady's magazine, implicitly and perhaps unconsciously bases the condemnation of Wordsworth's poetry partly on the phenomenon of women's writing for children previously discussed. It is the poet's school-girl hysterics, his "childish effusions," that the critic finds most troubling, labeling some of the 1807 poems "puerile beyond the power of imitation," and suggesting that it is "disgusting" to see mature men becoming the "copyists of children" (40–42).

5

North   Milton was a great poet; but a bad divine, and a miserable politician.
Tickler How can that be?—Wordsworth says that a great poet must be great in all things.
North   Wordsworth often writes like an idiot; and never more so than when he said of Milton, "his soul was like a star, and dwelt apart!" For it dwelt in tumult, and mischief, and rebellion. Wordsworth is, in all things, the reverse of Milton—a good man, and a bad poet.
Tickler What!—That Wordsworth whom Maga cries up as the Prince of Poets?
North   Be it so; I must humour the fancies of some of my friends. But had that man been a great poet, he would have produced a deep and lasting impression on the mind of England; whereas his verses are becoming less and less known every day, and he is, in good truth, already one of the illustrious obscure.
Tickler I never thought him more than a very ordinary man—with some imagination, certainly, but with no grasp of understanding, and apparently little acquainted with the history of his kind. My God! to compare such a writer with Scott and Byron!
North   And yet, with his creed, what might not a great poet have done?—That the language of poetry is but the language of strong human passion!— That in the great elementary principles of thought and feeling, common to all the race, the subject-matter of poetry is to be sought and found. . . .

This fictionalized conversation between Christopher North (John Wilson [1785–1854]) and Timothy Tickler (Robert Sym [1750–1844]) appears in 1825 in *Blackwood's Magazine* (nicknamed "Maga") as a part of the very popular series, written primarily by Wilson, *Noctes Ambrosianae* (1: 34). The series, published between 1822 and 1835, serves as a barometer of the contentious tastes of the literati as it ranges serio-humorously over the whole gamut of topics that concerned the educated classes of Britain. Although it is difficult to pin John Wilson down, for sometimes he eulogizes Wordsworth while at others he disparages him as he does here, his exaggerated and conflicting assessments of Wordsworth indicate the kind of intense debate about

Wordsworth's poetic nature, and about the nature of the poet in general, that is carried out during the time, especially from the publication of *Lyrical Ballads* to the end of the teens.

Actually, by the time Wilson pens this nocturnal conversation, Wordsworth, rather than being "one of the illustrious obscure," has gained a substantial following as "the Prince of Poets," especially among young writers, and more importantly he has played a crucial role in establishing the terms of discourse about the nature of a poet. Even as North–Wilson rejects Wordsworth's idea that "a great poet must be great in all things," he uses Wordsworthian language to measure the poet's failure: "had that man been a great poet, he would have produced a deep and lasting impression on the mind of England." That North–Wilson has fully embraced Wordsworth's "philosophical creed" is clear, and this despite the fact that Wilson is an extremely dogmatic Tory writing for perhaps the most conservative periodical of his day. As North–Wilson adopts wholeheartedly Wordsworth's "creed," the origin of that creed in revolutionary politics becomes wholly muted, partly as a result of Wordsworth's own muting of its potential radicalness. As Donald Reiman points out, all the young critics writing for "Maga" during the 1820s, including Wilson, John Gibson Lockhart (1794–1854), and William Maginn (1793–1842), "whatever their political or social views or their personal qualities . . . [,] were among the first group of critics who had been fully infected with the Romantic doctrine that poetry was essentially as important to human life as theology, or political economy, or historical study, or any other honorable human pursuit" (*The Romantics Reviewed* Part A 56). I would go further and say that the romantics are able to transform poetry-writing into a vocation that can be glorified by individuals of all political stripes exactly because they base their doctrine on the idea that poetry transcends the world of political strife even as it guides and directs that world.

Tickler is hardly exaggerating when he suggests that "the youngsters, in that absurd Magazine of yours [*Blackwood's*], set [Wordsworth] up to the stars as their idol, and kiss his very feet, as if the toes were of gold" (*Noctes Ambrosianae* 1: 35). In a *Blackwood's* review of *The White Doe of Rylestone* in 1818, the reviewer's conception of the poetic vocation is so close to Wordsworth's that it could have been written by the poet himself. The reviewer, probably Wilson, names Scott, Wordsworth, and Byron "the three great master-spirits of our day." They are poets "of perfectly original genius,—unallied to each other,—drinking inspiration from fountains far apart,—who have built up superb structures of the imagination . . . and who may indeed be said to rule, each by a legitimate sovereignty, over separate and powerful provinces in the kingdom of Mind" (*Romantics Reviewed* Part A 78). Infected with the romantics' metaphors of masculine quest and conquest, the review demonstrates to what extent romantic ideology has established its "sovereignty" in the literary world. The reviewer says of Scott's "domain": "War, as he describes it, is a noble game, a kingly pastime. He is the greatest of all War-Poets. His Poetry might make a very coward fearless" (79). Ironically, war becomes the "pastime" as poetry becomes the maker of kings, warriors, and cowards. Scott's kingly war-poetry "prevents History from becoming that which, in times of excessive refinement, it is often too apt to become—a dead letter" (79). Appropriately, the reviewer pictures Byron as holding "converse with the mighty in language worthy to be heard by the spirits of the mighty."

As Wordsworth is being canonized in *Blackwood's* and other journals, the Wordsworthian agenda of transforming the vulnerability of passive emotion into the power of manly heroic action becomes absorbed and naturalized in literary discourse. Writing in 1823 in a much more obscure and short-lived periodical *The Monthly Censor* (1822–1823), one reviewer employs the language from Wordsworth's prefaces ironically to prove the greatness of Wordsworth, once again demonstrating the circular nature of the process of canonization.

It is somewhat amusing for those who consider poetry as nothing more than a pleasant recreation—a refuge from sterner pursuits—to observe the machinery of preface and disquisition, and all the science of classification employed by Mr. Wordsworth in the various editions of his poems. But to such as look upon it as a *study,* and feel it to be one of the noblest of studies, and one which exercises a deep and abiding influence upon the character of man;—to all such the care and scrupulousness of Mr. Wordsworth will not appear a vain and contemptible labour. They will regard it as a becoming and necessary providence about that fame, which the consciousness of genius assures him is his due, and which must be accorded to him, when all the petty spite and malignant sarcasms of meaner spirits shall have sunk into oblivion. (*Romantics Reviewed* Part A 654)

So many of the reviewer's words are borrowed from Wordsworth himself that it would be pointless to try to separate them out. Implicit in the review is the distinction between the Public, "those who consider poetry as nothing more than a pleasant recreation," and the People, as the reviewer goes on to claim that "[n]ine tenths of those who read poetry and by whose decrees poetical reputations must be fixed and perpetuated, are persons of ordinary capacity" (655). The reviewer justifies Wordsworth's "science of classification" by tacitly appealing to the rigor of poetic activity, like Wordsworth, claiming its place alongside the "sterner pursuits" of those *other* occupations.

We cannot overestimate the tremendous influence that these periodicals play in establishing and sustaining romantic, especially Wordsworthian, ideology, and in supporting the myth of poetry-writing as a powerful vocation. On the other hand, it is all too easy, standing on this side of history, to overestimate the *unanimity* of opinion concerning the group of poets who propagated romantic ideology, a group which at the time is not seen as a single school. In other words, romantic ideology began to dominate the literary establishment *before* the romantic canon, as we know it, was established, and, in fact, it was the rise to power of romantic ideology that eventually enabled the consolidation of one of the most closely guarded canons of literature, the small group of male poets who have come to represent the apex of a whole literary tradition. Even with the ever-widening sway of the Wordsworthian creed in the 1820s, Wordsworth could still be, as we have seen, an object of ridicule. And other poets, with an agenda markedly different from romantic ideology, could be offered as the greatest reigning monarchs of literature. "I do not know whether my gallantry blinds me," Tickler says later in the dialogue that began with a comparison of Wordsworth and Milton, "but I prefer much of the female to the male poetry of the day" (*Noctes Ambrosianae* 1: 35). As North and Tickler go on to praise the group of female poets that we shall examine in Chapters 5 through 8, we realize that there was indeed a war being waged, quite loudly but politely, for and by women poets who are now forgotten, largely because of the romantic ideology that was formed partly in reaction to their real influence.

2

The Will to Write:
Inventing the Sources of Poetic Anxiety

We have seen how the romantic poets attempt to reinvest the poetic calling with sociopolitical influence through tropes of power that are based on categories of gender. Within this larger domain of cultural rivalry among professions is the microcosm of poetic rivalry itself. The obsessive self-imaging of the romantic poets is not only a way of asserting poetry-writing as a vocation and asserting primacy within culture over other vocations; it is as much a way of asserting primacy over other poets. Convinced that writing is more a matter of compulsion than a matter of choice, one of the romantic poet's foremost concerns, ironically, becomes his own motives and motivations for writing. And as he begins to ask why it is necessary to write, he also begins to ask what it is necessary to write, one question spilling over into the other and both becoming the subject of the poetry itself, as well as the focus of his critical analyses. Both questions contribute to, rather than allay, the trauma of poeticizing and the anxiety of influence. Once the romantic begins to believe that poets are compelled by overriding force, he must worry about how to connect the act of writing to the conventional forms and contents he has inherited, for the act of writing itself lies beneath or beyond convention in a realm circumscribed by, but not limited to, the desire-empowering self. As David Perkins has suggested, what the romantic poet desires is the freedom of desire unleashed from the historical conditions that define his desire:

To disclose the experiencing self in its full individuality, poetic style must above all be free. It must be free from the control of an audience, of traditions, of forms determined at the start. The freedom is claimed at every level, in the large structure of a poem and the least details of diction and versification. (*Wordsworth and the Poetry of Sincerity* 16)

But instead of inscribing the free play of desire, the romantic poem must contend with the contingency of the very desire that promises to free it from historical necessity. As he attempts to give himself fully, freely to desire, he intensifies the rift between his conscious productivity within history and the unconscious desire that fuels productivity. In other words, as he "apotheosizes" (Wordsworth's word) the vision of the individual self, he broadens the rift between the desire-engendering self and already engendered culture, between the creating self and the already created literary tradition that emanates from that culture, between the creating self and the literary fathers already deposited as models for his emulation. The romantic poet intensifies the anxiety associated with the poetic vocation by making himself, in each instance, the ultimate arbitrating voice of that vocation, in each instance, having to validate the supreme status of that vocation by reaffirming the supremacy of his own individual and unique vision.

Now that we have examined the romantic poet's attempt to empower his vocation, it would be instructive to consider the obverse relation, the anxiety created by his claim to such overwhelming influence. By examining how anxiety becomes both a cause and an effect in the romantic poet's desire to write, we can begin to see how anxiety contributes to the sense of his own eccentricity as a unique talent and to his self-perception as a cultural liberator.

1

Although poets in preceding generations certainly worry over such irritants as their fame, their influence, their originality, and their status in relation to contemporaneous poets, these worries are subsumed by a conception of the poetic vocation that tends to submerge individualizing anxiety and to bring to the surface a more socialized or collective form of anxiety. In fact, before the romantics, poeticizing is conceived more as an avocation than a vocation, more as an arbitrary, and relatively self-indulgent choice, rather than as a calling predetermined by the individual's genius, by an individuated psychological drive, or by a felt need for his unique vision within culture in order to make (rather than just keep) that culture free and whole. The Augustans view the poet as a social entity, thoroughly conventional in nature, and succeeding as a poet by harmonizing his uniquely individual talents with the conventions of social intercourse. I am not suggesting that they do not desire to explore the individuated self, but rather that any such exploration necessarily entails the mask of social propriety, a mask worn both to protect the individual's sense of privacy and to ritualize the essentially sociable nature of literary discourse. "The pressures against autobiographical disclosure required that writers conceal their self-discoursing practices by indirection," David B. Morris writes. "For Pope the difficulty was how to speak of himself, as he once put it, 'with decency.' This was no easy problem to solve in the decades before Rousseau in his *Confessions* utterly transformed the canons of self-disclosure" (*Genius of Sense* 20). The mask of the poet is a sign of his total commitment to and engagement in the socially instituted network of his culture. It indicates, moreover, that the intensified self-individuation that we witness in romantic ideology is inaccessible to the Augustans, tautologically because it is antisocial and because eighteenth-century ideology tends to preclude an opening to such self-involving discourse. The socializing function of the "pre-romantic" poet enables and subsumes his individuality, for as his poetry is the effect of his capacity to socialize, so it is also the most refined way to learn how to socialize well.

By *socialize* I mean to enter into predetermined civil and social institutions as a respected citizen and colleague, willing to foster reform of such institutions where necessary, but always cognizant of the privileges and opportunities already justly formed within such institutions. I mean the term to apply in both of its usual senses: to converse affably in desired social circles and to *be initiated* (to initiate oneself) into the rituals of one's culture. But I also use "socialize" in an extended sense: to help conserve civil and social institutions by conversing knowlegeably within and about them, to reaffirm cultural rituals by self-consciously practicing them. The Augustan poet, then, through socializing, gives homage to an already created whole, though that whole may certainly be seriously flawed, and accepts his individual vision as rightly circumscribed and modulated by that sociocivil whole.[1] In other words, the instituted social network provides him the freedom to write; indeed, if he has talent, is of the gentle classes, and has no more pressing sociocivil obligation, he is nobly obliged to write in order to signify his gratitude for that privileged freedom. His poetry-writing in turn enhances that freedom by refining the cultural institutions and rituals which grant that freedom as privilege. Morris explains the idea thus:

For Pope, the present "repays" the past by judiciously correcting or improving its legacy. This process, so crucial for understanding Augustan poetics, is what Pope describes in the ambiguous term *refinement*. Refinement does not imply an indiscriminate or artificial smoothness—as Romantic critics of Pope suggest in their attacks—mere high polish, fancy manners, or elitist taste. In refinement, the purpose of labor is to enhance value already existing in an original material. (9)

"High polish, fancy manners, [and] elitist taste" are certainly aspects of poeticizing refinement, but merely as signifiers of such refinement rather than as signifieds or ends. The ends of refinement entail the sustenance of mores, mentalities, and amenities that will ensure an enlightened culture and censure continual threats to that enlightenment. The word that becomes a negative concept for the romantics, signifying an emasculated condition in which poetry has cultivated its own narrow domain to the point of marginalizing itself and diminishing its power in the larger sociopolitical sphere, plays a crucial positive role in Augustan poetics.

The image (en)gendered by such a conception of the poetic (a)vocation is one of masculine bonding and camaraderie—the boys' night out—rather than the trope of individuated masculine potency that dominates the romantic conception of poetic productivity. We move from the "idle" pleasures of the Augustan coffeehouse with its men's club ambience to the romantic panorama. We move from an enclosed environment in which men succeed by an almost claustrophic collaboration and in which they attempt to tighten their circle of colleagues through cliquish "inside" conversation, to an outside ever-opening landscape where men, even when the best of friends, compete to prove the power of their discourse to grasp the centripetal universe. Finally, we move from a dominantly social and self-consciously artificial space from which women—if not feminine influence—can more easily be barred, a space where men rival congenially with men of equal status in a small "room" socially arranged for men's talk, to a natural terrain, where women cannot be denied entrance and where a more enunciated concept of the feminine is needed in order to make the picture whole. Although the female may still have her own room for a different, lesser kind of talk and rivalry, the romantic must relate to her as a poet within his own terrain as well. Not only has she claimed her own poetic status as she has begun to publish poetry in unprecedented numbers, but also she has claimed nature as an appropriate space for her productivity, though she does not conceive of her natural space in the same way that the romantic conceives his. Nature provides a common ground for male and female desire; if he is not to lose his grasp on that territory, he must assert himself all the more aggressively in her presence. Since he can no longer easily ignore her, he must give her a prominent position; he must prominently position her—making sure who is subject and who is object—in his natural landscape, in a landscape that is "naturally" his. Unconsciously the question becomes: how can the female be exploited to reaffirm the poet's own sense of the naturalness of his desire to write, his desire to conquer, his desire to desire.

The Augustans tend not to question whether poetic skill is a natural or artificial gift; they see it as a felicitous balance of both, but as a thoroughly social and socializing balance. Making poetry makes sense only within the context of social and civil institutions, only as man relates to man, much in the same way as making a chair or a parasol. Even as they compose poems in the setting of nature, they do so to socialize, and therefore they need not converse with nature as one self-desiring individual to another. Society, rather than nature, must provide the ultimate context for their discourse, for nature itself has ordained that they talk to one another, not to it.[2] The Augustans, then, tend to accept the social conventionality of poetry-writing as both its inherent nature and its supreme virtue. The conventional forms and contents of poetry emanate naturally from the conventional process of writing poetry, a process as ceremonial or ritualistic as the decorum of meeting for conversation in the coffeehouse. As opposed to the romantic conflict between historical contingency and self-liberating desire, Augustan ideology tends to celebrate the integrated correspondence between tradition and individual talent. Morris writes:

For Pope, as for Dryden, invention—the creative faculty which discovers and disposes new materials for art—was the indispensable collaborator in all worthy acts of imitation. . . . Thus the past, like nature, is an inexhaustible treasury of matter which the inventive poet will put to use, mixing genres, adapting characters, revising imagery, echoing thoughts to create a work simultaneously familiar and new, imitative and original. . . . Pope, while drawing nourishment from the past, found his main adversaries in the present—in the corrupt politicians and hack writers whose open rejection of established values he transformed into a sign of their duncelike irrationality. (5)

As opposed to the romantic's anxious desire to be free enough to create the taste by which he is enjoyed, the Augustan desires to refine the taste that has freed him to write intelligibly within a circumscribed social situation. Refusing to participate in this ritual is not merely irrational; it is more disturbingly insane. The spoilers, scribblers who have no sense of the freedom enabled by imitative poetics, always induce anxiety into poetic productivity by threatening to spread their insanity and to infect their culture with their own mania. Pope's willingness to imitate and to translate is a sign of his inventiveness, rather than a sign of thwarted desire (as it would be for the romantics), and more fundamentally it signifies the coterminous relation between his ostensible desire (his socializing mask) and the social tradition that has enfolded and cultivated that desire.

As the most refined form of social intercourse among a coterie of male equals, poetry-writing does not harbor within itself an alienating anguish; instead, it is an emetic to such anguish, which haunts on the fringes of the social network. As long as the poet is aware of his social bonds, and through his poeticizing pays tribute to the complex discourse that honors those bonds, he is embedded in a socialized network that keeps the anguish of alienation at bay. In other words, the psychology of individualized anguish is not considered inherent to the writing process itself, but exists *outside* the socializing process of which making poetry is an integral part, and that anxiety can intrude on the socializing process only when the poet is failing at his task. More precisely, poetic anxiety results from the intrusion of those writers who do not understand the decorum of socializing discourse, or who pervert that discourse in order to seek material, social, or political advancement. The good writer is the one who has been properly socialized, who understands the conventions, their applications and implications. Those who fail to understand are spoilers; they necessarily turn writing into warfare, for the properly socialized writers must be ever on their guard to keep the spoilers outside the fortress. By definition, spoilers cannot be good writers. If one lacks the social virtues, if one cannot learn the conventions of genial social intercourse, then one certainly cannot practice those virtues in the art of poetry, the most refined form of such intercourse.

Pope's *Epistle to Dr. Arbuthnot* is the classic instance of the kind of anxiety attached to writing in the Augustan age. While making his readers members of his coterie by identifying them with the urbane, magnanimous, admired Dr. Arbuthnot, Pope details the motives, manners, and morals of the incorrigible spoilers. As pointed out by Fredric V. Bogel, "the poem seems to express, in miniature, the essence of the poet's poetic identity. The central position that [it] occupies in Pope's poetry, moreover, permits us to take the poem as something of an Augustan paradigm, a point from which to plot one significant line of development in eighteenth-century English literature as a whole" (*Acts of Knowledge* 200–201). As readers of this poem, we are given three choices: 1) to identify with Pope's congenial and witty clique; 2) to feel outside the clique, but nonetheless to aspire to join its ranks by taking Arbuthnot and his colleagues as models; 3) to become offended by

Pope's hardhitting satire, feeling all its sharp edges but altogether missing its more subtle moral thrust, its warm geniality (especially as expressed in the prayer for Arbuthnot toward the end of the poem), its open invitation to converse and socialize. Either of the first two choices suffices, for each engages the reader in the socializing process. The third option, however, places the reader firmly with the spoilers, so that the poem becomes not socialization (talking to and with us), but ostracization (talking away from and at us). The readers who fall in the latter camp, however, have only themselves to blame, for they have not learned how to blunt a potential attack by turning with (conversing) the flow of instructive amusement, as the poem itself does by turning the attacks of its literary foes into pleasing repartee. Nor have they learned how to serve within (to conserve) prescribed sociocivil institutions. In other words, they have not learned how to socialize, and even such a socializing poem as the *Epistle* itself cannot teach them how if they are not willing to enter into the spirit of the ritual.

Pope expresses his frustration at being unable to teach (to shame) the spoiler with images of isolation, antisocial behavior, and madness:

> Who shames a Scribbler? break one cobweb thro',
> He spins the slight, self-pleasing thread anew:
> Destroy his Fib, or Sophistry; in vain,
> The Creature's at his dirty work again;
> Thron'd in the Centre of his thin designs;
> Proud of a vast Extent of flimzy lines.
>
> (89–94)

Because he is a little self-enthroning king, the scribbler cannot be shamed into virtue and likewise his "flimzy lines" can never be salvaged and made into great or even good poetry. The spoiler's failure, both as a writer and as a human being, lies in his self-centeredness, lies in the way in which he has unwittingly cut himself off from the give-and-take of congenial social intercourse, which is the source, substance, and consequence of good poetry. Poetry, for Pope and the Augustans in general, is a collaborative effort, many times literally, but always effectively, for the poem always implies, and often specifies, a coterie of friendly listeners, who will upon hearing respond in kind and thus continue the conversation and recuperate the fundamental sociability of poeticizing and thus help to sustain the social network that validates their individual enterprises.

The playfulness itself of Pope's poem—and of Augustan poetry in general—chastises the misdirected scribblers. Like coffeehouse conversation, poetry is a sort of bantering playfulness that is implicitly opposed to more productive work—even when it is most "serious" as in *An Essay on Man*. Only those who comprehend the inherent playfulness of the poetic avocation should participate, for all the others must necessarily pervert the process:

> Is there a Parson, much be-mus'd in Beer,
> A maudlin Poetess, a ryming Peer,
> A Clerk, foredoom'd his Father's soul to cross,

Who pens a Stanza when he should *engross?*
Is there, who lock'd from Ink and Paper, scrawls
With desp'rate Charcoal round his darken'd walls?
All fly to *Twit'nam,* and in humble strain
Apply to me, to keep them mad or vain.
Arthur, whose giddy Son neglects the Laws,
Imputes to me and my damn'd works the cause.

                                                    (15–24)

Like Byron after him, Pope satirizes according to categories of proper exclusion, those who should not write, but do. However, despite some overlap in
Byron's and Pope's categories—notably the "maudlin Poetess"—Pope necessarily focuses his arrows on those spoilers within the upper classes, for the
"common" writer has not yet burgeoned into an issue. Moreover, whereas
Byron is ambivalent about his readership and about the boundary lines between writing as a trade and writing as a gentlemanly avocation, between
writing as avocation and writing as prophetic calling, Pope is not as worried
by such issues. He can more confidently assume his audience to be men of
good breeding, good standing, and good humor, and, in fact, the poem can
only work when read by someone who takes such a role. He also more confidently assumes writing to be simply an avocation, one that certainly can make
money, but an avocation nonetheless.[3] The "Clerk foredoom'd" and the
"giddy Son" who "neglects the Laws" are called to our attention in order to
condemn them for giving up productive activities to write poetry, and poetry
that tautologically must be bad because it is written in defiance of its properly peculiar status as productive playfulness or playfully marginal productivity. It is difficult to imagine Pope condoning the popular romantic phenomenon of the shoemaker or shepherd turned poet because of a compelling
psychological drive to write, and Pope's grounds would be much more fundamental, categorical, and overdetermined than Byron's objections. Perhaps
even more than the class issue itself, Pope would have problems with the
conception of poeticizing promoted by this phenomenon; for him, the poet is
not an individual driven by self-generating desire to write in defiance of all
productive social duties, in defiance of all class boundaries, in defiance of the
prescribed social network that makes poeticizing meaningful. Poetry-writing
itself is not a calling, but an indulgence that can be justified, not according
simply to individual psychology, but rather according to the individual's place
within, and responsiveness to, the social network.

To defy one's productive duties in society is to disobey the Father. The
individual who scribbles when he should be clerking necessarily betrays, casts
himself out from, the social network. He "crosses" (meaning to make angry
and to countermand) not just the Father, but the "Father's soul," the actual
desires of the biological father and the hypostatized desire of the symbolic
father (as ideology), the Law of the Father, the divine will. "For Pope the
relation between fathers and sons did not conjure up themes or metaphors of
Freudian family romance," Morris writes, "but rather it referred mainly to
social, legal, and religious duties. Pope imagines the son primarily in the role

of heir. . . . [T]he father is both guardian and teacher; he protects the son, instructs him, and guides him towards eventual independence and maturity" (6). In Pope's scheme, poets become sons all, either obedient or defiant ones, according to their understanding of the socializing implications of the poetic avocation. A son must have special dispensation in order to indulge himself with poetry, but it is no less indulgence for having been dispensed by the Law of the Father.

Poetic activity, when entered into in the proper spirit, preserves the sanity of the individual and the standards by which society functions by keeping individuals and groups sensitized to what constitutes normative behavior. "The public sphere," according to Terry Eagleton, "acknowledges no given rational identity beyond its own bounds, for what counts as rationality is precisely the capacity to articulate within its constraints; the rational are those capable of a certain mode of discourse, but this cannot be judged other than in the act of deploying it" (*The Function of Criticism* 15). Eagleton connects this Augustan view to the ideal of *laissez faire* economic exchange, which is partly the source for its rationalization, an ideal that unhinges knowledge from politics:

Only in this ideal discursive sphere is exchange without domination possible; for to persuade is not to dominate, and to carry one's opinion is more an act of collaboration than of competition. Circulation can proceed here without a breath of exploitation, for there are no subordinate social classes within the public sphere— indeed in principle, as we have seen, no social classes at all. What is at stake in the public sphere, according to its own ideological self-image, is not power but reason. . . . It is on this radical dissociation of politics and knowledge that its entire discourse is founded; and it is when this dissociation becomes less plausible that the public sphere will begin to crumble. (17)

As we shall see in Chapter 6, Hannah More conceptualizes bluestocking conversation in a similar manner, using the image of circulation, and to a similar effect. The reality, of course, is that the Augustan "public sphere" of literary discourse, as Eagleton terms it, exists for the purpose of certain forms of subordination—of the individual to the state, of one class to another, of women to men. It is not true that anyone can join the conversation, any more than it is true that everyone within the culture has the resources to learn to read, or the leisure to engage in this "collaboration." The dark side of this sphere, then, consists not only in its tendency to hide the forms of domination which it preserves, but also in its tendency to punish verbally and psychologically those who fail to meet the norms of rational discourse as perpetuated within the socializing process. For Pope, this act of punishment becomes the moral responsibility of the good poet, as he separates the sheep from the goats, damning the latter to literary hell.

Repeatedly Pope associates the scribbling spoilers with the irrationality of disorder and its logical consequence, madness. His powerful image of the madman scrawling with desperate charcoal on his darkened walls transfigures the image of the scribbler as a spider spinning flimsy lines to enthrone himself. Both images derive their moral thrust from the vanity of self-centeredness and isolation, which results from perverting the sociableness of the poetic process. "Lock'd from Ink and Paper," the scribbler continues to write; incapable of possessing an appropriate conception of poeticizing, the scribbler poeticizes nonetheless. The scribbler errantly becomes his own sovereign, father of himself, father of his own little culture, and is not well enough socialized to see that what he has done is to isolate himself from genuine culture, from the Law of the true Father, from the sociocivil network that fathers him. How can he realize this when he has surrounded himself with the clutter of his own self-deceptively productive work? His poetry becomes the busywork of a deranged spider who spins a flimsy web to trap himself while he foolishly thinks that he is captivating the world.

Once the scribbler isolates himself by misapprehending the proper social function of the poet or misapplying his own poetic talent, he becomes a madman, angry and insane, attempting to aggrandize himself by belittling others, all the time isolating and belittling himself further. Nothing can be enjoyed or learned in isolation, and so the scribbler parodies unself-consciously the poet's charge to amuse and teach by instead complaining and ranting. Scribblers are compelled to attack genuine writers because their madness prohibits them from understanding the decorum of poetic discourse, and conversely they do not understand the ordering nature of poetry because of their disordering madness. "What Walls can guard me," Pope asks. "By land, by water, they renew the charge, / They stop the Chariot, and they board the Barge" (7, 9–10). The genuine poet's only protection is counterattack. "This Paper is a Sort of Bill of Complaint," Pope says about the *Epistle*. The scribbler's anti-socializing attacks draw even the genuine poet into a maddening spiral of counteroffensive maneuvers that threaten his own proper perception of the role of poetry. A poem like this one or *The Dunciad* skirts that ever-narrowing line between poetic decorum and scribbling madness.[4] It would be an error, however, for the poet to give in and exchange the task of instructive amusement, the nature of marginally productive play, the audience of congenial equals, the aim of genial social intercourse for the personal perversions of the maddening scribbler. This ever-present threat that the poet may slip into the madness of the spoiler constitutes Augustan anxiety, an anxiety placed *outside* of poeticizing itself; indeed, it is the perversion of poeticizing. By the time we get to the romantics, however, the dynamics between poet and hack have been inverted: the genuine poet becomes inherently contaminated with madness; it is the common (in all its senses) reader, or the inadequate poet like Southey, who comes to represent obsessive order and restrictive sanity.

To ask the question why write does not make much sense in Augustan ideology because the function of writing is assumed to be a socializing process that, through its socio-conventional genres and addresses and styles, overdetermines the individual urge to write. In other words, the question can only be asked in purely social terms, and the answer is readymade: to please and to instruct. Significantly it is an answer that any classical writer would have recognized without any difficulty, since it is a classical dictum. Rarely before the romantic period are writers concerned with the potential psychological thrust of the question. When Pope does ask the question in his *Epistle,* it answers itself:

> Why did I write? what sin to me unknown
> Dipt me in Ink, my Parents', or my own?
> As yet a Child, nor yet a Fool to Fame,
> I lisp'd in Numbers, for the Numbers came.
> I left no Calling for this idle trade,
> No Duty broke, no Father dis-obey'd.
> The Muse but serv'd to ease some Friend, not Wife,
> To help me thro' this long Disease, my Life,
> To second, Arbuthnot! thy Art and Care,
> And teach the Being you preserv'd, to bear.
>
> (125–134)

Pope's question could have a psychological bent here: why write when writing causes so much mental anguish? But it evades a psychological response, for the mental anguish is itself a form of social torture, not an individualized feeling experienced in the process of writing. It is anxiety created by scribbler madness, not by any distress inherent to poeticizing itself. Pope says that he writes because it is what he does well: "I lisp'd in Numbers, for the Numbers came." Although there is certainly an implicit appeal to nature here (natural talent, ordained ability), what Pope stresses is the social space that lies in the lap of nature's great expanse. Rather than proceeding to celebrate or recuperate nature's tutelage of the poetic genius, as a romantic would, he instead proceeds to the social space where poetry moves and has its being. Furthermore, his poetic right is asserted through a double negative: I could do this because I was *not* told *not* to. As John Paul Russo explains, Pope's "father had long since retired from business; hence no trade that he might ordinarily follow was spurned except his own, paradoxically, 'idle' trade" (*Tradition and Identity* 44). The Law of the Father, representing once again the socio-civil institutions that give rise to poetry and indulge its pursuit by a few gifted sons, does not intervene to stop him from poeticizing. He writes leisurely for his friends, not frantically to support a wife. Writing is a slight "sin," an "idle trade," but this does not mean that it does not play a *vital* role in society. Its role is crucial for Pope exactly because it lies in that marginal sphere of idleness, instruction, and amusement. Poetry vitalizes society from the margins, much like a parasite that provides a vital function to its host.

This is far from the focal cultural role given to the poetic vocation in the early nineteenth century. For the Augustans, poetry-writing is a tonic, assuring good mental health ("To help me thro' this long Disease, my Life"), a kind of Aristotelean social harmony, as it pleasurably teaches socialization. So the more appropriate question is not, why write, but why publish. Even the clerk or the giddy son may write presumably as long as he does not let this avocation become a vocation and interfere with his duties, presumably as long as he does not publicize his private pleasure beyond his own intimate clique. The problem is, of course, that this is exactly what Augustan poeticizing is: publicizing one's pleasurable discourse to an intimate clique. To write is necessarily to publicize, if not to publish, since writing is by nature a socializing process. It is only with actual publication (the makng public), however, that poeticizing becomes fraught with anxiety, for it is then that maddening readers—incompetent and made angry because of their incompetence—begin to pervert the poetic process.

Appropriately, then, Pope must sharpen his inquiry by asking why publish:

> But why then publish? *Granville* the polite,
> And knowing *Walsh,* would tell me I could write;
> Well-natur'd *Garth* inflam'd with early praise,
> And *Congreve* lov'd, and *Swift* endur'd my Lays;
> The Courtly *Talbot, Somers, Sheffield* read,
> Ev'n mitred *Rochester* would nod the head,
> And *St. John's* self (great *Dryden's* friends before)
> With open arms receiv'd one Poet more.
> Happy my Studies, when by these approv'd!
> Happier their Author, when by these belov'd!
>   (135–144)

Significantly, his answer is a series of names; he publishes to be read by *specific* men, more precisely by a specific network of men, as both the interconnectedness of his list and the summary phrase "great Dryden's friends" indicates. He writes and publishes for those who can read and respond in kind. He writes and publishes to amuse, to converse, to teach, and be taught by these colleagues in his coterie. Again, a primarily social answer to a potentially psychological question. Notice also the adjectives that accompany Pope's list of colleagues: "polite," "knowing," "well-natur'd," "Courtly," "ev'n mitred," "great," "with open arms." Even more than the learnedness (which can be assumed) of this coterie, Pope emphasizes their magnanimity, their civility, their congeniality. This list of names and virtuous epithets, Brean S. Hammond suggests, enables Pope to transfer these epithets to himself (see *Pope* 83).

Conversely, the spoilers whom Pope attacks help to establish, in Dustin H. Griffin's words, the "adversary as antiself." As Griffin demonstrates, Atticus, Sporus, and the other satirized characters serve to promote and sustain an image of the poet Pope and of the poet proper by repressing any potential similarities between them and himself. A satirical object like Sporus, representing the publicly bisexual Hervey, bolsters Pope's own sense of belonging within a manly coterie and bolsters the normative manliness of that coterie (see Griffin *Poet in the Poems* 172–190).[5] Thus, the intimate bond of masculine camaraderie can be distinguished from any "perversion" of manliness by repressing the actual similarity between homoeroticism and camaraderie. In other words, the manly strength of Pope's persona is established through the putative conventionality of his poeticizing ritual. And this strength is established by questioning the masculinity of his adversaries and by assuming the dubious correlation between heterosexuality and manliness, between homoeroticism and perversion, between homosexuality and impotence. Unlike his adversaries, Pope becomes a *productive* son in the patrimonial line that goes directly back to Dryden; he becomes an heir worthy of his father, capable of re-inseminating his culture for its continued growth and potency. Whereas the romantics are threatened by the feminine vulnerability of emotion that is intrinsic to their poeticizing and attempt to repress or purge that femininizing tendency by reasserting the power of their vocation, the Augustans are threatened by the feminizing implications of the all-male clique and attempt to repress those implications by reaffirming the conventional productivity of the patrilineal relationship. The father's (Dryden's) social nod of approval invigorates the son; the brothers' network of support enables them to ratify and mirror their potency to one another and to their literary enemies in other camps. This is why "Pope's relation to Dryden," as Morris points out, "does not reveal the strains of psychic and literary conflict that Harold Bloom discovers in Romantic and in post-Romantic writers" (4).

This does not mean that Augustan poetry-writing is not at all fraught with the competitiveness that becomes so important to romantic ideology. It stresses, rather, how the Augustans tend to "manage" or socialize competition by constituting themselves as competing social camps—my genial camp against your maddening camp—more than as individuals competing to impose visions on the world. Pope writes because the fathers approve his writing—a justification we cannot imagine most romantics giving. But here Pope is perfectly satisfied to take the filial role, because it means through time he will garner obedient sons for himself. He brings honor to himself by bringing honor to the paternal coterie with which he wants to be identified ("great Dryden's friends"). Because poetry is essentially socializing, poetic strength is collaborative, even when the poet writes alone; for he writes to celebrate the intrinsically conversational and conservational nature of writing poetry.

This is why all Augustan poetry is either occasional or imitative, why the great majority of the poetry is epistolary. The epistle readily defines the necessary social context, whether social occasion or superior rank or lateral affiliation as a brother (son) from the same poeticizing camp. Augustans write to mark a personage, a place, an event, whether trivial or monumental, as a means for social intercourse. Augustan poetry is civil poetry in that it commemorates acts of "state," acts that remind us of how we are civilly constituted as groups and classes—poet to patron, poet to colleague, poet to coterie, poet to estate or great house. Rarely are poems not addressed "to" or "on" specific individuals or places which represent embedded social relations. And those poems that are not so addressed are usually imitations or translations of specific classical models. "With the possible exception of Dryden," Russo points out, "Pope would devote more years of his life to translating another poet's work than any other English writer of his rank" (83). He could happily spend a decade of his life (1714–1725) doing translations and editions, rather than composing what we have come to consider "original" poems (*Tradition and Identity* 84). And even when he does compose "origi-

nal" poetry, in the words of Laura Brown, "Pope is creating his neo-classical
models out of his own poetry. He is both imitating the classics and making
the classics imitate him in a reciprocal move" (*Alexander Pope* 25). Because
imitation reaffirms the continuity of his patrilineage with an ever-refining tradition, "Pope would never outgrow or be embarrassed by his desire to imitate" (Russo 29). Likewise, the poet's relation to his patron in the eighteenth
century reaffirms the sociocivil essence of the poetic avocation. Even as
patronage is giving way to market publishing in the early eighteenth century,
the poet is eager to be perceived as writing in accordance with a patronizing
father's will, rather than simply out of self-possessing desire. As Hammond
argues, in the *Epistle to Dr. Arbuthnot* Pope appears to have "abandoned
every conceivable model of literary production. Any form of sensitivity to
what the government wants, or what a patron wants, or what the reading
public wants, is condemned as corruption or commercialism" (93). Attempting to halt the quickening pace toward commodity publishing, Pope represses
his own incipient commercialism in order to celebrate a mythic relation between the poet and his patron, here in the guise of Arbuthnot. The stability
of that social bond indicates the strength of the sociocivil body to ward off
the disease of scribbling anxiety, which haunts the outer region of poeticizing
in the self-centered spoiler and in the incipient uncivilized common reader.

2

In another rare moment when an Augustan examines the writing process
with a potentially psychological bent, Samuel Johnson explains how the attempt to compose "mocks us in the execution with unexpected difficulties"
(*Samuel Johnson's Literary Criticism* 24). In this particular essay (*Adven-
turer* no. 138, March 1754), Johnson's concern is "what degree of happiness
or vexation is annexed to the difficult and laborious employment, of providing instruction or entertainment for mankind" (22). Characteristically, Johnson presents the issue in order to prove that it is not really an issue. As
indicated by his balanced moderating conclusion, the writer's condition is not
a legitimate issue because it is no different from anyone else's lot in life:
"Upon the whole, as the author seems to share all the common miseries of
life, he appears to partake likewise of its lenitives and abatements" (26).
Rather than placing the writer in a unique position, as the romantics insist on
doing, Johnson places him alongside everyone else as indicated by those
words which are rhythmically accented by his rounded prose: "whole,"
"share," "all," "common," "partake," "likewise." No unusual degree of
anxiety is to be attributed to the writer, once he is viewed, as he must be, in
relation to the social whole.

Nonetheless, making an issue of the writer's anxiety affords Johnson the
opportunity of assessing the peculiar difficulties that constitute the writer's
normal degree of vexation as a member of the social species. "Composition
is, for the most part, an effort of slow diligence and steady perseverance, to

which the mind is dragged by necessity or resolution, and from which the attention is every moment starting to more delightful amusements" (24). Unlike Pope, Johnson confronts head-on that potentially painful psychological process of composition. He is addressing those "common distresses of a writer" (25) that become crucial to romantic ideology. But Johnson's splendidly apt description of the anxiety annexed to writing stresses the voluntary nature of composition itself. What is difficult is the *choice* of selecting words; "effort," "diligence," "perseverance" are his definitive terms. Composition is anxiety-producing because it is the difficult labor of choosing, of placing right words in right places. Like Pope—and this is more important than any difference—he views writing as a supremely sane activity, a process of making sane, making ordered, making just:

Sometimes many thoughts present themselves; but so confused and unconnected, that they are not without difficulty reduced to method, or concatenated in a regular and dependent series: the mind falls at once into a labyrinth, of which neither the beginning nor end can be discovered, and toils and struggles without progress or extrication. (24)

Johnson is describing what can go wrong ("sometimes") when writing, not how writing is constituted naturally by compelling anxiety. Paradoxically, writing is the tonic for the illness which *sometimes* accompanies it. Good writing results once the confusion is "reduced to method," made "regular," "concatenated." The labyrinth—Pope's scribbling madness—is an abnormal state that always threatens the normal process of making order through the process of writing. When the "mind is dragged by necessity [of making money, as in Johnson's own case] or resolution," the writer is voluntarily dragging the mind, and that to which the mind itself is dragged is "effort." Not surprisingly for Johnson, because writing is a method of purging disorder from the mind, the anxiety that sometimes attends that purging process only indicates how much more needed the process itself is. Like Pope's genuine poet, Johnson's author must, in the midst of threatening disorder that becomes intimately associated with composition, continue to compose if he is to retain any hope of sustaining sanity. The Augustan genius, then, is characterized by his sanity, by his ability to quell anxiety, which is itself extraneous. Through the method in his labor, he staves off the madness that mimics method.

The speaker of Pope's *Windsor Forest* represents well the socializing kind of sanity that the poetic avocation requires. Because it is a "nature" poem, *Windsor Forest* may at first be mistaken for a proto-romantic poem in which the individuated and isolated self confronts nature in an attempt to recuperate his individual power and assert his vision as uniquely ordained by nature. It is not. The urge to romanticize the poem is hindered immediately by the introductory invocation to nature.

> Thy Forests, *Windsor!* and thy green Retreats,
> At once the Monarch's and the Muse's Seats,
> Invite my Lays. Be present, Sylvan Maids!

> Unlock your Springs, and open all your Shades.
> *Granville* commands: Your Aid O Muses bring!
> What Muse for *Granville* can refuse to sing?
>   (1–6)

Nature "invites" the poet's "Lays." But it is Granville who "commands." The Muse is not to sing to or for nature, but to and for Granville. It is not so much that Granville stands above nature, commanding it and the muse, as that there is a full confluence, a total correspondence, between Granville's sociocivil authority to command and nature's tendency to invite. Nature is here socialized in a thoroughly different way from Wordsworth's movement from the love of nature to the love of man. For Wordsworth, that movement is temporal and psychological; it is something that must happen in time to him and within him. Nature hands him over to society. Furthermore, that movement is temporally disruptive and psychologically traumatic. It creates a breaking or turning point in his history and a schism or conflict in his mind which all of his poetry is devoted to mending. For Pope, the movement from nature to man is uninterrupted, seamless; the natural and the social have always existed harmoniously, each giving credence to the other, each providing value for the other; they are simultaneous and coterminous. This is why Windsor is both "At once the Monarch's and the Muse's Seats." The social space is seated in nature's lap, which is seated in the social space.

The poet's task here is to celebrate this harmony. "Here Earth and Water seem to strive again, / Not *Chaos*-like together crush'd and bruis'd, / But as the World, harmoniously confus'd" (12–14). Pope's "seem" is crucial. What to the spoiler would appear as maddening chaos, to the poet shows its true essence as order and sanity. "Where Order in Variety we see, / And where, tho' all things differ, all agree" (15–16). The poet's "natural" vision is contiguous with his "social" vision. Just as the poet's function in society is to pay tribute and contribute to the ordered wholeness of the sociocivil network through socializing, so the poet's function in "nature" is to celebrate the ordered wholeness of the natural network, which is an image of the social network, itself an image of the natural network, etc. *ad infinitum*. And just as the poet achieves his social function through socializing, he also achieves his "natural" function through socializing.

Like the *Epistle to Dr. Arbuthnot, Windsor Forest,* too, is an epistolary-occasional-civil poem, addressed to Lord Landsdown, written to mark not just a single state event, but the eventuality of the state itself, its coming into being, its beingness, its harmonious perfecting of itself in time and space:

> The Time shall come, when free as Seas or Wind
> Unbounded *Thames* shall flow for all Mankind,
> Whole Nations enter with each swelling Tyde,
> And Seas but join the Regions they divide;
> Earth's distant Ends our Glory shall behold,
> And the new World launch forth to seek the Old.
> Then Ships of uncouth Form shall stem the Tyde,
> And Feather'd People crowd my wealthy Side,

And naked Youths and painted Chiefs admire
Our Speech, our Colour, and our strange Attire!
Oh stretch thy Reign, fair *Peace!* from Shore to Shore,
Till Conquest cease, and Slav'ry be no more.

(397–408)

By the end of the poem the state of England has become the world eternal. "The pastoral Eden of *Windsor,* then," according to Laura Brown, "is a commodified vision of the English state, where imperial products are translated to the English countryside in a fantasy of power that makes all the world Britain" (33). England becomes, in the words of Thomas R. Edwards, "an image of the perfect human society because in it parties and sects can keep their identities within the embracing patterns of civil order and peace" (*This Dark Estate* 6). Just as the Augustan poet claims and solidifies his individual poetic power by associating himself both with the aristocratic patron as a father of the state and with his great literary precursor as a father of refined culture, he gladly sees his individual poetic strength as merely mirroring the freedom of a privileged social order. Rather than claiming that his strength lies in the priority and singularity of his poeticizing mission, he necessarily assumes that his individual poetic identity can exist and can be potent only as it is subsumed by the strains of a social harmony that always establishes itself before he begins to write. His task is simply to celebrate that harmony by replicating it in verse, by *rewriting* it.

Pope's imperializing vision turns Thames into the seamless thread that joins all humankind, and in so doing, he fulfills his function of both socializing and civilizing a world that seems disordered, "Chaos-like." Any sign of disorder (whether it be unsocialized nature, countries ignorant of or opposed to England's ordering presence, the new world striking out on a destiny untethered to England's, or the exoticism of feathered or naked Indians) must be ousted from the poem, or more accurately, must be reabsorbed and subsumed by English harmony, by the "Peace" that will flow from self-generating English culture. Wallace Jackson calls this ousting maneuver "the warfare against the darker powers of human energy," and he points out the "curious affiliation" between the "predatory" and "rapacious" darker passions, which Pope desires to purge from the poem, and the "aggressive element" of his "male role" within the poem (see *Vision and Revision in Alexander Pope* 22–25). Just as there is an inherent contradiction between the romantic's desire to disrobe the passionate self and his desire to assert an aggressive masculine stance, so there is an inherent conflict between Pope's aim of a fully harmonized peace that embodies perfect domesticity and his implicit appeal to the aggressive man of action who brings about this "harmony" through modes of belligerent imperialism.

As in the *Epistle,* the poet's potential anxiety resides at the borders of his poeticizing discourse, and the aim of that discourse becomes to purge that anxiety, as he effectively does by bringing the savage force (represented by the Indian) back to England. Once the Indian is mastered by the social network, he can be returned to the new world, literally and figuratively, for father

Thames will embrace him—socialize and civilize him—even from a distance. Pope's imperializing vision is purely social. Even as Pope propagates his own personal ideology—and this is certainly what he is doing in the poem—his conception of the poetic avocation requires that his ideology be presented as reflecting and as inflecting the social whole that substantiates his discourse. This is why he is compelled to close the poem with a self-effacing image of his humble role: "My humble Muse, in unambitious Strains, / Paints the green Forests and the flow'ry Plains" (427–428). He can "more sweetly pass [his] careless Days" (431) in this pastoral version of nature that concludes the poem exactly because that self-consciously artificial (summoned by his clever art) pastoral existence is validated by the imperial and universalizing vision that the poem has already adumbrated. The poet, at the end of the poem, is a figure of contentment, sanity, ease, and peace, the normal poetic condition, even of a bard who has just prophesied a mighty vision.

Although this conception of poeticizing may not represent the actual process that the Augustans enact as they compose, it does represent the self-image that the writer is anxious to promote in Augustan discourse. And it is a self-image effectively inverted by the romantic conception of poetic vocation. Haunted by the involuntary motions of his own desire, the romantic poet sees himself as an inherently confused and unbalanced—not to say mad—individual who writes poetry involuntarily according to the dictates of that desire. His is truly a *calling*, and one that is so productive that it undergirds the existence of all other vocations. Partly, it is the seriousness and import of his calling that makes anxiety—an anxiety always akin to insanity—so integral to authorship (as authority). Partly, it is the involuntary nature of that calling and the unbidden and uncontrollable nature of the desire that motivates his poeticizing. All three of these (the insanity, the import, the involuntariness of poeticizing), however, are interconnected with influence, both the influence of his vocation and his individual influence within that vocation.

3

The form of *Windsor Forest* flows, like the Thames, from the social categories that overdetermine its substance. It must be a reflective-pastoral poem not only because the fathers, classical poets, have already provided the model for the kind of statement Pope wants to make (as the epigraph from Virgil acknowledges), but also because his specific social status and his position as a loyal British subject demands that he image Windsor with urbanity balancing humbleness (Granville, not he, can write about Gods), flourishing society balancing natural growth, civility balancing potential wild(er)ness, ultimate peace balancing threatening chaos. Reflective-pastoral already provides the structure for these polarities; Pope need only provide the artistic reworking of that structure. Another way of stating this is that he conceives of his desire to order the world as being in every way coterminous with the world itself. To ask whether the pastoral form is natural or artificial—which to a romantic would mean questioning its inherent adequacy—doesn't make much sense, since artistic form inflects social form, just as society reflects nature, just as natural form re-reflects social form, just as society re-inflects art.

On the other hand, when Wordsworth is confronted with writing a poem to celebrate his own English history as a reflection and inflection of nature and society, he fumbles around not just for an adequate form, but also for the substance. As we step into the romantic panorama, we witness poets whose perception of themselves as self-desiring subjects problematizes their relations to poetic work, poetic form, poetic substance, and poetic influence. We witness poets who define their work as inherently traumatic work, always bordering on labyrinthine madness. They are poets who wander in natural isolation and who, to borrow Pope's words, scribble and scrawl because they think that they must.

The celebrated passages that begin *The Prelude* picture a poet beginning his career by beginning a poem that refuses to have a beginning. The career and the poem have already begun, and Wordsworth is caught, *in medias res,* searching for an origin in order to not begin in the middle of things. It is not simply that conventional epic will not do—though this is certainly part of the anxiety that initiates the poem; it is more importantly that no form whatsoever will suffice. There is nowhere that Wordsworth can turn for a form that matches perfectly naturally his individual desire, and this is partly because he fears that he cannot fully know his desire. He begins the poem only with the irrepressible desire to write, not knowing what substance, what structure, or what audience should situate his writing. This aimlessness of purpose, design, and effect results directly from his sense of poetic calling, producing his wandering pose and intensifying his anxiety.

> The earth is all before me. With a heart
> Joyous, nor scared at its own liberty,
> I look about; and should the chosen guide
> Be nothing better than a wandering cloud,
> I cannot miss my way. I breathe again!
> Trances of thought and mountings of the mind
> Come fast upon me.
>
> (Book 1, lines 14–20)

Only in the most superficial sense is Wordsworth at liberty, only in the most specious way is he not scared. His sense of leisure inverts Pope's leisure in *Windsor Forest*. Whereas Pope is free to write his poem at any time and in any place (his relation to the social whole cannot change with time or place), whereas he is free to write or not to write, whereas his culture will be free regardless of whether he writes or not, Wordsworth believes that this specific moment of leisure is ordained so that he can begin to begin his mission as a poet. The poem itself represents the struggle for his personal freedom and for the liberty of his culture (his nation, his tradition, his people). Not to write is to abdicate that chosen status, to betray himself and his culture.

Wordsworth's clever strategy of "choosing" natural objects that float and wander helps to stress his anxious predicament. Nature will guide him, but only insofar as he chooses the proper objects of discourse. Wordsworth must reject Milton, as he effectively does in this torturous beginning, because Milton is just an effect of that ordaining process. In order to find his proper materials, Wordsworth must know his causal origin, beyond Milton, beyond Milton's doctrinal good and evil, beyond the paradise already lost. In order to know his destiny—why he has been destined to write—he must return to the origin of that destiny. He must return to the origin of himself, to the origin of self. And since it is his desire that has made the self press so palpably from within the flesh, this means returning to the origin of desire itself.

Returning to the origin of his power—fathering himself—provides a subject (both a hero to write about in himself and a subject matter), but not a form. "The ambitious Power of Choice" (166) thwarts the actual act of choosing. As he serializes the potential themes available for "such an arduous work" (147), he wanders over the theme that he has already unconsciously chosen:

> Sometimes it suits me better to invent
> A tale from my own heart, more near akin
> To my own passions and habitual thoughts;
> Some variegated story, in the main
> Lofty, but the unsubstantial structure melts
> Before the very sun that brightens it,
> Mist into air dissolving!
>
> (221–227)

To "invent" a tale "from [his] own heart" means to forgo the socialized conventional structures so dear to Augustan ideology; moreover, it means to re-invent structure itself. As the poet must father himself as a subject, he must also father a form that is formed by, that informs and reformulates, the fathering of himself. "The unsubstantial structure" melts and dissolves. The wandering formlessness of the beginning of the poem announces Wordsworth's assault upon socialized conceptions of poetic structure. His theme becomes "variegated." It wanders in a labyrinthine wilderness, going wherever "nature" leads, choosing by not choosing, giving guidance by being guided. If he wanders long enough and far enough, he must stumble across the path that has been ordained for him. As we shall see, however, such wandering requires the idleness of leisure, which in itself becomes problematic since it accentuates the condition of poetry's marginality and ineffectuality, the very condition that the romantic poets want to countermand.

The disavowal of apparent structure must accompany a poem whose aim is determined by aimless desire. It is, after all, Wordsworth's frenzied desire to poeticize that forces his pen to paper, not a predetermined socializing end. Desire itself is boundless, formless, elusive; it is an "unsubstantial structure" that "melts / Before the very sun that brightens it." The poet must isolate himself, or at least he must begin in nature's isolation, for how else can he wander aimlessly toward the natural origin within himself? How else can he father his own vision? How else can he come to manage his aimless desire? Such isolation also helps to erect the barriers needed to quell the threat of influence. And yet, the poet needs a father, a comrade, and even a mother. And yet, Wordsworth needs Milton, Coleridge, and Nature, and the need for these others stresses and distresses the poet's attempt to father himself. These influential needs intensify the "natural" anxiety inherent in writing that seeks to liberate the self by regulating self-desire.

The "correspondent breeze" that becomes "A tempest, a redundant energy, / Vexing its own creation" (35–38) symbolizes the poet's isolation in nature and his need for a corresponding or conversant other within his isolation. The breeze also symbolizes, however, the anxiety that results from these needs and the anxiety inherent to the poetic vocation. The poet's inspiration, his involuntary desire to write, becomes a tempest, vexing itself, just as the storm-wind is a powerful breeze that struggles against itself. The wind, a self-energizing force that gains strength from its battle against itself, mirrors the poet's desire, a "redundant energy" that, in its self-struggle, empowers itself. The poet's desire, corresponding with nature's wind, generates a frenzied struggle to find objects to satisfy itself. Gaining power from the internal struggle, the wind/desire is caught in a spiraling assault upon the source of power, upon itself. However, since cause and effect are indistinguishable in these correspondent breezes, we could say that nature's wind vexes the poet's desire or that the poet's desire vexes nature's wind. Nature's influence makes the \ individual human into a genius by endowing him with "redundant energy" and in so doing marks him for the power of self-individuation and the anxiety that must accompany overdetermined self-consciousness. Nature teaches the poet to desire by depriving him of sufficient objects of desire. Conversely, the poet vexes nature's wind because once the poet's desire separates him from nature, it pits him against nature. For Wordsworth, writing is the activity of engaging with the chaos it struggles to order, and the writer must willingly accept the vexation that accompanies the chaos that gives birth to order. Thus the labyrinthine formlessness of the poem, its apparent wandering from spot of time to spot of time, is a natural result of the intrinsic anxiety-producing chaos of the process of composition, as well as the result of the poet's attempt to re-invent form and subject by tracing the limits of his desire, by fathering the self-desiring self.

Wordsworth's unruliness at the beginning of *The Prelude* is not "abnormal" for poetic sensibility, it is essential for it. Just as the lover's lunacy testifies that he is truly in love, the poet's malady confirms that he is a poet.

> But, oh, dear Friend!
> The Poet, gentle creature as he is,
> Hath, like the Lover, his unruly times;
> His fits when he is neither sick nor well,

> Though no distress be near him but his own
> Unmanageable thoughts.
>
>   (134–139)

The apt image of love-sickness, of desire out of control, stresses the poet's natural anxiety. Born in the labyrinth of nature, plunging into the labyrinth of his own mind, wandering aimlessly in order to aim his desire, the poet is a natural madman, vexed and often confused. From this fecund madness is born the natural order of culture itself. The poet's constant anxiety and his occasional madness are natural results of his liberty, his freedom within nature and his freedom to invent himself. In fact, liberty and anxiety feed each other, for the depth of his anxiety measures the height of his liberty. The deeper he goes into himself, the closer he gets to the origin of chaotic desire, the better he can manage that desire, tap its energy, and use it to free himself from the potential constraints of human nature, tradition, and the pressure of the present. Immersing in the origin of chaotic desire frees him for transcendence. On the other hand, his liberty enables him to quest for that origin; the freer he is, the closer he is able to come to the origin. Although both liberty and desire tend toward chaos and fuel the anxiety that naturally attends the threat of chaos, both are necessary conditions of poetic vocation, desire activating the will to write in the corridor of time, liberty providing the ample space in which to wander. The measure of both constitutes Wordsworth's promise as a poet and his potency as a prophet. Neither his liberty nor his desire is merely personal; each is intertwined with the fate of his culture, both mirroring that culture's shape and shaping that culture's destiny. This is why *The Prelude* must trace the path from the fecund bewilderment of the state of nature to the sobering duties of social intercourse, the path from leisure within nature to liberty within society, the path from liberty as personal leisure to liberty as sociopolitical liberation.

In this sense, then, *The Prelude* is a poem motivated by the search for liberty, or "Dear Liberty," as Wordsworth addresses it (31). It is a poem engaged in the process of liberation. Just as Pope is punning on the homeostatis between leisure and liberty, Wordsworth is punning on the disparity between leisure and liberty, between being at liberty and working toward liberation. Pope can celebrate his leisure unabashedly; because Britain already is a free country that is ordained to endow (impose) its freedom on the universe, the poet can enjoy his personal freedom in his own little pastoral corner of the garden, a garden that proleptically reaches to all corners of the universe and makes the whole world an image of pastoral social harmony. Liberty is much more problematic for Wordsworth. It is something, like desire, "ever more about to be." England is not yet wholly free, or more precisely, its leisure is enabled by various forms of enslavement. Book 7, "Residence in London," records the epiphany, already prefigured from the beginning in Book 1, of the poet's coming to see clearly the way in which the leisure of a great nation is yoked to its capacity to enslave a class of its people, to enslave itself. This epiphany is pregnant in Book 1 because it mirrors Wordsworth's personal condition as a human being and a poet: he is freed in order to be yoked to a task; he is at liberty in order to be enslaved to his calling. The poet can will to write only because he has been willed to write, a conundrum that the poem is devoted to struggle through as fiercely as it is committed to struggling through the relation between liberation and slavery in the geopolitical spheres of England and France.

As has been often noted, the city itself represents enslavement to most of the romantics (Blake being an exception in some cases, though not in the *Songs of Innocence and of Experience*); it represents the prison in which humankind places itself, and of course the irony is that the city, heart of human civilization, is the place where humanity is supposed to free itself from its barbarous urges, from its slavery to nature. Predictably, Wordsworth finds in the city an inversion of this topos: humankind is imprisoned by attempting to free itself from nature. And once again, we have the problematic of the personal mirroring the political, for Wordsworth's struggle as a poet is exactly an attempt to free himself from nature by fathering himself as a human entity and by engendering a social culture in which he can take a visionary role. Not surprisingly, then, Book 7 begins with the distress of his leisure, with the anxiety of his "idleness" amidst a city everywhere laboring to keep itself alive:

> Yet, undetermined to what course of life
> I should adhere, and seeming to possess
> A little space of intermediate time
> At full command, to London first I turned,
> In no disturbance of excessive hope,
> By personal ambition unenslaved,
> Frugal as there was need, and, though self-willed,
> From dangerous passions free. Three years had flown
> Since I had felt in heart and soul the shock
> Of the huge town's first presence, and had paced
> Her endless streets, a transient visitant:
> Now, fixed amid that concourse of mankind
> Where Pleasure whirls about incessantly,
> And life and labour seem but one, I filled
> An idler's place; an idler well content
> To have a house (what matter for a home?)
> That owned him; living cheerfully abroad
> With unchecked fancy ever on the stir,
> And all my young affections out of doors.
> (Book 7, lines 58–76)

The poet has time "at full command," but ironically his condition is actually the opposite. He is not in command of his life; he is "unenslaved" by "personal ambition" and "free" from "dangerous passions." As Book 7 proceeds, we discover that the poet is only as free as the city itself, that the incessant whirls of "Pleasure" are conversely tied to the oneness of "life and labour." The passage resounds with the language of leisure and idleness, closing with the image of homelessness, of the capacity to be "ever on the stir" with "unchecked fancy." Is the poet a well-contented idler, or is he a "self-willed" quester in search of a house to own him? What is a house that owns one if not a home? He is, of course, both—just as the city is both a prison and a quest for freedom, a swirl of pleasure and a machine of ceaseless labor.

"At leisure, then," Wordsworth "views, from day to day, / The spectacles" of idle pleasure afforded by the city until he is caught in his own web of idleness. To be at leisure means to have the time to think, to delve beneath the surfaces of things. For Pope, it means to recognize the sane harmony undergirding the seeming madness of variety; it means to escape the anxiety of manic scribbling through leisurely, voluntary social intercourse. For Wordsworth, on the other hand, it means to see into the heart of the "black storm upon the mountain-top" that "[s]ets off the sunbeam in the valley" (Book 7, lines 619–620). It means to be forced to write by the power of chaotic desire; it means to be forced to write according to the dictates of *natural* desire. Because desire's origin is nature, because desire *is* natural, the poet must write in the context of nature, even while he is immersed in the city, just as Pope socializes in the midst of nature's lap. The city—its superficial bustle, its artifice, its "blank confusion"—is something the poet must move beyond in order to motivate true social existence. The city is that artificial culture that the poet, through his natural propensity, transforms into genuine culture. So eventually, the city's ceaseless motion oppresses Wordsworth, rather than invigorating him. That ceaseless motion is an image of his own idleness, for it stresses the oppressiveness of desire that is unregulated by poetic endeavor.

> Thus have I looked, nor ceased to look, oppressed
> By thoughts of what and whither, when and how,
> Until the shapes before my eyes became
> A second-sight procession, such as glides
> Over still mountains, or appears in dreams.
> (Book 7, lines 630–634)

Instead of the pleasing network of a socializing whole perceived by Pope, Wordsworth, seeing into the life of things, perceives "[a] second-sight procession." He begins to see, by help of his imagination, the roteness, the tedium, the squalor, the enslavement, the falseness of refined city life. The city's ceaseless motion—its blank stares and idle pleasures confounded with crowded signs and degrading labor—represents the repression of genuine desire and the oppression of true liberty. Vision becomes a "second-sight procession," a regimented series of mediated sights, rather than the original and unmediated vision of natural desire. In *Wordsworth and the Figurings of the Real,* David Simpson argues that the city stifles the poet's desire because it prevents him from taking the "second look," the time for retrospection and reflection, and, as opposed to the country, the city limits his scope of vision, disables him from casting his glance into the wide expanse of unlimited and uncongested space:

[S]elf and world posit each other simultaneously at the moment of seeing, and this is why the environment of London is so threatening to those contained within it.

London provides, in its multitude of emblems and signs, too much 'outside', too many objects demanding assimilation by the mind. The mind therefore cannot keep up the steady pace of giving out and receiving back; there is not the necessary space and time to draw back for the 'second look' which has to happen if this cycle is to be maintained. (54)

In nature's expanse Wordsworth can more easily have the illusion that the world and the mind are fitted to each other, that his desire is ordained by itself and by the world, that there is no conflict between self-ordination and nature's ordering of self-desire. Nature's objects seem to offer themselves to his interpretation as a form of feminine sacrifice. In nature one seems freed into time and space, bound only by one's desire, to read the marks of nature as signs invested with meaning. It is only in nature that Wordsworth can seem to transfigure the ceaseless movement of desire into poetic progress. And it is only there that he can seem to transform incessant struggle between himself and his influences (the natural mother, the literary father, the rival brother, the enslaving culture) into a preordained harmony. The city, on the other hand, refuels desire by perverting it by fostering unproductive labor. It fosters the manic "redundant energy" that results when desire is traced and mapped and chartered (to use Blake's pregnant pun) until it cannot want what it wants. It is only away from the obvious signs of ideology—all of the futile attempts to structure desire, to place it on a grid—that the poet can claim his transcendence of ideology. It is only away from the city that Wordsworth, not realizing that ideology follows desire wherever it goes, can seem to escape the ideology that fosters an enslaved culture. Therefore, although Wordsworth's idleness seems a foil to the manic energy of the city, it is actually a mirror image. The city's ideologized desire resembles much too closely his own manic energy, his own inner tempest assaulting itself. The only way for Wordsworth to break this cycle for himself and for his enslaved culture is to return to the origin, where desire is unread, unchartered, and unregulated. The irony, of course, is that such a project cannot be managed without reading, chartering, and regulating desire, without casting ideology within a self-possessing vision that seeks to hide its ideological maneuvers.

If Wordsworth is to forsake the city for nature, he must come face to face with the city's obfuscation of nature's light. The poet outside the poem must somehow force the poet within the poem to have a vision in the city, where vision is impossible. Wordsworth's epiphany in Book 7 is capped with the sighting/citing of a beggar. The beggar allows him, for the first time, to read nature's signals beneath the city's arbitrarily oppressive signs. He is "smitten / abruptly, with the view. . . / Of a blind Beggar, who, with upright face, / Stood, propped against a wall" (637–640). On his chest the beggar wears a paper on which is written his life's story. Wordsworth cannot read the blank stares in city faces; they remain a mystery to him. But the beggar's story is spelled out, is written on him, so that Wordsworth can move from the arbitrary sign to the natural signal "written" on the beggar's face. Confronted with the writing on the wall, his eyes are opened by a view of blindness. "And, on the shape of that unmoving man, / His steadfast face and sightless eyes, I gazed, / As if admonished from another world" (647–649). With Wordsworth's revelation comes the capacity to see, as if from another world, the world of unbounded desire, the world of natural meaning, that the free-wheeling of the city is actually the motion of a cog. He begins to see that the ceaseless motion of the city despairingly mimics the fecund movement of desire itself and mocks the liberty ordained by nature. The same nature that endows his empowering desire has granted natural rights to these people in the city. Just as the city has temporarily oppressed his capacity to envision, to regulate desire, and has turned it from self-indulgent idleness to productive work, the city has also oppressed the people's capacity to regulate their desire by transforming tedious productive work into the pleasures of a liberated society.

Everywhere in the city the people's natural desire, their yearning for liberty, that pleasure derived from true freedom, is imprisoned by superficial leisure, that specious pleasure snatched in rare moments of holiday, in moments designed to lessen the tedium and incessant labor of life in an un-liberated, nonegalitarian society. But since desire is unquenchable, it breaks out in moments of desperation and in moments of play. It sometimes even threatens the kind of general chaos usually associated with the French Revo-lution:

> What say you, then,
> To times, when half the city shall break out
> Full of one passion, vengeance, rage, or fear?
> To executions, to a street on fire,
> Mobs, riots, or rejoicings?
>
> (671–675)

Riots and rejoicings are linked as the same movement of desire, like two eddies in the same river. Wordsworth then gives us one carnivalesque in-stance—"that ancient festival, the Fair" (676)—of the potential riot within the rejoicing. In the fair he also gives us, however, the oppression of desire that characterizes the city even in its moments of riot and rejoicing.

> Tents and Booths
> Meanwhile, as if the whole were one vast mill,
> Are vomiting, receiving on all sides,
> Men, Women, three-years' Children, Babes in arms.
>
> (718–721)

The Blakean image of the mill imprisons the momentary fire of the city. The "Babes in arms" return us to a previous image of imprisonment in the book, the image of a father "with a sickly babe outstretched / Upon his knee." The father has brought his babe out "to breathe the fresher air," but they are encased "in an open square / Upon a corner-stone of that low wall, / Wherein were fixed the iron pales that fenced / A spacious grass-plot" (604–610). His natural desire forces the babe to stretch outward, but the walls of the city fence and fix him within the iron pales of the enslaving city. Even the child's desire is vitiated by the city's aimless labor.

As the city becomes the "epitome" of "blank confusion" (722), as it represents the "Oppression, under which even highest minds / Must labour, whence the strongest are not free" (729–730), Wordsworth stands admonished by his idleness, and recognizes his own personal oppression within the guise of leisure. But because nature's meaning frames the city's confusion, natural vision must precede and succeed the blurring oppressiveness of specious social life. This is why the blank confusion at the heart of Book 7 is preceded by the pregnant signification at the heart of Book 6. This is why the oppressiveness of Book 7 must be followed by a natural book, a retrospective book, Book 8, "Retrospect—Love of Nature Leading to Love of Man." Book 8 prefigures the poem's ultimate conclusion by displacing a "realistic" view of social life in London with Wordsworth's own vision of true culture. The concluding lines of Book 7 serve as transition toward that greater understanding of culture by restoring the proper relations between natural freedom or the rights of man and leisure or the liberty of a few, between natural desire and the social management of that desire:

> This, if still,
> As hitherto, in freedom I may speak,
> Not violating any just restraint,
> As may be hoped, of real modesty,—
> This did I feel, in London's vast domain.
> The Spirit of Nature was upon me there;
> The soul of Beauty and enduring Life
> Vouchsafed her inspiration, and diffused,
> Through meagre lines and colours, and the press
> Of self-destroying, transitory things,
> Composure, and ennobling Harmony.
>
> (761–771)

This passage prefigures the natural harmony toward which Wordsworth, and humankind through him, must struggle. This aim is true "freedom" rather than the superficial freedom of leisure, freedom that does not violate "any just restraint." Moving from the "press / Of self-destroying, transitory things," from the anxiety of being at leisure, to the "composure" of self-generating "inspiration," Wordsworth, at the end of this book, comes to understand that he must compose himself: that he must calm himself by regulating his desire; that he must write about himself; that he must regulate desire by writing it in the same way that the blind beggar has written his life on the blank stare of the city; that he must harmonize desire by composing it.

In constructing a myth of poetic vocation, *The Prelude* rejects the Augustan idea that the poet is an idler, socializing in the civilized coffeehouses of London, an indulged son, choosing to engage in a crucial but marginal avocation. Instead, the poet is one whose work is crucial and focal for the making of a liberated culture. As the poet liberates his own desire, tracing it back to the origin of self and regulating the self that originates desire, he also teaches his culture to liberate itself. The poet's task is to teach his fellow citizens how to realize a "naturally" regulated state of desire. He must teach them to reject both extremes of unliberated culture, symbolized by the mill and the riot. The mill too easily accepts desire's tendency toward repetitive, redundant motion, and thus dooms citizens to be enslaved to mindless production. Because such a condition of repetitive labor is unnatural, the tyranny of the mill is sporadically disrupted by desire's other extreme, the riot, which expresses the citizens' refusal to subject themselves not only to repetitive labor, but also to all socially productive work. Unliberated culture attempts to prevent or circumvent the riot by providing its citizens with occasional, limited periods of leisure, but even these holidays are not enough to eliminate the riot. Just as holiday leisure is a form of deceptive liberty enforced to prevent riot, the riot, which too easily accepts desire's tendency toward aimless change and dispersion, is also a form of deceptive liberation. On the one hand, mindless repetitive labor may deceive Londoners into believing that they have achieved some productive function in society; both the riot and the holiday, on the other hand, may deceive them into believing that they have achieved a liberated community of desire, when, in fact, what they have created is the self-destructive anarchy that transpires when collective desire exhausts itself in communal death. The city, the symbol of false culture, then, alternates unpredictably between these two extreme states of desire, never reaching synthesis in what Wordsworth considers the natural condition of desire, energy that is liberated without unbridled license, energy that is bound to productive labor without also being enslaved to meaningless repetitive motion.

The conflict of desire that the poet discovers in London mirrors both the individual conflict within the sphere of poetic autobiography and the larger conflict within the sphere of international politics. This is why the French passages play such a large and pivotal part in this British epic. France represents an ideal and a threat. It represents a people liberated and enslaved. It represents the exhilaration of desire unbound and the anxiety of desire out of control. Although the French people have set themselves free, "Monarch and peasant" equalized (Book 6, lines 455–456), they have also enslaved themselves to the false form of liberty, a form that inevitably turns on itself and creates anarchic tyranny. Just as Wordsworth's personal leisure and labor must be reharmonized into the ordained freedom of a liberating vocation, just as London must transform its labor into genuine liberty, France must transform its liberty into genuine productivity. The poet must bring together his will to work with his compulsion to work, his sense of being at leisure (set free) to do as he will with his sense of being willed (set free) to do what he must. France and England must be brought together and reharmonized in the poet's self-possessing vision, despite their apparent discord in the world of realpolitik.

The storming of the Chartreuse in Book 6 represents the difficulty of harmonizing these polarities. The Convent of Chartreuse is a "sacred mansion" (423) resting "within an awful *solitude*" (419). As Wordsworth witnesses the "riotous men commissioned to expel / The blameless inmates, and belike subvert / That frame of social being" (425–427), he experiences his own casting out from the solitude of his own sacred mansion; he feels the frame of his own secure social being subverted. The priest's sense of sacred mission rests on his capacity for solitary leisure. With the coming of "liberty," does this mean that his sacred mansion must be sacked and that he must be placed in the mill, put to productive work in the city? Wordsworth wants to claim that nature's voice says no. " 'Stay, stay your sacrilegious hands!'—The voice / Was Nature's, uttered from her Alpine throne" (430–431). The poet's "conflicting passions" (440) urge him toward two seemingly opposed kinds of natural liberty: the freedom of the priest, of the highly talented man to fulfill his special mission, his holy purpose, without the press of daily labor experienced by the masses; and the freedom of natural equality, the rights of man. If the poet is special, is holy, does he not have special rights, ordained by nature itself in the form of his natural genius?

As France represents the one urge toward natural freedom, England represents the other, and so the poet is foredoomed to wander from his native land—the place where his genius is born and where he is ordained to renew traditional culture through his natural vision—to another kind of native land—a country being born again by attempting to abolish the tradition on which his renewed vision is focused. The war between France and England, the revolution within France and the repression of desire within English London, all mirror the war within Wordsworth. As M. H. Abrams has meticulously shown in *Natural Supernaturalism,* Wordsworth solves this conflict by turning inward. What cannot be resolved immediately "out there" in the political world, will be resolved eventually within the wise and patient soul. Appropriately, Wordsworth says that he begins to consider how "good and evil interchange their names, / And thirst for bloody spills abroad is paired / With vice at home" (Book 9, lines 352–354). We can think of this as France and England interchanging each other's names, each, in its turn, thirsting for blood abroad and creating vice at home. It is an unhaltable, nightmarish cycle that compels Wordsworth to deflect our attention away from its malignant operation, while focusing instead on the putative resolution of his own internal conflict, a resolution that, though it may be questionable in itself, is still more easily claimed than the resolution of international warfare and tyranny:

> We added dearest themes—
> The gift which God has placed within his power,
> His blind desires and steady faculties
> Capable of clear truth, the one to break
> Bondage, the other to build liberty
> On firm foundations, making social life,
> Through knowledge spreading and imperishable,
> As just in regulation, and as pure
> As individual in the wise and good.
> (Book 9, lines 354–363)

As nations are locked in an impasse that blocks them from achieving liberty, the poet spreads imperishable knowledge, encourages the "just" "regulation" of "blind desires" and purifies the "social life." Although Wordsworth, in this book and in this passage, has not yet fully recognized that it is the poet himself who epitomizes the wise and good individual who serves as the foundation for liberty, the poem struggles toward recognizing this truth already implanted in its inception. "I seemed about this time to gain clear sight / Of a new world" (Book 13, lines 369–370), Wordsworth says at the end of his penultimate book. The new world of liberty that France forbodes and forestalls is transfigured into the new world of his own poetic vision. It is a "world, too, that was fit / To be transmitted, and to other eyes / Made visible; as ruled by those fixed laws / Whence spiritual dignity originates" (see Book 13, lines 369–373). Ruled by the laws fixed by his own spirit, the poet transmits his vision to his people and enables them *spiritually* to inhabit the new world, which more physically powerful rulers, soldiers, scientists, and parliamentarians have been unable to father. Instead of binding the new world to the socializing/civilizing discourse of the old, as Pope does, Wordsworth fathers the new world out of the self-generating discourse of his own individual and sanctified desire. His original isolation within nature becomes the force of his social vision. As he discovers the power to father his own vision, he unconsciously prepares himself to liberate society through the strength of his self-originating discourse.

4

But if the poet is forced inward and compelled to write in isolating nature, how does he come to be the liberating force within society? Paradoxically, self-generating desire, "redundant energy," forces the poet toward his social mission, enables him to regenerate cultural desire for others, just as nonhuman nature goads him toward the love of humanity. From the very beginning, the poet must be situated within the context of society, even while he is isolated in nature. Nature, Milton, and Coleridge represent the limits of human desire in the context of human nature (Nature), of cultural tradition (Milton), of contemporary society (Coleridge); they serve as correspondents and conversants, influencing the poet's desire, turning it and turning with it, even as the poet attempts to advance the myth of self-generating poetic power. Nature, Milton, and Coleridge help to situate his boundless desire even as they implicitly subvert the myth that desire can be, in any sense, boundless; they are necessary threats. They enable the poet to turn in upon himself, to consecrate his infinite, inward spiral toward self-origin, because they mark the external terms of achievement that the poet must have in order to claim internal self-confirmation. In other words, they help to sustain the myth of his ordained cultural mission even as they subvert the myth of his own self-fathering. It is therefore more than expedient that social discourse be implied from the beginning, that his social role be seminal in his natural origin, for destiny means to possess the goal from the beginning. Wordsworth's relations to Nature and Milton and his addresses to Coleridge embed the poet in a network of social intercourse, and ensure that his (isolated) natural voice is always at the same time a voice with an appropriate audience, a voice that will be heard within the cultural sphere. But before we mistake Wordsworth's social intercourse with Pope's, we must point out the problematic, and even deceptive, nature of Wordsworth's intercourse. Cultural influences—the limits of human nature, historical tradition, and present society—must be purged from the poet's quest as they participate in, and indeed as they further, that quest. Wordsworth accomplishes this purging in a variety of ways, but we can understand the basic strategy through his relation with Coleridge, who represents the pressure of the present, the pressure of society itself. Coleridge, the poet's best friend, must be purged from the poem even as he is addressed:

> Thus far, O Friend! did I, not used to make
> A present joy the matter of a song,
> Pour forth that day my soul in measured strains
> That would not be forgotten, and are here
> Recorded: to the open fields I told
> A prophecy: poetic numbers came
> Spontaneously to clothe in priestly robe
> A renovated spirit singled out,
> Such hope was mine, for holy services.
> My own voice cheered me, and, far more, the mind's
> Internal echo of the imperfect sound;
> To both I listened, drawing from them both
> A cheerful confidence in things to come.
>   (Book 1, lines 46–58)

Wordsworth is speaking to Coleridge as a way of situating his own potentially fulfilled desire. Whether the allusion is conscious or not, he parodies Pope's line, "I lisp'd in Numbers, for the Numbers came." But instead of moving within the lineaments of social discourse as Pope does, Wordsworth flexes the muscles of his own poetic potency. Immediately, Coleridge, as equal comrade, is displaced by Nature, a greater self-generating other. Instead of simply telling his story to Coleridge, he is more crucially telling his prophecy to the open fields. But then Nature, too, is displaced by another listener, the poet's self. He does not seek approval from the fathers, from tradition, from Milton for instance, as Pope seeks approval from Dryden's friends. He does not identify himself with a coterie of equally talented son-poets, as Pope does. He is not even content to reside in nature's lap unquestionably as Pope does. The limits that nature would place on his human activity are obliterated as the poet turns inward away from nature to converse with his own desiring self. The poet's only limits become those that his own desire dictates. Poetic numbers come spontaneously and they come "to clothe in priestly robe / A renovated spirit singled out." Wordsworth is here laying the hands upon himself, ordaining himself, reaffirming his own sense of vocation as ordained by his own self-generating desire. It is not Coleridge's (society's) or Milton's (tradition's) or Nature's voice that cheers him and offers him confidence, but his own voice. The happiness that Pope finds in pleasing his brothers, in being approved by the fathers, in celebrating the natural-social mirror of harmony, Wordsworth controverts into an "internal echo," a dialogue with self. "To both I listened," he says, and he draws "cheerful confidence" from them both. In all of romantic literature, we have no better self-image of the romantic's sense of poetic vocation. Speaking to himself in the panorama of nature, he seeks to recover the origin of the echo, "the imperfect sound," that he hears issuing from his own mind; he seeks to find the origin of himself in himself, and in so doing he casts out the demons of influence that would shrink his world and blur his mighty vision.

This comparison of Wordsworth and Pope is not to suggest an absolute difference in the contours of Augustan and romantic masculine desire. Obviously, Wordsworth is working within a tradition as much as he is against one, a tradition that includes Pope as a major voice. However, this comparison does indicate some crucial transformations within that tradition, not the least of which is the romantic poet's attempt to defy tradition by inventing his own unique relation to poetic work, not the least of which is the romantic poet's redefinition of poetic willingness and his resituation of poetic anxiety. The sources of poetic anxiety are only one way of detecting the faultline that comes to separate Wordsworth from Pope, and Pope and Wordsworth are only two of the poets involved in this radical historical change. The difference between Pope and Wordsworth helps us to see more clearly how those "external" and sociohistorical pressures described in Chapter 1 are internalized by the romantic poet. The pressure to formulate a natural (in every sense of the word) vision is hardly experienced by Pope because of his conception of poetry as a socializing avocation; the pressure weighs so heavily on Wordsworth, however, that it becomes a "natural" pressure of poeticizing itself, spawning forms of anxiety alien to Pope. The pressure of poeticizing is experienced, of course, in different ways among the romantics; but for all of them, it is intimately and intricately connected with the pressures of influence. And since the poet's calling (his will to write) is essentially a myth of his natural self-generation, the reality of influence becomes a crucial threat, and perhaps the primary anxiety of poeticizing. The next three chapters examine in more detail how the romantic poets attempt to cope with different forms of influence, both masculine and feminine.

3

Fathers and Sons, Brothers and Lovers: Engendering Desire from the Margins of Masculine Rivalry

When in *The Prelude* Wordsworth rejects Milton's stance by inventing his own subject(ivity) and structure(lessness), when he displaces his immediate listener Coleridge with the mediation of Nature, and then displaces Nature with his own poetic voice, he is not only attempting to purge the poem of its natural, traditional, and sociohistorical limits; he is also attempting to purge the poem of influence of every kind. Once poeticizing is conceived as an involuntary activity, once it is seen as driven by chaotic desire and tugged by transcendent imagination, the fear of losing control becomes unavoidable. Once poetry is defined as the aggressive power of individual self-generating desire, the threat of poetic impotency becomes endemic to the poetic nature. Perhaps the easiest way to lose control, to be made impotent, is to have one's own vision wrenched from one by another whose presence is palpable. The anxiety of influence is exactly this kind of fear of the needed other. Wrestling to retain his vision, the romantic poet inevitably combats those who are most responsive to and responsible for his vision. Whether he perceives his major foe as the literary fathers, who provide a tradition without which he cannot enact his compulsion to write, or as his literary colleagues, the capable others who provide the context without which his feats become meaningless, the romantic poet engages in a contest whose very rules he seeks to determine through his own powerful manipulation of his influences.

Because the object of his grasping is the world itself, because his view is panoramic and natural, the romantic cannot afford to ignore any relation, for all relations, especially those that seem most natural, become threats. His relation to the female other, then, becomes particularly distressing. It is easier for Wordsworth to devise strategies for purging the influence of his father Milton and his brother Coleridge than it is for him to purge maternal Nature, that inexorable force that everywhere asserts itself as his dominant feminine other. As he takes the world in his grasp, he must necessarily take the feminine as a part of that world. Characteristically, the romantics are able to exploit this most troubling relation between themselves and their feminine others, and they do so by relying on the "natural" condition of the feminine as subordinate other. In other words, the relation that, in actuality, is most threatening, partly because it is most intimate, becomes in their myth of self-engendering desire the least threatening. The received male–female hierarchy not only serves as a convenient way of repressing feminine influence and rivalry; it also serves as a convenient way to deal with other kinds of influence and rivalry. Gender difference becomes a model for distinguishing the strong poet from other male poets. The feminization or emasculation of the rival male poet was already used by earlier writers like Pope as a way of normalizing their own socializing poetics and of masculinizing their relations with their closely-bonded male coterie. It also becomes a convenient and seemingly natural way for the romantic poet-persona to heighten his own potent self-sufficiency, as we have already seen in Byron's *English Bards and Scotch Reviewers* and in the leavetaking passages from *Childe Harold's Pilgrimage* and *Don Juan*. The threat of the brother can be diminished by feminizing his position as a rival. Because the split into male and female seems wholly natural to the romantic, the secondary split into male–male and male–female relations also seems wholly natural. From this secondary split flows the power of his myth to transform the anxiety of his influences into the horizon of his own visionary potential. Accordingly, when Coleridge wants to praise his rival, he does so by exploiting categories of gender: "Wordsworth has the least femineity in his mind. He is all *man*." As Jean Hagstrum points out, Coleridge tends to envy his friend's "virility," "sometimes morbidly and mischievously" (*Romantic Body* 73).[1] Coleridge's torturous relation with Wordsworth provides an instructive instance of how gender assumptions inform and formulate romantic poetics. But before examining how gender-based influence and rivalry manifest themselves concretely in Coleridge's poetry, we must briefly consider from a theoretical vantage point how influence itself is conceptualized, and how this conceptualization is at least partly constructed along the lines of gender difference.

1

Influence supposedly determines whether one has control over one's own, and thus power over others', destiny. When Harold Bloom speaks of the "anxiety" of influence, he is, of course, speaking of the fear of not having influence, the fear of being influenced: from this perspective one must either influence or be influenced. Influence is based on a hierarchized dichotomy as fundamental to Western culture as good/evil, body/soul, or male/female. The ideal state is one of absolute influence, the power to sway without ever having been swayed, the final cause that has no cause outside itself—the state of God. We tend to conceive of influence as the most powerful kind of power. It constitutes the top rung on the power-ladder, strength the bottom rung. For influence is the capacity to affect an object without the need to exert physical strength. It is the power to make an object (a material thing, a vehicle for exploitation) of the other supposedly without becoming oneself an object. It is the power of spiritual effect, and inasmuch as the spirit takes priority over the body in Western thought, influence is valued by that much over mere physical strength. Influence—a Latinate, high word—is allied etymologically to spirit, just as strength—an Anglo-Saxon word—is to body. Influence is the influx of the spirit, the power to give breath to another by a flow magically untainted by physical contact. Influence is naturally a masculine quality, though of course it can be unnaturally coopted by the feminine, just as Adam erroneously allows himself to be influenced by Eve. In its purest state, influence flows in one direction only: from God to man, from father to son, from male to female. Thus, influence often implies generation and succession. God breathes life into man and in doing so grants him the power of physical re-creation through the phallus; man inseminates life in woman and grants her the power of physical re-creation through childbirth. From God to man to woman: at each stage influence as spiritual capacity is displaced by power as physical capacity; woman is more tied to the physical than man and man moreso than God, and so in order for her to rise to the sphere of influence, she must somehow overcome a more binding physical burden, one that can be overcome only by perverting her destiny as woman, just as man can assume his divinity only by denying the limits of his body. Woman's proper power over man is merely physical: her sensuous and sensual allurement, her ability to provide comfort and consolation, her capacity to bear children and raise them, her fate to fulfill masculine desire. She can only affect others insofar as her power partakes of one of these physical functions. To ensure that her destiny is not easily controverted, however, man is also given greater physical strength itself, just as God has greater strength than man. Their greatest power, however, is in their refusal, except in times of crisis, to display that strength to their lessers, remembering that such a refusal itself constitutes influence, since what defines influence is its effectuality without physical exertion.

As Bloom makes clear, poetic influence derives from this paradigm of influence as the unidirectional, spiritual power of generation and succession, the power of the phallus. Bloom, influenced by his own romantic fathers, sees influence as tragic because it is no longer (or never has been?) possible. The divine state of absolute influence becomes more difficult (more impossible?) to achieve as succession progresses, as influence moves relentlessly from father to son in an uninterruptable deferral of power. Every father has been a son, and no son has the power of self-generation. Not being physical, influence can leap across centuries, across countries, across cultures. Like desire itself, it is an elusive force, spawning itself, and generating its own infinitely insatiable progress, or perhaps more precisely, regress. Like the relation between desire and its irrepressible products, the relation between the influential subject and its objects is adversarially binding. Influence always offers the promise of unbounded subjectivity, but a troubled subjectivity threatened always by the objects it needs in order to exist. The father needs the son, and

so becomes influenced by him, becomes a son to his own son; the male needs
the female and so becomes influenced by her. And in romantic ideology, God
becomes dependent on man, the creature he has created as the object of his
absolute influence. Or, as Shelley so frequently expresses both implicitly and
explicitly in his work, God becomes the creature of creator-man. Influence
becomes so pervasive that the only way of coping with it is to accept its limit-
less operation by exploiting it. To be influenced becomes a necessary evil, but
one that a great man can manipulate to advance the myth of his own self-
possession. In other words, to achieve enviable power at a time when the influence of others is so pervasive becomes the ultimate heroic feat for the
romantics.

The historical self-consciousness of the romantics—Bloomian belatedness—makes influence crucial to their poeticizing and tinges romantic heroism with the tragedy that arises from modern anxiety. A Dryden or a Pope
can be satisfied with translating a Virgil or a Homer, giving homage to the
classics through obvious imitation and looking back to a golden age whose
values represent a gauge by which they can measure their own merits and
flaws. A Wordsworth or a Shelley, however, is exhilarated and distressed by
the impossibility of relying on a past age to provide values that the poet can
simply translate into the language of his time. Because history has intervened,
the romantic poet sees his circumstances as unique. Historicism mandates
originality. Translation (except as a secondary pursuit) is failure; imitation is
even worse. And yet the intervention of history also forces the romantics to
accept the influence of the past as inescapably distinctive. Milton cannot be
translated or imitated, but he must be confronted. Milton cannot provide the
distinctive vision needed in present historical circumstances, but he has provided a vision for his own circumstances, and a vision so trenchantly influential that it threatens to stifle the progress of history itself. The idea of never
getting beyond Miltonic vision is traumatic to the romantics because such a
failure not only reflects their own impotence but also reveals the treachery of
historical process. Because desire is the motor of historical change, the failure
to meet the demands of history is itself a failure of desire, the obverse of the
failure to transcend history. Time can proceed relentlessly, presenting ever-
new problems, yet human beings can be stuck repeating the old answers in
the newness of time. It is a frightening vision of eternal recurrence that we
see enacted in romantic tragedy and that romantic comedy refuses to accept.
The romantic poet must learn to accept past influence (the influence of the
fathers) by heroically demonstrating how the present refuses the terms of the
fathers' past.

Historical consciousness also contributes to intensified anxiety over influence because it forces the poet to apprehend the present as a privileged
state of contestation. At this very moment, in its monumental uniqueness, history is being decided. Although the poet has no power over past vision, he is
able to shape the present relation to that past, in other words, to shape the
future through prophecy. His influence will depend directly on his capacity to
influence others in his present, his capacity to deflect their influence over him,

in determining that undecided future. This is why the romantics rely heavily on the prophetic stance, which itself is another instance of a masculine trope of power. Classical prophets like Cassandra notwithstanding, the conception of the prophet has close ties to vocal virility. The prophet is one who is able to enforce his vision on others, to convince them that he is strong enough to be a conduit for divine intervention. His influence becomes a form of masterful self-sufficiency, for he will find himself alone on mountaintops, misunderstood and often jeered and despised. His strong voice metonymically indicates his capacity to influence, his power not reliant on physical strength. To paraphrase Wordsworth, the prophet strikes blows with his words, and so his words become a powerful way of acting in the world, rather than merely a form of rhetoric. His influence is feared not only because it represents a greater divine influx, but also because his words become acts, fulfilling themselves as his prophecy is fulfilled in material reality. Because divine effluence is miraculously contained within the material body and the immaterial words of the prophet, he becomes a crucial paradigm for the kind of influence attributable to the poet. It is not the Cassandras that poet-prophets like Wordsworth, Shelley, and Blake turn to, but the Isaiahs, whose mighty voices confirm their potent visions, whose influence lies not in the disparity between the accuracy of their predictions and the ineffectuality of their voices, but in the irony of their forceful voices having so little *immediate* effect on their listeners. The masculinely-defined prophet suffers disrepute not because his voice is too soft or timid to make hearers of listeners, but rather because it is too strong and aggressive, because it is so overpowering that it frightens weak people away from the truth it so masterfully handles in words.

Whether the poet-prophet is pushed into solitude because of the little-mindedness of society, like Byron, or because of the greatmindedness of his own natural vision, like Wordsworth, his strength in solitude becomes a gauge for his impending influence on society. Many times, it is only the intimate female other who is capable of appreciating the paradox of his position—possessing the greatest capacity to influence and the least immediate effect—and it is her feminine appreciation that helps to reaffirm the masculine power of his voice. But, as frequently, the romantic poet is willing to feminize the intimate male other in order to assure the myth of his own prophetic influence. Prophetic solitariness itself is a romantic myth. All of the romantics communicate their strongest prophecies in a network of fellowship; whether that fellowship is the dreaded influence of fellow writers—as with Shelley and Byron or Coleridge and Wordsworth—or the influence of past male writers who are imagined to be present, as Blake imagines himself conversing with Milton or as Keats less fancifully converses with the picture of Shakespeare above his desk; or whether that "fellow"ship is the repressed influence of sympathetic sister-wives, or of more independent women writers. The rivalry with the fellow poet, in this way different from the coffeehouse congeniality of the Augustan coterie, even as it is manifestly dialogic and socializing, is conceptualized as a solitary pursuit: two champions wrestling at the margins of the other's territory or the snake and eagle wreathed in f(l)ight.

Although Bloom has stressed the rivalry between the poet and his literary father, he could have as easily stressed the sibling rivalry, the competition that ensues between the poet and his contemporaries, his *fellow* (compatriot, co-equal, male) poets, who represent as much a threat to his self-creation and self-possession as his progenitors. Because the progenitor's work is complete, the posthumous rivalry with the progenitor is more or less settled before it begins. That work can be viewed in its totality, assessed, manipulated, and assaulted without the risk of counterattack. The poet's failure becomes an error of hindsight, in which all the weapons of the competitor are already laid out for him. The rivalry with the brother, in some ways, becomes more intense and more immediate. The brother lays claim not just to the same inheritance, but also to the same temporal territory of the estate, for history confines them to common ground and imposes on them a shared discourse. Although the fellow poet can appropriate as well as be appropriated, the interaction needed to stimulate the growth of both minds always threatens to become each poet's fathering of the other. The potential of the fellow poet, as opposed to the actual power of the dead father, is itself unsettling because its claims are unpredictable and its territory always renegotiable. Because the fellow poet is so similar, his failures and successes are duplicitous: each failure potentially reflects the poet's own failure and serves potentially as a counter-gauge for the poet's potential success; likewise for each success. They become opposed twins with fates so intertwined that each must wish the other's success to signify his own, and also must desire the other's defeat in order to prevent his own. Therefore, an odd, paradoxical relation develops between the two: where the rival poet is weakest, the first poet can read both his own weakness and an opening for his own display of strength. The poet becomes weakest where the other is strongest, and vice versa, and he himself becomes weakest where he is strongest, as his strongest stance becomes the most compelling point of attack for another poet desiring to prove his strength. The most successful poet is the one who best sublimates the fear of his own weakness while advancing the myth of his self-possession, or it is the one who—as we shall see with Coleridge—is able to exploit his own perceived weakness as a point of leverage.

Through the seemingly predetermined and natural relations of male to female and male to male, the poet finds his anchor and his compass. As a compass, the fellow poet helps to chart the poet's course, for the poet must steer away from the route taken by his fellow; either that, or he must retrace the same route to demonstrate his fellow's occasional wrong turns. Because the best friend is viewed as the same, he can serve better as a representative rival, as a twin whom the poet must battle in order to struggle and to grow; ironically, because the woman is seen as different, she can serve better as an extension of the self, as an ideal, a "higher" or "deeper" form of consciousness that must be integrated with the self in order for it to achieve completeness, to fully know its limits and its power, to fully know itself. The poet's male counterpart functions aggressively to define the contours of the poet's own desire, to clarify and validate what makes his desire distinctive; the female companion functions to fulfill that desire, or to represent the potential for consummated desire. She is desire itself externalized or the outer goal (which must exist for desire to be motivated) internalized. She allows the poet an external object (as an aspect of her otherness) to move toward in order to make real (to realize) his internal need (because she is also seen as an aspect of the self).

The dynamics of influence operate here in predictable ways. Although the fellow poet is capable of influencing his brother, the female has no such power. Her "power" or "virtue" is always "physical," even when it is spiritual. That is, she is an internalized object, affecting the poet by her closeness, her contact, with him. As the fulfillment of the poet's desire and the completion of the poet's self, she figures in his poetics as territory always already claimed. Her power is also physical in that it is only instrumental. She serves to help the poet over his moment of trauma, the moment when self-possession is threatened by the influence of the other. She becomes a tangible and stable other, always ready to stand in when the myth of his self-possession is about to collapse. As his anchor of desire or his territory of self-expression, there is direct contact, a verifiable relation, a physical tie between them—exactly the kind of tie that cannot be assumed of the male counterpart without the risk of losing self-possession. As we shall see, Coleridge exploits this cultural conception of the tangible relation between the male and his stabilizing feminine other for his own aggression against his more virile rival.

As self-possession and influence become crucial determinants within the discourse of romanticism, categories of gender take on an intensified role, a role that can be examined through the basic permutations of gender relations (where the ">" denotes the direction of influence): male > male, male > female, female > male, female > female. It is the first two relations that are exploited in romantic poetry, while the latter two tend to be repressed, exactly because they threaten the myth of influence that these gender relations are being used to prop up. In romantic discourse the male > male and male > female relations manifest themselves specifically in these forms: influence of a celebrated poet on a poet struggling to achieve fame (father > son), the influence of fellow poets on each other (brother > brother), and the influence of struggling poet on a female other who serves to confirm the power of his vision (brother > sister). As he represses other relations—such as mother > son, sister > brother, or sister > sister—the poet succeeds in establishing the myth of his relative influence (since absolute influence is impossible), even as his works themselves must reveal the reality of others' influence over him.

2

We have seen how Wordsworth purges Coleridge's rivalry from his epic by making Coleridge the ears of the poem. But since Coleridge's listening implies the capacity to respond in kind, Wordsworth permanently forestalls response by subtly making himself both the voice and ears of the poem.

Fortunately, we have Coleridge's response to *The Prelude* in "To William Wordsworth, Composed on the Night after his Recitation of a Poem on the Growth of an Individual Mind." The title of Coleridge's poem indicates how successful Wordsworth has been in coopting Coleridge's anticipated response. Wordsworth's voice has been so strong, his vision so totalizing, that Coleridge's poem becomes almost a parody of the epic, as it wanders aimlessly along the same path Wordsworth has set out. On the surface, Coleridge's motivation in writing the poem is to praise Wordsworth. It quickly becomes clear, however, that beneath the sea of praise lies a whirlpool of envy, a whirlpool that bursts to the surface at the poem's climax and resubmerges to enable closure. It is almost as if Wordsworth's voice has conquered Coleridge, has drowned him in a sea of self-doubt, and turned the rivalry of male equals into the pseudorivalry of female other with male subject.

No doubt Coleridge's anxiety is exacerbated by the fact that Wordsworth's great poem takes as its subject the growth of a poet's mind. What Wordsworth can assert with such self-assurance leaves Coleridge little space to chart his own growth. Once Wordsworth casts himself as the poet who represents his generation, his era, and indeed the progress of all humankind itself, Coleridge cannot acknowledge Wordsworth's power without also acquiescing to Wordsworth's centrality. Once Wordsworth places himself at the center, Coleridge must either fight for that heroic place or make his own place on the margins of history and discourse, on the margins of poetic creation. But since Wordsworth has already forcefully and convincingly placed Coleridge within his realm, it is more difficult for Coleridge to take the first course. The second option, of course, is unsatisfactory if it means that Coleridge must become, like the female, always marginal, always secondary, always an echo, or, to use Virginia Woolf's metaphor, always a magical mirror reflecting Wordsworth's achievements back to him at twice their actual size. If Coleridge is to compete with Wordsworth without denying Wordsworth's poetic achievements, then he must somehow manage to leave Wordsworth's self-centralizing vision at least ostensibly intact while claiming significance and power in marginality. He must somehow manage to compete from an eccentric position, allowing Wordsworth to have the center, but problematizing the relation between the center and the radius. Because Wordsworth has made himself the hero not only of his own tale, but of all tales of poetic growth, Coleridge must re-usurp his own capacity for heroism by ironically dislocating or relocating the heroic stance itself. This is exactly what he does in "To William Wordsworth." In *The Hamlet Vocation of Coleridge and Wordsworth,* Martin Greenburg points out how Coleridge's statement "To admire on principle, is the only way to imitate without loss of originality" could be applied to Coleridge's own writing practices. Coleridge "admired and imitated on principle," Greenburg says, "without losing his distinctive qualities of thought and feeling" (23). In "To William Wordsworth" Coleridge admires and imitates out of desperation for a distinctive voice, and it is that desperation (as potential despair) that motivates his embracing of a principle to imitate and admire.

Coleridge deals with Wordsworth's rivalry in three ways: 1) through complex images of absorption and reception, submission and conquest, subjection and subjectivity; 2) through language borrowed from Wordsworth and revitalized from Coleridge's own eccentric position; 3) by repeatedly introducing a third term into the discourse, another figure that turns the one-on-one duel into a more complicated rivalry. Each of these strategies tends to make Wordsworth's centrality problematic even while accepting it, and each places Coleridge in a position similar to, but not equal to, the marginal female. For, unlike the female, Coleridge wants to claim for himself a kind of tragic heroism in marginality. It is the tragedy of influence, the tragedy that only a male can experience, since only a male can be cast out of his originally ordained state of masculine influence and be forced into exile in the land of feminine subjection, marginality, and echoing silence.

If Wordsworth combats the anxiety of influence by purging his rivals from the poem, Coleridge deals with influence by tragically absorbing rivalry. He accepts the brother's powerful voice and becomes the ears of his own poem, even as he subtly asserts his own eccentric power to speak. Absorption itself is a complex process that is not simply the reception by a passive medium of an active agent. The "softness" of the medium disposes it to receiving a harder intrusive agent; however, the capacity to absorb can itself become a kind of power. As the "active" agent asserts its power by permeating the "passive" medium, it also gives itself to that medium and becomes possessed by it. As the medium is infiltrated by the agent, the medium establishes its own form of power. Furthermore, *ad*sorption necessarily accompanies *ab*sorption. They are different conceptions of the same process. The harder intrusive agent that permeates the softer one, overpowering the medium by adding it to itself (adsorption) can also be seen as the inverse: the taking in of the harder agent by the softer medium (absorption). The hardness (the "d" in adsorb) becomes as much an incapacity as a strength; the softness (the "b" in absorb) becomes as much a capacity (or virtue) as a weakness. The subject-agent, as it influences, is influenced by the object-medium.

The poem begins with an image of absorption which enwombs the very power struggle that the poem seeks to abort. "Friend of the wise! and Teacher of the Good! / Into my heart have I received that Lay" (*Poetical Works* 1–2). From the beginning Coleridge's relation to the poet, to the poem recited, and to the power that makes the poem is problematic. Originally, the first line read: "O Friend! O Teacher! God's great gift to me." The revision blurs the more definite relation inscribed in the original version. Wordsworth is transformed from a "great gift" to a friend and teacher of the "wise" and "Good." Are the nouns "wise" and "Good" concrete synecdoches for the abstract virtues of wisdom and goodness (in which case, why is "wise" not capitalized like "Good")? The original version tends to verify this reading. Wordsworth is a great gift in that he teaches wisdom and goodness to Coleridge. However, the ambiguity of the preposition "of" unsettles the tidiness of that reading, and the possibility that the nouns are substantives adds to the ambiguity. Wordsworth is a friend and a teacher to the wise and Good. What does it mean to befriend and teach someone who is already wise and Good? What exactly is being taught, if not wisdom and goodness? Are wisdom and goodness the cause or the effect of the befriending? As "wise" and "Good" become adjectives modifying the poet–listener (Coleridge) rather than attributes of the poet–speaker (Wordsworth), the relation between listening and speaking threatens to become inverted. As listening absorbs speaking, it steals from the power of speaking without losing its own peculiar capacity. Just as Coleridge becomes a poet–listener, who speaks in order to praise the poet–speaker, so Wordsworth potentially becomes a poet–speaker who must listen, not only to the praise due him, but also to the wisdom and goodness of a friend and teacher of the wise and Good. The first line raises the question, which shall be addressed later in the poem, of Wordsworth's prophetic self-sufficiency. Has Wordsworth recited the "growth of an individual mind," or the growth of a collective mind, a mind that has imbibed (adsorbed) wisdom and goodness from his intimate fellowship with others? Even before Coleridge acknowledges that he has "received" Wordsworth's great lay, he has problematized the terms of reception.

At least five years before "To Wordsworth," Coleridge has already determined that "we receive but what we give." Does this mean that Coleridge is receiving from Wordsworth what he has already given? (As we'll discover when we examine "Dejection," the question is much more complicated than it appears.) The first stanza of "To Wordsworth" may seem to reject the potential complications of "receive" for the simplicity of unalloyed praise. Wordsworth is the "first" to sing "aright" that "[m]ore than historic, that prophetic Lay." Wordsworth has "dared" to tell thoughts that others may feel but are unable to articulate. Considering Wordsworth's own use of the word "dare," this is indeed high praise, placing Wordsworth among his own "earliest poets," who "generally wrote from passion excited by real events," who wrote "naturally, and as men," and whose "language was daring, and figurative."

As Thomas McFarland has noted, Coleridge's lines are "pure Wordsworth, both in their cadences and in their great Wordsworthian abstractions. . . . [H]ardly anywhere else does Coleridge achieve this peculiar Miltonicity of style" (*Romanticism and the Forms of Ruin* 59–60).[2] Borrowing from Wordsworth's language, Coleridge seems to accept the imitative, secondary, reflective, less daring condition of his own discourse. It is as if Wordsworth has stimulated Coleridge to speak by providing a register for his voice to make itself heard. But Coleridge's imitation forces us to attend all the more closely to his own articulations, to the fineness of difference between his voice and his rival's. For instance, Coleridge changes Wordsworth's statement "[t]houghts that do often lie too deep for tears" to his own "[t]houghts all too deep for words." By exchanging a vital and figurative image "tears" for an abstract and seemingly feeble word "words," Coleridge seems to mock his own lesser imagination, his own weaker power of figuration. He selects a word that fails to summon an image. Coleridge's choice, however, stresses the weakness within Wordsworth's own language, and we should perhaps note that the image stressed through its omission, "tears," is itself an image of feminine vulnerability. It is as if Coleridge is acknowledging the tyranny of words over thoughts, acknowledging how words, as they fail to articulate deepest thoughts, gain power to articulate only themselves. Possessing the power (and necessity) of iteration, words diminish the power of those who would express the uniterability of desire, who would articulate thoughts deep within the unique, self-originating experience of the poetic self.

Does Coleridge's statement exclude Wordsworth from or include him in the failure of articulation? Has Wordsworth overpowered words themselves by revealing to the mind the thoughts that lie deep within the heart? Or has he merely revealed to the mind that there *are* thoughts that lie too deep for words, quickening those thoughts within the heart but not disclosing them to the mind?

The poem refuses to answer the question, so that as Coleridge imitates Wordsworth's language, he also diffuses its strength, and stresses the failure of articulation that lies always dormant within the apparent success of the great poet-prophet. Words themselves become a rival for power, an intermediate rival standing in between the two poets and wrestling from each the innate and originary power of his poetic desire. Once again, Coleridge's original version is less ambivalent: "Thoughts that obey no mastery of words, / Pure self-beholdings." As he changes the language to imitate, perhaps mock and praise, Wordsworth, he also pushes it deeper into the self where words lose their magic power. Coleridge's ears may be fated to obey the mastery of Wordsworth's poetic vision, but Wordsworth has no final mastery over words, over the very material that supposedly enables his vision to conquer his listener. Wordsworth's words, in the original version, are called "pure self-beholdings." This reminds us of one of Wordsworth's own word-borrowings: his "Nature never did betray / The heart that loved her" in "Tintern Abbey," echoing Coleridge's "Nature ne'er deserts the wise and pure" in "This Lime-Tree Bower." Wordsworth's version emphasizes the reciprocal love between the self and nature, a love that is *not* unconditional. Nature selfishly loves those who return her love. Does this mean that human love is conditioned by the same self-interest? Coleridge's prior phrase not only stresses the egoism of Wordsworth's natural philosophy but also offers a corrective to Wordsworth's self-interested love, just as he is correcting his own self-pity within the poem. Nature's loyalty, Coleridge suggests, is based on the merits of wisdom and purity, or as he says in "To Wordsworth," wisdom and goodness. As Wordsworth is busy "building up" a "Human Spirit"—his own—Coleridge is busy "seeking"—to use a crucial word from "Frost at Midnight"—wisdom and goodness. The "pure," then, in "pure self-beholdings" becomes suspect. Is it the purity of unstained goodness, or is it the purity of unmitigated and unquestioned self-indulgence, the kind of self-involvement that Coleridge castigates himself for in "This Lime-Tree Bower"? In the latter reading, Wordsworth's poetic vision is revealed as pure narcissism, the poet echoing to himself the sounds that issue from the self, the poet looking out to the world, to his best friend, to his literary fathers, but beholding only the self-contained self in every image. Where the wisdom and purity of nature should be reflected, they instead become "bestowed" on the self by the self for the self.

Coleridge's adoption of Wordsworth's words suggests how the flattery of imitation always threatens to become the parody of praise. It is not that Coleridge is insincere, but that his sincerity cannot disengage itself from the disingenuousness of the serious rival. Words are transferable, and as such, they refuse to be possessed, they refuse loyalty. In *Coleridge's Blessed Machine of Language,* Jerome Christensen shows just how crucial this idea is to Coleridge's whole enterprise. Even though Christensen is here speaking specifically of Coleridge's prose, his insightful argument applies as well to the poetry:

[T]he writer's possession of his language is precisely what Coleridge's prose puts in question. Even fidelity . . . can produce a mimesis of text and commentary that verges on a more deeply disturbing infidelity: if not a rivalry at least a duplicity, as figure echoes figure and digress counters digress. (27)[3]

It is as if Wordsworth's words betray him, and Coleridge is only an innocent (disingenuous) bystander, a listener–disciple who unwittingly discloses the unclosable lapses in his teacher's lesson. After all, Coleridge's iterated words betray him as well, for they reveal his own envy, his self-doubt, his desire to wrench success from Wordsworth even as he garlands his rival with the native flowers that must decorate his own bier. As Wordsworth's words betray him and allow themselves to be possessed by Coleridge, they necessarily simultaneously betray Coleridge not only because they reveal his desire to steal his rival's success but also because they can be no more loyal to their second speaker than they were to their first.

Coleridge's word-borrowing acknowledges how he has accepted Wordsworth's putative centrality and representativeness while relocating heroism itself to the margins as the tragedy of the influenced. When Coleridge uses Wordsworth's words, he seems to say that Wordsworth has said what Coleridge should have said, and would have, if only. . . . What Wordsworth has dared—and managed—to do is to wrestle Coleridge's own potential poem from him; he has revealed to Coleridge what was already in his own mind. Coleridge receives into his heart "[w]hat may be told, to the understanding mind / Revealable." On the other hand, such a locution also establishes listening or reading as a virtue. "Surely it is a curious thing to say of a poem— that it speaks of things too deep for *words,*" Jean-Pierre Mileur writes. "The statement serves to point up the necessary incompleteness of the genuinely prophetic poem, redefining the prophecy and its fulfillment away from Wordsworth's previous life . . . toward a fulfillment outside [*The Prelude*] in the self-recognition occurring in the heart of the reader" (*Vision and Revision* 122–123). If no poet can embody in words the deepest things within the mind and heart, then doesn't the reader–listener provide what the poet's words cannot?

Finally, Coleridge's word-borrowing helps to problematize the relations of influence within the poem by subverting the unidirectional power of mind over heart, of speaker over listener, of strong brother over self-doubting brother. Mind and heart, often conceived as foes, work together in the stanza. At first, our attention is drawn to Coleridge's heart and mind, the heart accepting gratefully what Wordsworth has to offer, the mind understanding what the heart graciously receives. However, as the stanza achieves closure, both mind and heart—like words—become unpossessed, capable of belonging to either poet or to both. Hasn't Coleridge rejected here the most obvious way of imaging the relation between Wordsworth's active recitation and his own reception of it? A neatly logical outlay of relation between mind and heart would look something like this:

```
mind     = Wordsworth              = active speaking   = seminal understanding
  ↓                                       ↓                   ↓
wisdom   = poet–prophet             = generous giving   = original truth
                                          ↓
                        permeates = informs
                          absorbs = forms into
                         quickens = stimulates
                          bestows = teaches
                           drives = admonishes
                           shapes = disciplines
                  flows into/over = influences
                                          ↓
heart    = Coleridge               = passive listening  = implanted knowledge
  ↓                                       ↓                   ↓
goodness = poet(?)–disciple         = grateful receiving = imitated/reflected truth
```

The adsorbing mind of Wordsworth conquers the absorbing heart of Coleridge. Wordsworth's wise poetic vision permeates Coleridge's good and open heart. The aggressive strength of Wordsworth's poem drives Coleridge to recognize his own failure. Wordsworth's self-possessing mind inspires Coleridge to discipline his own willful heart, his own desire, and allows him to shape a disciplined response (not only the difficult discipline of completing a project in writing the poem but also of restraining his self-doubt and self-pity in order to celebrate his rival's success). Wordsworth's poem influences Coleridge's corresponding poem. Wordsworth's speaking sets the boundaries for Coleridge's attempt to speak his listening. All of these straightforward relations are complicated and countermanded by the poem: mind and heart, wisdom and goodness, active and passive, speaking and listening, giving and receiving, originating and imitating, bestowing and reflecting. Rather than the image of the mind disciplining and admonishing the heart by teaching it what the heart cannot know, Coleridge turns heart and mind into co-workers, just as he will turn the two rival poets into interdependent co-operating entities.

In this way Coleridge is able to turn tropes of subjection (bowing down to praise a stronger poet) into images of subjectivity (creating his own power of self-possession). As stanzas 2 and 3 recount the Wordsworthian themes of *The Prelude,* they retrace the perilous path taken by Wordsworth in his epic.

This summing up of Wordsworth's epic delivers a mini-epic or perhaps even a mock-epic, for as Coleridge rehearses the "theme hard as high," he also must soften and lower that theme, not only in that he must shift from the hard and high position of epic to one of the smallest and lowliest of literary forms, the eulogistic lyric, but also in that he must revise the expansive wanderings of Wordsworth's mighty excursion into a brief jaunt. Whereas Wordsworth's epic claims to rise to the eternal and universal and claims as its audience not just Coleridge but all of nature and humankind, past, present, and evermore about to be; Coleridge writes an occasional lyric, a little personal poem, apparently limited by its moment of conception, shadowed by time, directed to a specific listener in a contained context (more allied to Augustan poetic forms).

The lyric of praise is difficult to carry off because it must pretend to be directed at the one praised, for his ears only, when in fact it directs itself to all who will listen. While pretending to be an intimate communication from an admirer to a great man, it must publicize the greatness it intimates. Like the love poem, then, it is troubled by the demons of insincerity and one-upmanship. Does the lyricist write to unveil another's light to the world, or does he write to unveil his own virtue in being able to discern the brightness of that light, in being able to accomplish the feat of combining intimacy and publicity. Just as Wordsworth has personalized the epic, given it an intimate listener in Coleridge, named it with the rubric of his own private signature, Coleridge must expand the occasional lyric so that it becomes large enough to contain the greatness of epic. Eulogy is closely linked with elegy, for such hyperbolic praise is usually saved for those who are safe on the other side of death. So Coleridge's task is made even more difficult in that he writes to praise one, not at the moment of loss, the moment from which he begins to be forgotten by a mindless world, but at the peak moment of his self-canonization. How does one write a poem to celebrate the greatness of a poet who has just recited a poem celebrating his own calling to greatness? That Coleridge manages to do so enables him to reclaim his status as a true rival even as he bows to honor a greater one.

Stanzas 2 and 3 grant Wordsworth the masculine potency that he claims in his own epic, but they do so under the shadow of influence and under the predictable constraints and contradictions of eulogy. Wordsworth sings:

> Of tides obedient to external force,
> And currents self-determined, as might seem,
> Or by some inner Power; of moments awful,
> Now in thy inner life, and now abroad,
> When power streamed from thee, and thy soul received
> The light reflected, as a light bestowed.
>
> (14–19)

Part of Wordsworth's project in *The Prelude* is to trace his reconciliation of external force with self-determined desire, to reveal his self-anointment as natural genius, to embrace the outer by subjecting it to his ever-expanding "inner Power." What Wordsworth joins, Coleridge subtly tears asunder. The rift between "tides obedient to external force" and "currents self-determined" seems unbridgeable. How can Wordsworth's desire be both "obedient" and "self-determined"? The paradox that Wordsworth spends thousands of words weaving, Coleridge unravels in a dozen. The river imagery of the passage is apt here. It is the imagery that Wordsworth uses repeatedly to promote his own poetic persona. It is an appropriate image for the contours of masculine desire, the stream of influence, the forceful flow of masculine insemination— all self-consciously promoted as tropes for poetic vocation by Wordsworth, and self-consciously imitated/mocked by Coleridge. The equivocation "as might seem" can be read either as an affirmation of Wordsworth's paradox (internal currents of power seem to be external forces of influence) or as a devastating denial of the paradox: What seems to be a self-determining current must be revealed as an external force. Coleridge's passage can easily be read admonishingly. Wordsworth has mistaken externally derived power for self-generated power; he has mistaken a "light reflected, as a light bestowed."

We cannot overlook the part imitation plays in the process of reflection. Whereas bestowal implies the granting of an honor or gift, and would hold out the possibility for the poet's worthiness as a cause for the bestowal, reflection is much more duplicitous. The poet imitates (nature, another poet, history, perhaps all three) by mirroring his influences, but he also represses that mirroring act, taking the light as a gift bestowed by nature rather than as a theft taken from the world. Reflection valorizes the relation between two subjects and tends to resist any separation that would be made between them. The image that returns from the other to the self becomes the image of the self. The image of the other becomes an image of the self within the other, and vice versa. Making it impossible to mark the self without remarking the resemblance between self and other, reflection calls into question the metaphysics of originality and teleology. That is, it does so as long as the relation is recognized as an indeterminate interaction between two nonsequential subjects. Once one of those subjects is made subordinate, reduced to a secondary subject, taken as an object, placed within a sequence, reflection becomes the affirmation of originality and teleology. The problematic relation between two subjects is reduced to a relation between an original subject and an imitative object, a real self and a distorted other, speaker and listener, master and pupil, poet and critic, male and female. This conception of reflection makes resemblance itself an arbitrary effect, rather than a foundational cause of the relation between two subjects. The other can never really give my image back to me, because my image is always prior to—more real than—the image within the other. Imitation becomes a sleight of eye played by the other, one that the astute self can see through. In order to believe in this kind of originary reflection, the self must repress the problematic of the relation and the problematic of the origin, turning every relation into a misrepresentation and taking itself as the always anterior subject of every image that returns it to itself. Narcissus fails to understand the problematic of the reflective relation and of the origin, for he immediately takes the other's image as an image of the other, separate from the self. Ironically, Narcissus comes to epitomize the solipsistic subject, the subject incapable of moving beyond the self; he *should,* however, represent the opposite fallacy, the subject incapable of recognizing the ineradicable relation that always must exist between self and other. Narcissus is a child who has not yet reached the Kristevan/Lacanian mirror stage where the subject forms a self by realizing a relation with the not-self. Wordsworth is at the opposite end of the spectrum, where Narcissus is usually placed. When he sees an image of himself in another, he does not, like Narcissus, begin to desire the image as though it were a separate being detached from himself; rather he represses the symbiotic relation itself in order to retain mythic self-autonomy, reading every other as an emanation of the subject's original image.

Therefore, although Wordsworth's poem is supposed to trace an outward movement to the "Social Sense / Distending wide, and man beloved as man," his outward movement becomes once again "pure self-beholdings," viewed "[f]rom the dread watch-tower of man's absolute self." Mirroring Wordsworth, Coleridge returns the poet's image back to him, but, as mirroring tends to do, Coleridge's image transposes Wordsworth's. Coleridge moves inward the more he appears to move out, falling prey to Wordsworth's solipsism and to Wordsworth's power as he mocks and attempts to correct Wordsworth's error. Coleridge recuperates the relational necessity of reflection by restoring the subjectivity of Wordsworth's object-relations; he reminds us that nature, the other, and history are always born(e) with(in) the subject. Coleridge's poem itself becomes an instance of such reflection, returning the image of Wordsworth back to Wordsworth as though it is the image of a self-reflecting subject. That is, the reflected image of Wordsworth is not simply Wordsworth's image of himself, but always also Coleridge's image of Wordsworth and Coleridge's image of himself, each image mirroring the other. It is as if Coleridge has surfaced Wordsworth's nature with fragmented mirrors that make the original self impossible to locate within a barrage of images all claiming to be the self.

It is appropriate, then, that Coleridge should commit the inverse of Wordsworth's error as he attempts a critique of that error. The more Coleridge moves inward to the self, the more he moves outward to a mirror-image of self, to Wordsworth's image rather than to one that could ever be his own. As we move inside Coleridge's poem, as we move deeper inside Coleridge, where words are not supposed to be able to go, we discover only a relation. We can find no self-originating desire because his desire is always predicated by a desire to articulate his self in relation to an other. Behind Coleridge's image of himself is a mirror reflecting his image back in Wordsworth's language, which Coleridge has borrowed from Wordsworth in order to articulate his own desire. Within Coleridge's self resides the image of Wordsworth, or more precisely, resides a relation between two inextricable images of both poets. One cannot desire without the other's desire; one cannot die without the other's death. This is why Wordsworth's eulogy automatically becomes his elegy, why Coleridge's elegy automatically becomes his eulogy, why

Wordsworth's transfiguration becomes Coleridge's and the latter's death becomes the former's.

Inside this lyric of eulogy resides the eulogy of elegy. We become witness to one apparent transfiguration without death, and one death without apparent transfiguration, as the mock-epic of stanzas 2 and 3 gives way to the lyrical outburst of stanza 4:

> O great Bard!
> Ere yet that last strain dying awed the air,
> With stedfast eye I viewed thee in the choir
> Of ever-enduring men. The truly great
> Have all one age, and from one visible space
> Shed influence! They, both in power and act,
> Are permanent, and Time is not with them,
> Save as it worketh for them, they in it.
>
> (47–54)

As the poem rises to its climax, it raises Wordsworth to sainthood among the undying gods of poetry. And yet the passage begins with a dying—notably with an allusion to Shakespeare's *Twelfth Night,* rather than an allusion to anything by Wordsworth. It is Wordsworth's recitation that dies upon the air. Following Wordsworth, Coleridge turns unavoidable human mortality—the last dying strain—into the permanence of eternity and truth. The master's poem outlives its own dying strain, and so the master himself is transfigured into an "ever-enduring" man who "shed[s] influence" ceaselessly "from one visible space." Coleridge seems to grant his rival that supreme state, to shed influence without being influenced. And yet Wordsworth is not cast as a solitary god, but as a member of a choir. "The truly great / Have all one age." Wordsworth's work "[m]akes audible a linked lay of Truth, / Of Truth profound a sweet continuous lay." As Coleridge links Wordsworth's work to a "continuous lay," he calls into question the self-possessing desire of the self-anointed prophetic stance. He calls into question the internality of poetic power and puts into perspective the communal nature of influence. Jean-Pierre Mileur has identified this move as "negative apotheosis": "Coleridge's writings can be seen as a striving after the negative apotheosis of poetic greatness. The conclusion that we are invited to draw from such a conception of Coleridge's work is that poetry culminates not in great poets but in tradition itself—that literature is the last and greatest of poets" (122). What Coleridge does in this maneuver is to place a third term—literary tradition—between Wordsworth and himself, making any enduring poet merely a member of a great choir of history, which subsumes him. As Wordsworth tries to put all of history into perspective by making himself the hero of poetic tradition, Coleridge reminds him of his place within a community of voices.

In fact, the whole passage takes on the onus of putting-into-perspective. It is Coleridge who views Wordsworth in that choir of ever-enduring men. It is Coleridge whose "eye" and "I"—coming together with the force of repetition—are "stedfast." From what "dread watch-tower" is Coleridge viewing this mighty vision of transfiguration? Where is the poet who inscribes the rival poet within the "sacred Roll . . . [a]mong the archives of mankind"? The doubling eye/I reminds us and the writer of his own position, and turns us inward as we supposedly go out to praise another.

> Ah! as I listened with a heart forlorn,
> The pulses of my being beat anew:
> And even as Life returns upon the drowned,
> Life's joy rekindling roused a throng of pains—
> Keen pangs of Love, awakening as a babe
> Turbulent, with an outcry in the heart;
> And fears self-willed, that shunned the eye of Hope.
>   (61–67)

At the heart of the poem lie the secret breathings that quicken thoughts too deep for tears in Coleridge's own heart. He chooses the apt image of life returning upon the drowning man. As Wordsworth's stream of power rushes over Coleridge, it quickens his own desire and inspires him to write this poem. Yet it is a poem flooded with the seemingly unidirectional influence of the strong brother Wordsworth over the drowning Coleridge. Supposedly, as the drowning man comes up for his final breath, his life floods his mind momentarily, offering to him a reprise—a moment of potential salvation, a moment of possible recovery. Intermingled with the life's joy is the "throng of pains," and Coleridge can separate them no more than he can separate himself from Wordsworth, or that Wordsworth can separate himself from Coleridge.

Contrasted with Wordsworth's apparent transfiguration without death is Coleridge's death without apparent transfiguration:

> And all which I had culled in wood-walks wild,
> And all which patient toil had reared, and all,
> Commune with thee had opened out—but flowers
> Strewed on my corse, and borne upon my bier
> In the same coffin, for the self-same grave!
>   (71–75)

The duplicity of these lines transmutes a poem of praise into an elegy of despair. It also transforms Wordsworth's preceding transfiguration into a communal death. Coleridge, overcome by "fears self-willed," by his lack of self-generating desire alongside his desire for self-possession, intimates to Wordsworth the waste he feels within his own life, and figures that waste as poetic death. The communal death also publicizes, however, the interdependence of influence. Coleridge has wasted all which communion with Wordsworth had opened up. But likewise, Wordsworth has exploited that communion for the ends of self-possession. The flowers that are strewn on Coleridge's bier have been used to crown Wordsworth. As Coleridge sacrifices himself, as he pictures his own death, writes his own elegy in Wordsworth's eulogy, he also brings Wordsworth to the inescapable universality of death. Death should not follow, but should precede transfiguration. By moving from transfiguration to death, from death to communal influence, Coleridge subverts Wordsworth's everlasting life within the poem—meaning both that he disrupts the Wordsworthian vision of poetic immortality and that he forces every future reader of the poem to associate the image of Wordsworthian power with a reflected image of Coleridgean dying. One image leads the other inexorably to the "same coffin, for the self-same grave." Coleridge becomes a sacrificial victim who heroically gives up his own voice in order that his friend's voice may be heard. And, of course, the poem itself enacts this sacrifice, as Coleridge uses his poetic voice to celebrate and *disseminate* (as opposed to Wordsworth's prior *insemination*) his rival's greatness instead of his own.

Although Coleridge admonishes himself in the following pivotal, transitional stanza, he cannot wipe out the communal death that detransfigures Wordsworth and turns himself into a sacrificial hero of his own/Wordsworth's elegy/eulogy. Because Wordsworth's triumph has been a communal one, the intertwining of "triumphal wreaths" with funereal flowers is not inappropriate, but apt. Triumph itself is duplicitous. It signifies not only victory, but victory *over*. Someone must be defeated so that someone else may excel, so that the relation between the victor and the defeated itself becomes a kind of mirroring, the victor needing the defeated in order to claim his victory and needing to see himself in the defeated—needing to see his potential defeat—in order for the victory itself to be significant. The only fair fight is between equals; the more the victor sees the defeated as an image of himself, the more victorious he will feel himself to be. Coleridge's image of self-defeat, then, as it serves to remind Wordsworth of their shared desire, also encourages Wordsworth to see himself in his defeated rival.

As Coleridge moves toward resolution, however, he must suppress these thoughts, or at least he must appear to do so. Nevertheless, the axis of praise has been permanently shifted by the weight of the coffin. Even as the poem traverses the open grave toward reconciliation and restitution, death rides along. And once the poem recuperates, it must do so at Coleridge's expense, for the attempt to suppress death from the poem implies that Coleridge himself must also be suppressed, that the image that Coleridge reveals to us as his own true image must be masked again. As Coleridge casts the demon death out of his poem, he also casts himself out of his own poem, acknowledging that it is not *his* poem, but another's. Coleridge becomes, then, the sacrificial victim in a ritual where he must serve not only as the unholy victim but also as the priest who offers up the sacrifice. We read the final stanzas with fractured consciousness, with fourfold vision: giving homage to Wordsworth for his triumph, struggling to exonerate Coleridge from the error of wasting, struggling to exonerate Wordsworth from his "Pure self-beholdings," and giving homage to Coleridge for his heroic sacrifice. The poem itself re-enacts the sacrifice contained within it, as Coleridge reprimands himself and praises Wordsworth's egotistically sublime success. But Coleridge will not let Wordsworth or us forget the true internecine, intercollegial nature of influence even as he moves toward closure:

> Nor do thou,
> Sage Bard! impair the memory of that hour
> Of thy communion with my nobler mind
> By pity or grief, already felt too long!
>
> (82–85)

Coleridge's mind has had its nobler hour, not to be forgotten or muted by pity. But what Wordsworth is not to forget is the *communion* that he has exploited. The distressing ambiguity of "nobler" cannot be overlooked—nobler than Wordsworth's?—and the insistent possessives—"thy" communion, "my" mind—contributes to the sacrificial shadow of influence.

In the penultimate stanza, Coleridge returns to the stream of power, this time willing his feminine position under the surge of Wordsworth's mighty voice, and placing himself (in)voluntarily in the darkening margins of Wordsworth's brilliant vision. He returns himself to the position of an obedient, silent listener—"a devout child"—who allows the sea of his rival's assurance to spread and swell into the final stanza. That stanza, however, brings us back to a communal vision, this time a blessed, rather than a funereal, communion. The final stanza stresses the moment of silence that comes at the end of Wordsworth's recitation of his poem, and it implies the silence that must also swallow up Coleridge's own closure. The greatest praise for Wordsworth presumably would be silence, for it would not only indicate how he has wooed his male rival into a feminine position, but also how he has enraptured his rival and silenced him into astonished, dumbfounded worship of the divine presence within the poet's prophetic voice. But the silence at the end of Wordsworth's recitation and Coleridge's eulogy is, as silence always is, ambiguous. Is Coleridge "blended" and "absorbed" by the song, or since the song has ended, is it the silence itself which absorbs and swallows him? "Scarce conscious, and yet conscious of its close / I sate, my being blended in one thought" (108–109). The silence is necessarily shared, like influence itself. This moment of communal transcendence imitates/mocks the closure of *The Prelude,* which wills transcendence through the aggression of a deceptive "we":

> Prophets of Nature, we to them will speak
> A lasting inspiration, sanctified
> By reason, blest by faith: what we have loved,
> Others will love, and we will teach them how.
>
> (Book 14, lines 444–447)

Repeating Wordsworth's final self-confident lines in the context of Coleridge's wasting into silence emphasizes the strength of Wordsworth's voice to demand silence. That "we" is deceptive because it includes his listener Coleridge only rhetorically. Perhaps Wordsworth is entirely unaware of the potential force of these concluding lines on his friend and fellow poet, a man who has given up poetry in despair, who has begun to doubt both nature's power and his own, who does not feel sanctified by reason, but defeated by it. It is highly unlikely, however, that having lived through Coleridge's nadir of self-doubt with him, Wordsworth would not be aware, to some degree, of the excluding effect of these lines. They tend to assert an absolute dichotomy between subject and object, between those who teach and those who are taught. Those lines, perhaps unintentionally, include Coleridge as a prophet of nature only to stress the difference between speaking prophet and silenced pupil. Appropriately, Coleridge, too, concludes with a "we," but it is the equivocal plurality of indeterminate influence. Coleridge is not even sure about what he has blended with. "Thought was it? or aspiration? or resolve?" With whose thought or aspiration or resolve? As soon as he begins to speak again (in the poem that serves as voiced response), he begins necessarily to articulate the duplicity mimed within the silence. Mirroring Wordsworth's thought, aspiration, and resolve—all enunciated in *The Prelude*—is Coleridge's desire for his own thought, aspiration, and resolve.

As he has absorbed Wordsworth's poem, he is (un)willingly, (un)consciously adsorbed by Wordsworth. Rising, he finds himself in prayer, the position of supplication, of subjection, of submission. The silent prayer that ends the poem perfectly images the tragic heroism of a great man brought to his knees before another, yet rising to the moment. Mileur has described this movement toward prayer as a "new propheticism":

As Wordsworth stops speaking, the intensity of Coleridge's listening perpetuates the effect of Wordsworth's voice beyond its actual limit, revealing that the origin of this special moment is in Coleridge's capacity to respond at least as much as in Wordsworth's poetic power. When a balance is struck between speaking and listening, when hearing becomes as important as speaking (perhaps more important than speaking), then speech is transformed into prayer. For Coleridge, prayer, rather than the more militant, self-enhancing stance of Wordsworth, becomes the paradigm for a new propheticism. (128)

Mileur's parenthetical "perhaps" is crucial, for the "balance" itself is precarious and even dubious. Coleridge's intense listening allows Wordsworth's speech to echo, to be deflected from Coleridge back to the speaker. It is that awkward moment when the rival's poem comes to an end. It is the moment of necessary response, when the other poet must either praise or condemn, acknowledge his rival's success (his own potential failure or success) or failure (his own potential success or failure). Within the poem, he answers silence with silence. But as we step outside the poem, we recognize that his feminine speechlessness—his silence willed for the speaking of a "naturally" stronger superior—is ambivalently inscribed. For he has indeed through the silent prayer begun to speak himself. The poem itself becomes his answer. And it is not an answer that can come from the position of the female, who is told to accept her silent and marginal space as natural. Such an answer can only come from another self-possessing male whose silent prayer is both a congenial gift of homage and a competitive plea for the other's attention. For prayer is a kind of voiced silence. It enables Coleridge to bow to a higher power and at the same time to plead within the contours of his own desire, to beam with the reflected light of revealed vision and utter devout words from one sanctified by heroic suffering and devotion.

As Coleridge resituates heroism within marginality, silence, passiveness, he rewrites the tragic version of Wordsworth's comic vision, transposing the image of poetic influence without really transforming it. As he mirrors Wordsworth's image he reaffirms the potency of that image; as he defines his heroism as the desire for masculine desire, he glorifies the myth of poetic success as the fulfillment of masculine desire. He assumes a "feminine" position in order to attain a distinctively "masculine" triumph. And even though he begins to question the logic of those seemingly natural oppositions—listening/speaking, influencing/influenced, voiced/silent, central/marginal, original/imitative, masculine/feminine, strong/weak, mind/heart—his tragically triumphal resolution hangs upon those oppositions, just as his prayer hangs upon the difference between the end of Wordsworth's recitation and the beginning of pregnant silence. Just as that prayer signifies a potentially awkward moment when either a wholly new revision can be demanded or the old vision can be accepted as whole, so "To William Wordsworth" becomes a potentially awkward response (is it praise or is it blame?), which can wholly revise those oppositions or accept them as whole. Coleridge ultimately chooses the latter option. He does not create a new hierarchy (silence over voiced, feminine over masculine, radius over center) or destroy hierarchy itself (silence is speech, masculine is feminine, margin is center). Such radical revisioning would call into question the very basis of poetic power that the romantic poet needs in order to continue to write himself into the world.

Coleridge's implicit acceptance of masculine vision is all the more disappointing because he has at his disposal within the poem itself all the materials necessary for revision. He considers all the crucial elements needed for a feminization of poetic practice, but he chooses instead the safer route of heroic self-emasculation. He considers the limits of language—how words delimit the world—only to resituate himself within the received limits, rather than to push them outward. As he suggests the communal nature of influence, he holds out the potential for transforming poetic rivalry into poetic collectivity and mutuality. But he does not give up the war of influence. Instead, he sacrifices himself as a brave soldier in that war.

3

That Coleridge depends on gender difference to create his tragic heroism of influence is verified in "Dejection: An Ode." Once again, Coleridge is responding to Wordsworth's poetic self-assurance and to his own marginal and imitative position. Coleridge's many revisions of the poem, his constant reworking of it for various friends to whom it is addressed at different times, only amplifies the unsteadiness of his voice in the poem. He does occasionally identify with the feminine in the poem, such as when he uses the Aeolian harp, which, as George Dekker indicates, "might itself be considered the very type of trembling feminine passivity" (*Coleridge and the Literature of Sensi-*

bility 107). Nonetheless, "Dejection" refuses even to wander near the edge of marginality and self-silencing the way the later "To William Wordsworth" does. His search for an appropriate listener for the poem indicates the distress that is openly explored as the poem's subject. Whereas Wordsworth's "Intimations Ode" works toward a comic resolution (like *The Prelude*), "Dejection" sacrifices its poet for the sake of another's joy, turning a self-indulgent poem about the author's self-pitying failure into a self-possessing poem of tragic heroism. As Coleridge revises the poem, he purges at first his specific rival Wordsworth (named in the original version), then a more general masculine rivalry itself ("Edmund"), finally ending with a tragic masculine voice speaking to a mute feminine listener. Rather than writing a poem where he must risk taking a marginal position, Coleridge opts for Wordsworthian centrality, however tragic the outcome, by erasing all visible traces of masculine rivalry from his discourse. Unlike Wordsworth, Coleridge ultimately is too insecure to fight for centrality by making the brother the ears of his poem. Instead, he *assumes* centrality. Just as Wordsworth in "Tintern Abbey" exploits the feminine in order to forestall his confrontation with the ultimate rival, mortality, so Coleridge exploits the feminine to evade the lesser rivalry of masculine competition.

Where "To Wordsworth" is ambivalent and testy, "Dejection" is self-assured in its assertion, for as the poet experiences the nadir of poetic self-assurance, he becomes all the more convinced of the reality of "inner Power," of transcendent influence, of self-generating desire:

> Ah! from the soul itself must issue forth
> A light, a glory, a fair luminous cloud
>   Enveloping the Earth—
> And from the soul itself must there be sent
>   A sweet and potent voice, of its own birth,
> Of all sweet sounds the life and element!
>   (53–58)

In this context, "we receive but what we give" takes on a different meaning from the way I interpreted it in the context of "To Wordsworth." Here we become trapped in Wordsworthian self-beholdings without the assurance of Wordsworthian self-possession. The conversation between Coleridge and Wordsworth is here purposely misdirected toward a silent "Lady," one who seems to have no desire to respond, who in fact by the end of the poem is silenced further with the undisturbed peace and joy of childlike sleep. As William Heath points out, "The Lady could be almost anyone, and is addressed in such a way that her anonymity seems entirely appropriate" (*Wordsworth and Coleridge* 163). The psychology of the poem implicitly assumes that the Lady need not, perhaps cannot, answer, that "William" or even "Edmund" would be far more likely. Whereas "blameless William" or "virtuous Edmund" can experience joy, because they are not afflicted with the "visitation" that "Suspends what nature gave me at my birth, / My shaping spirit of Imagination" (85–86), the Lady experiences joy because she is incapable of being afflicted in the first place. Her purity, stressed in the poem, is the purity of the feminine state of ambitionlessness.

This can be seen best through the revisions of the final stanza of the poem. The original versions, addressed to men, celebrate the capacity of the listener to speak in turn:

> And sing his lofty song and teach me to rejoice!
> O Edmund, friend of my devoutest choice,
> O rais'd from anxious dread and busy care,
> By the immenseness of the good and fair
>   Which thou see'st everywhere,
> Joy lifts thy spirit, joy attunes thy voice. . . .
>
>   . . . .
>
> O simple Spirit, guided from above,
> O lofty Poet, full of life and love,
> Brother and Friend of my devoutest choice,
> Thus may'st thou ever, evermore rejoice![4]

"William" or "Edmund" must rise above "anxious dread," and is able to do so. Coleridge's heroism here consists in his clear vision in the midst of failure, his heroic sacrifice of self-indulgence in order to bless a rival. So just as the rival rises above dread to poetic success, Coleridge rises above poetic failure to heroic self-sacrifice. The rival male is given the power to teach through his song, but of course it is really Coleridge who is teaching the rival here. And whereas the rival would teach joy from a position of joy, Coleridge is able to teach joy from a position of dejection. How much more difficult! How much more heroic! As masculine influence is purged from the poem in the revisions, Coleridge also loses this ironic edge.

The female listener is not a rival. She is simply a listener. She becomes a "simple spirit," rather than a "simple Spirit," a "lofty Poet," or a joyful teacher of joy. Heath points out how "the slightly patronizing remark about 'simple spirit' is expanded by six lines to give [Edmund] literary rather than maternal qualities, and the speaker pays tribute to him as a poet" (*Wordsworth and Coleridge* 163). By putting the female companion to sleep, Coleridge further represses the real rivalry she could represent. There is no awkward silence at the end of the poem, for there is no male there to judge the poet's attempt at self-possession. There is no longer even a listening person to disrupt the impending and pregnant silence. Coleridge has learned well from William's use of Dorothy in "Tintern Abbey." Instead of the prayerful position, we get an image of Coleridge bending over the sleeping woman offering his benevolent blessing. Yet this silent, sleeping woman has enabled his self-possessing desire as surely as the masculine rivals whom he wipes from the text in an act of "self-willing fear."

Ultimately we must step out of the poem, and so must Coleridge. On that outer edge is silence, a threatening silence that waits at the end of every poem. And within this silence the repressed returns. The masculine rivals whom Coleridge would keep at bay return. And the feminine voice has always the potential to awaken within that silence. We might view women poets of Coleridge's day as the feminine voices awakening within the silences of these romantic poems, awakening within the stream of masculine desire. They, even moreso than Coleridge at the end of Wordsworth's recitation, must find a voice of active passion even as they are involuntarily enraptured by the stream of masculine desire. We shall see, in Chapters 5 through 8, how these women, in a different way from Coleridge, record their own awakening from silence amidst the clamor of masculine choirs.

4

The Limits of Rivalry:
Revisioning the Feminine in
a Community of Shared Desire

As we move from the first to the second generation of male romantics, we move into a web of influence even more entangled but also more self-consciously addressed by the poets themselves. As the second generation of poets offer a critique of their immediate precursors, they also inevitably offer a critique of themselves. As they acknowledge the immediacy of influence from their older rivals, they also grapple more openly (perhaps even more honestly) with the reciprocal or communal nature of influence. Even as they hold tight to the myth of self-possessing desire with one hand, they let go of that myth with the other. Shelley is perhaps the epitome of this split process. For more than any other male romantic, he overtly worries over the poetics of influence in his prose works as well as his poetry. Perhaps even more importantly, Percy is confronted with a feminine other, Mary, who makes repression of brother–sister rivalry more tenuous. Furthermore, he is confronted with a feminine mother, Mary Wollstonecraft, who, by politicizing the desire to categorize the feminine, makes it more difficult for him to take gender difference as a natural part of the landscape. Through Marys Shelley and Wollstonecraft, the recalcitrant feminine impinges on Percy's life, and unsettles the movement of his desire in ways that Wordsworth's wife and sister seem not to.

I am tempted to attribute this to a material cause: Mary Shelley makes feminine desire real because she embodies its most trenchant demands and contradictions. Wollstonecraft's philosophy is ambivalently mirrored in her daughter, who, in reacting so equivocally to the influence of her mother, makes the mother's influence all the more palpable. As Mary Poovey has demonstrated, Mary Shelley engages in a partly conscious, partly unconscious struggle with her mother's influence.[1] Shelley is torn between two conflicting desires, one derived from the utopian natural woman that Wollstonecraft looks forward to in her *Vindication of the Rights of Woman,* the other derived from social reality. As both Mary and Percy seem to sense, Mary's un- usual position as the daughter of two libertarian visionaries gives her a kind of psychic freedom to become her own woman, the first daughter of feminine desire, the first daughter born of feminine influence in the literary and socio- political sphere, and yet this psychic freedom is itself imprisoned within a darker reality of patriarchal society and is tortured by Mary's own internaliza- tions of that society's strictures and demands. In fact, this potential freedom itself becomes a massive burden, an anxiety of influence more intense than even the most contentious father > son relation. To accept fully such unprece- dented feminine freedom ironically would require Shelley to enslave herself to a personal project of cultural liberation through self-defiance, a project that would be the inverse of Wordsworth's, for it would necessarily explore how the self is a mirror of culture, how an individual man cannot possess his own desire any more than a woman can possess hers.

1

Shelley's first novel *Frankenstein* can be read as just such an explora- tion. In Poovey's analysis of the novel, she argues convincingly that the monster represents Shelley's own tortured ambivalence and "expresses the tension she feels between the self-denial demanded by domestic activity and the self-assertiveness essential to artistic creation" (138). In *Bearing the Word* Margaret Homans interprets the demon as "a revision of Eve, of ema- nations, and of the object of romantic desire. . . . Its very bodiliness, its identification with matter, associates it with traditional concepts of female- ness. Further, the impossibility of Frankenstein giving it a female demon, an object of its own desire, aligns the demon with women, who are forbidden to have their own desires" (106). Although these interpretations tend to con- tradict each other, both readings offer insight into Mary Shelley's self- consciously problematized relation to romantic ideology and her troubled relation to her own feminine desire. As an emanation of Shelley's own tor- tured desire, the monster demonstrates the conflict between masculine self- possession, which Shelley feels she must emulate if she is to fulfill the genius that has been claimed for her by her peculiar circumstances, and feminine affection, which she feels is the proper and happiest sphere of conduct for both men and women. The demon that her Frankenstein creates is not only the masculine monster that women writers often feared becoming (as we'll see in Chapters 6–8); it is also the monstrosity of masculine desire itself, the tendency of males (such as Percy) to disrupt the potential harmony of feminine space idealized for Shelley as the domestic arrangements of nineteenth-century society. As the object of masculine desire, the monster demonstrates how men tend to ignore the potential of feminine influence even when they are nurtured within feminine space. By objectifying his desire in his monstrous creativity (representing male romantic poetry), Frankenstein separates himself forever from the potential reconciliation between his self-defeating desire and feminine influence. In order for his desire to retain its aggressive, self-totalizing nature, it must consistently defeat itself by denying the power of the feminine other it has objectified.

In addition to tortured feminine desire and the object of masculine desire, I would argue that the monster must also represent masculine desire itself. The demon is the embodiment of Frankenstein's self-possessing (romantic) urges. Shelley demonstrates how such desire leads men astray and eventually disrupts their attempt at genuinely shared community by destroying all forms of feminine influence. What Walton is attempting to understand, and what Frankenstein learns too late, is the necessity of domestic affection and shared space. The solitary conqueror, whether a scientist like Frankenstein or a discoverer like Walton, not only severs needed human bonds but also necessarily looses his own unrestrained desire upon the world, a desire that is relentlessly aggressive, anarchic, and destructive, even when what is desired is itself a humanitarian ideal.

Frankenstein, like Godwin and Percy, desires to perfect humanity, but in the quest of that goal he ironically threatens already established human bonds, which are the only true basis for human harmony and happiness. Opposed to Frankenstein's monstrously self-consuming desire is Clerval's feminized desire. Clerval is a rare type, a man whose desire has been shaped by feminine influence without an aggressive, resistant counter-reaction, and as such he represents one side of Percy, as much as Frankenstein does. Clerval is an aspiring poet, who is compared from the very beginning with Frankenstein's fiancée Elizabeth. Both offer an alternative to self-possession; both retain their loyalty to domestic bonds; both gaze at nature wondrously and respectfully from the security of their appropriate domestic sphere, as opposed to Frankenstein and Walton, who attempt to master nature by denying the proper limits of human influence; both attempt to nurture Frankenstein, to prevent his self-obsessive desiring. Significantly, it is Clerval who nurses Frankenstein back to physical health after his breakdown upon completing the monster; it is Clerval who brings his friend back to the family and the potential influence of the feminine, but too late. It is Clerval whom the monster murders in retaliation when Frankenstein destroys the female mate whom he has promised the demon. As the homoeroticized version of Elizabeth, it is appropriate that Clerval should be so identified with the mate that Frankenstein cannot allow the monster (himself) to have, as well as with the actual mate (Elizabeth) whose influence Frankenstein fatally represses. Because Clerval represents the femininely influenced male, he must die as a forewarning of Elizabeth's death. Neither he nor Elizabeth can halt the process of self-possessing desire, for both are powerless in comparison to the monster, in relation to the power of masculine desire.

If Shelley's *Frankenstein* explores the destructiveness of romantic self-possessing ideology, it also explores the inadequacies of the vocations that the romantic poet is anxious to ally himself with, the industrial capitalist and the scientist-explorer. Shelley sees these professions as implying a desire to increase human power by controlling nature, as threatening not only domestic calm and happiness but also the survival of the human species. In her fascinating essay, *"Frankenstein:* "A Feminist Critique of Science" (reprinted in *Mary Shelley*), Anne Mellor demonstrates how Shelley's novel distinguishes between "bad" science, "the hubristic manipulation of the forces of nature to serve man's private ends" (287), and "good" science, "a careful observation and celebration of the operations of nature with no attempt radically to alter either the way nature works or the institutions of society" (292). In the former kind of science, represented, of course, by Frankenstein's creation of the monster, there is an attempt "to penetrate, possess, and control Mother Nature" that "entails both a violation of the sacred rights of nature and a false belief in the 'objectivity' or 'rationality' of scientific research" (310). I think the novel goes further than this to ask whether even "good" science is possible without such violation. Walton's journey toward the North Pole could easily be classified as "good" science, since it does not necessarily imply an assault of nature, but rather entails merely an attempt to understand the secrets of polar magnetism. And yet, Walton's exploration, like Frankenstein's experiments, leads to domestic trauma, isolation, and potential death for his crew and himself. The question becomes: What is the line between "mere" observation of nature and mastery of nature? Like Wordsworth, who says that he strives to keep his eye steady upon nature, Frankenstein and Walton immediately slip over that line into self-possessing conquest. As we shall see, this is because "observation" ("good" science) itself—or what I call spectatorship—is, like "bad" science, based on a conventionally masculine stance that accentuates the difference between active subject and passive object.

Even when the object is given a sacred life of its own, as Mellor notes that Wordsworth and Erasmus Darwin do, the question of the use of knowledge remains. If knowledge of the natural object is not to be exploited to control the world or reform society in some way, then of what use is it? As Byron points out in *Don Juan,* the gaining of knowledge can never be innocent, but rather re-initiates a cycle of cure leading to new disease. Likewise, as Frankenstein's creature gains knowledge, his desire to understand presents a cure (a mate for him) which can only lead to a new disease (the need to create another monster). The creature desires a mate, desires a human community—both very good things in Shelley's eyes. But necessarily he also desires to know more—a desire that Shelley sees as problematic since it inevitably disturbs the stability of human community. As Frankenstein himself comes to recognize, the cycle of knowledge, like the cycle of desire, is a threat. Because the consequences of knowledge are always unknowable, progress in knowledge itself ironically becomes a form of exponential regress into ignorance. It is also ironic that what the male creature desires most, a mate and home, is what Frankenstein cannot give him, because it would only refuel the cycle of knowledge, forcing Frankenstein to experiment further in creating a female monster. The only thing that can save the monster is domesticity, the very thing that Frankenstein has repressed in order to conduct his experiment, and the very thing that he would have to repress further in order to bring about the cure (if he were to provide a mate for the creature). In denying his creature a domestic environment, Frankenstein compounds his own denial of domesticity, and yet if he creates a mate for the creature, he compounds the cycle of knowledge. Frankenstein can learn that knowledge is dangerous only *after* he has already begun his quest for it; he can realize that domesticity is sacred only *after* he is no longer protected by its absolute security.

On the other hand, Elizabeth implicitly understands the dangers that lie in wait outside the domestic circle. She wants Frankenstein's younger brother, Ernest, to become a farmer: "A farmer's is a very healthy happy life; and the least hurtful, or rather the most beneficial profession of any" (*Frankenstein* 59). Elizabeth's dream for Ernest would prevent his becoming a Frankenstein by domesticating his masculine desire and subjecting him to nature's power. According to Mellor, "Nature nurtures those who cultivate her; perhaps this is why, of all the members of Frankenstein's family, only Ernest survives" ("Possessing Nature: The Female in *Frankenstein*" 228). Although I agree that Ernest can be seen as surviving as a result of this potential relation to nature, neither Elizabeth nor Clerval survive, despite their harmony with nature. Perhaps survival requires more than respectful cultivation of nature; perhaps it also requires a kind of separation from nature, subjection to its will, and protection from it through a human community. Farming is by far the most domesticated profession. It requires the man to settle on one spot, and to limit his attention there, as opposed to the questing of the scientist and capitalist; it requires a certain subservience to nature, as opposed to the spectatorship and objectification of scientists and the speculation and assault of capitalists. Finally, since Elizabeth's vision of the farmer is bucolic, suppressing the tendency of farming in the early nineteenth century toward "improvement" based on the discoveries of scientists and the theories of *laissez faire* economists, farming is seen as encouraging neither the quest for knowledge nor the greedy seeking after profit and power. Farming alone of the masculine professions remains unthreatening to domesticity in the novel. The boy Frankenstein's homelife is so perfect because his father has retired and spends his time within the home. Only Frankenstein's thirst for knowledge, and the father's inability to slake such a thirst (for as we have seen desire tends to intensify itself), can destroy the felicity of domestic calm.

Unfortunately, in Mary Shelley's view domesticity cannot survive the assault of masculine desire. Accepting the tragic consequences of the male's heroic effort to achieve absolute influence, Mary Shelley diminishes within her own parable of feminine desire the potential for the feminine to alter the destructive nature of masculine desire. Caught within the strong forcefield of romantic and patriarchal ideology, she allegorizes that strength by depicting the feminine primarily as weakness and victimized vulnerability. She rejects the possibility for the cultural transformation of desire and instead pleads for a complacent acceptance of desire as it is patterned by early nineteenth-century ideology. Mellor is exactly correct when she points out that Shelley's idea of "good" science entails "no attempt radically to alter either the way nature works or the institutions of society."

So Shelley herself is caught in the double bind portrayed in her own novel. The domesticity she wants to celebrate in the early life of Frankenstein and in the DeLacy family is and is not the early nineteenth-century patriarchal family. It is not in that the men in these families are kept at home, their desire to quest disarmed. It is the patriarchal family in that the hierarchy of husband over wife, father over children, elder son over younger, son over daughter, is sustained. In order to defeat the destructiveness of self-possessing masculine desire, the domestic institution itself must be radically altered. But to alter that institution requires disturbing the domestic calm that the institution supposedly ensures. Shelley's perfect domestic spaces, therefore, turn out to be fantasies. Because they remain *patriarchal* havens, they cannot protect their inhabitants from the assault of masculine conquest, being the origin and effect of such conquest. Because they are feminized *havens,* they are not strong enough to protect their inhabitants from the assault of masculine conquest, whose object is to constrain the feminine in marginal havens, lest it alter radically the course of desire itself. Ironically, then, by depicting accurately the reality of feminine vulnerability in a patriarchal society, Shelley resists her mother's call to alter radically social discourse, and by resisting her mother's influence, she also resists the course of feminine desire itself, the potential for a feminine order of influence. Instead, similar to Coleridge, she ultimately conceives of the feminine as the radius of masculine power, and domesticity as a space deposited by the countermovement of masculine desire.

Mary Shelley's response to such a burdensome challenge is quite understandable. In effect, she is being asked to complete the life of the woman who died in giving birth to her as much as she is being asked to create a space for desire that is differentiated (that can be experienced by an individual) even as it is unshackled from the myth of masculine self-possession and wholly shared by both sexes. Realizing such a task, even as the stuff of fictive dreams, is perhaps too much to demand of anyone trapped within her personal and social conditions. Even Wollstonecraft herself, as Poovey notes, is unable to rise totally above the masculinist ideology that she has helped us to see through and gradually to move beyond.[2]

2

Dying in order to give birth to new life, Wollstonecraft nonetheless represents the potential for a new order of influence, a feminine order based on the natural movement from birth to death to rebirth in an other, who continues the work already begun by inseminating it, incorporating it, sharing it, and giving birth to new work. Patriarchal influence is based on the masculine movement of desire. The father implants his seed and then becomes a spectator at and a speculator on the process of production. His conception of production and reproduction is conceived in terms of distance between subject and other, in terms of natural alienation between himself and his production, between his work and its influence, between his desire and its object. The father's child is an alien being, so much like him and yet not born out of him. And the father's son, even more like him, becomes the ultimate threat. For the father, the process of birth is a miracle. He has given birth miraculously without physical contact; it is birth by the potency of influence (as defined in Chapter 3), rather than birth as a physical process. And so the father speculates on (re)production. He sees the tie between mother and child, the umbilical cord that is never totally cut.[3] He watches the sharing of space in the womb; he watches the sharing of desire in the child's training and development; he sees the child growing in the mother's space, incorporating the mother's knowledge, and he sees the mother willingly, gently pushing the child beyond her space, the child incorporating her as she or he moves outward. The father, more distant from this physical natural process, must speculate on it, no matter how closely he watches it. And through his speculation, through his abstract relation to it, he comes to believe in his superior relation to it. He comes to value the distance he must have in order to repress the envy he must possess. What he cannot immediately share he will devalue. As he speculates, the father also comes to believe that he can be above the natural shared process and its consequences. He comes to believe that he can give birth miraculously without the taint of the physical (birth by influence) and that he can reproduce above the natural processes of birth, rebirth, and death. Homans points this out as a myth which claims that "the child originates in and belongs to the father and that the mother provides merely the environment in which the child grows" (see *Bearing the Word* 153–160). The father's work (his productions and reproductions) becomes transcendent work, the work of spectating and speculating, and his aim becomes influence, the capacity to reproduce objects without sharing the desire of others. He constructs a myth of self-possessing desire, of desire that moves beyond the mother, that moves beyond shared space, that moves deeper and deeper into a self that is miraculously free of influence, that is itself influential.

As we have seen, conceptualizing the self in this way stresses the priority of self over others—over nature, over tradition, over fellow workers. Self-possession necessarily gives way to rivalry, and rivalry thrives on aggression. Masculine rivalry, then, can be seen as based on assumptions of alienation (the uniqueness of one's space), scarcity (the limitations of space), and priority (the desire to possess as much space as possible). Rivalry assumes the need to compete for limited resources in a hierarchy of rewards, the need to divide up the terrain rather than to share it. Crucial to this conceptualization of influence is the refusal to accept birth as the beginning or death as the end. Just as the male's prerogative and obligation are to expand his space outward, he is also compelled to elongate his span backwards and forwards in time, signifying his desire for immortality. This is why romantic poeticizing, despite the apparent appeal to nature, tends to refuse the naturalness of fatality, and instead constructs an elaborate evasive myth of immortality through the representation of an ever-expanding vision. It is almost as if nature is made an ally for the purposes of diffusing or diverting "her" will to death, or repressing desire's inexorable self-exhaustion within the merely individual. Ultimately, the father feels that he must aggress against the mother, for rather than the son, she is the real threat. She represents the reality of his relation to natural processes, to birth, and to death. His transcendence is, in effect, another form of aggression, his way of suppressing the influence of the mother. It is his way of asserting the limits of the physical. If he cannot reproduce himself by sharing the desire of another, even better he can reproduce himself by living on (eternally) in his work; he can live above the physical in the immortality of his speculative productions, in the work that expresses his unique, potent, influential, undying desire.

Feminine influence, on the other hand, can be seen as based on the necessity of shared space (the womb), on the necessary limits of beginning (birth) and ending (death) in time and space, on the need to share knowledge without a hierarchy of rewards (the training and nurturing of children without remuneration). In "Family Structure and Feminine Personality," Nancy Chodorow has argued that "[w]omen's biosexual experiences (menstruation, coitus, pregnancy, childbirth, lactation) all involve some challenge to the boundaries of her body ego ('me'/'not me' in relation to her blood or milk, to a man who penetrates her, to a child once part of her body)" (59). Compounded with this biosexual difference is, of course, the effect of her cultural role on her perception of space and influence. The mother's sociohistorical obligation is to provide a habitat of plenty even when resources are scarce. She is to attend as equally as possible to the very unequal needs of her children. The child does not attempt to contest or supercede the parent's (mother's) work, but to incorporate it as she grows according to her own inclination, but always cognizant of others' (the siblings' and the mother's) desire manifest within her own desire. Chodorow calls this "double identification": "A woman identifies with her own mother and, through identification with her child, she (re)experiences herself as a cared-for child" ("Family Structure" 47). Such a process encourages feminine vulnerability and self-sacrifice, as it also enables empathetic nurturing. The mother passes on to the child a creative impulse and encourages the child to grow according to the child's own inclination. This is why Wollstonecraft focuses on the natural education of women in society. The children's creative capacity is limited by the conditions of the mother's upbringing, both how she is brought up and how she brings up her children. As long as the mother is enslaved to superficial and pernicious forms of influence (such as flattery and seductiveness), society itself will be a prison for all, and natural equality will be impossible. The parent's task, whether mother or father, is to grow, to create, to pass on creativity, and to die. We are immortal only insofar as we live on in the process of generation and regeneration in the others who necessarily move beyond us. As opposed to the masculine paradigm of influence in which the father asserts his immortality and the son must attempt to usurp the father's superior place, the potential for feminine influence acknowledges and accepts the parent's death so that the child may find her own space.

Whether or not we go all the way with Chodorow and claim that "women are less individuated than men," that "they have more flexible ego boundaries," and thus that "feminine personality comes to define itself in relation and connection to other people more than masculine personality does" ("Family Structure" 44), we have to recognize the potential for such difference, and more importantly, I think, to realize how revolutionary such a potential is. I am not suggesting that this is the actual course for all women, any more than rivalry is the actual course for all men. Rather than a dichotomy, we should conceptualize these paradigms as existing on a complex continuum, and always keeping in mind that this differentiation interpolates these paradigms as manifestations of historical process. This paradigm, or ideal, of feminine influence must be contextualized, placed amidst the circumstances of personality, history, ideology, and all other relations that give meaning to the paradigm itself. The relation between Wollstonecraft and her daughter could no more be free of masculine rivalry than the relation between the Shelley couple could be free from the self-possessing conflict inherent in nineteenth-century patriarchal family arrangements. Mary Shelley's relation to her mother is conditioned both by the absence of feminine precedent and the presence of masculine precedent. In other words, that there were so few *publicly recognized* incidents of a daughter writing under the influence of either a metaphorical or real mother affects the mother > daughter relation as much as the fact that there were innumerable and unavoidable instances of father > son literary rivalry. The Wollstonecraft > Shelley (both Mary and Percy) relation is trapped within the ideological field of masculine rivalry, even as it maps out a possibility for another ideological field beyond the scope of rivalry.

The internalized conflict within Mary Shelley embodies for Percy the reality of resistant feminine desire, desire alien to his demands but vulnerable to his conventionally aggressive masculine gestures. He necessarily sees in his wife not merely the promise of her own natural genius, but also the promise of Wollstonecraft and of womankind. Mary's and Percy's courtship at the site of Wollstonecraft's grave could well serve as the icon for the physical reality of feminine influence and desire in Percy's life. Wollstonecraft is present not only as a shadow of competitive influence from the past, like Milton or Aeschylus, but also as the promise of a new order of influence, a new community of shared desire within the future. Appealing to a material cause, however, seems too facile, especially if taken as the sole explanation for Shelley's greater consciousness of feminine resistance to the totalizing tendency of romantic (masculine) desire. We must remind ourselves of the reality of ideology itself. Wollstonecraft's ideas are real to Shelley because they fit into his ideological matrix, because his ideological field pulls and is pulled by Wollstonecraft's ideological magnet. We must also remember that an ideological field cannot interact with another field without resistance, friction, contradiction, even opposition. Such is the case with Shelley's attraction to Wollstonecraft's Enlightenment philosophy. Blessed (or burdened) with a rival mother and a rival other, Shelley develops a higher consciousness of feminine influence than his male colleagues, but at the same time he also seems unable to give up the gender hierarchy, which is so convenient for the myth of romantic poetic creation.

3

Percy Shelley questions masculine rivalry also because of his interest in revolutionary communitarian change. Philosophically he is pushed toward an understanding of the collective nature of all human activity, even as he engages in the intensely individualized self-questing endeavor of romantic poetry-writing. Even more than Wordsworth, Shelley believes that his personal desire must spread itself wide, becoming a flood of cultural liberation. But how is it possible for his desire to transfigure itself into mass liberation if it is at the same time taking women or readers as captive objects? His poetry, therefore, becomes a record of eloquent struggle against the tyranny of masculine desire, even as it hesitantly takes on the contours of that desire. Even as he attempts to remake masculine rivalry into a community of shared desire, he appeals to tropes of masculine potency that disrupt the community he seeks to assemble. This conflict between self-possessing desire and collective desire foregrounds the contradictions within romantic myth, contradictions that the first generation ultimately accepts as seamless paradoxes.

We can see Shelley's fractured ideology in the nervous prefaces he attaches to his poems. For instance, when he introduces *Prometheus Unbound* to his readers, he feels compelled to defend the originality of his work. "One word is due in candour to the degree in which the study of contemporary writings may have tinged my composition," he says, "for such has been a topic of censure with regard to poems far more popular, and indeed more deservedly popular, than mine" (*Works* 205–206). He proceeds to offer far more than a word, however, with more than half the introduction being given over to this issue. There are two ironies here. First, *Prometheus Unbound* is a rewriting of Aeschylus's lost play and of Milton's epic, and yet the poet seems less concerned about the charge of imitating either of these literary fathers. Second, *Prometheus Unbound* is so unusual a poem that it could hardly be mistaken for the work of any of Shelley's contemporaries, and yet this is where he expresses his greatest concern. The implicit brother > brother relation is more threatening to him than the overt father > son influence. The rivalry of brothers is so unsettling that he sets about revising the terms of such shared desire for brothers working together in the close quarters of a common historical moment.

Shelley's characteristic gesture in the introduction is toward humility and "candour": humbly he admits that his work does not deserve the attention given to some of his more popular contemporaries (no doubt notably Byron), and candidly he acknowledges that his work has been necessarily influenced by his contemporaries. Already we can see in Shelley a reformulation of the influence relation, a reformation of the relation between subject and other, originality and imitation. Like Coleridge, he will image influence and orginality in communal terms, rather than in the egotistical, inward movement toward naturally originating desire that Wordsworth appeals to. But unlike Coleridge, he will not take a circular route back to Wordsworth's self-possessing stance; he will instead remain fundamentally divided, trying to move forward within opposed ideological fields. Notice here the impending shift from the peculiarity of the creative self to the peculiarity of a communal network:

It is impossible that any one who inhabits the same age with such writers as those who stand in the foremost ranks of our own, can conscientiously assure himself that his language and tone of thought may not have been modified by the study of the productions of those extraordinary intellects. It is true, that, not the spirit of genius, but the forms in which it has manifested itself, are due less to the peculiarities of their own minds than to the peculiarity of the moral and intellectual condition of the minds among which they have been produced. Thus a number of writers possess the form, whilst they want the spirit of those whom, it is alleged, they imitate; because the former is the endowment of the age in which they live, and the latter must be the uncommunicated lightning of their own mind. (*Works* 206)

By distinguishing between "form"—which must include both the formal and material contents of the work—and "spirit," Shelley hopes to salvage individual originality at the same time that he erodes its foundation. The writer is "endowed" with conditions of production which she or he cannot escape. Like Coleridge, Shelley is here inquiring into the relation between bestowal and mimesis. Where does the light (or lightning) of genius come from? Is it a reflection or an endowment? There is no doubt that Shelley wants to come down squarely on the side of endowment. Genius, he suggests, is "the uncommunicated lightning of [the writer's] own mind."

However, it becomes clear that Shelley is actually waffling. He is driven to hold onto originality, but effectively it is no longer originality since it has lost its primary meaning: newness. The writer does not create new forms and materials; these are always produced beforehand within a collective, reciprocal matrix of minds, a choir, to use Coleridge's word. What then does the poet create that is new? He creates anew. That is, as Shelley says in *The Defence of Poetry,* he synthesizes relations, recombining these already existing elements into apprehensions that can be seen as though they are new. The newness is what occurs in the perceptual relation between the writer and the world, between the reader and the work, between the reader and the world, between the writer and the reader; it is a process of renewal, rather than a process of producing new "forms." Shelley's justly famous passage from the *Defence* stresses both the internalization of influence that is itself externalized from inner influence and the communitarian nature of that influence, the way it is shared:

All things exist as they are perceived; at least in relation to the percipient. . . . And whether it [poetry] spreads its own figured curtain or withdraws life's dark veil from before the scene of things, it equally creates for us a being within our being. It makes us inhabitants of a world to which the familiar world is chaos. It reproduces the common Universe of which we are portions and percipients and it purges from our inward sight the film of familiarity which obscures from us the wonder of our being. . . . It creates anew the universe after it has been annihilated in our minds by the recurrence of impressions blunted by reiteration. (*Political Writings* 193–94)

We are portions and percipients of a common universe. Poetry provides an ever-new relation to that common universe by continually reappropriating it in language, itself a reflection of that common universe. What I have omitted from the first elipsis, however, is this contradictory, wish-fulfilling statement: "But poetry defeats the curse which binds us to be subjected to the accident of surrounding impressions" (193). Surrounding impressions become a curse and an accident rather than an intentional leverage for socializing desire. Earlier in the *Defence* he has been even more retrograde when he claims that the first function of poetry is to create "new materials for knowledge and power and pleasure" (191), or when he speaks of the poet as a solitary nightingale singing to itself (171).

Nevertheless, Shelley has begun to flesh out what Edward Said calls "affiliation"—the network of unavoidable mutual influences that makes originality in its truest sense impossible. "In the end," Said writes, "originality has passed from being a Platonic ideal to becoming a variation within a larger, dominating pattern" (*The World, the Text, and the Critic* 134). Originality becomes almost its own opposite. "Thus the best way to consider originality is to look not for first instances of a phenomenon," Said points out, "but rather to see duplication, parallelism, symmetry, parody, repetition, echoes of it" (135). What Said sees as the "contemporary literary situation," Shelley has already begun to suggest 150 years before Said is writing. Shelley has begun to shift away from Wordsworth's emphasis on the poet's stabilizing re-creation of form out of the tempest of self-generating desire to an emphasis on the necessarily unstable relations between the poet's desire and the objective articulation of that desire in forms, between the poet's desire and the reader's resistant counterdesire, between the formed desire of the poet and the worldly conditions that inform it. For Shelley, there is no way of escaping those relations, nor can we deny the essentially imitative nature of those relations.

From Shelley's idea that poetry is fundamentally mimetic, what follows is a more radical reformulation of the relation between self and generation, originality and imitation:

As to imitation, poetry is a mimetic art. It creates, but it creates by combination and representation. Poetical abstractions are beautiful and new, not because the portions of which they are composed had no previous existence in the mind of man or in nature, but because the whole produced by their combination has some intelligible and beautiful analogy with those sources of emotion and thought, and with the contemporary condition of them. . . . A poet is the combined product of such internal powers as modify the nature of others; and of such external influences as excite and sustain these powers; he is not one, but both. Every man's mind is, in this respect, modified by all the objects of nature and art; by every word and every suggestion which he ever admitted to act upon his consciousness; it is the mirror upon which all forms are reflected, and in which they compose one form. (*Works* 206)

Shelley has begun, however ambivalently, to socialize the "sources" of poetic inspiration. Not only does he give equal emphasis to "internal" and "external" sources; more importantly, he insists on the mimetic nature of poeticizing itself. "Every word and suggestion" becomes a part of the repertoire of influences that condition the poet's capacity to recombine those very influences. Just as the poet becomes an undeniable network of influences, the reader, too, becomes such. The poet's task is influence, to "modify the nature of others," but it is not the ideal unidirectional influence that Wordsworth and Coleridge ultimately appeal to, but a reciprocal influence that moves across an age and succeeds from generation to generation. Readers constitute a part of those "external" sources that are imbibed by the consciousness of the writer, mirroring back to the writer the influence they have imparted, just as the writer mirrors their influence back to them.

Shelley's transformation of masculine desire and rivalry can be seen in four ways. First, he begins to problematize the search for the origin of desire within the self. Desire, for Shelley, begins to become a process that is always beforehand a relation between two subjects, rather than the birth of a subject that moves toward society only once it has created itself. Second, when Shelley looks back to the origin of poetic experience, he finds it not in individual daring poets the way Wordsworth tends to, but in the social construction of perception and language itself. He speaks of those original poets collectively as a class that functions integrally within a social network, rather than as linguistic Hannibals marking individual and original paths up unchartered mountains. Third, the necessity of influence becomes, not a tragedy that must either be purged (as Wordsworth does) or willed as heroic sacrifice (as Coleridge does), but a comedy, which celebrates the renewal that results from repetition in the midst of continuous change. Fourth and finally, Shelley begins to understand the problematic role that masculine influence and rivalry play in the making of a community of shared desire, and so he attempts to polymorphize sexual desire itself, so that feminine desire can enter the discourse and disrupt the self-possessing disposition of masculine desire.

4

Even though Shelley, influenced by the ideas of Mary Wollstonecraft, attempts to carry out a radical project of natural equality between the sexes, the undertaking for him is not an easy one. In fact, part of his attraction to his second wife may have been due to the fact that she was the daughter of the famed duo Wollstonecraft and Godwin (just as part of his attraction to his first wife entails his perception that she is being tyrannized by her father and needs a deliverer). In both his life and work the drive for masculine self-possession and conquest tends to override his well-intentioned gestures toward natural equality.[4]

We can see the conflict in Shelley's first major poem, *Queen Mab,* a didactic poem which self-consciously preaches natural rights and sexual equality, among other things. Ianthe, the heroine, falls asleep at the beginning of the poem and experiences a prophetic dream in which the secrets of past, present, and future are exposed to her by Mab. The poem can be read as an attempt to educate women in the manner suggested by Wollstonecraft, for Shelley does not hesitate to use syllogistic reasoning and to load the poem with a barrage of footnotes, referring his readers to a host of philosophers in several languages. Mab's task, and Shelley's, is to prepare the young Ianthe for the work of rationalist, meliorist Godwinian reform and the poem reasserts Wollstonecraft's claim that the liberated, egalitarian society can be brought about only when both women and men have learned to act in accord with the disinterest of reasoned principles.

This objective is transmuted, however, by the dictates of masculine desire at work thematically and formally in the poem. The female > female, mentor > pupil, prophet > disciple relationship between Mab and Ianthe is framed by two maneuvers that characterize romantic masculine desire. The Mab > Ianthe portion of the poem consists of a dream, an otherworldly, magical span and space which, though it contains its own charms and truths, derives its existence from the empirical reality that frames the poem. That empirical reality is constituted by two pairs of male > female relationships, the first in the Dedication from Percy to his first wife Harriet, the second in the poem's closure between Ianthe and her lover Henry, the second displacing the first and representing an ideal not experienced in the actual relationship between Percy and Harriet. The gendered relations are embedded into the structure of the poem thus:

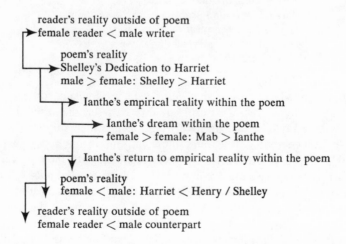

reader's reality outside of poem
female reader < male writer

poem's reality
Shelley's Dedication to Harriet
male > female: Shelley > Harriet

Ianthe's empirical reality within the poem

Ianthe's dream within the poem
female > female: Mab > Ianthe

Ianthe's return to empirical reality within the poem

poem's reality
female < male: Harriet < Henry / Shelley

reader's reality outside of poem
female reader < male counterpart

As we move farther inside the poem, we also move farther inside the dream, a fantasy of female > female influence. The increasingly real male > female relations that frame the dream serve to vitiate the feminine influence at the core of the poem. Just as Ianthe's role represents Harriet's inside the poem, Harriet's represents the reader's role first in the poem and then in relation to the world outside the poem. The reader, even if male, is to take a feminine position, for she is to identify first with Harriet, toward whom the poem is directed, and then with Ianthe, who learns the lesson within the poem. Likewise, Mab's role as prophet–teacher to Ianthe is prefigured first by Shelley as prophet–teacher to the (feminized) reader, and then by Shelley's dedicated relation to Harriet. As we leave the dream within the poem, we also leave behind female > female influence within the poem for influence that at first appears to be female > male influence, as Harriet returns to her lover Henry. But as we shall see, this female–male relation turns out to be the conventional relation between man and woman (female > male). As the (feminized) reader leaves the poem, she then is to relate to her real lover as Ianthe has been taught to relate to Henry, again a female < male relation. What is especially notable about this final relation embedded in the reader's return to her empirical world is that instead of being encouraged to change the world (female reader > male world), she is told to nourish the male, who needs her salvaging love.

Accordingly, the focus of the Dedication is the poet's growth enabled by the wife's nurturance:

> Whose is the love that gleaming through the world,
> Wards off the poisonous arrow of its scorn?
> Whose is the warm and partial praise,
> Virtue's most sweet reward?
> Beneath whose looks did my reviving soul
> Riper in truth and virtuous daring grow?
> Whose eyes have I gazed fondly on,
> And loved mankind the more?
> Harriet! on thine:—thou wert my purer mind;
> Thou wert the inspiration of my song;
> Thine are these early wilding flowers,
> Though garlanded by me.
>
> (1–12)

The conventionality of this invocation is itself evidence of its inappropriateness for a poem celebrating natural equality between the sexes, for the convention is based on the courtly love tradition in which the lady inspires the knight to the good, the true, and the beautiful through her own beauty, modesty, purity, and chasteness. One of Wollstonecraft's most powerful arguments is that such separate feminine virtues lead to all kinds of superficial and injurious behavior. Whereas the male is the physical protector, the female becomes the spiritual protector; she wards off the arrows of the world so that he can quest toward self-understanding and creativity. She, representing virtue, becomes his reward for virtuous action. That Shelley did not fully understand the ramifications of chivalric love can be seen in the *Defence of Poetry*, where he argues that chivalry was a form of feminine liberation because it compelled men to respect and understand women.

The true relation borne to each other by the sexes into which human kind is distributed has become less misunderstood; and if the error which confounded diversity with inequality of the powers of the two sexes has become partially recognised in the opinions and institutions of modern Europe, we owe this great benefit to the worship of which Chivalry was the law and poets the prophets. (*Political Writings* 184–185)

Although Shelley is essentially right that the error is to mistake difference for inequality, he does not go quite far enough. He still holds to some kind of categorical differentiation between the sexes, rather than refusing the categories themselves. The crux of his problem is to maintain differentiation according to individual desire and individual needs without either categorizing those individuals into classes that facilitate tyranny, or disrupting the capacity for polymorphously shared desire.

Although *Queen Mab* is supposed to be a poem about a woman's education, a woman's discovery of self-identity, a woman's movement toward virtuous action and its reward, feminine influence is usurped—even before the poem begins—by the male's own overriding claims and desires. Percy needs a woman to represent the ideal he moves toward, the object-goal he desires; Harriet, with her "purer mind," becomes that ideal, that object-goal in her own poem. The irony here is that Harriet actually fails to fulfill Percy's need. Though at first she responds enthusiastically to his attempts to educate her and to interest her in his reformist projects, the longer they are together, the more her own interests become salient. The Dedication, then, is also conventional in the sense that it is a social ritual expressing an ideal behavior that is contradicted by the messiness of actual life.

We can see this clearly in the sublimation that occurs in the poem's closure. At the end of the poem the soul of Ianthe, disembodied for the duration of the dream, is reunited with her body, emphasizing how the otherworldly dream, the allegory, derives its existence from the empirical reality. Mab is influential in the terms that I defined in the previous chapter: she is a spiritual being who exerts her power through spiritual means with one who has been spiritualized. Ironically, however, once Mab has exercised her influence, the embodiment of that influence in Ianthe tends to subvert the unconventionality of Mab's position. Ianthe's "influence" on Henry is as dubious as the wish-fulfilling influence of Harriet on Percy. In both cases, the women are returned to conventional tasks that eschew their own spiritual development by emphasizing their physical bond to worthy and needy males. Their influence is an ersatz version of genuine masculine influence. Ianthe is told to return to Henry and to nurture her love for him, a very confined task for one who has past, present, and future seen: "Go, happy one," Mab says, "and give that bosom joy / Whose sleepless spirit waits to catch / Light, life and rapture from thy smile" (Part 9, 209–211). In effect, she has been idealized in the dream, purified by Mab, in order to make her capable of representing the object-goal of Henry's desire, in order to provide "Life, light and rapture" to the awaiting male. The emphasis on touch (bosom) and sight (smile) indicates how Ianthe's influence is erratically and suddenly reconstituted as physical effect, as subtle sexual allurement even. Conveniently, she functions dually in the poem: as the spiritualized goal and as the physical reward. What Harriet is not for Percy, Ianthe has been made to be for Henry, his inspiration, his "purer mind," "Virtue's most sweet reward."

5

Shelley's maturer poems reveal also this pattern of masculine conquest disrupting his attempt to move toward a feminized or more polymorphous discourse. In *The Revolt of Islam* he bifurcates the traditional male quest-hero into a male–female pair, each sex necessary for the revolution to transpire, each in quest for a mutual other-identified self, rather than merely a self-identity. A revolutionized culture is possible only when the two, each reflecting the influence of the other, are reunited on equal ground. The poem is a review of the French Revolution, and as such, it is a critique not only of that revolution, but of all revolutionary endeavors. *The Revolt* also offers a critique of the Wordsworthian conception of the relation between self-identity and cultural liberation, and as such, it can serve also as a critique of the French cantos of *The Prelude*. (Of course, Shelley could not have known *The Prelude,* but he was acutely aware of, and increasingly disappointed by, Wordsworth's general attitude toward revolutionary change.) For Shelley, as for Wordsworth, masculine questing is intimately tied to social liberation; however, Shelley ultimately cannot accept the route taken by Wordsworth any more than he can accept the Reign of Terror and its consequences.[5] Moreover, it is the interjection of feminine desire into his discourse that enables Shelley to explore more tenaciously than Wordsworth the failure of the French Revolution and that enables him to highlight Wordsworth's own failure in responding to revolutionary disappointment.

At the beginning of *The Revolt* we are introduced to an anonymous narrator who is attempting to rise "from visions of despair." Since Shelley was too young to experience the immediacy of revolutionary failure, this narrator would have to represent historically a poet–prophet of the previous generation, someone who has experienced the revolution directly and as a result can feel sudden disillusionment rather than the pervasive and more distant regret that tends to characterize Shelley's generation of belated Jacobin sympathizers. Shelley begins the poem where normally the romantic writer locates either the climax or the closure, on the mountaintop. Ironically this narrator must ascend not because he has a prophetic vision to relate, but because his inner vision has failed him in tandem with the failure of the French Revolution. From the very beginning of the poem his desire is socialized and the outer expanse of nature itself is implicated in the complex cultural allegory in which he participates, even though he cannot read that allegory as yet. So the poem begins at a juncture of confusion in the context of a nature that is unreadable because social meaning itself has become unintelligible. We do not begin with a quest for originary desire that gives meaning to social experience by forcing us deeper within the aboriginal self; we begin, instead, with the quest for objective or collective desire that will give meaning to the experience of the social self. Shelley's prophet must look ever outward in order to conduct his claustrophobic desire back to the world from whence it came, whereas Wordsworth must look ever inward to find the world contained by his agoraphobic desire, a world that he can then feel safe to enter after it has been conquered as his own. In this sense, Shelley has returned to an Augustan-like belief in the priority of collective desire, but with a crucial difference: he must somehow reaccommodate the anxiously individuated romantic self to its natural home in socialized desire.

Therefore, even as *The Revolt* opens with a Wordsworthian pose, it immediately begins to subvert that pose within the first stanza:

> When the last hope of trampled France had failed
> Like a brief dream of unremaining glory,
> From visions of despair I rose, and scaled
> The peak of an aëreal promontory
> Whose caverned base with the vexed surge was hoary.
> (Canto 1, stanza 1)

The "I" at first appears to be a conventional romantic narrator, who will rehearse his tale to us, who will return us to the origin of his own desire by recounting his growth into a despairing soul, who will prophesy from the present moment of despair a future of hope based on a lost holistic past. The "I" situates himself predictably on the mountaintop, taking the romantic visionary stance. Immediately, however, that stance is literally shaken from under his feet: "for sudden, the firm earth was shaken, / As if by the last wreck its frame were overtaken" (Canto 1, stanza 1). Like Wordsworth, who ironically turns the physical ascent into a spiritual fall in Book 6, Shelley's hero reaches the top only to be toppled. But whereas Wordsworth's irony serves to reveal how desire turns to disappointment when the quester relies on the external expanse (nature, society, others) for spiritual fulfillment, Shelley's irony reveals the inadequacy of self-questing solitude, the utter impossibility of vision that is solely internal. Whereas Wordsworth's quester must turn within to self-motivating desire as he descends the mountain and symbolically descends into himself, Shelley's quester must look to a point higher than his own ultimate ascent, and that higher point can be apprehended only once the self has been disoriented and shaken from its self-involvement, and only through the mediation of another's desire.

As Shelley's "I" witnesses "[a]n Eagle and a Serpent wreathed in fight" (stanza 8), his attention is riveted from his own desire, his own disappointment, to a higher point of reference. The eagle and the serpent, wrapped together in combat, represent not only the revolutionary battle between the forces of oppression and liberation, but also the essential sharedness of that battle. The romantic I/eye of the poem is incapable of solitary prophecy. He needs the voice of another to emblematize the sight he has observed from his cherished mountaintop, to allegorize the vision that is unreadable to a prophet who is internally "shaken." Accordingly, the "narrator" becomes fascinated by a mysterious woman who takes the fallen serpent to her breast. From this point on, the "narrator" gives up his voice to others; he becomes, as opposed to Wordsworth in *The Prelude,* an active listener in his own poem, for it is only through listening that he can come to understand the serpent and the eagle that enrapture him from above, the despair that haunts him at the beginning, and the prophetic hope that is available to him in the end.

It is no coincidence that his first teacher is a woman. It is she who first tells the story of her development into a poet-prophet-liberator. It is not simply that the roles have been reversed—male poet has become silent listener being enraptured by the voice of a female poet–revolutionary—but also that the usual movement toward masculine self-possession is perpetually deferred in order to chart the female poet's course. The relation between the female allegorist and the listener-narrator is mimetic and parallel. Both are in a state of disappointment as a result of revolutionary failure; both have situated themselves in solitude in order to come to terms with that failure. Each can read his or her own desire in the face of the other, and therefore each makes real, makes palpable, the desire of the other.

Characteristically, not only does Shelley stress here the mimetic interrelation of the sexes—how male despair is a mirror image of female despair, and vice versa—but also, and more importantly, he asserts the mimetic interrelation between individual desire and social desire. This male narrator turned silent listener, this female listener turned romantic quester cannot look within without also looking outward because the despair within is an individualized reflection of the failure outside. This vicious circular movement is crucial for understanding Shelley's critique of revolutionary failure. When individuals look outward, they see oppression because that oppression is the outward expression of internalized oppression. In other words, as Deleuze and Guattari argue, sociopolitical oppression is the cause and effect of the collective repression of individual desire. The trick is somehow to break the chain of repressive oppression and re-form a revolutionary circle—which is why the snake, which the female prophet holds in her breast, is a fitting image for revolutionary endurance. The male-female pair must learn to look at each other and see reflected there the potential liberation that exists potentially in/outside. In this circle and cycle of desire, each individual is a link in an enclosed social chain; genuine revolution occurs only when the chain is broken without also breaking the links that bind each individual to the other in a community of shared desire. The relation between male and female equals, then, becomes the perfect symbol for this potential process of liberation. Individual human beings can exist only insofar as they exist in a community of others who confirm their individuality and make possible the expression of their desire. What the male listener-narrator sees in the female prophet's eyes—and hears in her voice—is the allegory of his own desire liberated from the chain of oppression. She, then, can read in his eyes the allegory of her desire liberated.[6] And as a new link is formed between them, the old chain that had warped that potential link gives way. The collective circle of desire is there—must be there—from the beginning, but it had been warped into a chain of slavery, a burden of influence, an anxiety of self-limits. In Shelley's poetics, the wound made by the rival's tugging on that chain becomes an opening for the revolutionary circle.

The sister = brother link of Laon and Cythna is the exemplary community of shared desire, especially by the end of the poem when that relation has produced a child. This child is physically the offspring of Cythna and the evil tyrant who has raped her. However, because the tyrant has no influence over Cythna—or more precisely has only physical strength over her—she can will the child to be Laon's, a child of revolution and communitarian desire, rather than a child of tyranny and warped desire.[7] The tyrant exploits the link of shared desire; he demands that the link between them be used to satiate his lust, be used to assert his individual will over Cythna's; it is a form of *missharing*. Cythna's will, however, is out of the tyrant's reach, and so the rape that is supposed to represent the tyrant's potency actually becomes a sign of his impotence, a sign that the self-possessing individual can be limited by his physical limitations.

It is not that the physical—the material precondition—does not count in the poem. It is rather that the physical can count only insofar as it has influence over human will. Indeed, one of the major causes of revolutionary failure in the poem is the tyrant's shrewd decision to starve the revolutionaries into defeat. Along with famine comes the accumulation of corpses, the spread of the plague, and eventually for some rebels the loss of the will to endure. The child then represents the inextricable link between physical desire and influential desire, one turning into the other so dizzyingly that it would be correct to equate them—almost. In a revolutionized society, they are harmoniously synonymous. In a tyrannical culture, they are out of tune with each other. An oppressive culture is one in which the power of strength is pitted against the power of influence, in which the strength of individual desire is used to rape the community of desire from which it gains its strength. Cythna's sharing of spiritual desire (with Laon) even in the midst of rape, even in the midst of the missharing perpetrated by the tyrant, is a sign of the capacity to break the chain, to (re)form the circle even in the midst of despair and tyranny.

If the brother = sister couple can be seen as an ideal mirror reflecting always the potential for shared desire to a fallen world, then we can also understand how the two opposed forces—the "mob" of rebels and the "conspiracy" of tyrants—are mirrors reflecting each other's distortions of shared desire. The tyrants have banded together through an astute understanding of their need for one another. They realize that if one fails, the other will eventually go—the domino effect. The tyrants are able to establish lines of communication through a complex series of signals and codes as though they are members of one body receiving messages from a central brain; indeed, they are one body, members of the Hobbesian leviathan body of tyranny:

> With secret signs from many a mountain-tower,
> With smoke by day, and fire by night, the power
> Of Kings and Priests, those dark conspirators,
> He called:—they knew his cause their own, and swore
> Like wolves and serpents to their mutual wars
> Strange truce, with many a rite which Earth and Heaven abhors.
> (Canto 10, stanza 7)

The historical referent of this passage is the unholy alliances entered into by the monarchs of Europe in an attempt to quell French-exported revolution. The normal internecine state of affairs—"mutual wars"—is suspended so that the tyrants can present a single face to the rebels. The "strange truce" that seems to come so easily to the tyrants blots out the true internecine character of their relations with one another. They are usually at war not simply because they choose to be, but more fundamentally because their common ideology dictates their self-questing conquest for power over others, especially over their most powerful brother tyrants. They may be enemies in war, but they are spiritual allies in every other way, and this spiritual alliance daunts the rebels, blinds them to the fracturing rivalries that must reside within tyrannical ideology, and disables them from exploiting the tyrants' own ideology against the rule of tyranny.

The reference to the Israelites' trek through the desert is apt here. The Israelites are summoned to create a unity of desire after generations of slavery, but they repeatedly fail, due to their factiousness, due to the corruption and splintering of desire that slavery breeds. On the other hand, the enslavers are able to create such a unity of desire. Not only do they have the advantage of material strength on their side; they also have the advantage of greater ideological consistency. In order to survive as tyrants, they hire specialized workers to cultivate the ideological field that nourishes their rule. The ideological field appears so seamless, especially to the slaves, that it looks like a perfect system designed by God, rather than a patchwork of circumstantial beliefs, assertions, and assumptions sewn together by all who participate in the ideological field, slaves included. This is why the priests—those specialists hired to refine the field into a seeming system—have such power over the rebels. Just as Cythna's poetic speech has power over the female slaves, and Laon's has power over the male slaves, the priests also have the power of poetic persuasion, and unfortunately undergirding that power is the deceptive seamlessness, the internal logic, of their ideology. Laon and Cythna must necessarily forge alliances of shared desire in the midst of ideological confusion, openness, and uncertainty, just as the listener–narrator and the female prophet must forge a link despite their mutual despair at the beginning of the poem. The priests are spared such a predicament, and thus they have the advantage. The missharing desire of the tyrants—their "strange truce"—is enabled both by this ideological systematization and by their net-work of common needs, by their practical understanding of what must be done in order to survive and by the theoretical justifications that are as real as the physical weapons that mutilate the bodies of their slaves.

Fragmented and splintered, unsure and untested, the rebels have neither ideological wholeness nor a practical understanding of what can be done in order to win. In breaking their chains, they have also damaged the links that bind them together. Looking at their tyrant foes, they see the unified front of a powerful system, but they cannot see what is actually reflected in the mir-ror of tyranny. The tyrants are a distorted image of the rebels, and vice versa. The mass of confusion and anarchy that the tyrants see in the rebel mob is actually the confusion and anarchy that the tyrants create. They look in terror at the mob but fail to see that the rebel mob is a mirror in which they actually are viewing themselves. Likewise, the rebels look in horror at the tyrants and see a unified front, not realizing this front of shared desire is really created by the factiousness of the rebels themselves. As long as they see the tyrants in that mirror and not themselves as well, they will fail to understand that their own fragmentation enables the unity of tyranny. It is almost as if the tyrants have stolen magically from the rebels only what the rebels can possess.

Nevertheless, no ideological field, no matter how closely its fences are mounted, can become closed. More to the point, when the tyrants construct an ideological fence so strong that it appears impregnable, they fence them-selves in, as well as the masses whom they oppress. Shelley brings home this point with the force of irony. The priests tell the rebels that the famine is God's way of punishing them for attempting to break out of the ideological field. The tyrannical logic carries weight. The rebels begin to see that they have brought this upon themselves, but they fail to see that just as they have the power to punish themselves, they are empowered to bring themselves back to health. Even in their misery, or especially in their misery, they see their own desire warped in the warped desire of others:

> It was not thirst but madness! Many saw
> Their own lean image everywhere, it went
> A ghastlier self beside them, till the awe
> Of that dread sight to self-destruction sent
> Those shrieking victims. . . .
>
> (Canto 10, stanza 22)

As the self-fulfilling prophecies of the priests come true for the rebels, as the rebels begin to believe in the power of the tyrants, the tyrants begin to be-lieve in their own theoretical justifications for their physical dominance. The tyrant priests, too, are pierced with the poison of their own arrows:

> The Princes and the Priests were pale with terror;
> That monstrous faith wherewith they ruled mankind,
> Fell, like a shaft loosed by the bowman's error,
> On their own hearts: they sought and they could find
> No refuge—'twas the blind who led the blind!

> So, through the desolate streets to the high fane,
>   The many-tongued and endless armies wind
>   In sad procession: each among the train
> To his own Idol lifts his supplications vain.
>
> (Canto 10, stanza 26)

The intercorrelation between spiritual influence and physical strength is nuanced by the paronomasia of error/arrow. Within tyrannical ideology is the internal error of its logic that will eventually cause the arrow to stray, that will eventually bring the weapons of tyranny to bear on the tyrants themselves. Stricken with the plague that they read as God's curse, they are driven to believe in the power of the Idol-God that they have invested with power. They pray to that God for forgiveness, not realizing that the power lies within themselves, just as the rebels look to the unified front of the tyrants and are unable to see their own empowerment reflected.

Shelley's logic is itself impeccable here. The tyrants cause the famine. The famine causes the plague. Although the tyrants are able to escape famine by storing up all the food and wine in the palace, they are unable to escape the plague, which seeps into the palace like the resistance of revolutionary desire seeping through the cracks of systematic oppression. As with the rebels, the potential for the tyrants' own defeat both is and is not an internal or external cause. The death of the rebels causes the plague, which assaults the tyrants from the outside (that is, the rebels must cause the defeat of the tyrants). On the other hand, the plague is the result of the internal flaw within the tyrants' own ideological field, a flaw that cannot be eradicated except through their own demise (that is, the tyrants potentially cause their own defeat from the inside). Because their ideology necessarily asserts the necessity of the oppressed without also asserting the dependence implied in that necessity, that ideology will always work against itself even as it serves to sustain itself. So we come back to the circle, the cycle that the tyrants mistakenly think they can avoid. Their desire is linked to the desire of the mob as a misshared desire. Whatever they do to the mob, they ultimately do to themselves. The circle of the physical and the spiritual is also completed by this cycle. The physical deprivation of hunger that encourages spiritual weakness in the rebels turns into the physical disease that causes spiritual retribution on the tyrants. The chain of desire linking the tyrant to his slave is distorted and destructive, but it can never be broken. The chain can be turned into the living sinews of freed desire, but it can never be severed.

Both the slaves and the tyrants, then, are distorted reflections of the mirror of shared desire experienced by the revolutionary family circle—Laon, Cythna, and their progeny. As the revolutionary circle leaves the physical world of failed revolution, they retire to a higher place to await another ripening within time. The revolutionary family becomes a community of unbounded "converse," the obverse of distorted communities below:

> And ever as we sailed, our minds were full
>   Of love and wisdom, which would overflow

> In converse wild, and sweet, and wonderful,
>> And in quick smiles whose light would come and go
>> Like music o'er wide waves, and in the flow
> Of sudden tears, and in the mute caress—
>> For a deep shade was cleft, and we did know,
> That virtue, though obscured on Earth, not less
> Survives all mortal change in lasting loveliness.
>> (Canto 12, stanza 37)

Like the tyrant family, the revolutionary family communicates almost telepathically from a pool of shared motives, aims, and signals. The only difference lies in the capacity for enlarging that pool of desire. As long as shared desire is limited either to the exemplary revolutionary family or as long as it is repressed by the anti-exemplary tyrant family, oppression will persist and desire be contorted into visions of anguish, famine, plague, and death for all.

Shelley has begun here to create a feminine order of influence. The revolutionary family is a community that replaces rivalry with shared space, replaces a hierarchy with egalitarian discourse, replaces the speculation and spectatorship of the father with the incorporation and participation of the mother, replaces the self-articulating subject with the conversational subject, replaces self-generating desire with a desire that is always mimetic, socialized, and other-identified. And this feminization of the quest discourse is indicated as much by the original narrator's willingness to give up his voice so that other voices can narrate within his space as by the integration of feminine subjectivity into the revolutionary process.

Shelley has even managed to strip the masculine urge toward romantic transcendence of some of its force in the poem. The urge is still there, however. As the actual revolution fails within history, Shelley feels compelled to move out of history where revolutions cannot fail because they cannot be tested. Revolutionary desire itself becomes hypostatized, stripped of its fundamental temporality, and made into a Platonic form of potentiality, existing in a state of stasis rather than in a process of becoming. As the revolutionary family is burned at the stake, they miraculously re-emerge above history inside the eternal temple from which they are narrating this history to the initial "I" of the poem. The irresistible urge to transcend threatens to overtake the meticulous logic of the intertwining of the physical and the spiritual by giving the spiritual unexplained dominance in the closure of the poem. It is not, however, the single "I," the romantic poet-quester, the conquesting authorial presence, who transcends, but a community of ideal shared desire. The narrator is left behind—in fact, forgotten—in history, purged from the poem by the end. We even forget that he is listening. He has died so that we as readers may be born, as we become those potential rebels viewing the holy family and potentially seeing our desire in their shared discourse. Perhaps it is necessarily an ambivalent ending, for Shelley must have some way of communicating the fecundity of desire that exists even at the moment of revolutionary failure without allowing his readers to mistake historical failure for final defeat. He does this by allowing the revolutionary family to transcend history, to overcome death itself, and so he strays in the opposite direction, for he debatably separates desire from the historical process that is its sole source of vitality.

We can see how fractured Shelley's ideology really is if we consider once again the convention of dedication. Although the poem's dedication to Mary is more attuned to the implications of masculine desire than his previous dedication to Harriet, the influence of social reality breaks into his song. Just as he is careful to represent Cythna freeing a mighty band of women rebels inside the poem, he is anxious to assert a mutuality of experience, labor, and love between his wife and himself. Laon needs Cythna to free self-enslaved womanhood, to free herself; Cythna needs Laon to free self-enslaved manhood, to free himself; Laon needs Cythna to free him; Cythna needs Laon to free her. Mary is to Laon what Cythna is to Percy, and vice versa. Percy pictures Mary's liberation in terms very similar to the liberation of the oppressed women within the poem (see Canto 9, stanzas 9–19), as we can see in *The Revolt*'s dedicatory stanzas:

> How beautiful and calm and free thou wert
>   In thy young wisdom, when the mortal chain
>   Of Custom thou didst burst and rend in twain,
>   And walked as free as light and clouds among,
>   Which many an envious slave then breathed in vain
>   From his dim dungeon, and my spirit sprung
> To meet thee from the woes which had begirt it long!
>   (Dedication, stanza 7)

Mary is both the Cythna liberator and the oppressed women who are freed. The "and" that connects the speaker's liberation to Mary's is ambiguously causal. Is it Mary's self-liberation that propels the speaker's? Is it the speaker's that propels hers? Are they one and the same? No doubt, the answer is yes to all three questions.

We can see the difference between Ianthe–Harriet and Cythna–Mary through the following passage:

> And in thy sweetest smiles, and in thy tears,
>   And in thy gentle speech, a prophecy
>   Is whispered, to subdue my fondest fears:
>   And through thine eyes, even in thy soul I see
> A lamp of vestal fire burning internally.
>   (Dedication, stanza 11)

Mary has taken on the attributes of Mab as well as those of Ianthe. She is both an active prophet and an object of desire. Like Ianthe, Mary is the object of Percy's gaze; she is described as a sensual, alluring other who comforts the male's "fondest fears." The word which best indicates Shelley's fractured ideology here is "vestal." Ultimately it is that old chivalric standard of chastity that qualifies the female for the gaze of the male. Cythna has escaped the hearth. She ventures out from the home, as she must if she is to be an effective revolutionary. She also escapes the burden of chastity, for Shelley carefully describes the passionate, guiltless premarital lovemaking that she and Laon enjoy. How ironic, then, that Mary should be imaged as a chaste goddess of the hearth. The fire is Percy's symbol for prophetic speech, but it is also here a symbol for the light and warmth of the domesticity for which Mary is responsible. One further irony is that Mary, like Cythna, has escaped the hearth and has accepted the brand of an adulterous woman for eloping with a married man. Percy could have resorted to their personal history in depicting his wife's risk-taking role, but his own conventional masculine desire prevents him from more thoroughly representing the force of feminine resistance.

The Dedication ends, like the poem itself, with an image of reciprocity, an image of a revolutionary family existing eternally above the adverse circumstances of history:

> Like lamps into the world's tempestuous night,—
> Two tranquil stars, while clouds are passing by
> Which wrap them from the foundering seaman's sight,
> That burn from year to year with unextinguished light.
>
> (stanza 14)

This image of reciprocal lights burning eternally may suggest shared desire, but it also indicates the light of self-possessing dominance. Although the Dedication and the poem achieve some sort of feminine reordering of influence, the temptation for masculine rivalry is too great to overcome entirely. We can see how this is true if we return to the beginning of the dedication, which opens with an image of Percy returning to "mine own heart's home; / As to his Queen some victor Knight of Faëry, / Earning bright spoils for her enchanted dome" (stanza 1). As he returns from masculine combat in the world, fighting to become "a star among the stars of mortal night," he asks her to accept his "doubtful promise" by allowing him to unite his labor to her "belovèd name, thou Child of love and light." The chivalric trope returns insistently as a means of signifying the poet's desire. His light is the fire of masculine victory over his poetic rivals; hers is the light of "bright spoils," the light he brings to her as she is decorated with his achievements, the light reflected on her from the "enchanted dome," the domestic scene in which she is trapped, but to which he returns. Predictably it is Percy's bildungsroman that centers the Dedication and Laon's that focuses the poem. Percy narrates his development into a poetic hero in the Dedication, just as Laon is the primary narrator of the poem, turning it over occasionally to Cythna. Those double quotation marks that surround Cythna's narration remind us of how her desire is still contained within his.

6

With *Prometheus Unbound* Shelley moves closer to a genuine community of mimetic influence as he celebrates the tendency of desire to spawn itself and as he appropriates that tendency as a vehicle for revolutionary discourse. Like desire itself, the poem practices proliferation at every juncture. Multiple spirits leap up from unitary minds and every figure has at least one double reflecting its desire back to itself in a playful deferral of identity. Not only does he bifurcate the hero; he also triples the heroine. Asia is reflected in Ione and Panthea. Prometheus sees Jupiter in himself through Jupiter's double, the Phantasm of Jupiter, just as Asia sees Prometheus in the image of herself, her sister's dream, and just as Prometheus comes to see Asia as the empowerment of himself. Asia reads her own liberation in Demogorgon's mind, just as Prometheus sees his own crucifixion in the Furies' vision. The poem is a sphere of see-through mirrors reflecting the inside to the outside and the outside in, reflecting every character in every other. This is why Prometheus can be the single mind with all the action taking place within his "head" and simultaneously can be an individual within the poem's mind. This is why we can travel through Shelley's multivoiced lyrical drama—it is hardly a narrative—and feel that we have constructed the drama ourselves within our own minds.[8] By forsaking narrative, Shelley is able to replace the narrator with the reader; by forsaking authorial "didacticism"—as he calls it in the preface—for the playful deferral of intention, he can more readily bring the reader's desire to bear on the poem's outcome and design. We are brought into a realm where desire is uniquely ours but simultaneously collective, as the poem serves as a link binding each reader's desire to the other's. Every reader may be his or her own allegorist,[9] but no allegory can escape the influence of any potential other, for no single allegory can complete the poem; only the infinity of possible readers reading can come close to the complete allegory. This is a poem in which the burden of influence has become the praxis of communal desire.

In order to indicate that a new order of influence can be effected only through the self-transformation of other-identified desiring subjects, Shelley partially reverses the expected gender roles of Prometheus and Asia. Prometheus learns the potential and limits of emotion when he begins to control his masculine thirst for revenge and replaces that destructively aggressive emotion with feminine pity, when he learns that he must share desire even with his rival foe. As he hears his curse thrown back at him, he sees himself in his enemy and recognizes that the desire for revenge is a form of missharing, encouraging his enemy toward greater aggression while victimizing himself. The ridicule that so many critics—beginning in Shelley's own day and moving through Matthew Arnold to the American new critics—have directed at Shelley derives largely from his attempt to demonstrate the power of feminine pity. Thus, Shelley has been characterized as weak, ineffectual, puerile, unmanly, soft, and undisciplined—the very epithets that Wordsworth and Byron work so hard to avoid through their manipulation of emotion as a conduit of masculine empowerment.

Similar to Coleridge, Shelley allies the male hero with feminine vulnerability. But unlike Coleridge, Shelley makes the more radical move of claiming this feminization of the romantic quester as a necessary end-result of the quest. Prometheus can be truly heroic only once he incorporates his feminine vulnerability into a project of constructive reform. What critics have castigated, then, as Shelley's self-pity in poems like *Adonais* and "Ode to the West Wind" must be understood in this context of self-transformation toward a new order of influence. The moment of pity in Shelley's poetry represents the moment when the individual recognizes the limits of self-possession and accepts the capacity to be influenced as a partly voluntary, partly involuntary act of renewal. Just as pity makes the self vulnerable to the other's suffering, inviting the other in and identifying the self as other and the other as self, self-pity identifies the essential otherness within the self, accepting that the self must suffer in isolation if it does not make the necessary link with the others that define it. This is exactly what happens to the prophet at the end of "West Wind" as he moves from vulnerable self-pity to a renewal of shared desire with the wind and the readers who join in the incantation of the song. This is also what happens to Prometheus, as he enacts the natural movement from self-identified pity, to other-identified self-pity (compassion for Jupiter, who is the other of himself), to other-identified love (for Asia, who is the *other* other of himself). What *Prometheus Unbound* suggests is that such emasculation is the beginning of heroic responsibility for one's own desire and responsiveness to the desire of others.

Prometheus is also feminized as he learns to wait and suffer virtuously, as he learns to quell his need to strike out and conquer. Ironically, Shelley makes this point by binding Prometheus so that he cannot act physically. Shelley's drama is a prime example of the romantic awareness of the importance of the musculature of the mind. Prometheus's struggle is entirely a mental one, a matter, however, not of intellectual astuteness but of emotional dexterity. This is why Shelley changes Prometheus's torture from a vulture eating at his liver to one eating at his heart. Until the heart is whole, until the mind can learn from the heart, as the female from the male, as the prophet-speaker from the silent listener, then the heart will be eaten by the vultures of tyranny. Shelley's male hero, then, must, like the chaste maiden of chivalry, learn to be physically inactive as he practices the arduous task of emotional integrity. He must learn the power that the heart can give the mind, and that the mind and heart together can give the other-directed self.

We realize how crucial this point is to Shelley's ideology when we place it in the context of his statement in *The Defence:* "We have more moral, political, and historical wisdom than we know how to reduce into practice; we have more scientific and economical knowledge than can be accommodated to the just distribution of the produce which it multiplies." What we are missing, he goes on to say, is "the creative faculty to imagine that which we know; we want the generous impulse to act that which we imagine; we want the poetry of life" (*Political Writings* 190). Shelley, Hazlitt, and Keats all identify imagination directly with the "generous impulse," with sympathy, with pity. "Until the mind can love, and admire, and trust, and hope, and endure," Shelley suggests in the preface to *Prometheus Unbound,* all is hopeless.

Asia learns to move out and embrace power as she encounters the symbol of Necessity/Power in Demogorgon, and she learns the potential and limits of intellectual struggle as she becomes the metaphysical interlocutor of Demogorgon. Whereas Prometheus's act, Act 1, is stationary, drawing its victory from emotional endurance, Asia's act, Act 2, is driven by physical movement and intellectual progression, normally attributes of masculine heroism. Asia makes her trek to the underworld like an epic hero confronting Death in order to save his people. Asia's trek represents both the liberation of desire from the depths of repression and the incorporation of power into the intellect that has alienated itself from its own power and thus has become the victim of its own oppression.

Appropriately, then, Act 2 begins with the reading of dreams, with the intensification of desire. Asia demands of her sister, "Lift up thine eyes, / And let me read thy dream" (II.i.55–56). Panthea's dream itself images the release of desire in sexual terms:

> . . . from his soft and flowing limbs,
> And passion-parted lips, and keen, faint eyes,
> Steamed forth like varopous fire; an atmosphere
> Which wrapped me in its all-dissolving power,
> As the warm aether of the morning sun
> Wraps ere it drinks some cloud of wandering dew.
> I saw not, heard not, moved not, only felt
> His presence flow and mingle through my blood
> Till it became his life, and his grew mine,
> And I was thus absorbed. . . .
>
> (II.i.73–82)

Absorption here, unlike in Coleridge, is not a threatening experience, but an essential moment in the movement toward a revolutionized culture, which can exist only if desire is fully shared. Characteristically, Shelley uses the fusion of sexual intercourse not just to represent that moment, but to indicate how crucial reformed sexuality is to a reformed society. Panthea's dream of unrepressed desire awakens her sister Ione, and topples her, too, momentarily into a world of uncircumscribed desire. Unused to such a state, Ione is disturbed by this feeling of aimless, unmotivated, generative, shared yearning. Shared desire is contagious; it moves from Panthea's dream of her intermingling with Prometheus to Ione's dream of her intermingling with Panthea and finally to Asia's dream of her union with Prometheus.

> [I]t is thy sport, false sister;
> Thou hast discovered some enchantment old,
> Whose spells have stolen my spirit as I slept
> And mingled it with thine: for when just now
> We kissed, I felt within thy parted lips
> The sweet air that sustained me, and the warmth
> Of the life-blood, for loss of which I faint,
> Quivered between our intertwining arms.
>
> (II.i.99–106)

What Ione understandably mistakes for witchcraft is actually unleashed desire taking its natural course in dissolving the limits of individuated self-identity. The dream manifests itself as it becomes a character in the play and drives the sisters deeper into the collective mind, into the secret cavern of power's home, into the heart of desire itself.

Just as Prometheus must confront the Phantasm of Jupiter before he can feel his emotional vulnerability, Asia must confront Demogorgon in order to understand her intellectual responsibility. Those tough metaphysical questions that Asia directs at Demogorgon all return to her, for only she can answer them, as she herself comes to recognize:

> *Asia.* So much I asked before, and my heart gave
> The response thou hast given; and of such truths
> Each to itself must be the oracle.
> One more demand; and do thou answer me
> As mine own soul would answer, did it know
> That which I ask.
>
> (II.iv.121–126)

Asia's catechism enables the heart, the soul, the mind, each corresponding with the other, to respond to itself. It is a mockery of religious catechism where the questions are merely rhetorical because all the answers are known beforehand. Asia's answers are the responses of desire itself. It is the mind taking control of itself, generating its own real questions and fulfilling itself with its own real responses. It is the project of rational Enlightenment brought home to the energetic empowerment of liberating desire.

The final act of *Prometheus Unbound* is often considered problematic because it seems anticlimactic, but from the perspective of transformed desire, the act is both necessary and successful. The act is a sexually charged celebration of polymorphous desire, discourse, and community. The final scene of Act 3 prepares us for this orgy of song and dance and love. When the Spirit of the Earth asks Asia a precocious sexual question, she responds teasingly:

> Peace, wanton, thou art yet not old enough.
> Think ye by gazing on each other's eyes
> To multiply your lovely selves, and fill
> With spherèd fires the interlunar air?
>
> (III.iv.91–94)

Asia assumes that the Spirit of the Earth is yet untrained in lovemaking, but his response indicates that he understands more than she thinks he does: "Nay, mother, while my sister trims her lamp / 'Tis hard I should go darkling" (95–96). At the heart of the revolutionized culture is transformed desire, desire that refuses to wait for the chaste maiden to trim her lamp.

This is why Shelley portrays the lovemaking of Laon and Cythna; sex itself, as the ultimate sharing of desire, as the ultimate way to combat tyrannical missharing, is not something that these lovers do apart from their revolutionary mission; it is integral to that mission. And accordingly this is why once

the revolutionized culture is achieved, Prometheus and Asia retire with their
entourage to their cave to sometimes conversation make and sometimes love.
Prometheus's description of their future life in this "simple dwelling" is, in my
opinion, one of the most lyrically beautiful passages in the romantic canon:

> We will entangle buds and flowers and beams
> Which twinkle on the fountain's brim, and make
> Strange combinations out of common things,
> Like human babes in their brief innocence;
> And we will search, with looks and words of love,
> For hidden thoughts, each lovelier than the last,
> Our unexhausted spirits; and like lutes
> Touched by the skill of the enamoured wind,
> Weave harmonies divine, yet ever new,
> From difference sweet where discord cannot be. . . .
> (III.iii.39–39)

Even discourse itself must become sexualized in utopia, suffused with the
playfulness of desire and enthused with the wonder of endless difference that
characterizes the process of desire unregulated except by its own perpetual
movement.

    Shelley infuses his pastoral here not only with the innocence expected
within the genre, but also with something not so expected: the celebration of
difference as the current of experience that enables harmony. Shelley's utopia
is not a place or a state, but a process of continuous delightful change in
which "common things" and divine "hidden thoughts," in which smiles and
tears, are interwoven. The enemies of this process are the static hierarchies of
tyrannical culture. Such hierarchies, spawned by the fear of unregulated desire, attempt to contain difference, to circumscribe desire, by freezing them
into stable unchallengeable categories. But in Shelley's utopia, only desire itself can rule, and desire forbids the stabilization of difference. The final act,
therefore, announces that "Love rules . . . / Forcing life's wildest shores to
own its sovereign sway" (IV.410–411). The exuberance of the final act is
not only the actualization of shared desire; it is also the realization of a new
order of influence. New arts must be born, arts that sustain individual desire
without fearing the influence of the other, arts that spring from difference, not
from discord, and that invite the other into the space of self:

> And if ye sigh, then I will smile; and thou,
> Ione, shalt chant fragments of sea-music,
> Until I weep, when ye shall smile away
> The tears she brought, which yet were sweet to shed.
> (III.iii.26–29)

Like the communal dreaming that retains the differentiation of individual desire experienced by the sisters in Act 2, these utopian arts are communal
while respecting differences in mood, personality, and talent. "Fragments of
sea-music" is the perfect expression for this differentiated commonality that
is based on other-identified selfhood. This is why the dominant form of Act 4

is the operatic chorus, which retains the individuality of voice while celebrating the sharedness of harmony. It allows for recitative, the recombina-
tion of voices, a cacophony of contrast without discord. The act is a series of
ever-recombining choruses, spirits joining together to bring about a common
world, joyful in their democratic reciprocity, unafraid of the seemingly chaotic nature of their enterprise, for that chaos is "made calm by love, not fear"
(IV.171).

For this final act, Shelley changes the primary image for mimetic influence from the mirror to the sea:

> Leave Man, who was a many-sided mirror,
> Which could distort to many shape of error,
> This true fair world of things, a sea reflecting love;
> Which over all his kind, as the sun's heaven
> Gliding o'er ocean, smooth, serene, and even,
> Darting from starry depths radiance and life, doth move.
>
> (382–387)

The mirror no longer serves, for it always has the potential for erroneous distortion. On the other hand, the sea "distorts" necessarily, naturally; or more
precisely, the sea is incapable of distortion, for the concept of distortion no
longer applies to its ever-malleable condition. The sea is an image of polymorphous reflections, single and yet various, constant and yet everchanging,
whole and yet differentiated. It is the ebb and flow of desire itself. Shelley for
the same reason rejects the plural from "men," for the term "Man," a word
that is both singular and plural: "Man, oh, not men! a chain of linkèd
thought, / Of love and might to be divided not" (394–395). "Man" is "one
harmonious soul of many a soul, / Whose nature is its own divine control, /
Where all things flow to all, as rivers to the sea" (400–403). In this "anticlimactic" act Shelley banishes many signs of the "masculine" order of influence: rivalry, hierarchy, scarcity, division, conquest, self-possession. He
chooses instead to celebrate the potential of influence as shared space and
other-identified desire.

At least one critic, Edward Bostetter, has recognized the significance of
feminine influence in the play and in Shelley's whole canon:

Almost all masculine characteristics and activities have been subordinated; the point
of view at the end of the third act is primarily female—the final description of the
transformation of man is by the Spirit of the Hour who is female. Indeed, Shelley's
conception of the ideal society, as of the universe, is by the very nature of his
conception of Intellectual Beauty strongly matriarchal. The simplest symbol of
the ideal state is that of the lady and the garden in *The Sensitive Plant*.

In sum, his conception of universal and social love is simply the projection
of his own extraordinarily intense and limited desires. (*The Romantic Ventriloquists* 217)

Bostetter's summary statement is characteristic of the way critics tend to view
Shelley's incorporation of the feminine pejoratively as a kind of limitation or
weakness. If we overlook Bostetter's implicitly masculinist bias here, however, his statement offers an insightful commentary on Shelley's ideology. The

ideal community is a garden full of sensitive plants, and the keeper of that garden is a woman. This is because, as Shelley says repeatedly, love is the means through which utopia may be achieved, and as he says implicitly in *Prometheus Unbound,* it is the feminine principle activated into motion, which brings love—as sexual play, as social sympathy, as moral compassion—through the axis of power and into the province of shared desire.

Finally, what Shelley has here rejected is the focal romantic assumption that influence itself is tragic and must be purged or overcome. Like the influence from his contemporary rivals that Shelley willingly accepts in the preface, or the influence that Asia sheds on Prometheus, or the influence that the sisters have on one another, or the influence joyfully shared among the singers in the chorus, the influence of the final act is celebrated as the shared experience of human endeavor. Without it, desire would have no recourse but to burrow deeper and deeper into a self that may be potent in its energy but will be ultimately infertile because it has become self-isolated. Without it, utopia would be impossible.

Despite Shelley's gender-role reversals in the poem, Prometheus is still the primary focus. It is primarily Prometheus's liberation that we experience, and only secondarily Asia's. We can see this in the nature of Asia's final question to Demogorgon: "Prometheus shall arise / Henceforth the sun of this rejoicing world: / When shall the destined hour arrive?" (II.iv.126–128). Furthermore, self-possessing rivalry still animates the movement toward revolutionary victory. Prometheus asserts self-identity and lays claim to his own distinctive voice by demarcating himself from his archrival Jupiter, whom he almost becomes in his inordinate thirst for revenge. The Prometheus–Jupiter relation is conceived as masculine rivalry, for Prometheus must do battle with his evil twin in order to establish the territory of his reign and make the world safe for his progeny. Asia acts in his behalf since he is bound; she does his bidding since he cannot do his own. She has no rival in the poem. Rather, she serves as an extension of him, that better part of him that can never be bound by the mere physical restraints of his twin's tyranny. Her relation is first to Prometheus and then to her sisters, who are pale images of herself, who constitute an entourage or concubine of comforters for the fallen hero. Why doesn't Asia have a direct relation to the tyrant? After all, she is as oppressed as her lover? Jupiter has no power over her symbolically, because she is Prometheus's higher self, tied to her lover and thus has a relation to Jupiter only through him. It is her role that is already determined by his need, rather than a genuine reciprocity of each equally determining the function of the other.

The consummating image of the first act indicates how Shelley's discourse is not entirely transformed by a new order of influence. After Prometheus has been tortured, spirits come to succor him, and their reviving power, though helpful, is not enough to secure the hope he needs:

> *Prometheus.* How fair these airborn shapes! and yet I feel
> Most vain all hope but love; and thou art far,
> Asia! who, when my being overflowed,

> Wert like a golden chalice to bright wine
> Which else had sunk into the thirsty dust.

(I.807–811)

The physically sexual relation between male and female here predicates their structural and thematic relationship in the poem. Without her, his power and productivity, represented by his sexual prowess, would waste. She is the golden chalice that prevents his seed from wasting, that contains and makes fertile his desire—a beautiful image, but nonetheless one which derives its potency from a limiting masculine perspective. His overflowing is the initial act, just as his repentance, his emotional overflowing, is the act that initiates the poem. The need to intensify and then fulfill his desire is what determines her form as a salvational chalice and her role in the poem as a *reactive* subject in the second act. Despite its admirable egalitarian transformations, the structure of *Prometheus Unbound* is still based on an implicit foundation of the chivalric quest. So even though Shelley is extolling feminine vulnerability, his tendency to assert masculine priority is not fully erased. How can it be, when his ideology grows dialectically out of the dominant ideology that undergirds the patriarchal society against which he pits himself?

7

It may at first be surprising when Shelley pits "Poetry" against "the principle of Self" as "God and Mammon of the world" (*Political Writings* 190–191), especially in light of romanticism's tendency toward poetic self-possession. But when we consider Shelley's attempts to transform individuated self-identity into socialized self-identity, this passage becomes crucial for understanding the ideological contradictions within his poetics. It is once again a matter of limits. "[A]nd man, having enslaved the elements, remains himself a slave" (190). In *The Defence,* Shelley directly connects "the principle of Self" to the repression of individual desire and to sociopolitical oppression. If the physical body is taken as the limits of selfhood, then we necessarily enslave ourselves to a metaphysics of "accumulation" that will continue to lead to "the abuse of all invention for abridging and combining labour to the exasperation of the inequality of mankind" (190). Desire itself becomes enslaved by the limits of the body in its self-possessing greed, or as Shelley puts it: "The body has then become too unwieldy for that which animates it" (191). How can he achieve a poetics that retains the integrity of individual desire while encouraging the active sharing of desire in the very process of reading?

Romantic criticism has often interpreted the Alastor poet as a critique of the romantic—or more specifically the Wordsworthian—poet quester, but I don't think that it has noted how radically Shelley is dissenting here from the romantic ideology of self-possession.[10] His critique is perhaps more harsh on himself than on his father Wordsworth. Shelley's comments in the preface to the poem have often puzzled critics because they seem self-contradictory and because they seem to conflict with the poem.[11] As an attempt to transform his own view of self-identity and its relation to human liberation, however, these ideological conflicts make sense. The inconsistency, which Shelley is surely aware of, is not between the life of poetic imagination and the life of human intercourse, as some critics would have it, and as Wordsworth would have it. The conflict is instead between two views of the self-identity of the poetic subject, one the self-possessing Wordsworthian poet, the other not yet defined at the point that he is writing *Alastor,* but becomes much more clearly sketched in later poems like *The Revolt, Prometheus Unbound,* and *Julian and Maddalo.* In other words, *Alastor* offers only what Shelley is capable of offering at this early stage in his career: a negative poetics of the self-possessing poet–prophet, rather than a reconstitutive poetics of the other-identified self.

The poem is a deeply moral and moralistic tale, as the preface acknowledges in the same way that the preface to *Prometheus Unbound* seeks to disclaim the didacticism of that poem. Shelley has not yet figured out that part of his problem is the authorial authoritarian stance implied by didacticism. The exchange between poet and reader, in a revolutionized literary experience, cannot be based on a rivalry between the two, on an attempt to conquer the other by spreading wide one's vision to the point of swamping the other.[12] In the preface, Shelley traces a line of development that converts the Wordsworthian comedy into a tragedy:

The poem entitled *Alastor* may be considered as allegorical of one of the most interesting situations of the human mind. It represents a youth of uncorrupted feelings and adventurous genius led forth by an imagination inflamed and purified through familiarity with all that is excellent and majestic, to the contemplation of the universe. He drinks deep of the fountains of knowledge, and is still insatiate. The magnificence and beauty of the external world sinks profoundly into the frame of his conceptions, and affords to their modifications a variety not to be exhausted. (*Works* 14)

This pattern follows exactly the typical Wordsworthian development of the poetic sensibility. It is at the point of the poet's internalization of the "external world" that the problem seems to arise, both for Wordsworth and for Shelley. It is a problem that Wordsworth never fully works out because he simply ceases to struggle with it. Shelley, however, faces the problem squarely, and enunciates it thus:

So long as it is possible for his desires to point towards objects thus infinite and unmeasured, he is joyous, and tranquil, and self-possessed. But the period arrives when these objects cease to suffice. His mind is at length suddenly awakened and thirsts for intercourse with an intelligence similar to itself. (14)

The poet must move from the love of nature to the love of mankind. However, the similarity is deceptive, and this can be seen in Shelley's specifying that the poet "thirsts for intercourse with an intelligence similar to itself." The "solitude" which appears to enable the development of the poetic soul becomes the avenging "spirit" (which is, of course, what Alastor means) that ruins the poet.

Shelley astutely adds a third term, which has actually been there from the beginning: the otherness within the self. The poet mistakes solitude for self-possession—a tragically fatal error—not recognizing that self-possession is a mythical animal that kills the self even as it seems to animate it. In his solitude the poet has internalized the external world, and so when he turns outward to that world, he grasps at a simulacrum, a false double that looks like the vision he has internalized. In other words, like Wordsworth, the poet has learned to hear in nature's voice only his own voice, to see in the mirror of the world only his own face. It is a trap impossible to escape once it is fallen into. When he checks his inner vision to make sure that it validates the world outside, he gets a matching response, unable to see that the two visions correlate because each is the false replica of the other. The fate of the poet, then, is unavoidable, even as he attempts intuitively to correct his vision by seeking the other. "He images to himself the Being whom he loves." What else can he do? Because he is "self-possessed" (to use a word that Shelley fortunately also uses), he is incapable of conceiving of his relation to the other in terms other than narcissistic possession. The poet is experiencing the process of "accumulation" that Shelley bemoans in *The Defence*. Mistaking the world for his individual internalization of it, he cannot help but seek an other who is the externalization of his inner ideal of himself, a female whom he can add to himself and be his better half, his salvational mirror. Once he adds her to himself, once he internalizes her, he thinks that he shall be whole again. "He seeks in vain for a prototype of his conception. Blasted by his disappointment, he descends to an untimely grave" (14–15). That which the Wordsworthian poet tries to avoid at all costs, Death, is what overtakes him with a vengeance. The vision that becomes immortal—that lives happily ever after—because it has no point of reference outside itself, is for Shelley a fatal vision that is doomed to self-destruct. And no doubt, one impetus for the writing of *Alastor* is Shelley's horror at seeing Wordsworth's promising vision self-destruct into the lifelessness of *The Excursion*. Shelley brings his point home: "The picture is not barren of instruction to actual men. The Poet's self-centred seclusion was avenged by the furies of an irresistible passion pursuing him to speedy ruin." This is the more tragic version of Keats's "egotistical sublime" (15).

This pattern and critique are duplicated narratively in the poem. Critics are right, however, to be puzzled by the narrator's stance. He, too, seems to duplicate the error of the poet. The narrator begins the poem with an invocation to "Earth, ocean, air, beloved brotherhood" and "Mother of this unfathomable world." Yes, there is a contradiction here. The narrator seems to be imbued with the same spirit of solitude, the same self-possession that dooms the hero-poet.

> Mother of this unfathomable world!
> Favour my solemn song, for I have loved
> Thee ever, and thee only; I have watched
> Thy shadow, and the darkness of thy steps,
> And my heart ever gazes on the depth
> Of thy deep mysteries. I have made my bed

> In charnels and on coffins, where black death
> Keeps record of the trophies won from thee,
> Hoping to still these obstinate questionings
> Of thee and thine. . . .
>
> (18–27)

The Wordsworthian phrase "obstinate questionings" indicates how the narrator like the poet is trapped in the Wordsworthian pose. He, too, is self-obsessed, and his self-possession weds him to Death, the charnels and coffins that are the scene of his self-deluded quest for life.

Why should the narrator be as deluded as the doomed hero? Because Shelley himself is still confused, is still attempting to work through to an alternative conception of self-identity. With the hindsight of Shelley's own career before us, we can see the error of the early poet. What Shelley later recognizes and explores in detail in *The Revolt* and *The Defence,* for instance, is that the self is socialized from the beginning, that poets are socializing agents, that there is no prior moment before the moment of social intercourse, that there is no origin for desire within the self except insofar as the self is the identity created by its relation with, its influence from, others. Because Shelley does not understand this crucial point as he composes *Alastor,* the narrator cannot understand either. Thus, his narrator appropriately, and perhaps self-consciously, mimics the error he sets out to rectify through poetic example.

The feminine that is incorporated—even if not fully—into the discourse of *Prometheus Unbound* is both self-consciously and unself-consciously repressed in *Alastor.* The poet is nurtured by an "Arab maiden," who watches his "nightly sleep, / sleepless herself," and then "to her cold home / Wildered, and wan, and panting, she returned" (see 129–139). Shelley demonstrates how the poet is incapable of recognizing the maiden's love and thus incapable of responding to it.[13] Instead, he dreams of a "veilèd maid" who is the externalization of his inner ideal of himself. She, too, is a poet, and she sings to him: "Knowledge and truth and virtue were her theme, / And lofty hopes of divine liberty" (see lines 129–191). Shelley stresses the failure of narcissistic desire not only by contrasting it with the poet's thoughtless rejection of the actual maiden, but also by heightening the illusory nature of self-possessing desire by portraying the poet wasting within a wet dream, rather than enjoying the full connectedness of sexual intercourse with an other (see 149–191). As night "swallowed up the vision," the poet himself is swallowed by the darkness and emptiness of his visionary solitude. "[S]leep, / Like a dark flood suspended in its course, / Rolled back its impulse on his vacant brain" (189–191). This vision of desire fulfilled is actually a vacancy that can never be filled by a dream; it can only be fulfilled as it is shared with an other whose reality is as palpable and different and irreducible as the poet's own.

The poet intuitively senses the void within him that cannot be filled. When he sees a swan, he sees—as always—a narcissistic image of himself:

> And what am I that I should linger here,
> With voice far sweeter than thy dying notes,

> Spirit more vast than thine, frame more attuned
> To beauty, wasting these surpassing powers
> In the deaf air, to the blind earth, and heaven
> That echoes not my thoughts?

> (285–290)

Although the poet recognizes his "wasting," he does not know how to cure it. Nature has become blind, deaf, and unresponsive, ironically at the very point that he begins to realize his own emptiness within. But how else could it be? Once the void within is felt, the external world must also become a void, since it is but an externalization of his internalization of its own image. Appropriately, this self-defeating process is imaged with the Wordsworthian echo, but unwittingly Shelley reverses the echo passage of *The Prelude*. Whereas Wordsworth's inner vision was confirmed by nature's echo of the internal voice that is his alone, Shelley's poet speaks to a nature that cannot return his voice because it cannot hear, because the voice itself is thrown into a vacuum from which it cannot escape, the vacuum of the isolated self.

If we return to the preface, then, we see that Shelley has made the same error there that the narrator makes and that the poet-hero experiences. Like Wordsworth, he begins his summation of the poet's life in a mythical nature that fosters mythical self-possession. He describes the poet as a youth "uncorrupted" who is "led forth by an imagination inflamed and purified." Only after he begins to work through to a new origin grounded in social experience can Shelley leap across this impasse blocking his route to a new conception of the desiring subject. But until that step has been made, Shelley, his narrative voice, and the Alastor poet, all will only reflect one another's confusion, and will not be able to see beyond the blinding limits of self-possessing identity.

8

In *Julian and Maddalo* Shelley presents not only the blinding limits of self-possession but also the limits of masculine rivalry in the relationship between Julian, the Shelleyan revolutionary optimist, and Maddalo, the Byronic historicizing cynic. Julian describes Maddalo as a self-possessing narcissist: "The sense that he was greater than his kind / Had struck, methinks, his eagle spirit blind / By gazing on its own exceeding light" (50–52). In a more subtle way, Julian, who narrates the poem, is also hemmed in by his own kind of self-possessing vision. His love of "all waste and solitary places" alludes to the Alastor poet's self-deluding obsession, the solitariness that leads to waste. These companions are faces of the same self-possessing coin, facing each other as they lovingly converse, each seeing himself in the other's face, but failing to see how the other reflects the limits of himself. These two visions may represent the rivalrous collaboration between Byron and Shelley, but they also represent the irresolvable tug-of-war within Shelley himself, as he attempts to write the revolution without repressing history, to write within history without suppressing the revolution.

Shelley incorporates the figures of desire into his text through two un-
named characters: a musical madman who rants ceaselessly and a taciturn
daughter who refuses to articulate the pain that she has witnessed. Just as
Julian and Maddalo represent the two faces of civilized poetic discourse, the
madman and the daughter represent the two faces of desire. Shelley places
him in the poem as desire's subject. He is the topic of the poem; he is desire's spoken text. Thus, his words form the center of the poem, but that center is devoid. Like the Alastor poet, the madman's desire is an overflowing
void, a state of illusion and elusion, full of emptiness and darkness. The madman is the masculine principle of desire taken to its extreme, desire that has
become pure energy without a circle (to use a Blakean image), motion without a course, an agent without an aim. He represents desire set loose. In this
sense, the madman is the shell of nature, its chaotic wildness, its apparent
cruelty, its unrelenting productivity and potency. But this does not mean that
he is desire unrepressed, for the madman also represents the shell of civilization. He is a sort of civilized savage. Maddalo has provided him with all
the acoutrements of highest society—"busts and books and urns for flowers . . . / . . . And instruments of music" (254–256). Indeed, these are
the things "which had adorned his life in happier hours," for he is educated,
noble, and was once wealthy. The madman's language also indicates how he
is a shell of civilization. He is learned in philosophy and poetry, as evidenced
by his elaborate tropes, his self-conscious taking on of the poetic figure of the
unrequited lover, his unself-conscious parody of "serious" (to use Shelley's
phrase about Julian from the preface) philosophical problems. "What Power
delights to torture us?" he asks. "I know / That to myself I do not wholly
owe / What now I suffer, though in part I may" (320–322). Viewed as a
whole, his talk does not cohere, though it has the cogency of learned discourse as we move from line to line. In this way, the madman is a parody of
Julian's and Maddalo's conversation. "[M]y judgement will not bend / To
your opinion, though I think you might / Make such a system refutation-
tight / As far as words go" (192–195), Maddalo says to Julian, and Julian
could as well say to Maddalo. When we take each character separately, his
vision is cogent, but as we move to view the whole, their visions fail to cohere.

The madman, then, is the radicalized masculine principle of desire in
both nature and art. Intensely self-conscious but senselessly wild, he combines Western society's view of the male's conflicting dual role as the maker
of civilization who is responsible for all intellectual refinement and material
progress and as the keeper of natural innocence who is the victim of the female's wiley seductions and coy, unnatural social refinements. This dual role
is brilliantly represented through the madman's musical talent. Music is the
apex of civilized accomplishment and also the expression of natural feeling.
Does it calm the savage beast by gratifying his natural instinct or by bringing
him into the embrace of civilized aesthetics? We can ask the same question
about the effect of the madman's music on his fellow inmates in the asylum.

> "And those are his sweet strains which charm the weight
> From madmen's chains, and make this Hell appear
> A heaven of sacred silence, hushed to hear."— . . .
>   . . . his melody
> Is interrupted—now we hear the din
> Of madmen, shriek on shriek, again begin.
>
>   (259–267)

The wonderful irony, of course, is that the madman's music, whether it produces silence or shrieks, hides what lies within him. Julian would say that it produces beauty and indicates the power of the human mind to create harmony, peace, and joy even in the midst of madness. Maddalo would say that it produces shrieks and indicates the history of humanity's discord, destruction, and pain. Neither the shriek nor the silence, however, is readable, and so both friends are confronted finally with the undecipherable thing itself. "I must remove / A veil from my pent mind" (382–383), the madman shrieks. But as he unveils in his ceaseless raving, the veil remains untorn.

Maddalo's daughter is no more forthcoming than the madman. She represents the feminine principle of desire. Unlike the madman, she is not presented as an extreme, but rather as a norm. She is desire's unspoken text, its object, its goal. She represents the circle without which masculine energy breaks loose into the overflowing void. For this reason, Shelley places her strategically toward the beginning and toward the end of the madman's ranting. She encircles his desire, as she represents the masculine hope for balance—between revolution and history, between metaphoricity and iteration, between civilization and its discontents, between tyranny and chaos, between the silence and the shriek, between the madman and his lover, between Julian and Maddalo, between the poet and his reader, between masculine desire and its fulfillment. The female is placed in Shelley's text as a mere extension, but she is actually its foundation (what the poststructuralist critics would call its supplement). She is an extension of Maddalo—as his daughter. She is an extension of Julian as well: "I had nursed / Her fine and feeble limbs when she came first / To this bleak world," he says (151–153). Julian (as Shelley) replaces the mother. He nurtures the child, as nature would. His optimistic nurturing vision promises her a glowing future, whereas Maddalo (Shelley's alter ego), as the father, has a realistic vision of the future, based on past oppression.

In order for this crucial divergence between them to be enunciated, the daughter is taken as an object of their discourse, much in the way that they take the landscape and the madhouse at the beginning and as they unsuccessfully attempt to take the madman in the middle. As a new day begins, Julian is still distressed by the unresolved argument he and Maddalo have engaged in on the preceding day. At first unable to get a response from the sullen Maddalo, who has no doubt become a bit tired of Julian's endless optimism, Julian realizes that he has the perfect example before his eyes:

                                    . . . See
        This lovely child, blithe, innocent and free;
        She spends a happy time with little care,
        While we to such sick thoughts subjected are
        As came on you last night—it is our will
        That thus enchains us to permitted ill—
        We might be otherwise—we might be all
        We dream of happy, high, majestical.
                                    (166–173)

"You talk Utopia," Maddalo responds cryptically. Their discourse on the
daughter comes rather quickly to a halt, for she is too much a blank slate.
She is yet unformed, and thus the question of whether she *can* be reformed is
moot. Furthermore, she cannot speak. She cannot, therefore, confirm for us
whether Julian or Maddalo has the more valid vision. She is the perfect example because she is so malleable, and for the same reason, she is the least
desirable example. This is the double bind of the male's exploitation of the
feminine principle: he wants her to be fully his own, to be the totalized object of his self-possessing vision, but he also needs her to resist, to remind
him of the separateness of the self, for his vision cannot conquer what is already held before it is reached after.

     In order to continue the argument at a higher level, Julian and Maddalo
need a more resistant object, an object that can speak itself and that can
own its own vision. This, too, of course, is a double bind—as the friends later
realize—for such an object is no longer an object, but a discursive subject itself. In this sense, the daughter is also an extension of the madman. Her quiet
simplicity forces Julian and Maddalo to turn to the madman's verbose complexity. She is the unspeaking pretext that leads to the madman's prolix text.
And she must also come after his manic speaking in order to purify and contain it, in the same way that Asia becomes a chalice purifying and containing
Prometheus's anguished overflow.

     Logically, the madman cannot serve as an example because he is not
representative of mankind. He cannot tell us whether Julian or Maddalo is
right because he himself is schizophrenic (withdraws from reality like Julian)
and paranoid (has tightly-rationalized delusions of greatness and of persecu-
tion like Maddalo). Finally, the extremity of his condition stresses to them
the vanity of their argument—its egotism, its futility, its pettiness. The madman creates in them a desire to act instead of talk, to treat him as an agent
who needs encouragement in order to progress, rather than as an object for
their gaze. Maddalo is compelled to provide him with a place to stay and with
the niceties of civilized life. "[Y]ou may guess / A stranger could do little
more or less" (256–257), Maddalo says, justifying the limit of his agency.
Julian, feeling overwhelmed by the madman's manic power and by his own
helplessness, "sought relief / From the deep tenderness that maniac wrought /
within" him (565–567). The maniac halts their argument rather than pro-
gressing it or resolving it not only because he is self-consciously abnormal,
but also because his own ranting discourse forces them into silence. They can-

not hear themselves think when he talks. They are forced out of their self-possessing visions by their horror and their sympathy, their need to bring him back to sanity and their fear of ending up like him.

As an object of discourse, the daughter is no less penetrable, and yet she remains an object within the text. As an extension of the madman, she knows his secret, but her silence denies that secret to us. As he is the wild potency of nature, she is its gentle, mystical aspect, inspiring both the male's desire to understand and his awe, his fear of knowing. Julian describes the daughter thus:

> A lovelier toy sweet Nature never made,
> A serious, subtle, wild, yet gentle being,
> Graceful without design and unforeseeing,
> With eyes—Oh speak not of her eyes!—which seem
> Twin mirrors of Italian Heaven, yet gleam
> With such deep meaning, as we never see
> But in the human countenance.
>
> (144–150)

A lovely "toy" designed by "sweet" Nature, the girl is naturally aesthetic, a natural object of desire in the same way that the maniac is the natural flow of desire. Julian expresses in the poem Western society's contradictory view of the feminine role: the daughter is an innocent child of untainted instinct more in tune with nature's mysteries than the male, and she is a sophisticated co-nundrum of social refinement who saves man from his basest natural instincts. She somehow is able to hold in balance the paradoxes of nature: its wildness and gentleness, its seriousness and playfulness, its subtlety and simplicity, its transparency and opacity.

At the same time that the daughter is the artifact of artless nature, she is the artifact of artificial civilization. Or, to metaphorize the paradox within Julian's thinking, she is the flower of civilization. She is the natural manifestation of society's arduous handiwork. Appropriately we see this aspect of her *after* the maniacal ranting, after the friends' argument comes to its ultimate impasse. Julian sees her for the first time "after many years":

> His child had now become
> A woman; such as it has been my doom
> To meet with few,—a wonder of this earth,
> Where there is little of transcendent worth,—
> Like one of Shakespeare's women. . . .
>
> (588–592)

She has become, for him, like a product of the greatest master-artist. Shakespeare, considered the epitome of natural craftsmen by the romantics, produces art that is artless, creates women characters who are unique and "transcendent." (As we shall see in Chapter 7, women writers also turn to Shakespeare when they attempt to record feminine experience.) Unlike the madman, Maddalo's daughter is not an abnormality; she represents the real potential of every normal woman. This is the ideal of the Alastor poet's dream, a version of himself and, like Venus, born from his own brain. She is really an illusion created by the male's desire to possess himself in possessing her. It is Julian's "doom" not to have met with enough of these women. And we can assume that it is the madman's curse not to have fallen in love with one of them.

As an extension of the madman, as a keeper of the mystery, as a harbinger of ultimate wholeness and balance, she must be privy to the madman's secret. She is the figure within the text who contains the key to making the center cohere, for only she can tell us the story whole, "[t]he stamp of *why* they parted, *how* they met" (610). Although she does not want to reveal that secret even to Julian, he is insistent: "I urged and questioned still, she told me how / All happened—but the cold world shall not know" (616–617). The poet regains control of his text and his vision by usurping the feminine myth he has created. By allowing her to remain silent for us (the readers), Shelley sustains the myth of her transcendence—the awe of nature, the wonder of civilization. Whether her knowledge can allow the poet to create transcendent wholeness—to join the maniac to his lover, to join Julian and Maddalo, to join the hope of utopia and the reality of history—remains in silence, in the poet's decision to remain silent. By refusing to speak, the poet claims a power over the daughter, over us, and over himself. She can return to her mythic silence, and he can regain a semblance of control over the poetic process. Even though Julian's (Shelley's) refusal to speak enables readers to assert their own desire by filling in the story however they will, that refusal still keeps the feminine voice trapped within a void of the poet's own making.

Like the madman, Shelley is caught in the double bind of language. No matter how fervidly he attempts to articulate the wholeness of shared desire, he becomes trapped by the very structures and figures that express the fragmentary nature of his present condition and the tortured history in which he has participated unwillingly. Like Frankenstein deciding to limit knowledge by refusing to create a female mate for his creature, Shelley limits our knowledge of the madman, lest we misuse what we come to know. But whereas Mary Shelley, all too aware of the destructive consequences of the male's quest for knowledge, graphically displays those consequences in Frankenstein's mutilation of the female mate and in the monster's murder of Frankenstein's newly-wed wife, Percy Shelley, torn between self-possessing desire and shared desire, grants both the male and the female knowledge and power to speak, but traps them mutually in a silence of their own making.

5

The Borders of Gender:
Emprisoning Feminine Art
through Rites of Poetic Passage

If the influence of Mary Wollstonecraft and Mary Shelley disrupts the traditional flow of masculine desire in Percy Shelley's works, we must wonder
about the larger context of women's influence in the literary world. How does
the emergence of women as successful competitors in the literary marketplace
of early nineteenth-century Britain affect the poetry of male romantic writers?
As noted in Chapter 1, this is a difficult question to answer because it involves
peering into the psyche of these poets. It is also difficult to answer because
the operation of influence in general is so labyrinthine. As Stuart Curran has
argued, the eighteenth-century cult of sensibility, which has such a tremendous influence on romantic poetry, "was largely a female creation. It was
unquestionably a central concern in writing by women, whether in the ubiqui-
tous romances or in poetry. The relative fame accorded Henry Mackenzie's
novella of 1771, *The Man of Feeling,* should not blind us to the crucial fact
foregrounded in his title: that men, too, can feel" ("Romantic Poetry: The I
Altered" 195). When we consider that earlier women writers not only *indirectly* influence the romantic poets through their influence on male writers like
Mackenzie whom we tend to identify with the cult of feeling, but also *directly*
influence the romantic poets and that the influence is mutual and multidirec-
tional; then we realize how exponentially compounded and complex a matter
we are confronting.

It is impossible for such a groundbreaking phenomenon as the emergence
of public women poets *not* to disrupt the usual patterns of desire expressed
in men's poetry. The question is: how exactly are those patterns altered? In
a poet like Shelley, where the influence is embraced as a more consciously
intentional political act, answering this question is easier than in poets like
Wordsworth, Coleridge, Byron, and Keats, who do not identify themselves
with the Wollstonecraft feminist program. When the influence is unconscious

and the resistance greater, the effect on the poetry is no less disruptive (and perhaps it is even more disruptive) but is all the more difficult to chart.

Whereas the first generation of romantic poets begins to write during years when the bluestocking is still the prevailing image of the female writer, when Keats begins to write, women's participation in poetic production has not only increased dramatically, but also changed significantly in kind. As we shall see in more detail in the succeeding chapters, by the end of the eighteenth century women poets have begun to view themselves as *feminine* poets with a voice and an agenda uniquely their own. They also have begun to see themselves as the beginning of a new *feminine* tradition rather than as individuals who just happen to be women merely continuing the tradition of their fathers. Perhaps most importantly, by the time Keats has begun to write, women poets have established themselves and are embraced, however ambivalently, by the publishing industry and the reading public. This means that the potential to have poetic foremothers, as well as forefathers, is much greater for Keats than for Wordsworth, not only because it has become less unacceptable to see women as serious poets and potential mentors for young male poets, but also because the influence of these women has become so palpable and profound that to ignore them wholly would mean ignoring some of the most prominent figures in the contemporary literary scene.

The writing of poetry for Keats, then, is suffused with greater ambivalence than it is for Wordsworth. Wordsworth, much more directly linked to the male tradition of Dryden and Pope both in terms of time and class status, can see himself as rebelling against that tradition, improving it by renewing it, by returning it to its roots in manly action and away from emasculating refinement and sickliness. Wordsworth would be able to feel the threat of such emasculation as coming from the outside—whether from sickly German tales or presumptuous female romancers and their readers—and as infecting even the best writers of the tradition. This is why, as we have seen, Wordsworth feels compelled to purge the influence of feminine Nature, once it has been exploited to advance his myth of self-possessing desire. The women in his poems—Dorothy, Lucy, the Nutting maiden, the Highland girl, etc.—are all creatures who help him to claim his estate, for, being sacrificed to silence, they are unable to dispute the inheritance which they help to promulgate. Likewise, Wordsworth attempts to father his readers' vision for them, encouraging even his most astute critics (M. M. Abrams, F. W. Bateson, Geoffrey Hartman, Harold Bloom, to name a few) to become Wordsworthian disciples, passing the inheritance on to their own readers.[1]

In this period poetry begins to take on the symbolic cultural value that it still retains to this day. It becomes a ritual that marks the search for a mature self, a publicly private ceremony symbolizing the young person's composing of an adult identity by exploring the relation between developing self and already developed world. Whereas Wordsworth, who perhaps more than any other poet helps to establish poetry as such a ritual, can more confidently engage in this ritual, Keats's desire is split, like Shelley's, but for different reasons. While Keats is suspicious of Wordsworth's aggressive visionary designs, he is also not comfortable with the apparent alternative, the self-abnegating, decorative poetry being increasingly taken over by women like Mary Tighe. Keats, that poet who for Virginia Woolf represents the comfortable androgynous nature, provides us with a paradigm of the boy—awkward with his feelings, his sexuality, his potency, his position in society—who transvalues poetic aspiration into the gaining of a mature masculine voice. Mary Tighe, the female mentor whom Keats eventually feels compelled to outgrow, can represent here the emergence of a phenomenon that holds both a threat and a promise for the young male poet: the discovery of poetry as a fit medium for giving voice to (making public, communal, socially valued) the normally private ephemeral experience of women.

Whether it is voice (the discovery of a mature self), vision (the mature representation of the world), verse (the craftsmanlike mastery of the artistic medium) or some combination of all three that supplies the rationale for poetic maturation, we tend not to question the assumption that writing poetry is a naturally progressive, developmental process. Good poets must grow, and our critical studies of great poets are always evolutionary parables. We often use the word "master" to describe processes of maturation, implying the dominant role that both gender and class have had in poetic rituals of maturation. We conceptualize the experience as one of gaining control, enforcing discipline, establishing rank, and it is not by mistake that in nineteenth-century Britain one's sex and one's class status are the major factors determining the kind of maturity that is appropriate for an individual. The search for maturity in or through poetry is allied to the search for sexual identity—how to become a man or a woman—and because proper routes to maturity are defined by gender, writing poety can become a means for enforcing the boundaries of gender. Or, as for Keats and Tighe, it can become the obverse—a means for exploring the limits and for potentially violating gender boundaries. The question for the young poet ultimately becomes a second-order question: How can I master the rituals that signal to the world my possession of a maturity appropriate to my sex and status? For the obscure young poet the question becomes: How can I master the rituals that signal to my readers that I have mastered poetic maturation?

This, of course, is the question that obsessed Keats as he aspired to poetic greatness, and fortunately we have, both in the letters and in the poems, a record of his obsession. Keats's "development" can be seen as a self-conscious movement from literary apprenticeship to master craftsman, from uncertain ventriloquy of others' voices to masterful articulation of his own unique voice, from modish pictorialism of "thoughtless youth" to visionary gleams of profound prophecy. As opposed to Tighe, whose literary life was almost as brief as his, Keats needs both for himself and for his audience to construct an Oedipal parable of filial adoration giving way to paternal separation and patricide, and then of separation giving way to rightful inheritance of the father's acclaimed domain. As opposed to Tighe, who must always demonstrate her duty, her unseparable bond of affection (to her mother, her mother-in-law, her husband, her brother), Keats must instead prove his prowess for mastery of his own fate by heading out alone to stalk and overtake the dragons that threaten his claim to manhood and to poetic greatness. Starting from the premise that poets must go through stages before they can reach the ultimate stage of canonization, Keats self-consciously stages his own development, rehearsing each phase with precise determination. We shall see that Keats appeals to each of the paradigms of maturity, to verse, to voice, to vision, as well as to the psychology of influence, but not with the simplicity that such a reductive scheme might imply. As with Tighe, other routes to maturity—supposedly off limits to the opposite sex—beckon from the wayside and disturb the happy fantasy of a straight and narrow path to poetic adulthood.

1

It is easy to see why the poetry of Tighe was so popular, and why it initially attracted Keats, as well as why its popularity was so short-lived, and why Keats felt the need to appear to advance beyond it. It is not quality that is at issue here, but rather the cultural and individual response to a woman's representation of poetic maturity. Tighe's poetry puts her audience, both male and female, at ease with their own feelings by formalizing and naturalizing those feelings. But in order to create this aura of ease, Tighe must sacrifice the risk-taking ambition and empire-building vision that Wordsworth makes the groundwork of poetic greatness. Instead, her poetry refuses to bring attention to itself. It appears satisfied to be as ephemeral as a moment of delightful sadness felt briefly, briefly remembered, a fleeting response to a particular, quotidian contingency, which can never become monumentally momentous—at least never in the context of what is valued in a patriarchal culture. In other words, her verse is written not to be remembered, which is *not* the same as poetry written to be forgotten. It is written to "linger"—to use one of Tighe's own words for it—in the heart, rather than to assert an immortal existence, to establish a self-perpetuating line, or to claim a lasting space in the mind as an immoveably essential truth. Tighe cannot press beyond this mode without also pressing her luck with the reading public. What is at stake is her definition as a mature woman. In order to be successful in any terms, she must identify herself as a woman disciplined by the poetic experience, rather than as someone who masters the elements of poetic experience. We see this in her versification: her diction, imagery, rhyme schemes, meter, narrative perspective—and all the other conventional components of style and form. We hear it in her voice—her tone, ideology, choice of theme and subject—and all of the more intangible signals that mark the presence of the personal search for a meaningful public persona. Versification and voice are many times at odds, for the former insists on submission to convention, while the latter pulls toward the demands of originality, self-assertion, and pride. Finally, we infer it from the virtual absence of vision: any attempt to construct a philosophical system, to transmit prophecy, to claim a hold on the wholeness of all experience. Instead, Tighe limits herself to (in)sight, which is detailed, fragmentary, evanescent, profound only in its depth of feeling and breadth of description, beautiful not in the Platonic sense that Keats appeals to but in the sense of delicacy, tenderness, gracefulness, refinement.

Contemporary reviewers predictably cherish her tenderness and melancholy, her niceness of description and cautious self-discipline. This passage from her husband's preface to her works—which he edited after her death—captures well the impulse of Tighe's poetry and the kind of response it evoked from her many readers: "To possess strong feelings and amiable affections, and to express them with a nice discrimination, has been the attribute of many female writers; some of whom have also participated with the author of Psyche in the unhappy lot of a suffering frame and a premature death" (*Psyche with Other Poems* iii). Tighe's delicate, suffering frame—an attribute practically demanded of these first female poets by their public—diminishes any threat that may surface in her voice because it establishes firmly the iconology of the feminine. Her domains of "polished language" (versification) and "amiable affections" (voice) also reduce the threat of the unfeminine. Tighe manages to bring her voice gently into the verse without violating cultural demands for feminine maturity; these are, after all, demands that she herself trusts, even if she might regularly feel betrayed by them or occasionally feel tempted to betray them.

Tighe begins writing poetry, at the latest, in her early twenties, probably just after her marriage to her cousin, Henry Tighe. She prints her poems privately and distributes them to her friends. Though she is not published until after her death, it is clear that she intends publication all along. Finally succumbing to a protracted illness (the result of consumption which she contracted around 1803) that lasts for at least the last six of her thirty-seven years (1772–1810), she does not live to experience the brief fame that follows in the footprints of death.

Except for *Psyche,* her poems are brief, and all of the poetry, including *Psyche,* evokes impermanence as the inescapable condition of reality, the only wisp of beauty or truth knowable. From beginning to end, there is no discernable difference in her versification, her voice, her insight or outlook, which refuses the visionary. She does not grow poetically; she does not raise the issue of poetic growth; she does not consciously or unconsciously stage a process of maturation. As Wollstonecraft first points out, and as later feminist writers like Nancy Chodorow and Carol Gilligan have verified, maturation in Western culture is routed differently for girls and boys. In nineteenth-century culture, womanhood is assumed from the first to be something stable—though definitely not static—and stabilizing. What defines feminine maturity culturally is a paradoxical relation between the constancy that derives from the commitment to self-restraint and self-sacrificing duty and the evanescence that derives from the demand for decorativeness, unsystematized feeling, dependence, and quotidian, repetitive labor. Supposedly, a woman achieves maturity not through the violence of separation, but through the gentle acceptance of dutiful bonds. In girlhood, she is to be virginal. In womanhood, she is to be chaste. She is to serve her husband and her children with the same loyalty she once reserved for her parents and her siblings. This constancy, however, belies the reality of violent change that characterizes her movement toward womanhood. She must leave her father's home and care, for the care of another man, whom she may not even know, whom she certainly cannot know well enough to diminish the fear that must accompany the demand to place herself fully in another's hands. In menstruation she experiences biological changes, which, if unexplained, can seem frightening, biological changes that have no real equivalent in boys. She can experience childbirth, a form of violent separation that both physically and psychologically men cannot replicate. She is supposed to be more in tune with the small changes as well, changes that she is trained to attend to: how many times a dress can be worn before it becomes unfashionable, what the best response is to her husband's barely noticeable gesture, whether the pitch of her infant's cry should distress her. Could this mixture of commitment to constancy and hyperawareness of evanescence help explain Tighe's attraction to Spenser, the consummate poet of constant mutability?

I think it most certainly helps explain Tighe's versification and voice, as we can see by examining the sonnet, dedicated to her mother, which significantly prefaces *Psyche,* her first poem. The sonnet praises the bonds of affection, which naturally bind the mother "whose tender smile most partially / Hath ever blessed thy child" to "the graces which adorn my first wild song / If aught of grace it knows" (1). The concluding conditional clause is typical of Tighe, characteristic of her gentle self-restraint. Those graces, Tighe says, belong to the mother, even though they are written by the daughter:

> since from thine eye
> The beams of love first charmed my infant breast,
> And from thy lip Affection's soothing voice
> The eloquence of tenderness expressed,
> Which still my grateful heart confessed divine:
> Oh! ever may its accents sweet rejoice
> The soul which loves to own whate'er it has is thine!

The almost unnoticeable punning on "own" in the final line is exactly the kind of modest acceptance of feminine maturity that Tighe constantly infuses into her poetry. Whatever the daughter accomplishes as her own belongs to the mother, and vice versa. This mutual ownership (if mutual possession can be considered ownership) serves to remind both women of the profound interconnectedness of their respective duties, loyalties, and loves, and at the same time it serves to remind them of their limits. Whenever the daughter is tempted into pride for her "graces," she reigns herself in with that pun.

The "soul that loves to own" could easily turn into the soul that loves self-ownership and self-assertion, but instead it becomes forever the soul that loves to own whatever the mother has made possible in her nurturing. The syllepsis in the final line also attests to Tighe's chastity, her commitment to self-restraint. "Whate'er it has" functions both as the object of the infinitive "to own" and as the subject of "is thine." It is a tangible linguistic link that can never be broken, either by the daughter who writes or the mother who is written to. In fact, the difference between writing and reading, addresser and addressee, is effectively suspended, just as ownership is. This reminds us of Coleridge's dispossessing moves in "To William Wordsworth." Tighe, however, rather than beginning with self-possession and then problematizing it, begins with problematized property and sustains it.

Even though this is her first poem written at an early age, Tighe is writing through the persona of a fully mature woman. The purpose of her verse is to elucidate that state of calm, stable, constant maturity, rather than to move from one stage of development to a higher one. The unique voice within is always kept gently restrained by the determined conventionality of the versification. The meter and rhyme are regular, except for the concluding word of the first line "partially." The images are conventional, even predictable, and mild: "tender smile," "willing ear," "beams of love," "infant breast," "grateful heart." There is a scarcity of metaphors, similes, and other figures of speech (in fact, there are none). This unself-conscious emphasis on versification characterizes Tighe's poetry from beginning to end. It would be a mistake, however, to think that this "unself-conscious" emphasis is sustained by an unconscious self. Just as the woman's maturity requires that she self-consciously present herself as an unself-conscious presence ministering to the ephemeral details of daily life, so poetic maturity for a woman in early nineteenth-century Britain requires that she unself-consciously versify without bringing attention to the self-conscious voice blended into the pattern of the poem.

Obviously it is not that Tighe could not be more daring and "original." The failed rhyme of "partially" could easily be corrected, and yet she insists on leaving it in "error." Though the succeeding poem, *Psyche,* is not the "wild song" that she suggests it is, the potential for wildness is always just beneath the surface of conventionality. The wild nonrhyme of "partially" is a glaring instance of this. So is the seemingly innocent pun on "own." It is impossible to read the line "The soul which loves to own whate'er it has" without being reminded that feminine maturity is exactly the repression of such ownership. It is the agreement not to desire independent individuality, not to seek attention–getting originality, not to assert the priority of self-ownership. Through her muted, arch-conventional style, Tighe manages to convince us of her constancy to mature feminine values, while exploiting the forms of an artistic medium historically marked as masculine.

This potential violation of feminine decorum is intrinsic to the procedure of early female poetry-writing. Tighe herself must be conscious of the issue. Not only is she using a classical myth; also she is using Spenserian stanzas. In her preface to the poem, she anticipates all the objections that men (and women trained to think with men) will raise about the poem. Because she writes "only for the more interested eye of friendship," she "may therefore be forgiven the egotism which makes me anxious to recommend to my readers" this tale. Moreover, though she may offer excuses for all other defects, she realizes that she cannot "be excused" for "the deficiency of genius" (ix–x). Lest we attribute such modesty simply to the genre of self-introductions common to young poets (the kind that both Byron and Keats write for their first editions), we should consider her next point. She realizes, she says, that "severer moralists" will "frown" on the subject she has chosen: "the beautiful ancient allegory of Love and the Soul." She asks these moralists to allow "that I have only pictured innocent love, such love as the purest bosom might confess." Quoting Rochefoucault's dictum that young women who do not want to become coquettes must never speak of love as something that they can participate in, Tighe suggests that it is only "the false refinement of the most profligate court which could give birth to such a sentiment." She, instead, equates love with purest morals, implying, of course, that this holds for both women and men (x–xi).

Tighe is hesitant, and yet desirous, to claim originality in versification and voice. Always aware that "my verse cannot be worth much consideration," she endeavors "to let my meaning be perfectly obvious." Although her "partiality for Spenser" encouraged her to adopt his stanza, she is "yet ready to own" that it has "many disadvantages," some owing to her own inadequacy ("difficult to the author"), others intrinsic to the form itself ("tiresome to the reader," "by no means well adapted to the English language"). Just as she is willing to deviate from standard practice by not using the kinds of obsolete words "found in Spenser and his imitators," she is also willing to acknowledge her debts while retaining the capacity for her own inventiveness. "If I have subjected myself to the charge of plagiarism," she says, "it has been by adopting the words and images which floated upon my mind, without accurately examining, or being indeed able to distinguish, whether I owed them to my memory or my imagination" (see xii–xiv). This is a pragmatic response to the burden of influence, which tends to disturb the male romantics more profoundly, but it is also a subtle way of shifting the question of influence away from its basis in patriarchal ownership and territorialism. This reworking of the order of influence is similar to Shelley's, but we shall see it is even more pronounced in later women poets, such as Felicia Hemans, whom Tighe influences.

Just as Tighe and her mother are bound by the bonds of affection and share each other's graces, so the mature poet must understand that she is bound to her parent poets and that she must share "ownership" of her poetry with them. Beneath the desire for a network of happy communal influences, however, Tighe voices the "masculine" desire for imaginative originality and full self-possession. Just as Shelley must fight hard to repress his "masculine" desire for total originality and fails, Tighe must fight hard to retain her desire for shared influence and fails. The limit for masculine maturity is a line whose other side is also the (obverse) limit for feminine maturity. It is as if the male and female poet stand on opposite sides of a mirror, seeing through it to the other's reflection and seeing only her or his own reflection at the same time, desiring to enter that alien terrain reflected in the mirror, not fully knowing that that alien terrain reflects her or his own as well.

Tighe's emphasis on versification makes sense for the cultural limits of feminine maturity, because verse itself has always potentially implied the feminine realm of the decorative, the ephemeral, the ineffectual. Isn't verse the dress that adorns the body of thought? We shall see that Keats will eventually want to answer no to this question, but influenced by the decorative tradition that Tighe makes her own, he at first thinks of poetry in just such terms. Tighe has little choice, if she wants to continue to write poetry confidently without being censured and feeling guilty for invading masculine terrain. There is not a better description of decorative style as a signal of the female poet's maturity than Tighe's own description of Psyche:

> Oh! how refreshing seemed the breathing wind
> To her faint limbs! and while her snowy hands
> From her fair brow her golden hair unbind,
> And of her zone unloose the silken bands,
> More passing bright unveiled her beauty stands;
> For faultless was her form as beauty's queen,
> And every winning grace that Love demands,
> With mild attempered dignity was seen
> Play o'er each lovely limb, and deck her angel mien.
>
> (11)

Like Psyche's physical presence, Tighe's verse is "faultless," demonstrating "every winning grace" but doing so with "mild attempered dignity." She strives for diction as pure and lucid as Psyche's "snowy hands," and she captures what E. V. Weller identifies as "languor" (*Keats and Mary Tighe* xv–xvi), like the wind that breathes over Psyche's "faint limbs." Like Spenser and the sentimental poets so much influenced by him (Thomson, Gray, Collins, Beattie, for example), the verse stresses the eye in every way. Tighe's pictorialism aims for an unveiled brightness and clarity, without straying too far toward the lush and sensual. She strives to be senuous without invoking too strongly the temptations of sensuality, and so her images are thoroughly conventional, using the directness and simplicity of sight to offset the underlying sexuality.

This is exactly the kind of poetry that William Wordsworth criticizes in his Preface to *Lyrical Ballads:* highly refined poetic diction and determined personification. Like Wordsworth, Tighe desires to plummet to a depth of feeling, but unlike him, she cannot boldly claim to leave the artificial behind in search of emotion recollected in tranquility and common language undefiled by civilized life. She understands that to move too far away from the decorative would be to move too close to unrestrained feeling and unladylike aggression. So instead of offering a theoretical discourse on the relation of pure poetic language to a life of deep, long thought, she offers "artificial" language tempered by absolute clarity ("to let my meaning be perfectly obvious") and tempering the dangers of heightened emotion. In other words, she offers sentiment—the evocation of genuine feeling for other human beings and other human situations, which are made accessible to every reader without the danger of stirring the reader's all-too-human emotions beyond control.

(We shall discover a similar aim clearly spelled out in Joanna Baillie's theoretical introduction to her first volume of plays.) Tighe describes precisely the kind of emotional tempest she hopes to help her readers avoid when she pictures Psyche blasted by the 'envy" which has "[p]oisoned her sisters' hearts with secret gall" as Psyche's fame for beauty increases:

> For she was timid as the wintry flower,
> That, whiter than the snow it blooms among,
> Droops its fair head submissive to the power
> Of every angry blast which sweeps along,
> Sparing the lovely trembler, while the strong
> Majestic tenants of the leafless wood
> It levels low. But, ah! the pitying song
> Must tell how, than the tempest's self more rude,
> Fierce wrath and cruel hate their suppliant prey pursued.
>   (13)

Unlike either Wordsworth or Keats, then, Tighe accepts the naturally "artificial" status of poetic language, accepts it both because it provides her a bower of protection in which to write her own poetry as a woman and because it can help protect her readers from the ravenous reality of envy, fierce wrath, and cruel hate. She brings attention to the limits of poetic language and voice appropriately in the very last stanza of the poem, where she must bid adieu to the bower of decorative verse that has helped to distinguish her voice:

> Dreams of delight, farewel! your charms no more
> Shall gild the hours of solitary gloom!
> The page remains—but can the page restore
> The vanished bowers which Fancy taught to bloom?
> Ah, no! her smiles no longer can illume
> The path my Psyche treads no more for me;
> Consigned to dark oblivion's silent tomb,
> The visionary scenes no more I see,
> Fast from the fading lines the vivid colours flee!
>   (209)

As opposed to Keats (in his final stage) and the other romantics, Tighe, with mild regret, accepts the ephemeral nature of her "visionary scenes." "Fancy" cannot cheat so well, so after a brief moment of feeling voiced and made heard, her lines "fade" fast. Only the page remains, but the page cannot restore the visionary gleam, which is swallowed by silence and the darkness of oblivion.

Beneath Tighe's conventional verse, we can hear her distinctive exploratory voice modulating the dominant tones and themes of her poetry: the delicacy of delight, the pang that sadness makes, the way that pleasure beckons melancholy and vice versa, the healing magic of memory that is itself always fragile, the emotional logic of a disciplined life, the fecundity of affectionate bonds, the finality of death. All of these themes are touched on simultaneously in her sonnet "Written at Scarborough, August, 1799":

> I think upon the scenes my life has known;
> On days of sorrow, and some hours of joy;
> Both which alike time could so soon destroy!
> And now they seem a busy dream alone;
> While on the earth exists no single trace
> Of all that shook my agitated soul,
> As on the beach new waves for ever roll,
> And fill their past forgotten brother's place:
> But I, like the worn sand, exposed remain
> To each new storm which frets the angry main.
>
> (220)

This sonnet, as remarkable as any written by Shakespeare, Spenser, Milton, Wordsworth, or Keats, explores the limits of voice without ever actually violating the cultural dictates of womanly maturity. The sonnet probes the depths of self secretly hoping to find an unmuted voice as individuated, as self-perpetuating, as self-owning as that of a Wordsworth or Keats. If the self is constituted by the "scenes" of life, then the feminine self is particularly vulnerable to "each new storm which frets." The feminine self becomes "a busy dream" that evaporates into the details of quotidian life; it becomes a series of waves, each wave, each self constantly displaced and forgotten by the next. But Tighe's explicit linking of the self is to the "worn sand," rather than to the waves. Her voice is the passive shore that lies exposed in her poetry and in her life. The transposition of "exposed" and "remain" in the penultimate line stresses both the fear of too much exposure and the fear of remaining exposed without the protection of significant "scenes." At the same time, it suggests implicitly a desire for exposure and permanence beyond what her culture prescribes for even the maturest female poet. The self remains, only to be violated by "each new storm," and Tighe's voice, her "agitated soul," can here be raised to a new pitch of anguish and complaint while still remaining protected by the carefully-followed conventions of verse. Keats sounds like this in his sonnets, too, and Shelley in his pensive poems. But beyond the tone and the sheer lyrical power of the verse here, the similarities end. They end because of the culturally-defined borderline of gender, which disables Tighe from stepping boldly into the male poet's terrain, although it can never prevent her from trespassing ever so gently.

One of the ways in which the male romantics signal their poetic maturity involves taking poetry itself as the subject for poetry, either as a way of claiming poetry as special territory available only to the imaginative mind, or as a way of heightening its power and value by investing poetic discourse with philosophical gestures. Poetic reflexivity comes to signal a mature mastery not only of the concrete poetic medium, but also of the abstract generality that grounds the medium. It enables self-authorization, the capacity to see oneself as the master of one's own fate, the creator of one's own influence. Poetry becomes allowable for women in the late eighteenth century because it becomes allied to the realm of private feeling. Like the decorativeness of verse, the ephemera of "mere" private feeling imply an association with women's experience. As long as Tighe and the women poets who follow behind her stay within the domain of what is perceived as feminine experience, they are relatively safe. But if they stray either into masculine feeling (such as expressing bold complaint or protest) or into visionary thought, perceived as intrinsically masculine, then they risk whatever security they have gained as maturely feminine poets. Since gender is no more a natural division than the distinction between poetry and philosophy, or voiced sentiment and visionary thought, it is impossible for Tighe to remain confined by the limits of feminine maturity as it is for her to avoid totally visionary reflexivity.

In one sonnet she explores the relation between "Fancy" and "Hope," between age and "staid Wisdom's reign," between the playful desire that fanciful poetry encourages and the sobering demands of feminine maturity. "Shall my distempered heart still idly sigh," she asks, "For those gay phantoms, chased by sober truth?" And she answers herself: "Ah, no! my suffering soul at length restored, / Shall taste the calm repose so oft in vain implored" (225). Although this poem definitely reflects her commitment to self-restraining constancy as constituting mature womanhood, it also implies a deep dissatisfaction with this limitation. "Fancy" is closely allied with poetry, just as her "brow, where many a line / Declares the spring-time of my life gone by, / And summer far advanced," is metonymic for the many lines of poetry written on the pages of her mind. In the succeeding sonnet, her assessment of poetry's powers and limits is even sharper:

> On images of peace I fondly rest,
> Or in the page, where weeping Fancy mourns,
>   I love to dwell upon each tender line,
>   And think the bliss once tasted still is mine;
> While cheated Memory to the past returns,
>   And from the present leads my shivering heart
>   Back to those scenes from which it wept to part.
>   (226)

In its ironies this poem is similar to Donne's "The Triple Fool," in which the persona ridicules his own attempt to heal love-sickness by writing poetry, only to be more sorely wounded when he hears the poem he has composed in agony happily set to music and sung by someone who cannot know the depth of pain that sparked the poem. And similar to romantic poetry, Tighe's sonnet reflexively reflects upon the powers and limits of poetry itself. Poetry is a power that ever deceives the fragile self into thinking that it can transcend the limits of self, that it can transcend the dwindling of time toward death, but always those limits reassert themselves, even within the poetic discourse that seeks to evade them. In returning to the fanciful scenes of youth marked on the page, the poetic self must necessarily also reenact poetic closure, which portends the closure of self and reintensifies the ever-approaching close of life itself. Unlike Keats, however, who feels compelled to conclude his Nightingale ode with the inability to discern a waking dream from visionary experience (what is a vision if not a waking dream?), Tighe's Fancy is both cheating and cheated at the same time. She is a "fond" girl who needs the bower her Fancy provides, but she is also a woman who fully understands the fondness (meaning both silliness and affection) of resting on images of peace. Poetry triggers Memory, and Memory, too, is cheating and cheated, for it triggers both the original joy remembered and the original sadness of having to part from that past bliss. The poem instigates a cycle of no return in which feelings mount upon feelings, in which the past invades the present and vice versa, and in which reality and poetry are both cheated by each other.

Ultimately, Tighe accepts the limits, even as she plays against and puns on them. As she suggests in the final stanza of the last poem written before her death:

> Oh! do not quite your friend forget,
> Forget alone her faults;
> And speak of her with fond regret
> Who asks your lingering thoughts.
> (310)

Remembering, for Tighe, is always a kind of "fond regret," and even the mature voice of a poet can only ask as much as "lingering thoughts," for to ask anything more denies the essential evanescence not just of feminine experience but of all human life.

2

Leaving Tighe for Keats, we do not quite leave behind the domain of the "passive heart" (Tighe 227), which Tighe (in)tends to inhabit. Rather, we take that domain with us. Just as Tighe's womanly verse has to have intercourse with masculine forms, so Keats's manhood is infused with what their culture perceives as feminine fecundity. And just as we cannot truly approach an understanding of Tighe without an exploration of some masculine counterpart, so we cannot really begin to understand Keats's obsession with achieving poetic manhood without having explored some feminine counterpart. (Regardless, the latter course has been taken many times.) Only through such interweaving of the sexes—and without relying on reductive, absolute categories as if gender and sex were coterminous—can we begin to debunk the assumption that a poet like Keats can represent a universal paradigm of poetic development.

We can use the same descriptive categories—verse, voice, vision, and influence—for marking the patriarchal conceptualization of maturity that we used for Tighe; we must attempt to delineate, however, any significant differences in how these categories function as markers of maturity for men and women poets. The first difference that we will notice is how the categories become hierarchized into stages or levels of development. Keats moves from verse to voice to vision in an attempt to get closer to the poetic greats who, in his opinion, are immortalized at the apex of the final visionary level. I am not suggesting that these categories are absolute or even that they are not extremely complex, more than overlapping; only that they are tendencies that can be easily identified in the poetry and letters, and that can easily help us identify the implications of the masculine conceptualization of poetic maturation.

Keats's first level I will call the bower stage. In this stage poetry is constituted solely as versification, and versification is valued in itself. This is due partly, of course, to Leigh Hunt's influence. For Hunt, poetry tends to be a process of stylizing already-invented narration or already-formulated feelings. *The Story of Rimini* is the perfect example of this poetic creed. But, of course, Hunt is not the first or only advocate of poetry as stylistic craftsmanship. Perhaps we could, for the sake of convenience, give Spenser the honor of fathering this line in British literature. Poetry is envisaged as a bower to which we go not to escape life but to enhance it through the unique poetic value of beauty combined with permanence: beauty can be found in the infinite profuseness and ever-changing vitality of lush sights in the bower; permanence can be found in the lucidity and stability of moral vision, which resides comfortably in poetic allegory but cannot be so easily discovered in actual life. Perhaps another factor determining this as Keats's initial phase (there is no reason why versification must come first) is his intimacy with and early admiration for Benjamin Haydon. In considering the development of an artist, it would be impossible for the susceptible young Keats not to correlate the painter's craft with the poet's, and to surmise that just as the painter must spend a preparatory period perfecting his technique, so must the poet. The co(i)nfluence of Haydon, Hunt, and Spenser would certainly encourage Keats's pictorialism, and would make a poet like Tighe appealing as a model versifier.

Tighe-like "feminine" senuousness is to be found everywhere in Keats's early poetry, and, as Weller has amply demonstrated, the Tighe influence is specifiable and various. But it is Spenser, a mentor much less disturbing to this young male poet's fragile poetic self, whom Keats names in his poetry. Unlike the second phase where influence becomes troublesome and disruptive, in this bower stage Keats is much more comfortable with the idea of shared influence and mentorship. How else can one learn the technique of versification, except through an apprenticeship of slavish imitation? In "Specimen of an Induction to a Poem" Keats looks to Spenser fondly with "girlish" adulation and affection. "I must tell a tale of chivalry," Keats says, "For large white plumes are dancing in mine eye" (1–2). Keats explicitly rejects a tale of "cruelty, / When the fire flashes from a warrior's eye" (23–24), for "the splendour of the revelries, / When butts of wine are drunk off to the lees" (35–36). His invocation to Spenser comes exactly at the point where it is obvious that he is incapable of continuing unaided, that he is faltering in the technique of narrative invention:

> Spenser! thy brows are arched, open, kind,
> And come like a clear sun-rise to my mind;

> And always does my heart with pleasure dance,
> When I think on thy noble countenance. . . .
>
> (49–52)

Does Spenser serve as his great mentor in this initial phase partly because he is, unlike the formidable Milton or the chameleon Shakespeare, so inviting? Is this why Spenser has so many imitators? In the early poetry Keats does follow rather meekly "with due reverence" (see lines 55–64). It is as if he is in a bower that can only nurture his young ambition and support his first "daring steps." "Sleep and Poetry" crystalizes this first phase, but at the moment of Keats's moving on to the next phase. The poem displays his reliance on the bower conception of poetry even as it gropes toward another conception. He pleads for a "bowery nook" that shall become "elysium—an eternal book / Whence I may copy many a lovely saying / About the leaves, and flowers" (lines 63–66). Or again: "th'imagination / Into most lovely labyrinths will be gone, / And they shall be accounted poet kings / Who simply tell the most heart-easing things" (265–268). Although Keats wants to believe that "the great end / Of poesy" is to "be a friend / To sooth the cares, and lift the thoughts of man" (245–247), he is also intuitively aware of the implications of this conception. It is a very apt description not only of Tighe's conception of poeticizing, but of the conception adhered to by all the later women poets of the period.

Haunting the edge of poetry as the bower of sentiment, ease, and delicate beauty is a harsh world of manly action. "And can I ever bid these joys farewell?" he asks himself. "Yes, I must pass them for a nobler life, / Where I may find the agonies, the strife / Of human hearts" (122–125). What pulls Keats away from this bower of potential bliss is what keeps Tighe (almost) confined to such a bower: the cultural rituals of gendered maturation. Just as Tighe must suppress her desire to explore the "masculine" realm of self-owning voice and formidable vision, so Keats fears his desire to remain in the realm of the "passive heart," and thus is compelled to repress that desire.

> Is there so small a range
> In the present strength of manhood, that the high
> Imagination cannot freely fly
> As she was wont of old?
>
> (162–165)

Unfortunately, the answer to Keats's question is yes. There is "so small a range / In the present strength of manhood" that a poet with Keats's "feminine" sensibility (or however we label his suspicion of the routinely masculine) must reject that part of himself and go in search of proper "manhood."

It is around 1818 that Keats begins to "mature" as a poet and as a man. What we witness both in the letters and in the poetry is an intensely feverish exploration of his poetic ambition. These are the celebrated letters that allow T. S. Eliot to consider Keats's greatness, as opposed to Shelley's, "much more the kind of Shakespeare" (see *The Use of Poetry and the Use of Criticism* 91). Could it be partly Keats's "penetrating" anguish over masculine maturation that causes Eliot to find these letters "true for greater and more mature poetry than anything that Keats ever wrote" (93)? What Keats has done for his literary tradition in these letters is to universalize, to justify, to penetrate to the core of the masculine experience of poetic progress. In penetrating this experience, however, Keats also helps us to penetrate its mythology and its historical-cultural contingency. Though there is much that could be said about these letters, I wish to emphasize four things. First, when Keats represses the "feminine" bower in order to move to the second phase, he internalizes that bower, returning to it despite himself. He cannot rid himself of it. Second, the second phase is marked by violent separations and divisions—especially between the sexes—that are not present in the bower phase, and the letters and poetry of this second phase display everywhere this violence. Third, this violence is a result of his fear of the "feminine" allure of the bower, and the potential impotence that it represents. Once the bower is repressed and internalized, his fear of it is expressed and externalized, transferred to " 'Dandy' readers, male & female" (*Letters* 1: 379). Finally, Keats never resolves—and probably cannot—the conflict between the demand for "manhood" and his desire for the bower, for to do so would be to erase the bower from both his conscious and unconscious self, an act impossible for any man, no matter how hard some try.

John Gibson Lockhart's infamous review of Keats's early poetry begins by associating Keats's poetic ambition with the "mania" of "many farm-servants and unmarried ladies" to write verse, as a result of the "just celebrity of Robert Burns and Miss Baillie" (see Reiman's *The Romantics Reviewed* Part C 90). In an attempt to stem the tide that threatens to feminize poetry totally, making it as pretty and ineffectual as womanhood and as common as the lower classes, Lockhart, reminiscent of Byron in *English Bards and Scotch Reviewers,* castigates Keats, advising him to fulfill his mandhood in a proper, respectable way: "This young man appears to have received from nature talents of an excellent, perhaps even of a superior order—talents which, devoted to the purposes of any useful profession, must have rendered him a respectable, if not an eminent citizen" (90). Lockhart can stand here for the voice of patriarchal culture, which speaks both from without and from within Keats, telling the young poet that, for him, poetry cannot fulfill the normal process of masculine maturation; if he stubbornly continues down this road, he may end up like the countless "superannuated" governesses who leave their rolls of unpublished and unread lyrics behind. Lockhart's series of articles on the "Cockney School" of poetry constantly attempts to separate the men from the boys. Hunt, Keats, and their ilk, who "exert their faculties in laborious affected descriptions of flowers seen in window-pots," are mere "uneducated and flimsy striplings, who are not capable of understanding [the merits of poets like Pope and Wordsworth], or those of any other *men of power*" (91–92, emphasis in original text).

It is probably not Lockhart's voice, but the patriarchal voice replicated by Lockhart and internalized within Keats, that causes him to enact his fantasies of violent separation, both from the feminine bower and from the father's controlling hand. In a letter written in May of 1817, Keats instructs Hunt to ask Shelley whether he has heard "Stories of the death of Poets," and he innocently suggests that Mrs. Shelley should "procure some fatal Scissars and cut the th[r]ead of Life of all to be disappointed Poets" (1: 140). Later that year, Keats writes to Reynolds about his longing "for some real feminine Modesty," the kind missing from "a set of Women," whom he calls "Devils," "who having taken a snack or Luncheon of Literary scraps, set themselves up for towers of Babel in Languages Sapphos in Poetry" (1: 163). By February of 1818, he has attempted to cut himself off from impotent masculine influences as well as from the feminizing influence of Tighe's bower. He tells Reynolds that modern poets are like an "Elector of Hanover" who "governs his petty state, & knows how many straws are swept daily from the Causeways in all his dominions & has a continual itching that all the Housewives should have their coppers well scoured." On the other hand, "the antients were Emperors of vast Provinces, they had only heard of the remote ones and scarcely cared to visit them.—I will cut all this—I will have no more of Wordsworth or Hunt in particular" (1: 224). We must note the repeated image of violent "cutting" here both in relation to the feminine which is called on to cut all disappointed (male) poets, and in relation to his own maculine cutting of impotent male mentors—both of whom threaten his progress toward literary greatness. Accordingly, he desires to give up Tighe (the feminine which he must outgrow if he hopes to avoid castration) and Beattie (the threat of effeminence or masculine impotence which he fears replicating), both of whom "once delighted" him. "[N]ow I see through them and can find nothing in them—or [but] weakness—and yet how many they still delight" (2: 18). His announcement to George and Georgiana Keats that "I hope I shall never marry" must also be viewed in this context of repression. This is the same letter in which he bemoans England's decline as a result of there being no longer any great men (see 1: 391–405).

In the second phase, Keats enters farther into the "Chamber of Maiden-Thought" (1: 281). He begins to think that "[t]hat which is creative must create itself" (1: 374). Attempting to find a voice that will create itself, he begins to construct a systematic philosophy of poetry, however fragmentary, and to take as the subject for his poetry the vision that makes poetry possible. Keats himself best describes this movement from verse and voice to voice and vision when he describes the difference between *Endymion* and *Hyperion:*

[I]n Endymion I think you may have many bits of the deep and sentimental cast—the nature of *Hyperion* will lead me to treat it in a more naked and grecian Manner—and the march of passion and endeavour will be undeviating—and one great contrast between them will be—that the Hero of the written tale being mortal is led on, like Buonaparte, by circumstance; whereas the Apollo in Hyperion being a fore-seeing God will shape his actions like one. (1: 207)

In the "Chamber of Maiden-Thought" Keats abandons the Tighe-like "bits of the deep and sentimental cast" for the Wordsworthian "march of passion." The snowy ladies, enticing nymphs, and languid boys that we encounter in the bower phase give way to explicit sexuality and aggressiveness, sometimes violent as in "Isabella," sometimes destructive as in "Lamia" or "La Belle Dame sans Merci," sometimes deceptively consensual as in Madeline's dream in *The Eve of St. Agnes.* The violence of feminine experience that Tighe must repress in order to be considered a mature poet, Keats must embrace as a sign of his manhood. The passive, sentimental hero must be exchanged for the "fore-seeing" visionary who "will shape his actions" like a god. Spenser is traded for Milton and Shakespeare. Like Moore comparing Byron's poetic career to Napoleonic conquest, Keats appeals to Napoleon, the grandest myth of the self-made strong man of his time.

What Keats is attempting in both *Hyperion* poems is to create a vision of the world from the strength of his own voice, to envision the future of his own poetic immortalization. Influence, therefore, becomes more problematic than in the bower phase. When he gives up the first *Hyperion,* it is because "there were too many Miltonic inversions in it—Miltonic verse cannot be written but in an artful or rather artist's humour. I wish to give myself up to other sensations" (2: 167). Rather than relying on Milton's verse, he must create his own genuine voice. No longer is it enough "artfully" to apply himself to the perfection of technique. Even if the poetry must become obscure and dense with the effort, as it does in the second *Hyperion,* he must not turn back. Unlike Tighe, he is willing to sacrifice clarity to originality. Writing poetry becomes not only an assault against the father's rule—and it is no coincidence that the *Hyperion* poems are about the overthrow of the old gods by the young ones—it also becomes an assault against language itself, which impedes total expression of voice and total display of originality. Poetry becomes a parable of masculine exploration into the dangerous unknown: "In Endymion, I leaped headlong into the Sea, and thereby have become better acquainted with the Soundings, the quicksands, & the rocks, than if I had stayed upon the green shore, and piped a silly pipe, and took tea & comfortable advice" (1: 374).

Even as Keats takes his headlong dive into the sea of self-creation, however, he takes the "feminine" bower with him. The chamber of thought that opens up to all those other dark rooms is a "Maiden" chamber. It is out of this conflict between Keats's desire for the feminine bower and his desire for masculine self-possession that his ambivalence for Wordsworth develops, and it is also out of this conflict that his paradoxical conception of poetic identity evolves. For him, poetry becomes not an expression of the "egotistical sublime," but an act of self-dispersal. It is not the kind of lingering, self-problematizing dispersal that Tighe engages in, but rather a kind of self-dispersal that enables the self to be re-erected in the temple of poetic delight. And even as Keats leaves behind the feminine bower, he finds himself emprisoned within that feminine temple, emprisoning the feminine as he is in turn emprisoned by it.

3

Whereas Wordsworth locates the feminine within nature in order to construct a myth of poetic power that enables the self-possessing man to progress beyond nature, Keats, suspicious of Wordsworth's aggressive self-possessing posture, transforms the Wordsworthian sublime by placing the feminine in a different spot, but within a similar structure. For Keats, the feminine becomes not a sacrificial victim, but a naturally inviolate sign (a presence that can be neither sacrificed nor victimized), which represents the possibility of existing within the "other" through art, and also represents the possibility of freezing natural process into the permanence and stability of artistic achievement. For Keats, the feminine is not so much that which intensifies and motivates desire toward a self-possessing end, but that which crystalizes the perpetual movement of desire into the permanent designs of art and thus reassembles the individual self into the grander framework of self-dispersing artistic vision. In his "mature" poetry he is forced to contain or crystalize the feminine as a sign of his manhood, as evidence of his self-control. The effect of Keats's placing of the feminine, nonetheless, brings him back full circle to Wordsworth's masculinist stance.

Like Wordsworth, Keats traces man's development from an originary experience of natural innocence (the "infant chamber") to a crisis of identity (the "Chamber of Maiden-thought") in which the individual is awakened to "the weariness, the fever, and the fret / Here where men sit and hear each other groan." It is in the midst of the maiden chamber that most of Keats's now celebrated poems are written. These poems enact the struggle to discover a vision that is whole without being merely self-possessed or egotistically sublime, that is visionary without being self-deluded. The key that Keats turns to repeatedly, of course, is "beauty." "What the imagination seizes as Beauty must be truth," he says (*Letters* 1: 184). Ultimately that is all we know, and perhaps it is all we need to know in order to progress. In a later letter, he states: "I never can feel certain of any truth but from a clear perception of its Beauty—and I find myself very young minded even in that perceptive power—which I hope will encrease" (*Letters* 2: 19).

"Ode on Melancholy" records the intensity of the struggle toward enduring participation. Characteristically, "when the melancholy fit" falls, as it inevitably must, we have only one course of action, to aestheticize the experience of pain itself, to articulate it as an artistic structure, to regulate the flurry of irregular desire by freezing it into the stability of artistic pleasure.

> Then glut thy sorrow on a morning rose,
>   Or on the rainbow of the salt sand-wave,
>   Or on the wealth of globed peonies;
>   Or if thy mistress some rich anger shows,
>   Emprison her soft hand, and let her rave,
>   And feed deep, deep upon her peerless eyes.
>   (15–20)

The first three images are natural figures, and so we need to ask whether this salve for melancholy is a sort of Wordsworthian (re)turn to nature. Although "Ode on Melancholy" does not seek to address—much less answer—this question, "Ode to a Nightingale" does. The latter ode serializes the curative options available to the aching heart, the drowsy numbness of pain. If the poet achieves self-dispersal at all, it is most likely in the seventh stanza. The bird is made immortal not so much as to fuse the human subject and the natural object, or to transfer nature's immortality to a self-possessing subjectivity; rather the apotheosis of the bird enables the poet to share his melancholy with other human subjects:

> No hungry generations tread thee down;
> The voice I hear this passing night was heard
> In ancient days by emperor and clown:
> Perhaps the self-same song that found a path
> Through the sad heart of Ruth, when, sick for home,
> She stood in tears amid the alien corn.
>
>   (62–67)

Those other human subjects (the emperor, the clown, Ruth, future generations) are imagined. They themselves are artistic representations of himself, subjects who, although in the midst of totally different circumstances, would be thrown into the same state of mind as the poet when hearing the song of the nightingale. As opposed to Wordsworth, the poet's desire becomes not a uniquely self-addressing voice in the midst of an internalized nature, but a choir whose common desire enforces a sympathetic bond across generations and geography and social class. It is the feminine presence at the climax of the text that assures the crystalization of artistic desire. What Keats provides us in Ruth is a moving simulacrum of the experience that has possessed him. As she stands "in tears amid the alien corn," we are each allowed both to keep our aesthetic distance (our degree of necessary alienation) and to traverse "through the sad heart" of this woman, to re-experience our threatening desire with the threat diminished by its artistic re-enactment in the scene. The import of aestheticization here is revealed in the concluding lines of the stanza:

> The same that oft-times hath
> Charm'd magic casements, opening on the foam
> Of perilous seas, in faery lands forlorn.
>
>   (68–70)

The path through human sympathy leads immediately into the desired retreat of imaginative play, as the mind momentarily is freed to experience its desire without the portentous desolation that must return as the poet is returned to "my sole self." Unlike stanza 4, where the poet ineffectually asserts the power of poetry, stanza 7 enacts that power by aestheticizing the real image of the poet into a feminine reflection, who enables both the gratification of similarity and the pleasure of distance and difference. Similar to Shelley, then, Keats refuses the quest for self-originating desire within a mythic aboriginal self, and in order to do so must fight a hard battle against the ineluctable self-possessing individuation that is ironically the very source for his desire for self-dispersal.

We can see also in "Ode on Melancholy" how Keats correlates the objectification of nature with the aesthetic salvation of feminine beauty. In the second stanza, the feminine is placed notably at the end of the series. It consummates the alternatives and creates a hierarchy with itself holding the top rung. Note also that the aesthetic experience of the feminine is *made* and not simply enjoyed. That is, the relation between the power of nature's beauty and the individual's perception of that beauty is ambiguous. Is that power derived from the mind's ability to create an artful vision from nature's mindless objects, or is it simply a naturally instinctual response to an object that is itself the creator of its own artful vision, to an object of discourse that is really a self-originating subject of desire? The relation between the individual's desire and the feminine object is much less ambiguous, and suggests that however much nature may be a subject in and of itself, the burden of creating aesthetic pleasure lies with the masculine mind. The main verbs of the last two lines indicate the kind of activity necessary for the poeticizing agent: emprisoning and feeding. The individual must hold desire ("emprison her soft hand") without stifling it ("let her rave"). By emprisoning desire within the structures of art, the individual can "feed" upon the beauty captured, can experience intensified desire without the threat of madness.

That this is a poem on "melancholy" should not go unnoted. Melancholy is a sort of temporary madness—often, of course, associated with lovesickness—that always threatens to overwhelm the individual and turn into a protracted insanity. By feeding desire and feeding upon it, the individual gains control—or a semblance of control—over desire. Instead of a threat, desire becomes an accomplice in the creation of aesthetic pleasure. Keats manages, like the other romantics, to exploit the anarchic tendency of desire while distancing himself from the disruptive quality that anarchy entails. Just as Wordsworth describes his natural frenzy as a kind of maddening lovesickness that must precede the self-possession of poetic creation, and just as Shelley frames the disordering ranting of the madman in *Julian and Maddalo* with the self-controlling urbanity of Julian's earnest conversation and resolute silence, so Keats feels that the mania of desire can be controlled by an act of discursive imagination.

What is the difference, then, between the desire of aesthetic pleasure and the desire of melancholy? One crucial difference is, of course, the element of control itself. Whereas artistic desire is desire that has been temporarily stabilized, melancholic desire is like the desire of the madman in *Julian and Maddalo* (schizophrenic, paranoid, anarchic, unself-possessing), or like the desire of Childe Harold (aimless and antisocial). More importantly, artistic desire is not real, but simulated desire. This is why we can read a poem articulating melancholy without necessarily experiencing schizophrenia, paranoia, anarchy, or the annihilation of self-identity. By substituting desire with a reliable simulacrum, the poet exchanges actual danger with pleasurable risk.

Finally, the structure—the process of emprisoning—enables some mediation between real desire and its simulacrum, artistic desire. The artifactuality of the poem does not efface desire, but it erects a medium between the subject and his desire. We usually call this aesthetic distance. It is the capacity to feel in control of the experience itself. It is the self-conscious sense of *making* the experience, the pleasure of being able to discern the *architecture* of the experience.

Whereas Wordsworth gains a semblance of control by victimizing the female, whose absence of control serves to accentuate his own self-possession, Keats gains a semblance of control of his desire by apotheosizing the feminine—making it impervious to history, to language, to desire itself—to the status of undying art(efact). "Peerless eyes" means both without peer, without equal, and unable to be peered into. Like the eyes of Maddalo's daughter, the eyes of "thy mistress" reflect the light of truth as they absorb that light into a profound chasm of secret truth. As we turn to the final stanza of the poem, we see how Keats makes the feminine a sign of the inviolable while not falling entirely into the trap of self-delusion. The "She" that begins the final stanza is ambiguous. Does it refer to "thy mistress" or to 'Melancholy" or to both? In any case, "She dwells with Beauty," but it is "Beauty that must die." Even as he emprisons desire and aestheticizes it in his mistress, it slips through his fingers and gets loose. Even as he conquers melancholy by distancing himself from it through its articulation in art, melancholy lives on outside of the artistic structure he has designed, lives on in the design of nature, which he cannot refashion. "Joy" is always "bidding adieu." "Pleasure" is always "aching" and "turning to poison while the bee-mouth sips." Aesthetic pleasure can only be a limited form of control because it, too, is vulnerable to the desire that calls it into being. Nevertheless, what Keats has managed to do is to bring "veil'd Melancholy" into the "very temple of Delight." Like the mistress's eyes that are "peerless," melancholy is veiled, indicating the correlation between these two feminine presences.

No one can enter the temple of delight that paradoxically houses melancholy "save him whose strenuous tongue / Can burst Joy's grape against his palate fine." The power of the poet enables him—if only temporarily—to take charge of his desire. The sensuousness of these lines combines with an aggression (the bursting motion of the strenuous tongue) and a delicacy (his fine palate) to represent the poet's relation to the feminine. He must emprison her soft hand, but he also must let her rave. He must burst into her temple, but he cannot dethrone her. The "sovran shrine," then, is ironically both the temple of art that is created by the poeticizing self and the shrine of desire that disassembles the self. It is the shrine of death itself. Desire's ultimate object is annihilation. For what is desire but the energy that disperses itself in accordance with the laws of thermodynamics? The "sovran shrine" is the artifact that the poet has created to enshrine his moment of control over desire and death, and it is the larger movement of uncontrollable desire that enshrines his artifact.

"His soul shall taste the sadness of her might." The feminine principle of desire, as it is enshrined as art, also enshrines itself above art's sway. He is able to "taste"—that is, to share and to restrain—her "might" temporarily through the power of his own vision. The final line of the poem capsulizes the paradox of this sharing of the power of desire, for she is able to hang his "soul" among her other "trophies." Yet, his soul has become that trophy. It has become an artifact that symbolizes his victory over her (over desire, melanchoy, death, oblivion) and therefore over himself. As he secretes his soul into his art, he creates an artifact that can represent his temporary and ambivalent victory, even as it fails to violate the law of desire itself. What is "negative capability," after all, but this very process of self-crystalization through self-dispersal? It is the ability to lose the self in another object—the song of a nightingale or an urn or a woman's peerless eyes—and therefore to reaffirm the previous reality of self-identity. It is the ability to be and not to be at the same time—the ultimate resolution to Hamlet's unresolvable dilemma.

4

In *The Eve of St. Agnes* Keats rehearses this same dilemma, but focuses on the shared desire, the collective human attempt to purge the threat of desire from life through religion and the attempt to crystalize that desire through art. This is why the poem is obsessed with ritual, with architecture, and with the embodiment of ritual within architecture, the frieze. The poem begins with the beadsman's telling of the rosary. It begins in the bitter cold of a medieval chapel, with all its attendant signs of death:

> His prayer he saith, this patient, holy man;
> Then takes his lamp, and riseth from his knees,
> And back returneth, meagre, barefoot, wan,
> Along the chapel aisle by slow degrees:
> The sculptur'd dead, on each side, seem to freeze,
> Emprison'd in black, purgatorial rails:
> Knights, ladies, praying in dumb orat'ries,
> He passeth by; and his weak spirit fails
> To think how they may ache in icy hoods and mails.
>   (10–18)

The beadsman is the antithesis of the madman of *Julian and Maddalo*. He is the masculine principle of actively repressed natural desire. As an ascetic, he is *almost* at home in the ritualizing structure of religion, which is embodied by the chapel. The chapel is a place that seems safe because desire has seemingly been purged from it. Religion counsels the acceptance of the death within life by also denying the life within life—the energizing force of desire. The perfect symbol of this view is captured in the "sculptur'd dead," who are "emprison'd" in "purgatorial rails." *Emprison* here implies the same process as it did in "Ode on Melancholy." It is the process of creating a structure that will allow us to gain control over desire, and, as we shall see, the concept of emprisoning returns again significantly in the poem's closure.

As the beadsman sits in the cold chapel among the ashes practicing his religious rituals, doing "harsh penance" for "sinners' sake," the revelers are just in the next chamber. Indeed, the beadsman can hear "Music's golden tongue," which tempts him, but 'already had his deathbell rung." The beadsman forces himself to choose death-dealing ritual over the risk-taking expression of desire. Music here represents the same ambivalent force as in *Julian and Maddalo* and "The Highland Girl"—the potential to contain naturally instinctual desire within the civilized designs of a highly accomplished art. The "argent revelry" that tempts the beadsman represents the world of art, the world in which desire can supposedly be emprisoned by substituting actual desire for its artistic simulacrum. Contrasted with the "sculptur'd dead" of religious ritual, we have another kind of frieze or freeze:

> Soon, up aloft,
> The silver, snarling trumpets 'gan to chide:
> The level chambers, ready with their pride,
> Were glowing to receive a thousand guests:
> The carved angels, ever eager-eyed,
> Star'd, where upon their heads the cornice rests,
> With hair blown back, and wings put cross-wise on their breasts.
>   (30–36)

The warm, bright, musical color of the revelry exists in striking contrast with the chilly, dark, deadly silence of the chapel. The "carved angels" are "ever eager-eyed," as they hold up the cornice. These angels are always ready and willing to fly, to flee their "carved" state into a sphere of released desire, but they hold themselves back. The "hair blown back," the "wings put cross-wise on their breasts" indicate their necessary ambivalence: a pose of self-emprisonment and of self-preparation for flight. But it would be a mistake to separate the artistic world of the angels from the religious world of the sculptured dead. They are part of the same mythology, the angels representing the heaven of fulfilled desire promised after life, the sculptured dead representing the purgatory of unfulfilled desire that life itself must be. The two spheres, like the cold north and sunny south, constitute a single world.

We can see this in the multivalent ironies of St. Agnes Eve itself. Religion attempts to turn desiring animals into moral citizens by purging desire from human activity, or more precisely by rechanneling (sublimating) that desire toward controlled acts of wise resignation—the kind the beadsman practices, the kind the old man and the poet advocate in *The Ruined Cottage*. The chaste female—in this case Madeline—becomes the sign of the inviolable sanctity of religion, the sign of its capacity to control human desire. It is, therefore, in the chamber of feminine chastity that the conflict between natural desire and socializing repression is played out. Like art, religion is a complex structure that contains within itself a door that admits desire while attempting to contain and exploit that energy towards its own distinctive ends. One of these doors is the ritual of St. Agnes Eve:

> . . . upon St. Agnes' Eve,
> Young virgins might have visions of delight,
> And soft adorings from their loves receive
> Upon the honey'd middle of the night,
> If ceremonies due they did aright;
> As, supperless to bed they must retire,
> And couch supine their beauties, lily white;
> Nor look behind, nor sideways, but require
> Of heaven with upward eyes for all that they desire.
>
> (46–54)

It is the "old dames" who spread this gospel, not necessarily official religion itself. Nonetheless, the ritual has become an established part of the religion, for it is true to the vision and intent of religion. St. Agnes Eve allows us to experience desire without experiencing it, allows us to possess desire without the fearful anarchy it portends.

The virgin dreams of fulfilled desire, but it is only a dream, and more importantly it is a dream protected by religious ritual itself. The virgin's lover can come to her only if she has fasted, only if she has repressed in actuality what she consummates in her dream. She cannot have a vision of desire if she is not chaste, and she cannot taste the nectar of love if she has not taken the poison of ascetism in fasting the day before. The ritual "visions of delight" correlate to the designs that art erects for the enjoyment of simulated desire. The dream, protected by St. Agnes, serves the same function in religious terms, as aesthetic distance does in art, but, appropriately for religious ideology, the power to envision is taken out of the hands of the individual dreamer and put in the hands of St. Agnes or God. Aesthetic distance, for Keats, has no authority outside itself, and this is why Keats is so dismayed by his own struggle to acquire taste, to seize the beauty of art. No one can give it to him or ordain it for him; he must discover it himself through the arduous process of creative endeavor and artistic refinement, stepping from chamber to dark chamber and learning with each step.

Madeline, "her maiden eyes divine" (57), has carefully followed all the rituals of denial, and thus she hopes to remain unviolated and unviolating. It is "young Porphyro, with heart on fire" whom she hopes to dream of, and does. Porphyro represents the masculine principle of desire in its extremity. He is the madman in the text, not in that he is schizophrenic, but in that he is lovesick, in that he will violate all conventions, rituals, even honor itself, to possess Madeline, to consummate his desire, and in that he must violate the feminine principle in order to achieve his goal. He is the purely active man, whom Keats must write about in order to control his desire to be such a man. Porphyro idolizes Madeline—literally. He has put her in the place of divinity, and so he represents a threat to the control that religious ritual provides. It is not that Porphyro self-consciously violates religious ritual and belief, but that his lovesickness blurs the factitious distinction between self-possessing desire and religious conviction. This is indicated by the fact that he prays for what, according to his faith and to the authority of society (in Madeline's father, who has forbidden their love), he should not possess: "he . . . implores / All saints to give him sight of Madeline . . . / That he might gaze and worship all unseen" (77–80).

Even though Porphyro is the antithesis of the beadsman, he, too, is surrounded by *memento mori*. Indeed, because he is the masculine principle of desire unbound, he embodies perhaps even more the ultimate self-exhaustibility of desire. This is why when the old beldame leads him to a chamber, he finds himself "in a little moonlight room, / Pale, lattic'd, chill, and silent as a tomb" (112–113). In the heart of desire, even in "Love's fev'rous citadel"—as Keats calls it—is the chapel of the sculptured dead, is the "sovran shrine" of death itself.

As Porphyro invades Madeline's chaste chamber, he is invading the temple of a "mission'd spirit" (193); he is seeking to turn that chaste place into a temple of delight. But this is not such a difficult task, for just as within Porphyro's fiery desire is the chamber of death, so within Madeline's chamber of religious chastity is the temple of artistic delight. As we move into her chamber, we move again into the architecture of aesthetic pleasure:

> A casement high and triple-arch'd there was,
> All garlanded with carven imag'ries
> Of fruits, and flowers, and bunches of knot-grass,
> And diamonded with panes of quaint device,
> Innumerable of stains and splendid dyes,
> As are the tiger-moth's deep-damask'd wings.
>   (208–213)

These "carven" artifacts become "craven" idolatries, as Porphyro turns the chamber into a pleasure palace. As Madeline kneels to pray, "[s]he seem'd a splendid angel, newly drest, / Save wings, for heaven" (223–224). This vision of Madeline causes Porphyro almost to faint, and as she undresses, he spies her, both of them "stol'n to this paradise"; she "dreams awake" of him and he "entranced" by her. They exist momentarily in a "silver twilight" where desire can be, for once, fulfilled. They exist inside her dream, inside his trance, and so they can experience the ardor of his real desire while being protected by the ritual of her religious vision. Porphyro consummates this vision—as religion and as art. He prepares a feast, heaping delicacies on golden dishes, and he plays music to her "in chords that tenderest be." And yet he still resides within her chaste vision. "Thou art my heaven, and I thine eremite," he says to her (see stanzas 30–33). This statement, of course, has the force of irony, for he is the very opposite of an eremite, engaging in this hedonistic feasting as a prelude to his passionate lovemaking.

At the heart of the poem is the problematic climax of sexual (un)fulfillment. It is problematic because it is real desire cast in the form of simulated desire. It is problematic because history returns with the force of the repressed, disrupting their vision and ejecting them into the harshness of time. "Her eyes were open, but she still beheld, / Now wide awake, the vision of her sleep" (298–299). He, too, is entranced, and "into her dream he melted"

(320). By violating the feminine sign that is supposed to assure the sanctity of religion and the imaginative power of art, Porphyro unsettles the very distinctions that enable a myth of controlled desire. His violation is even more problematic and disquieting when we consider the question of consent. In religion, it is, of course, a paradox of the function of the will in faith. In art, it is the Wordsworthian paradox of choosing a calling. Madeline has chosen to dream, but whether that dream results is beyond her power. She has willed her chastity (her refusal to feast, her refusal to realize desire), but she cannot will the vision within the dream. To what degree Porphyro wills his actions is even more ambiguous, for his violation disrupts the neat categories that both art and religion thrive on, and that desire dissolves in its polymorphous movement.

At the literal level, it is a question of rape. If Madeline is indeed in that state between sleeping and waking, between dream and reality, then she cannot consent. Although there may be some question about Porphyro's mental volition (how much he is actually aware of and in control of his actions), there is little doubt that Madeline is in such a volitionless state:[2]

> Her eyes were open, but she still beheld,
> Now wide awake, the vision of her sleep:
> There was a painful change, that nigh expell'd
> The blisses of her dream so pure and deep:
> At which fair Madeline began to weep.
>
> (298–303)

The "painful change" is the difference between Porphyro idealized in her dream and his real face: "And those sad eyes were spiritual and clear: / How chang'd thou art! how pallid, chill, and drear!" (310–311). In an attempt to regain the ideal vision of her dream, but still in the confusing "silver twilight" between dream and reality, she asks him to make love to her: "Give me that voice again, my Porphyro, / Those looks immortal, those complainings dear! / Oh leave me not in this eternal woe" (312–314). Or is she only asking for the resumption of his "voice," "made tuneable with every sweetest vow" (308–309)? As Porphyro perhaps unwittingly, definitely unmaliciously, exploits the "woofed phantasies" of both religion and art, he himself becomes "entranced" by his vision of Madeline. He, perhaps self-consciously, plays every role: the lovesick knight who has lost control of his will and therefore cannot be blamed for his actions, the "eremite" worshipping the embodiment of divine presence, the artist creating a harmless vision from the chords of his "hollow lute." All categories are blasted in the fire of his passion, and his dissolution invades the sacred space of feminine chastity. Just as his dissolute state is transferred to Madeline and she begins actively to desire outside of the ritualized contexts designed to regulate desire, so too her state of anarchic passion is transferred back to him and feeds his desire. "Upon his knees he sank, pale as smooth-sculptured stone" (297). Within his adoring pose is combined the religious attitude of the sculptured dead, the aestheticizing posture of the carved angels, the pose of Madeline herself, as earlier "she knelt, so pure a thing, so free from mortal taint" (225), "a splendid angel, newly drest, / Save wings, for heaven" (223–224).

As he robs her of chastity—in the temptation to share the feast he has set out, in the seductive designs of his musical art, and in the climactic act of sexual intercourse—she threatens to rob him of motivation itself. The question is whether they can keep at bay the ideological categories that fashion desire and separate male from female by turning the male into desiring passion and the female into desired passivity. The question is whether they can keep at bay the natural progression of desire toward fatal self-exhaustion. They have only two options. 1) They can attempt to remain in the silver twilight of abandoned categories and divisions, which means that they risk a brief existence in the highly energized realm of desire feeding upon itself. In such a realm, civilization is avoided, as the lovers live to love, as they live without counterdesire, without being bound to the production of productivity in society. But to live within desire's own production, eschewing the productivity of civilizing products, is a dangerous enterprise. It means living without the stabilizing products of ideology, and thus without the motives and aims granted by the pull of ideological patterns. It means to exist within the anarchic licence of liberating desire. This, to me, and I think to Keats as well, is impossible. For desire to fuel itself without producing the products of counterdesire would necessarily mean that desire would have to feed upon its own energy in order to maintain its momentum. And, of course, desire would exhaust itself in death. This is one way to read the ending of the poem, as the lovers escape into the oblivion of the storm, into the self-exhaustion of tempestuous desire. 2) They can return to society in the hope of living without society's constraining and divisive restrictions. This second option, though it is at least possible to attempt, seems doomed. At best, they may, like Shelley, hope to form new ideological categories that will reform desire and reshape the world. But Keats seems doubtful of this option as well.

Within the poem, despite Porphyro's optimism, they return to those adamant categories that bind them to society, to history, and to nature. At the moment of climax also comes the moment of real repression, instead of ideal liberation. "[M]eantime the frost-wind blows / Like Love's alarum pattering the sharp sleet / Against the window-panes; St. Agnes' moon hath set" (322–324). The real difference between Madeline and Porphyro, between the male and female in society, is accentuated, as she predicts her fate: "A dove forlorn and lost with sick unpruned wing" (331). Whereas she is all too aware of the reality of their predicament, he attempts to repress reality—a much easier task for a man, who is free to wander, than for a woman, who will be left "to fade and pine" (329). He appeals to the chivalric code, which he has violated in violating her:

> Say, may I be for aye thy vassal blest?
> Thy beauty's shield, heart-shap'd and vermeil dyed?
> Ah, silver shrine, here will I take my rest

> After so many hours of toil and quest,
> A famish'd pilgrim,—saved by miracle.
>
> (335–339)

Porphyro wish-fulfills himself into the "sovran shrine" of the "Ode on Melancholy." And just as Keats, in that ode, wants to have it both ways, to violate that shrine with his strenuous tongue and to keep it intact as an inviolable sign of artistic impregnability, so Porphyro wants it both ways, to violate his lady and to gaze yearningly on her in the light of her purity without "mortal taint." She represents to him salvation as he once again sacrilegiously appeals to the language of pilgrimage. She saves him from famishing, from expiring into the nothingness of exhausted desire. Miraculously, however, she does not become tainted by the satiation of desire. In his eyes, she remains a worthy object of the quest, even though the quest is over once he has obtained her, a worthy object of his worship even though she has become a participant in the pilgrimage, rather than simply the objective of his journey. By dissolving the distinctions between dream and reality, religious faith and lovesickness, ritual and passion, art and life, desire desired and desire fulfilled, Porphyro also claims to dissolve the distinction between masculine and feminine desire. As he melts into her dream, he no longer remains the suitor and aggressor, any more than she remains the passive receptacle, the awaiting chalice, of his love. Her perspective, however, is not so romantic (in the pejorative sense of baseless optimism). Within her perspective, all those categories reassert themselves and desire is returned to the ideological field in which those categories have their being.

Madeline has no choice but to hurry "at his words, beset with fears" (352). Although he can view her still as an inviolable sign—as "beauty's shield," as a "silver shrine"—she cannot afford to view herself in such a mythic light. Much more than he, she recognizes that they are emprisoned by the reality that they have made and that has made them, by the very dream that he appeals to as though it is the reality. But he is determined to sustain the myth that the prison can be escaped. "By one, and one, the bolts full easy slide:— / The chains lie silent on the footworn stones;— / The key turns, and the door upon its hinges groans" (367–369). As they flee this prisonhouse of social restriction, they flee into the storm, into the dark, chilly, vacant prison of nature itself. Just as society conspires to delimit and distill their desire, so the laws of nature dictate the self-exhaustion of desire, that energy must dissipate into the prison of death. Accordingly, the final stanza of the poem returns us to the beginning. This time, however, we have been evicted from the neat categories of both religious and artistic ritual. We are brought into the nightmarish realm of the unknown, into the realm of uncompromising death.

5

In *The Eve of St. Agnes* Keats has not only explored the ritualizing limits of religion and art within the poem, he has also self-consciously offered the poem itself as just such a self-limiting ritual. In *The Subterfuge of Art,* Michael Ragussis suggests that the narrator "is engaged in a quest himself—the creation of romance—and thereby describes, as it were, the poem's sub-plot. He is caught, like most storytellers, between the worlds of imagination and reality, and it is here that he is most like Madeline" (73). I would suggest, rather, that the narrator is most like Porphyro, not Madeline. Like the poet of the "Ode on Melancholy," the narrator struggles self-consciously to create a tale that balances real desire and its artistic simulacrum. He hopes to distance himself from the necessary fall that comes with romance closure by heightening the distinction between desiring subject and desired artifact, by complicating the relation between the poem and its genre.

The narrator reminds us repeatedly within the romance itself that the experience of romance is a simulacrum that sublimates desire. Toward the beginning (in stanza 5), we are introduced to the first such warning: Keats describes the "argent revelry" as "[n]umerous as shadows haunting fairily / The brain, new stuff'd, in youth, with triumphs gay / Of old romance" (39–41). The romantic image within the poem becomes a mere shadow haunting the poem, haunting the brain that seeks to stuff itself with the shadows of the poem. "These let us wish away" (41). Can we wish those shadows away, once their nature as shadows has been articulated? Can we return to the myth of desire-fulfilling romance, once the poem has pierced the form that seeks to contain the desire, once the romance has pierced itself? The narrator again pits the poem against itself toward the end. Porphyro says to Madeline: "Hark! 'tis an elfin-storm from faery land, / Of haggard seeming, but a boon indeed" (343–344). Attempting to put Madeline at ease and to assure himself, he transforms the real storm that patters at their dream into an "elfin-storm," one that will mask their escape from the guards, from the "sleeping dragons all around," one that will not harm the lovers, for they are the heroes of the tale. Porphyro's unwilling self-deception within the poem becomes the narrator's willing self-deception as the maker of the poem. His romance of desire fulfilled is, and yet cannot be, our romance.

Finally, the narrator forces us to move outside the romance before the romance itself has ended not only by the suggestive imagery of death in the final stanzas, but also by the disorienting shift in narrative perspective that introduces the concluding stanza: "And they are gone: ay, ages long ago / These lovers fled away into the storm" (370–371). By shattering the convention of the progressive present and throwing us into the reality of our own present outside the narrative frame, the narrator jolts our romance sensibility and unsettles the aestheticization of desire that the poem struggles to design. Madeline and Porphyro, who have stuffed our brains, are nothing more than "phantoms" of delight, self-deceptive images that give us pleasure because they seem to imitate our desire while containing it in the conventional structures of art. As Susan Wolfson points out, "Keats's narrator so fore-grounds the devices of romance and romance tale-telling that fiction-*making* becomes as important a part of the occasion as the fiction itself" (*The Questioning Presence* 101). By stressing the fictive nature of the tale, the narrator acknowledges the simulated nature of romance desire, and yet this maneuver is itself an attempt to assert control over the fiction of making desire. Like Julian withholding information in order to retain the narrator's control over the reluctant and maddening desire manifest within the poem, Keats's narrator destroys the fictive cover in order to protect himself from discovering the disappointment of manic desire, which accompanies the conclusion of romance and reentry into reality. Like Porphyro, the narrator wants to have the romance of desire fulfilled but wants it without the reality of desire exhausted, once fulfilled. But unlike his character, the more self-conscious narrator hopes to distance himself from self-deception by happily accepting the artfulness of his self-deception.

Just as Porphyro hopes to escape the categories that limit his desire, we readers come to the poem in the hope of escaping the very same categories through the ritual of art. As readers, we are most like Madeline though. The narrator works his art on us like Porphyro playing his hollow lute to Madeline, who wants his love, but does not want to be seduced. Porphyro's lute must be hollow in order for it to make its full sound, in order for it to sing. The ritual of romance is also hollow, a form or genre to be filled with an appropriate fable, a vacuous form haunted by its own desire for fullness, and the narrator, so conscious of this hollowness, alerts the readers, placing them in Madeline's drowsy condition between desired dreaminess and fearful recognition of pale reality. Like Madeline, we can see Porphyro for what he is, a wan phantom promising delight that he can deliver only at our peril, or we, like her, can place our trust in his heroism and follow through to the dark conclusion. Just as Keats allows the lovers to escape the prison of social reality only to escape into the larger prison of nature, he allows his readers to escape their social reality only to return them to the larger reality of unfulfilled desire. Like the "silver twilight" between reality and dream, the poem occupies that delicate space between desire always fulfillable and desire always expended. Keats makes it difficult for us to sustain the myth that Porphyro so pitiably appeals to. As we come to the end, he jolts us, much in the way Madeline is jolted into realizing that she has no option but to rely on Porphyro's chivalry once she has accepted, however much without culpability, his passion. We must accept the narrator's disillusioning conclusion. Even if we choose to romanticize it, to refuse to see its darkness, we cannot refuse closure. We cannot refuse to return to the reality of our individual histories, to our individual desire, marked and chartered by ideology. Perhaps our only consolation here is that—like the speaker of "Ode to a Nightingale"—our condition of self-exhausting desire is a shared state, a condition shared by all the readers who deceive themselves by reading to wish desire away by wishing it fulfilled.

Although Keats is troubled by Wordsworthian self-possession, his relation to the feminine within his texts is ultimately not that different from Wordsworth's or Coleridge's, though it is certainly closer to Shelley's. In all four poets, the myth of the feminine is sustained. It is hard to give up because it gives shape and meaning to the cultural processes that engage them. If we are to move beyond the myth that romantic men create of the feminine, we must attempt to see romantic ideology for what it is. We must be able to view the horizon of masculine desire, how at its limits resides the feminine desire whose suppression enables the male to proceed apace toward his claim to self-possessing individuality or self-dispersing immortality. This means exploring the margins of romantic poetry, listening to the voices of women too long muffled by their brothers' voices, and recovering history that has too often been covered over by our own enamorment with masculine power and romantic myth.

6

The Birth of a Tradition:
Making Cultural Space
for Feminine Poetry

> Sweet Psyche, many a charmed hour,
>   Through many a wild and magic waste,
> To the fair fount and blissful bower
>   Have I, in dreams, thy light foot traced!

Included in Tom Moore's "Juvenile Poems" is this stanza from "To Mrs. Henry Tighe, on Reading Her 'Psyche' " (see *Complete Poetical Works* 1: 95). Like Keats, Moore is enamored by the "blissful bower" created by the feminine poet. It is not only Psyche's "light foot" that Moore traces "through many a wild and magic waste," it is also Tighe's "light foot," the delicate meters of her poetry which purely trace the course of Psyche's love. He praises Tighe in the first and third stanzas of the poem thus:

> Tell me the witching tale again,
>   For never has my heart or ear
> Hung on so sweet, so pure a strain,
>   So pure to feel, so sweet to hear.
>
>   . . .
>
> Did ever Muse's hand, so fair,
>   A glory round thy temples spread?
> Did ever lip's abrosial air
>   Such fragrance o'er thy altars shed?

What impresses Moore is the aura of bewitching femininity—so sweet, so pure, so fair, so fragrant—which Tighe manages to infuse into her poem. Moore, in a "juvenile" mood, can afford to be bewitched by Tighe's lovely poem on love. But just as Keats feels compelled to outgrow the feminine bower, lest he be emprisoned within it, Moore's praise of Tighe, like the praise of all women poets during the early part of the nineteenth century, is tenuously ambivalent. In 1806 he writes, "I regret very much to find that she is becoming so *furieusement littéraire;* one used hardly to get a peep at her blue stockings, but now I am afraid she shows them up to the knee" (*Memoirs* 8: 61). As long as Tighe remains within her feminine bower, as long as she remains the poet of pure and sweet feeling, she is safe for masculine praise. When Moore suggests that Tighe has begun to show those blue stockings "up to the knee," he is suggesting that she has crossed the boundary of gender into masculine terrain.

Moore's attitude toward Tighe represents a general change of attitude toward the "poetess" that occurs in the romantic period. During the middle part of the eighteenth century, women begin to organize occasions so that they can discuss fashionable intellectual and literary topics among themselves and with men. These fashionable discussion circles bring the male cliques of the Augustan coffeehouse into the feminine parlor, where women can take themselves seriously as thinkers and men can be seen to profit from free intellectual dialogue with them. The bluestockings (as they are called with both wonder and derision) self-consciously set out to make learnedness and literariness respectable attributes for British ladies. The first-generation blues—Elizabeth Vesey (1715?–1791), Elizabeth Carter (1717–1806), Frances Boscawen (1719–1805), and Elizabeth Montagu (1720–1800)— are scribbling women who suffer ridicule in order to prove that women, too, can think and write. They not only help to refocus literary culture within the feminine parlor; they also help to refocus literary discourse on topics in which women can participate with less derision from the wider public by helping to foster the age of sensibility. Bringing poetry into the comfortable and fashionable sitting room where men are encouraged to articulate the virtues of gentle (if not genteel) feeling, the blues are able to espouse the intellectual equality of the sexes and the import of learning for women while stressing the significance of feeling for *both* sexes in a civilized society.

Previous to the bluestocking circles, the woman who pursues a literary avocation is more prone to scandal, for if she is willing to ignore the norms by becoming a female scribbler, then what prevents her from breaking other rules established by the law of the father. Indeed, her tendency to scribble, because it places her outside the social norm, is seen as a sign of her general abnormality. She becomes a literary crossdresser, a woman wearing the ill-fitting literary apparel intended for men. That Aphra Behn (1640–1689) and Eliza Haywood (1693?–1756), the two most famous British women writers before the 1750s, lead lives plagued by scandal only serves to confirm the taboo against women poets. Throughout the Augustan period, women's public participation in the literary establishment is so rare that their very scarcity makes public censure of them all the more the norm.

The bluestockings begin the process of making literary women *as a group* more visible and respectable by making their intellectual, moral, and financial support influential to aspiring young men. Though the degree of formality varies in these circles, all of them studiously avoid gossip and scandal, concentrating their efforts on the development of a literary culture that nurtures wit, learnedness, collegiality, refined feeling, and common sense. And although there is definitely some emphasis on gentility and fashion, a cardinal rule of these groups is that individuals are to be valued and nurtured according to their talents, rather than to their economic or class status, or to their gender. The women who organize these circles are sure to appear in print after, if not before, their celebrity as literary hostesses; their fame, however, consists as much in what they nurse in others as in what they themselves author. A bluestocking, however, is still too easily perceived as a kind of literary crossdresser. As writers, the bluestockings are problematic to the larger public because they, primarily Augustan in outlook, emphasize learning and because they tend *not* to discriminate between traditional (masculine) discourse and proper feminine discourse. Or, as we shall see in the case of Hannah More, they are only beginning to open that faultline which by the 1820s separates proper feminine writing from masculine discourse.

As the psychic space in which male poetic activity is conceptualized moves from the Augustan coffeehouse to the bluestocking parlor, from the parlor to nature, the terrain of poetry becomes divided into two complementary spheres, masculine and feminine, which are seen to exist as naturally in the realm of literature as in the realm of nature. The consensus becomes that women can write poetry without being abnormal, as long as they write as proper ladies, to use Mary Poovey's apt phrase. Needless to say, this gendered division is a sort of defense mechanism whereby the literary establishment can adjust itself to the inexorable movement toward feminized male poets like James Beattie (1735–1803), who is a protegé of Elizabeth Montagu's bluestocking circle, and toward increasingly visible women writers, like Hannah More (1745–1833), also a protegé of Montagu. By granting women their own space for poetry-making, distinctly theirs, distinctly feminine, the literary establishment is also able to reaffirm the dominance of male poetry-making. As we have seen in Chapter 1, by affirming the difference between masculine and feminine poeticizing, romantic writers are able to consolidate the concept of poetic vocation, distinguishing between (male) poets who are called to guide culture and (female or effeminate) poets who merely dabble in poetry as a fashionable pastime, placing the powerful male (romantic) poet over both his lesser domesticated brother and his lesser domesticating sister. In the most troubled years when both men and women are attempting to find their literary footing (from around 1790 to 1820), there are actually four categories: the powerful male poet, the feminized male poet, the abnormal bluestocking poet, the normalizing feminine poet. Just as the concept of the domesticated male poet serves as a foil to reclaim normalcy and virility for men aspiring to poetic greatness, so the concept of the bluestocking serves as a foil to normalize the feminine poet and to diminish the male poet's fear of feminization by segregating literary production according to "natural" spheres of gender. In effect, a hierarchy is established with the virile male poet at the top, the effeminate male and proper female poet in the middle, and the bluestocking at the bottom. This is why in 1806 Moore wants to claim that he can easily distinguish between the bluestocking and the feminine poet, that he can point to that line across which the normalizing female poet cannot cross without immediately becoming an object of public derision, a bluestocking, and why in 1830 he feels confident in defending Byron's poetic fame by appealing to the manliness of the poet's character and life. Thus, as successful and fully respected feminine poets take over from bluestockings the arena of female writing, "bluestocking" itself becomes an entirely derisive label, against which the feminine poetess can position herself and delineate her own normality, and through which the literary establishment can accommodate the broadening of the literary market without plunging into frightful gender confusion. This fear of crossing over the line, of becoming a literary crossdresser, not only serves *against* women writers as it keeps them hemmed in by masculine demands; it also serves *in favor of* women writers by creating a new space in which they can experiment, excel, and express the uniqueness of their own desire.

This chapter focuses on the transitional phase in which women writers and their sociohistorical condition are transforming the bluestocking into the feminine poetess. By considering briefly one female poet who practiced her craft entirely under the aegis of the Augustan coffeehouse and then by examining two women who, themselves nurtured by the bluestocking parlor, help to redefine female poeticizing so that it can claim its own space within culture, we shall better understand the feminine poetesses who come to reign over the literary market during the romantic period.

1

In *A Room of One's Own,* Virginia Woolf asks why women turn to the novel instead of to poetry when they first begin to write publicly—when they first begin to conceive of themselves as authors. Although it first may appear ingenuous—as Woolf must have intended—the question is actually ingenious, requiring that subtle analysis be applied simultaneously to two contested terms: gender and genre. Woolf's answer to her own question, though instructive, is not quite as rigorous as the question itself. Woolf convincingly demonstrates how individual women's predicament in the early nineteenth century contributes to the rise of the novel as a congenial "feminine" form, but in the process of doing so she hypostatizes poetry and fiction into immutable genres with categorically inherent qualities that transcend historical evolution. Need the composing of poetry require total concentration, as opposed to the composing of a novel, which Woolf claims can be more easily written despite constant interruption? Need poetry require a looking inward to express the depth of an experiential self, as opposed to the outward-oriented observation of character and event that Woolf claims constitutes the novel? Does tighter organic structure inhere in poetry more than in fiction? Woolf's own "novels" help to answer these questions, since they are novels which stress internal experience over external observation of character and event, since they impose a concept of organic unity more astringent than many poems, and since they require an intensity of self-concentration in both writing and reading more demanding than most poems. Woolf also tends to ahistoricize gender as she posits innate "manly" and "womanly" styles of composition, but she does not fully address the question of how such "natural" gender differences would interact with generic forms. What happens to "poetry" once women, despite obstructive and constrictive social conditions, begin to publish poems? What happens to the "womanly" mode of writing when women, from the moment they begin to write poetry, are implanted in the thriving tradition of "manly" poetic forms?

Although Woolf begins to reconstruct the general social conditions under which women begin to write (in a common sitting room where the kind of concentration supposedly required of poetry would be difficult), she tends to emphasize the *personal* situations of unusually talented individuals like Jane Austen and Charlotte Brontë rather than broader social configurations and their causes; moreover, she tends to ignore, and has been followed by later feminist critics in this way, a significant group of female poets working alongside the first women novelists in the adverse social milieu of early nineteenth-century Britain. That there *are* extremely successful female poets publishing *before* most of the novelists that Woolf mentions indicates how problematic her answer may be. Many of these poets certainly do experience the common sitting room syndrome—the lack of money, privacy, and self-confidence—that Woolf describes so well; they manage, however, to write poetry and to conduct enviable (to their male counterparts) careers as poets while also taking care of the domestic duties that weigh so heavily on women of the time.

It is not coincidental, though it is certainly ironic, that the conception of poetry Woolf refers to is the kind of poetry being written by men at the point when women are beginning to publish. What Woolf takes to be transhistorical, universal, categorical qualities of poetry turn out actually to be a particular and peculiar historical manifestation—romantic poetry—that has come to be synonymous with poetry itself. The paradox of Woolf's stance— consciously ignoring the first published female poets because her premises about poetry are unconsciously based on the romanticist assumptions that originally subordinated and eventually suppressed women's poetry—is so instructive because it pressures us not only to recover these first feminine voices but also to reassess the critical assumptions that have caused these women poets to be covered over within history, even by feminists themselves.

As Woolf points out, there were always women—solely eccentric aristocrats or royal women—who were willing to risk the pain of ridicule by gaining a reputation as women who presumed to write poetry, but these women were only a handful from the most privileged class, and their urge to write was usually limited to the privacy of their diaries and journals. After 1780, women like Anna Barbauld (1743–1824), Hannah More (1745–1833), Anna Seward (1747–1809), Charlotte Smith (1748–1806), Anne Grant (1755–1838), Helen Maria Williams (1762–1827), Joanna Baillie (1762– 1851), Amelia Opie (1769–1853), Mary Tighe (1772–1810), Sydney Owenson (1776–1859), Mary Brunton (1778–1818), Lucy Aikin (1781– 1864), Mary Russell Mitford (1787–1855), Felicia Hemans (1793–1835),

Letitia Elizabeth Landon (1802–1838), and Sara Coleridge (1802–1852) could conduct impressive careers that included poetic composition as a major component.[1] Though the existence of the blues partly explains why these following generations of women poets could be so successful and why their numbers could increase so quickly, we have to construct a larger picture which will enable us to view women's poetry as a sociocultural phenomenon, as well as a literary one.

The bluestockings are still operating partly under the ideology of the Augustan coffeehouse. Like Dryden, Pope, Swift, and Addison, they see themselves as writing primarily for a literary coterie, which represents the best minds of their society, and which sets the standards that other readers and writers can emulate. Their freedom to scribble is seen as a part of the larger freedom to converse; their liberty to risk literary crossdressing derives mainly from their class status. They do not so much desire to change literary discourse, its themes and forms, as to alter the practice of that discourse by making women active participants within it. By the time the next generation of women writers (those born in the mid-eighteenth century) have begun to achieve their fame, the role of the coterie as the organizing institution of literary production has diminished, and the bluestocking parlor, which has given them their literary credentials and has made their connections with male writers, is being left behind for the larger twin worlds of domestic duties and state politics. And it is not a coincidence that as we move from the bluestocking matrons to their daughters, we also move from the highest class to the middle classes, from married women with expendable wealth and leisure to spinsters who are pressured to make a living and housewives who have pressing duties within the home, from women who talk about the need for female education to women who set up schools and serve as schoolmistresses and governesses, from women who have a more relaxed eighteenth-century view of religion to women who are more fervent about religion; from women who serve as patrons at a greater distance from politics and poverty to women who lead lives immersed in politics and social service to the middle and lower classes.

As the publishing industry, which views the poem as a marketable commodity, erodes the role of patronage and subscription, and the common reader supplants the coterie, so the face of female writing changes dramatically from aristocratic scribbling (poetry conducted as a leisured avocation in the security of a stable hierarchy) to bourgeois publishing in which the writer is seen as a sort of freelancing handmaiden who has indirectly a sociomoral obligation to the state because she writes to civilize, moderate, and chasten an increasingly factionalized and fractious citizenry. Although this evolution corresponds to the movement from Pope to Wordsworth, the female writer's desire to nurture culture as a sociomoral handmaiden competes with the romantic's claim to father culture from the power of isolated natural desire. And whereas the male romantic sees his problem primarily as the capacity to break continuity in order to establish the self-fathering strength of his own voice over culture, the female writer's problem is primarily one of establishing continuity in the midst of her own attempt to give birth to a new voice, the feminine poet, who wants her power to emanate not from the isolated experience of self but from the vested authority of culture as a whole.

Even though they write as women, the Augustan foremothers, and to an extent the bluestockings, do not tend to think of themselves as constituting a feminine tradition separate from the male tradition; indeed, their point is to inhabit as thoroughly as possible male tradition while making it amenable to female scribblers. Since the feminine itself is still defined as inherently non-literary and subintellectual, for women to write *feminine* poetry would seem to defeat their purpose, and yet it would be impossible for any woman living during the early eighteenth century to write without being made self-conscious that she is a woman writing.

2

Take for example Lady Mary Wortley Montagu (1689–1762), a woman who is able to achieve notoriety in her own time only by entering the fray of Augustan infighting and jeopardizing her reputation as a lady. Lady Mary, born a generation before the central blues, could have taken advantage of the bluestocking syndrome toward the end of her life, but she refuses to, preferring instead to work under the paradigm of the masculine Augustan coterie. Her identification with the established masculine tradition is evidenced as well by the strategies, forms, and subjects of her writing, where she everywhere pleads for acceptance even as she demands recognition. Ironically, as she makes herself visible and influential (sometimes admired, sometimes scorned) in the warring male camps of Augustan literary life, she sacrifices her more "militant" feminist voice either to anonymous or post-humous publication. In order to be an equal, she moderates her feminine voice by speaking conventionally as a male writer is expected to, and accordingly whenever she speaks as a woman for women, she makes herself even more invisible by actually pretending to be a male writing or by not publishing what she has written.

Lady Mary is introduced to the world of the Augustan coffeehouse at an early age, but appropriately her entry into that world is made in jest. Louisa Stuart (1757–1851), Lady Mary's granddaughter, proudly records the incident in her "Biographical Anecdotes" for the first collected edition (1837) of Lady Mary's works. Lady Mary's father, Lord Kingston, "[a]s a leader of the fashionable world, and a strenuous Whig in party, . . . of course belonged to the Kit-cat club. One day, at a meeting to choose toasts for the year, a whim seized him to nominate [his daughter], then not eight years old, a candidate; alleging that she was far prettier than any lady on their list." Lord Kingston has the girl "finely dressed" and brought to the tavern. "The company consisting of some of the most eminent men in England, she went from the lap of one poet, or patriot, or statesman, to the arms of another, was feasted with sweetmeats, overwhelmed with caresses, and, what perhaps already pleased her better than either, heard her wit and beauty loudly extolled on every side" (*Essays and Poems* 9). Lady Mary cherishes this day, according to Louisa Stuart: "never again, throughout her whole future life, did she pass so happy a day" (9). Whether this event sparks Lady Mary's desire to make her presence felt in the wider world of politics and letters usually closed to women we cannot say, but it perfectly emblematizes the situation of a woman writer in Augustan England. Even when she is praised for her wit (and beauty), she is taken as a rare object to be admired; even when she is allowed to enter the male terrain of the coterie, her entry is a suspension of the rules, rather than a normative act, and her presence becomes a vehicle for paternalistic jesting.

Collegial learning is so important to the bluestocking and her predecessor because in Augustan ideology, poetry is produced, transmitted, and valued as such, and because this is exactly what she is denied as a result of her gender. The irony of the father's attention is not missed on Stuart, who points out that his admiration is not followed up with education:

There can be no dispute that Lady Mary showed early signs of more than ordinary abilities; but whether they induced Lord Kingston to have her bred up with her brother and taught Latin and Greek by his tutor, is not so well ascertained. . . . Most likely not; most likely her father, whose amusement in her ceased when she grew past the age of sitting on a knee and playing with a doll, consigned all his daughters alike to the care and custody of such a good home-spun governess as her letters describe. (*Essays and Poems* 9–10)

Complaining of her own education as "one of the worst in the world," Lady Mary becomes an advocate for women's education. As she labors "to acquire what may be termed masculine knowledge . . . , she was by no means disposed to neglect works of fancy and fiction, but got by heart all the poetry that came in her way, and indulged herself in the luxury of reading every romance as yet invented" (10–11). By the time Louisa Stuart is writing, the distinction between "masculine knowledge" and other fanciful (feminized and marginalized) discourse can almost be taken for granted; for Lady Mary, however, poetry, fiction, and even romance would be more readily subsumed as a kind of masculine knowledge that the young woman must labor to acquire or must beg to be given. Fortunately for Lady Mary, she possesses "that eager devouring appetite for reading, seldom felt but in the first freshness of intelligent youth," and she has access to men, such as her uncle William Fielding, "who perceived her capacity, corresponded with her, and encouraged her pursuit of information. And she herself acknowledges her obligations to Bishop Burnet for 'condescending to direct the studies of a girl'" (10).

In Augustan England a young lady with literary ambitions could easily be silenced as much by the father's benign neglect as by his conscious command. And since the husband's neglect or command could be even more stifling to her ambition, the choice of a spouse is crucial in determining how much space she will be given to scribble in. Unfortunately, as almost in the case of Lady Mary, the choice of husband is not hers to make. Whether it is love or literary ambition, or some combination of both, that leads Lady Mary to betray her father's command cannot be known, but it is clear that she is determined not to be totally ruled by the law of the father. When she expresses a desire to marry Edward Wortley instead of her father's choice, her father threatens to cloister her and reduce her inheritance to "a moderate annuity. Relying upon the effect of these threats, he proceeded as if she had given her fullest and freest consent; settlements were drawn, wedding-clothes bought, the day was appointed, and everything made ready, when she left the house to marry Mr. Wortley" (18). It may be difficult for us fully to imagine "[t]he father's rage," as Stuart requests, just as it may be difficult for us to realize the degree of courage entailed in Lady Mary's disobedient act, the kind of courage, however, that would also be required if she were to attempt literary production.

Furthermore, in choosing her own desire over her father's command, Lady Mary is taking a calculated, but audacious risk, for Wortley himself was a relatively unknown factor. Her knowledge of him by social necessity could not have been intimate, having come primarily through secret letters exchanged through the auspices of Wortley's sister. "Polite literature was his passion," according to Stuart, and he socialized with "such companions as Steele, Garth, Congreve, Mainwaring, . . . [and] Addison" (14). From Stuart's description of their meeting, however, it is clear that Lady Mary could surmise that Wortley would be relatively supportive of her endeavors as a learned lady:

His society was principally male; the wits and politicians of that day forming a class quite distinct from the "white-gloved beaus" attendant upon ladies. Indeed, as the education of women had then reached its very lowest ebb, and if not co-quettes, or gossips, or diligent card-players, their best praise was to be notable housewives, Mr. Wortley, however fond of his sister, could have no particular motive to seek the acquaintance of her companions. His surprise and delight were the greater, when one afternoon, having by chance loitered in her apartment till visitors arrived, he saw Lady Mary Pierrepont for the first time, and, on entering into conversation with her, found, in addition to beauty that charmed him, not only brilliant wit, but a thinking and cultivated mind. He was especially struck with the discovery that she understood Latin and could relish his beloved classics. (15)

Alluding to the effect of the bluestocking circles of her own day, Stuart brings attention to the markedly different relations between men and women before these circles are organized. Even though male "wits and politicians" continue to express surprise on discovering learned women far into the nineteenth century, the chances of encountering such women become greater, partly as a result of the bluestockings, in turn giving women greater opportunities both to find supportive male mates and to influence the masculine world of politics and letters. Lady Mary's opportunities for such encounters depend much more on chance and on her own individual determination than on social arrangement. It is through her husband that she meets Addison, who, impressed by her critique of his play *Cato,* allows her to contribute an essay to the *Spectator*. Notably, Addison does not allow her critique of *Cato* to be published, even though he "altered his play in several ways to conform to her suggestions" (see Halsband and Grundy, *Essays and Poems* 62–68).

Perhaps Lady Mary's most daring publication is a weekly newspaper *The Nonsense of Common-Sense* printed from December 1737 to March 1738. According to Robert Halsband and Isobel Grundy, the editors of *Essays and Poems:*

The title of her paper could have been suggested by an essay in *Common Sense* (the Opposition paper) on 10 December 1737: 'I am Nonsense, a Terrestrial Goddess, your avow'd and irreconcileable Foe. . . . I have the Ladies, the Poetasters, and the M[inistry] on my side.' One week later the first issue of *The Nonsense of Common-Sense* appeared. Although its anonymous author poses as an impartial commentator on manners, morals, and politics its purpose was clearly to defend Walpole and his ministry from the attacks of the Opposition press. (105)

Taking up arms against the Tories, Lady Mary poses as a *male* commentator, even though she is *always* careful to address her audience as "Gentlemen and Lady Readers" (106). Exploiting the pose of an educated, disinterested gentleman who is capable of rising above politics to address issues of concern to the whole nation, Lady Mary examines wide-ranging matters, including taxes, interest, trade and manufacture, corruption, censorship, literature, opera, virtue, treatment of laborers and the poor, women's education.

Like Pope and the other Augustan scribblers, Lady Mary, even as she identifies herself with one camp, attempts to exempt her own discourse from the internecine cycle of attack and counterattack engaged in by manly warring cliques:

[A]s this author [of *Common Sense*] takes the Liberty of blameing whatever he dislikes, I will positively praise whatever I think right, thô I foresee that I shall be supported in this design by no party whatever. The usual way of answering one Satyr is by another, and the conclusion drawn from reading both sides, by any Indifferent Man, is, that there are Rogues on both sides, which is no very comfortable Refflection. Now I will leave *all* Rogues to the remorse of their own consciences, and the confusion that is the natural consequence of ill concerted Villainy without any mention of them at all, and proceed to the defence of any reasonable attempt I see, thô it should be attended with the most unreasonable Murmurs against it. (106)

Just as she intones a disinterested voice above party faction, she claims a voice above the prejudice of gender. Ironically, in order to speak *authoritatively* about and for her own sex, she finds that she must speak as a man, as an "Admirer" of women, which means as a male who can be charmed by their wit as much as bewitched by their charms. Lady Mary purposively inverts the usual mode of praise that men practice. Instead of viewing those little feminine vanities as a naturally charming consequence of woman's real beauty, she sarcastically but sympathetically points to those vanities as a natural consequence of an "imaginary Empire of Beauty," which keeps women placated, powerless, and uneducated:

I have allways been an Humble Admirer of the Fair Sex, nay, I beleive [*sic*] I think of them with more tenderness than any Man in the World. I do not only look upon them as Objects of pleasure, but I compassionate the many Hardships both Nature and Custom has subjected them to. I never expose the Foibles to which Education has enclin'd them; and (contrary to all other Authors) I see with a favourable Eye the little vanitys with which they amuse themselves, and am glad they can find in the imaginary Empire of Beauty, a consolation for being excluded [from] every part of Government in the State. But with all this fondness for them, I am shock'd when I see their Influence in opposition to Reason, Justice, and the common Welfare of the Nation. (109)

Even without knowing that this is actually a woman writing, the ironies are rich. Lady Mary ridicules the prototypical male author who favors women so much that he would never dare expose the foibles that result from their education. Cleverly, Lady Mary makes her male persona both the butt of her gentle ridicule and the source of correcting masculine misprision. The man who *never* takes women to task for their foibles is as guilty as the man who sees women as morally and intellectually defective. Indeed, the logic derives from the same premise: that it is natural for women to have such foibles. Ironically the man in this essay does take women to task, even as he claims he never does, by positively demanding a higher standard of behavior, encouraging women to exchange their obsession with an "Ornamental" life for a concern with the economic welfare of the nation. By noting women's occasional and indirect "Influence in opposition to Reason, Justice, and the common Welfare of the Nation" through their vain concerns with ornament, Lady Mary's male persona ironically brings attention to how women *should* be allowed a healthier kind of direct influence within the system of government itself. In a later essay, Lady Mary anticipates Wollstonecraft's argument against double-standard education, ending her essay with this call to arms: "Begin then Ladies by paying those Authors with Scorn and contempt who with the sneer of affected Admiration would throw you below the Dignity of the Human Species" (134).

Like her prose, Lady Mary's poetry derives its force from imitation of the masculine Augustan tradition, and the tension between her masked feminine voice and aggressively masculine Augustan forms gives shape to much of her literary production. According to Halsband and Grundy, "[t]he tradition supplied her not only with forms but with satirical or moral stances based on inheritance from or reaction against the past. She had the gift of successfully embodying her idiosyncratic opinions and attitudes in a verse style heavily influenced by her contemporaries and immediate predecessors, especially Dryden and the Pope of the 1717 *Works*" (172). As a result, much of her poetry is allusive, satirical, topical, and occasional, possessing the socializing characteristic of Popian verse described in Chapter 2. Even though she knows well the dangers that await a woman who enters as a combatant in Augustan polemical poetry, she probably feels that she has no choice, if she is to be taken seriously. Halsband and Grundy write: "As a woman and an aristocrat, Lady Mary frequently expressed horror at the idea of writing for print. Yet she may well have connived at or even arranged for the publication of her verse attacks on Pope and Swift" (172). As the blue-stockings bring poetry into the parlor, they help to diminish this inimical aspect of poetry-making; by facilitating the idea that serious poetry can be as much the sincere expression of refined natural sentiment as the hardhitting match of wit or the battleground of sociopolitical dispute, the bluestockings also make it easier for women to write poetry without being compelled to conceive of themselves as warring camps.

Even when Lady Mary exploits the gunpowder of Augustan satire, there is a timbre of wistful sentiment that is audible. For instance, her poem "On a Lady mistaking a Dy[e]ing Trader for a Dying Lover" is clearly a rewriting of Pope's *Rape of the Lock*. Just as her strictures against affectedly admiring men apply well to Pope and his satire, so her poem is as much a subtle complaint against Pope's view of women as it is an ostensibly compliant rewriting of his poem. Pope writes in the preface to the *Rape of the Lock,* the poem "was intended only to divert a few young Ladies, who have good Sense and good Humour enough, to laugh not only at their Sex's little un-guarded Follies, but at their own" (*Poems* 217). Pope introduces Belinda, the lady he will allow us to toast in admiration and in jest, in the following manner:

> *Belinda* still her downy Pillow prest,
> Her Guardian *Sylph* prolong'd the balmy Rest.
> 'Twas he had summon'd to her silent Bed.
> The Morning-Dream that hover'd o'er her Head.
> (Canto 1, 19–22)

Lady Mary alludes to Pope's beginning when she has her heroine reclining in the same way at the beginning of her poem:

> As Chloris on her downy Pillow lay,
> 'Twixt sleep and wake the morning slid away,
> Soft at her Chamber door a tap she heard,
> She listen'd, and again; no one appear'd.
> Who's there? the sprightly Nymph with courage cries.
> Ma'am, 'tis one who for your La'ship *dies*.
> (1–6)

Just as Pope appears to be merely ridiculing the little fanciful world of women's "Empire of Beauty," but is actually goodhumoredly praising that empire, so Lady Mary appears to be doing the same, but her satire is laced with the ridicule of modulated indignation. Pope brings to life a machinery of sylphs and nymphs, gnomes and salamanders to help us delve into the psychology of woman's superficial kingdom of vanity. Lady Mary *names* Chloris a "sprightly Nymph," but only in order to stress the real difference between Chloris's dreamlife and her dreary reality. Just as Lady Mary has attacked women's "ornamental" life in *The Nonsense of Commonsense,* urg-ing them to forsake their vanity and idleness for intellectual and economic productivity in the life of the nation, so here she subtly condemns Chloris's life of idle, dreamy leisure. As Chloris is comfortable on her "downy Pillow," the morning slides away. The heroine is so comfortable in her little world trapped between fanciful silken dreams and idle reality, that she mistakes the flesh-and-blood tradesman at her door for one of Pope's soft guardian sylphs.

The joke is on Chloris, who, like Belinda, looks in the mirror to appraise her own bewitching beauty. A woman who is silly enough to think that women's beauty is so powerful that it literally kills their lovers is also self-deceived enough not to be able to see the superficiality of the mirror's world. Lady Mary, too, is dealing with social psychology, but her analysis is quite different from Pope's. If women are silly, how much are men also to blame, for how often have poets claimed to die when denied their ladies' embraces? "Mankind the more you Court the farther fly, / And 'tis for me and only me they dye" (18–19). Chloris's words are truer than she realizes. As we shall see in another poem, Lady Mary is very suspicious of the logic that requires women to ally themselves unquestioningly to "constancy" and chastity, forever fleeing the courting lover. It *is* only for womankind that men *dye*. And as Lady Mary points out in her essays, whole industries have been based on dying and ornamenting expensive apparel for women, *foreign* industries that directly compete with the domestic wool and cotton industries of Britain. This is what she means when she criticizes women for their wasteful vanity, which indirectly negatively influences the economic productivity of a nation.

Like Pope, Lady Mary ridicules the facial masks that women create to enhance their beauty. Chloris asks: "Why were these Eyes for such destruction giv'n? / 'Tis not my fault, I did not make one feature" (25–26). The question of blame reverberates throughout the poem. To what extent is Chloris at fault for her foibles? Previously she says she "must blame" "Prudence" for not allowing her to receive the dying lover as warmly as otherwise she might. If she is to blame, then it is a cruel fate, to be so impotent and at the same time so at fault. This is clear from the "tempestuous Scene" that ensues when Chloris discovers her mistake.

> She wept, she rav'd, invok'd the powers above
> Who give no Ear when old Maids talk of Love,
> Fruitless her prayers and impotent her rage
> Yet fierce as when two Females do engage.
> (34–37)

Her rage is a cause of her impotence, as much as it is a result of it. She is powerless because of her moody feminine temper, which takes trifling matters seriously and ignores serious matters.

But Chloris is also angry because of her impotence, as we see in the final section of the poem. As Chloris turns to address her female audience, the tone of the poem changes slightly from bantering ridicule to wistful sympathy (similar to Pope's tone change at the end of *The Dunciad*).

> 'But let us to our selves for once be just
> 'And see our own decays and wrinkles first,
> 'When e'er to melting sighs we lend an ear

'Think youth and beauty make the Man sincere,
'No other powers their stubborn hearts can move,
'Did ever Vertue light the torch of Love?
'From sad experience I this truth declare,
'I'm now abandon'd, thô I once was Fair.'

(55–62)

By transforming the beautiful young Belinda into a deceived old maid, Lady Mary also transforms the genre and its pointed lessons. These lines, even as they remain in character, remain in Chloris's quoted voice, also speak *for* all women's "sad experience." Since men are too busy admiring women to tell them the truth, women must tell it to themselves *"first,"* for man's way is to flatter women in earnestness first and then to blame them in jest after women have begun to take themselves all too seriously. As the blame shifts from self-deceived women to deceiving men, the poem interconnects that burden of guilt for women *and* men. Man's sincerity and insincerity alike lead to woman's self-deception, just as her "Vertue" leads to both his "Love" and his refusal to love, leads to his "stubborn" heart. It is appropriate that the poem, in an attempt to break this cycle of missharing, to use the concept that we applied to Percy Shelley's poetry, concludes with a simple truth. Chloris's capacity to see herself for what she is—an old maid abandoned by the men who once saw her as beautiful—only begins the process of re-claiming power out of the rage of impotence. Although the conclusion of the poem verges on the kind of sentimental poetry fostered by the bluestockings and their feminine descendants, the poem technically remains within the bounds of Augustan poetics and ideology.

As we have already seen in Tighe's poetry, the acceptance of inconstancy and fleeting nature is a crucial theme for feminine poets. Lady Mary also anticipates this concern while remaining within the bounds of Augustan poetics. In "Satturday: The Small Pox" from her *Eclogues,* Lady Mary ex-ploits traditional pastoral to write verse that teeters between Popian satire and the kind of sentiment fostered by the daughters of the bluestockings. Flavia, the heroine of "Satturday," is similar to Chloris, but her beauty is threatened by disease rather than time. It is important to note also that Lady Mary was no stranger to the ravages of smallpox. Not only had she herself experienced the fear of being marked by the disease; she also played a vital role in legitimizing the smallpox innoculation in Britain as she conducted experiments on her own children to prove the effectiveness of the vaccination and as she attacked the timid and inept medical establishment in a pseud-onymous article in a major periodical.

Like Chloris, Flavia is forced to realize the impotence of her feminine situation, but without the profound psychological deepening that Chloris experiences. Even though Flavia remains on the surface, the reader is en-couraged to delve beneath.

Monarchs, and Beauties rule with equal sway,
All strive to serve, and Glory to obey,

> Alike unpity'd when depos'd they grow,
> Men mock the Idol of their Former vow.
>
> (85–88)

Deflating the world of political conquest by equating it with the "Empire of Beauty," Lady Mary again anticipates the insights of later poets like Barbauld, Tighe, Baillie, and Hemans. As we shall see, they will carry this idea much further as they articulate the relation between domestic affection and civil duty.

Because Lady Mary's poems overtly embrace the socializing rituals of male Augustan poetry, many can be printed in her lifetime, but others, more defiant, can not. "Epistle from Mrs. Y[onge] to her Husband" is one such poem. The poem alludes to a scandalous trial in which William Yonge sues his adulterous wife and her lover. Even though Yonge himself was a notorious libertine, he wins the case and gains most of her fortune after having his wife's love letters read to the House of Lords (see Halsband and Grundy 230). The poem is an enraged complaint in the voice of the victimized wife, criticizing the double standard which allows men to gratify their "high Ambition" in the "Sweets of . . . recover'd Freedom," while "[t]he Judging World expects our Constancy" (see lines 14, 69–80). Unlike "On a Lady" or the *Eclogues,* "Epistle from Mrs. Y[onge]" bursts the seams of masculine Augustan ideology.

Even though Lady Mary is cautious in moderating her feminine desire so that it harmonizes with masculine Augustan expectations, her poeticizing immediately makes her a target for men's jesting. When she is embraced by John Hervey (1696–1743) and his coterie, she becomes an enemy to Pope. As we have seen, Hervey is noted for his effeminacy, which Pope exploits to delineate the productive virility of his own clique and line of descent. It is difficult to say whether Hervey's gender-bending public image makes him less threatened by a female scribbler; certainly it must have made him an even easier target for Pope's satire. When he calls Sporus "that Thing of silk" who speaks "florid Impotence," and pictures him in the role of Milton's Satan, "at the Ear of *Eve,*" Pope is lashing out at Lady Mary as well as at Hervey (see *Epistle to Dr. Arbuthnot* 305–367). When Pope is lambasting another woman writer, Eliza Haywood, in *The Dunciad,* he suggests that female spoilers are more "shameless scribblers" than male spoilers, because "That sex . . . ought least to be capable to such malice or impudence" (see *Poems* pp. 384–385 and 741). That Lady Mary probably collaborates with Hervey in writing satires against Pope, such as "Verses Address'd to the Imitator of the First Satire of the Second Book of Horace" (see *Essays and Poems* 265), only makes her all the more vulnerable. Lady Mary has neither the security of a well-defined feminine role, nor the comfort of a coterie that is fostered by women for both sexes. Instead, she is forced to write as a fellow scribbler even though she is not fully embraced as a fellow (a male, an equal, a supported scholar), and conceiving of poetry as delimited by the men who hold sway over its tradition, she has to find ways of expressing the uniqueness of her difference within a gendered society by exploiting poetic forms that assume the homogeneity of the writer's socializing status and function.

3

Even though the bluestockings, too, conceptualize literary activity in primarily Augustan terms, by redefining the coterie to include both genders, they also begin to redefine the practice of writing poetry. Just as the blues are nurturing aspiring young male writers, they are also nurturing aspiring young female writers both by their example and, by their support. The generation of women writers nurtured by the blues are freer to assert themselves as writers, but ironically part of that freedom derives from the distinction that can be made between a learned crossdressing lady writer and a more appropriately feminine writer, between the militant, pushy newcomer and her more welcomed compliant, conformable daughter. By examining the work of two prodigies of the bluestockings, Hannah More and Anna Laetitia Barbauld, we can see the difference that having visible, influential foremothers makes. Not only are More and Barbauld strong enough to begin to reject the tradition of masculine poeticizing as a uniform paradigm to which women writers must unilaterally adhere; they are also self-confident enough to revise the outlook of their immediate foremothers, the bluestockings. As they reorient the relation between the female poet and masculine tradition, and as they begin to emphasize the relation between the female poet and her traditional role within culture, writers like More and Barbauld also begin to establish, for the first time in British history, a discernable tradition of feminine poetry. What we see in these two transitional figures, then, is not the relatively smooth ideological field that characterizes the next generation of feminine writers like Baillie, Hemans, and L.E.L., but rather an extremely unsettled configuration in which contradictions abound.

Hannah More is perhaps the most important pivotal figure in the movement from the Augustan and bluestocking scribbler to the feminine poetess, for she more than any other establishes the nineteenth-century woman writer as the conscience of culture. I would suggest that More's influence in counter-revolutionary England is as crucial as Madame de Stael's influence in revolutionary France, but whereas de Stael exerts her influence primarily among the politicians and wits of Europe, More finds ways of also spreading her influence down and directly to the masses. She helps to mobilize the nineteenth-century publishing phenomenon, bringing the power of print to the lower-class reader, and bringing to bear the increasing power of the common reader on the publishing process. As Richard Altick has pointed out in his classic study on this topic, the Sunday-school movement, of which More herself was a prime force, brought literacy to the lower classes. And during the pamphlet wars of the 1790s, millions of cheap political tracts, revolutionary and counterrevolutionary, directed at these new readers, are sold in unprecedented numbers. Holding guard against vanguard writers like Thomas

Paine, More is the most successful writer for this market, producing anti-jacobin tracts that sell millions of copies in just a few years (see *The English Common Reader* 67–77). Ironically, it is political factionalism—one of those forms of behavior that women are supposed to avoid—which lowers More's sights to the emerging market of common readers and raises her writing career to a level of popularity not experienced before by women or men. Because More's tracts, however, are aimed at calming a volatile situation, rather than fanning the fires of political dissension, and because they are concerned with the plight of the poor—a justifiable and even obligatory feminine concern—their implications for women's changing political status are submerged beneath their more overtly feminine motives, objectives, and appeals. Appealing to the most traditional conception of women's place, More ironically takes the bluestocking adventure a step farther by insisting that the female writer is the guardian of mass sociomoral culture, as well as the nurturer of high literary culture.

Appropriately, Hannah More's literary career begins when she at the age of sixteen composes a pastoral drama for the girls at the private venture school in Bristol, a school which she manages along with her four spinster sisters. According to M. G. Jones, these venture schools become common during the latter part of the eighteenth century to accommodate "the steady rise in wealth, numbers, and influence of men engaged in trade and commerce on an ever-growing scale" (*Hannah More* 5). While the male school focuses on more utilitarian kinds of knowledge than the traditional endowed grammar school in order to prepare boys for their new positions in trade and manufacture, the girls' school serves a more symbolic function. It represents the hope of bourgeois families, beginning to make their fortunes and exert their influence, to rise into the gentle classes. Thus, the female schools focus on the kinds of ornamental and fashionable knowledge that would be expected of young ladies, rather than on the more "masculine" kind of learning which the bluestockings themselves promoted. "Women of all sorts and conditions, with or without character or intellectual qualifications, found in the private venture school a not too ill-paid means of livelihood," writes Jones. "Among them the More sisters, who set up their school on the crest of the wave, held an honourable place" (7).

Ironically, in setting up her school, More must repress the desire to engage her own students in the kinds of masculine discourse that she herself desired as a child. Jacob More, Hannah's father, a schoolmaster at a charity school, responds to his daughter's "eager request to study classics and mathematics." But, according to Jones, his instruction "came to an abrupt end when he discovered that Hannah's ability was superior to that of the schoolboys under his care. Mathematical prowess such as hers threatened to be was unfeminine and not to be encouraged. Deprived by parental disapproval of the astringent training which mathematics is alleged to bestow, the eager child, as she grew older, gave full rein to the 'velvet studies' of history and of literature" (12–13).

Her work in the Park Street School represents her unusual class position. As the school grows and More's name becomes known for her literary accomplishments, the gentry begin to send their daughters there, increasing her links with the upperclasses with whom she desires to associate. Bristol, with its growing intellectual, fashionable, and literary life, also affords More with opportunities to make connections and be admired as a literary lady. Perhaps the most important opportunity, however, which determines her independence and enables her to leave schoolmistressing for a life of social service and literary entrepreneurism, is created by a situation that is otherwise humiliating. After her fiancée postponed their wedding date two times, he does not show up at the church, but instead sends a note of apology through his groomsman. After More breaks the engagement, he arranges to give her an annuity without her knowledge. "It was this settlement which, when time had softened the bitterness of so humiliating an experience, gave a provincial schoolmarm . . . financial independence" (Jones 16). More's outlook remains that of a "provincial schoolmarm," however, even as she mingles in the bluestocking circles of London, helps Edmund Burke to win his parliamentary seat in Bristol, gives advice to the royal family on the education of Princess Charlotte, sets up and oversees a large, complex network of working class schools for children and adults, is consulted by bishops and state ministers in a time of national crisis, and becomes entangled in various public controversies as a result of her tremendous influence and fame. From beginning to end, Jones writes, "[s]he professed no interest in [politics] and regarded them as a man's province and unfitted for women" (20). Much of her writing is devoted to working out this paradoxical creed in which a woman could be, in terms of religion, politics, education, and literature, one of the most influential individuals in the nation and yet not see herself as intruding on masculine terrains of power.[2]

More's book *Strictures on the Modern System of Female Education* published in 1799 calls women to arms in the same way that Burke calls men to the defence of British custom and "liberty" in his *Reflections on the Revolution in France*. More creates the same sense of urgency, so that her treatise becomes not just another how-to book on the education of girls, but rather a rallying summons to make women aware of the crisis their culture faces and aware of what they can do to avert that crisis:

In this moment of alarm and peril, I would call on them with a 'warning voice,' which should stir up every latent principle in their minds, and kindle every slumbering energy in their hearts: I would call on them to come forward, and contribute their full and fair proportion towards the saving of their country. But I would call on them to come forward, without departing from the refinement of their character, without derogating from the dignity of their rank, without blemishing the delicacy of their sex; I would call them to the best and most appropriate exertion of their power, to raise the depressed tone of public morals, and to awaken the drowsy spirit of religious principle. . . . For, on the use which women of the superior class may now be disposed to make of that power delegated to them by courtesy of custom, by the honest gallantry of the heart, by the imperious control of virtuous affections, by the habits of civilized states, by the usages of polished society; on the use, I say, which they shall hereafter make of this influence, will depend, in no low degree, the well-being of those states, and the virtue and happiness, nay perhaps the very existence, of that society. (*Works of Hannah More* 1: 313)

Like the romantics, More is emphasizing the role of mental influence over physical strength in the sustenance and advancement of "civilized states." The best way to avert revolution in England, she suggests, is for women to use their influence over "private" moral life to redirect the political course of the nation. "Your private exertions may at this moment be contributing to the future happiness, your domestic neglect, to the future ruin of your country" (1: 322). Like all of her writings, More's *Strictures* is addressed to a specific audience, "women of rank and fortune." More writes: "Among the talents for the application of which women of the higher class will be peculiarly accountable, there is one, the importance of which they can scarcely rate too highly. This talent is influence" (1: 313). By considering influence a "talent" that can be put to use in civil life, More is exploiting the chivalric tradition, but at the same time she subtly shifts the focus of that tradition from feminine passivity to feminine activity: "The general state of civilized society depends, more than those are aware who are not accustomed to scrutinize into the springs of human action, on the prevailing sentiments and habits of women, and on the nature and degree of the estimation in which they are held" (1: 313). More is careful to distinguish what is required of the sexes in her period from the "excesses of the heroic ages": "I do not wish to bring back the frantic reign of chivalry, nor to reinstate women in that fantastic empire in which they then sat enthroned in the hearts, or rather in the imaginations of men" (1: 315). Even as More reaffirms Edmund Burke's appeal to ancient hierarchical values as the source of resolution for present cultural crises, she deflects his nostalgia for "the frantic reign of chivalry," when women's influence was limited by men's admiration, limited by the way ladies were "enthroned" within the imaginations, rather than the hearts, of men. Instead of bemoaning the death of the age of chivalry, as Burke does, More attempts to exploit the supposed moral influence granted to ladies during that reign but without also "reinstating" the "excesses" of that reign, which reduced women's real talents to an imaginary influence by lifting them above the world of realpolitik in which genuine influence is exerted. Like Lady Mary, More recognizes the disadvantage of being in the position of looking "down on her adoring votaries from the pedestal to which an absurd idolatry had lifted her" (1: 315). But neither is she advising ladies to take to the streets:

At this period when our country can only hope to stand by opposing a bold and noble *unanimity* to the most tremendous confederacies against religion, and order, and governments, which the world ever saw, what an accession would it bring to the public strength, could we prevail on beauty, and rank, and talents, and virtue, confederating their several powers, to exert themselves with a patriotism at once firm and feminine, for the general good! I am not sounding an alarm to female warriors, or exciting female politicians: I hardly know which of the two is the most disgusting and unnatural character. Propriety is to a woman what the great Roman critic says action is to an orator; it is the first, the second, the third requisite. (1: 313)

And yet has not More herself, as one of the most prolific polemicists of her day, become a politician in the truest sense? More's rhetoric is designed to repress this question both from her readers and from herself. This paradox, that a woman must exert the most public influence without becoming a public spectacle, is the stumbling block which More transforms into a stepping stone, and the paradox applies not only to overtly political writing but also to more "ornamental" activities like writing poetry.

At the heart of her project, then, lies More's defence of, if not defensiveness over, the femininity of her own publicity:

A woman may be knowing, active, witty and amusing; but without propriety she cannot be amiable. Propriety is the centre in which all the lines of duty and of agreeableness meet. It is to character what proportion is to figure, and grace to attitude. It does not depend on any one perfection, but it is the result of general excellence. It shows itself by a regular, orderly, undeviating course; and never starts from its sober orbit into any splendid eccentricities; for it would be ashamed of such praise as it might extort by any deviations from its proper path. It renounces all commendation but what is characteristic; and I would make it the criterion of true taste, right principle, and genuine feeling, in a woman, whether she would be less touched with all the flattery of romantic and exaggerated panegyric than with that beautiful picture of correct and elegant propriety which Milton draws of our first mother. . . . (1: 313–314)

Though Milton's Eve may not be the best example she could have chosen, More furnishes here the ideological stance and the tone that will characterize women's presence in literary discourse for the duration of the nineteenth century. "Strictures," then, is the perfect word for her treatise, for it indicates how More is educating women to enforce on themselves the propriety that will allow them to forge a new role in an increasingly literate culture. And although her suggestions for feminine education are traditional to the point of being reactionary, the "talent" displayed in order to extend feminine "influence" speaks louder than her words. There is no topic that she cannot broach, no idea that she cannot propose, no audience that she cannot address, as long as she does so with "propriety."

Like Lady Mary, More is concerned with the tendency toward viewing feminine virtue as ornamental virtue. Much of *Strictures,* and also of her treatise *Hints for Forming the Character of a Young Princess,* is devoted to combatting the idea of an *accomplished* young lady, since, she suggests, this phrase implies that feminine virtue lies in accomplishing merely the "ornamental" or fine arts. For the same reason, More is an enemy of the cult of sensibility, though ironically her circle included writers like Beattie, Henry Mackenzie, and Horace Walpole, whom we associate with this cult. Like Wordsworth, More believes that the popularity of German tales is eroding British taste and morals. When More rails against these writers of "sensibility," however, she is primarily aiming at the school of natural rights promulgated by Rousseau and the perfectibilists in England, naming Wollstonecraft's *Wrongs of Women* as the major offender (see 1: 318–321). Like Jane Austen, More places "sense" over "sensibility" not because she does not value tender feeling, but rather because she thinks that "sensibility" has become a pejorative word encouraging excessive and affected modes of behavior (see especially Chapter 16 "On the danger of an ill-directed Sensibility" 1: 378–385). Also aware that women have been taught to feel as a substitute for thinking and judging, More is anxious to redress that imbalance. "It is prudent," she writes, "to endeavour to discover the natural bent of the individual character: and having found it, to direct your force against that side on which the warp lies, that you may lessen by counteraction the defect which you might be promoting, by applying your aid in a contrary direction" (1: 379).

The biggest problem with "ill-directed Sensibility," in More's eyes, is that it fosters self-indulgence, which in turn causes women to seek "flattery" and "celebrity," whereas "sober studies" direct her attention outward. A true bluestocking, More refuses to see the kinds of dangers in book-learning that men traditionally prognosticate for women. "The great uses of study to a woman," she says, "are to enable her to regulate her own mind, and to be instrumental to the good of others" (1: 363). The key is the idea of *regulation,* which means something quite different for More than for Wordsworth. For More, and the affectional poets who follow her, the internalization of passion and sentiment, practiced by Wordsworth, perverts the individual and culture itself. For her, feeling is not an inward-motivated or inward-moving process, but rather when properly directed is *always* both outward-motivated and outward-moving.

Like Lady Mary, More wants to erase the dreamworld of Belinda's mirror in order to bring the female outward into a more productive relation with culture:

> She should pursue every kind of study which . . . will lead her to be intent upon realities. . . . She should cultivate every study which, instead of stimulating her sensibility, will chastise it; which will neither create an excessive or a false refinement; which will give her definite notions; will bring the imagination under dominion; will lead her to think, to compare, to combine, to methodise; which will confer such a power of discrimination, that her judgment shall learn to reject what is dazzling, if it be not solid. (1: 363)

We could say that More's project is the converse of the romantic poet's. Whereas he wants to masculinize an increasingly marginalized and feminized activity, she wants to feminize an activity formerly perceived as a sign of masculine strength. Whereas he wants to make poetry powerfully productive by purging its tendency toward feminine delicacy, she wants to make feminine knowledge powerfully productive with*out* diminishing the aura of delicacy that it may be gaining; for the same reason that ornamentation is a threat to his bid for self-possession, it is the bane of her cultural marginalization.

More goes so far as to connect women's inferior education with their tendency to scribble: "It is because the superficial nature of their education furnishes them with a false and low standard of intellectual excellence, that women have too often become ridiculous by the unfounded pretensions of literary vanity" (1: 363). Men, of course, make the opposite charge: women scribble too much when they have intellectual pretensions. By discriminating between genuine feminine genius and pretension to genius (categories men will immediately recognize), she can claim proper literary pursuit for women while denying the necessary connection with presumptuous ambition and a crossdressing mode of life:

The truth is, women who are so puffed up with the conceit of talents as to neglect the plain duties of life, will not frequently be found to be women of the best abilities. And here may the author be allowed the gratification of observing, that those women of real genius and extensive knowledge, whose friendship has conferred honour and happiness on her own life, have been, in general, eminent for economy and the practice of domestic virtues. . . . (1: 364)

Needless to say, despite her conservative intention, the implication is radical. Women's literary genius is derived, she says, exactly from that sphere from which Thomas Moore wants to salvage masculine genius. More, however, has to assure her readers that feminine genius will not disrupt the traditional order of things: "Superior talents, however, are not so common, as, by their frequency, to offer much disturbance to the general course of human affairs" (1: 364). Because a lady genius is so concerned about her domestic duty, she often unjustly "tacitly accuses herself of neglecting her ordinary duties because she is a *genius*" (1: 364). On the other hand, false genius is found in the "romantic girl with a pretension to sentiment" whose study has been "her desultory poetical reading, in an elegy on a sick linnet, or sonnet on a dead lap-dog." Because she is "surrounded with fond and flattering friends," the overly sentimental girl blooms early and withers away when her poetry is placed in the public light by an "impartial critic."

While those more quiet women, who have meekly sat down in the humble shades of prose and prudence, by a patient perseverance in rational studies, rise afterward much higher in the scale of intellect, and acquire a much larger stock of sound knowledge for far better purposes than mere display. And though it may seem a contradiction, yet it will generally be found true, that girls who take to scribble, are the least studious, the least reflecting, and the least rational. They early acquire a false confidence in their own unassisted powers: it becomes more gratifying to their natural vanity to be always pouring out their minds on paper, than to be drawing into them fresh ideas from richer sources. The original stock, small perhaps at first, is soon spent. (1: 364)

More must create a pattern of development for female genius, for as we have already seen in Chapter 5 with Tighe and Keats, the female cannot simply follow established masculine rituals of literary maturation any more than the male can rely on emergent feminine rituals. We shall see that even for the later generations of affectional poets, this remains a serious issue. At the heart of the issue is the question of originality. "It will be necessary to combat vigilantly," More writes, "that favourite plea of lively ignorance, that study is an enemy to originality" (1: 364). It is especially important to combat this idea vigilantly because upperclass women cannot take for granted the education automatically given to upperclass men. Wordsworth, having taken advantage of such an education, can more easily celebrate natural ignorance as an ideal state from which to create without being stifled by influence.

Even though More says she is not "encouraging young ladies to turn authors," her example and her advice cannot help but lead them in that direction. While she warns them of the dangers, such as the fact that "her highest exertions will probably be received with the qualified approbation" entailed in "the mortifying circumstance of having sex always taken into account" (1: 365), More also lays down the boundaries which make it easier for women to compose in the security of feminine domesticity. She even goes so far as to argue that the "other sex . . . will be sure to be gainers" when women's understanding is improved.

> [T]he enlargement of the female understanding being the most likely means to put an end to those petty and absurd contentions for equality which female smatterers so anxiously maintain. . . . The more a woman's understanding is improved, the more obviously she will discern that there can be no happiness in any society where there is a perpetual struggle for power; and the more her judgment is rectified, the more accurate views will she take of the station she was born to fill, and the more readily will she accommodate herself to it; while the most vulgar and ill informed women are ever most inclined to be tyrants . . . . (1: 365)

It is not surprising that between 1790 and 1810, during the reign of her greatest influence, More herself is railed against by her enemies as something of a female tyrant. She accrues, through her working-class schools, social connections, and political tracts, so much power outside the state-church official hierarchy that she becomes embroiled in constant controversy. From the right, she is attacked for spreading Methodism and revolutionary dissent among the working classes through her schools, which are seen to be undermining the authority of the Anglican Church. From the left, William Cobbett attacks her as the most powerful enemy of reform, calling her "The old bishop in petticoats" (Jones 204). It is only through her feminine "propriety" that she manages to survive these assaults and to retain her influence over the public. Her later works, including the didactic novel *Coelebs in Search of a Wife, Practical Piety, Christian Morals,* and *An Essay on St. Paul,* all sold extremely well, popularizing religious fervor for the middle and upper classes, and preparing the way for the mood and outlook of the Victorian period.

It is the Bishop of London who requests the "old bishop in petticoats" to write something to counteract the popularity of Tom Paine's *Rights of Man* among the "lower orders of people" (see Jones 134). More's response is the pamphlet *Village Politics,* published in 1792. How could More rationalize the politics of the village as not stepping into the realm of masculine politics? *Village Politics* is political propaganda at its best. It speaks to the lower classes in their own language. It goes further by speaking through them as More creates a dialogue between Jack Anvil, a blacksmith, and Tom Hod, a mason. The tract fulfills More's feminine caretaking role through the act of chastening. Tom, the would-be jacobin rebel, is placated by Jack, More's voice in the dialogue. Jack moderates Tom, bringing him back to "common sense" by returning him to his limited private domestic duties. Jack warns: "But bear one thing in mind: the more we riot, the more we shall have to pay. . . : the more time we waste in meeting to redress public wrongs, the more we shall increase our private wants. And mind too, that 'tis working, and not murmuring, which puts bread in our children's mouths, and a new coat on our backs" (*Complete Works of Hannah More* 1: 60). By reminding Toms of their religious, moral, domestic duty, More domesticates them.

This process of domestication is even more apparent in her best-selling tale from *Cheap Repository Tracts, The Shepherd of Salisbury Plain*. At the same time that Wordsworth is working on his Salisbury Plain poem, More publishes this tract dealing with the same issues of homelessness, poverty, war, famine, and the changing relations between the classes. Whereas Wordsworth's poem is clearly aimed at the upper classes in an attempt to explore the limits of pity and charity in the changing economic-cultural environment, More's tract is aimed at both upper- and lower-class readers. More's shepherd is the idealized commoner, deeply religious, fully engaged with performing his duties for wife and children, literate enough to read and quote scriptures, but wise enough not to read anything seditious. It is the lower-class Shepherd who reminds Mr. Johnson of his responsibilities as a gentleman, much in the way that the Leechgatherer teaches Wordsworth's gentle poet. Ultimately, More's appeal in these tracts is not to reason nor to passion, the more violent provocation of emotion exploited by Burke, but to sentiment, the refining sympathy of the domestic affections. And like Wordsworth, More wants to transform the sentiment of pity into a kind of active regulating passion, but for the end of re-establishing a domesticated community of individuals who respect each other while retaining their respect for class values, rather than toward the end of Wordsworthian self-possession.

Toward the conclusion of Part I, Mr. Johnson comes to this realization:

On the whole, he was more disposed to envy than to pity the shepherd. I have seldom seen, said he, so happy a man. It is a sort of happiness which the world could not give, and which I plainly see, it has not been able to take away. This must be the true spirit of religion. I see more and more, that true goodness is not merely a thing of words and opinions, but a living principle brought into every common action of a man's life. What else could have supported this poor couple under every bitter trial of want and sickness? No, my honest shepherd, I do not pity, but I respect and even honour thee; and I will visit thy poor hovel on my return to Salisbury, with as much pleasure as I am now going to the house of my friend. (1: 195)

The Shepherd gently moves the gentleman beyond "words and opinions" to "common action." The tract brings the gentleman into the hovel, not for the sake of reform, but for the sake of charity and mutual respect, so that the gentleman can be taught by the Shepherd the lesson of his class duty and in turn return to reteach the Shepherd what the gentleman has learned through the commoner's example. And the message of the tract reduplicates its own convoluted class interactions: the middle-class spinster through her tract teaches the uncouth commoner how to teach the gentleman how to reclaim his function as a gentle man, how to shed gently his moral influence over a culture seemingly at the brink of shattering into warring class factions.

Conversation is the vehicle through which this domesticating refinement occurs. The importance that More attaches to conversation can be seen in her tracts to the commoners, in her treatises to the upper ranks of society, and in her poetry. In *Hints Towards Forming the Character of a Young Princess,* More writes:

Books alone will never form the character. Mere reading would rather tend to make a pedantic, than an accomplished prince. It is *conversation* which must unfold, enlarge, and apply the use of books. Without that familiar comment on what is read, which will make a most important part of the intercourse between a royal pupil and the society around him, mere reading might only fill the mind with fallacious models of character, and false maxims of life. It is *conversation* which must develope what is obscure, raise what is low, correct what is defective, qualify what is exaggerated, and gently and almost insensibly raise the understanding, form the heart, and fix the taste. . . . (2: 10, More's emphases)

As James Chandler points out, because print itself has been expropriated as a tool by jacobins and reformers, it comes to represent in counterrevolutionary Britain the tendency toward anarchy, a tendency which must be chastened by speech, bringing the individual back into an immediate community, which, because that community is defined by its customary relations, will serve to bind the individual to the traditional rule of law.[3] Whereas Wordsworth values speaking over writing because he sees voice as a better vehicle for asserting his self-fathering poetic power, More's interest in conversation is a factor of her bluestocking lineage. In *Bas Bleu,* the poem which celebrates the bluestocking circles of the earlier part of her life, she figures conversation as a new Reformation, bringing society out of the depths of the dark ages:

> Long was Society o'er-run
> By Whist, that desolating Hun;
> Long did Quadrille despotic sit,
> That vandal of colloquial Wit:
> And conversation's setting light
> Lay half-obscur'd in Gothic night;
> At length the mental shades decline,
> Colloquial Wit begins to shine;
> Genius prevails, and Conversation
> Emerges into *Reformation.*
>
> (1: 15)

Conversation plays the same vital role for More that socializing plays for the Augustans. More alludes to the self-balancing antitheses of Pope's system in the *Essay on Man,* for in *Bas Bleu* conversation becomes, like common sense, a mediating and refining force, making civilized order out of the babel of incessant babble:

> Hail, Conversation, heav'nly fair,
> Thou bliss of life, and balm of care!
> Still may thy gentle reign extend,
> And Taste with Wit and Science blend.
> Soft polisher of rugged man!
> Refiner of the social plan!
>
> (1: 17)

More's deference to Pope, whom she admires very much, is not incidental, but characteristic. Like Lady Mary, she still views poetry primarily in terms of Augustan poetics. More's poetics, however, have shifted ground, so that even though she is using Augustan strategies, themes, and forms, the context and aim of her poeticizing are different from Lady Mary's and Pope's.

In *Sensibility: An Epistle to the Honourable Mrs. Boscawen,* More transforms the context of the fraternal Augustan clique into a co-gendered coterie of friends, alluding self-consciously to Pope's *Epistle to Dr. Arbuthnot:*

> Though purer flames thy hallow'd zeal inspire
> Than e'er were kindled at the Muse's fire,
> Thee, mitred Chester! all the Nine shall boast;
> And is not Johnson ours? himself a host!
> Yes, still for you your gentle stars dispense:
> The charm of friendship and the feast of sense:
> Yours is the bliss, and Heav'n no dearer sends,
> To call the wisest, brightest, best, your friends.
> And while to these I raise the votive line,
> O! let me grateful own these friends are mine;
> With Carter trace the wit to Athens known,
> Or view in Montague that wit our own:
> Or mark, well pleas'd, Chapone's instructive page,
> Intent to raise the morals of the age:
> Or boast, in Walsingham, the various power,
> To cheer the lonely, grace the letter'd hour;
> Delany too is ours, serenely bright,
> Wisdom's strong ray, and virtue's milder light:
> And she who bless'd the friend, and grac'd the lays
> Of poignant Swift, still gilds our social days;
> Long, long protract thy light, O star benign!
> Whose setting beams with milder lustre shine.
>
> (1: 33)

Whereas Pope establishes a male line descending from Dryden to himself, More constructs a much more inclusive and heterogeneous grouping of inter-connected *friends*. In fact, her "votive line" is not so much a line of descent as a horizon of inclusive praise. Whereas Pope's "votive line" is determined more by those who must be excluded, More's line stresses inclusiveness, going on for thirty-five lines before the ones quoted and for several after. This is no surprise, since the bluestocking circles, though they are not in any sense democratic, are still the bringers of a new kind of inclusiveness. More's long list of male writers ends with Johnson, "himself a host." As Johnson is made a "host," his literary club is placed side by side with the bluestocking circles, indicating a kind of transference between the traditional male line and the new feminine hostesses. Then More proceeds with the bluestockings them-selves. Like Pope's *Epistle,* this poem is about claiming the right to literariness.

Like Tighe after her, More puns on the word "own," using it to mean her individualized right to claim entry into this network of friends ("let me grateful own these friends are mine"), while also using it to stress the impossibility of delineating exclusive rights since the network is *common* property ("that wit our own"). Just as Johnson is claimed ("And is not Johnson ours?"), though with a bit of insecurity (represented by the interrogative), "wit our own" is claimed. Montagu's wit belongs to all the bluestockings, for it can exist only in the context of the conversation among interdependent friends who encourage and appreciate that wit. It is women's wit, but *not* distinctively segregated feminine wit, since the poem everywhere replicates masculine Popian wit as closely as possible. These friends whom Boscawen can claim are also claimed by More; the object of the address (Boscawen), the subjects of address (all of the bluestockings named), and the vehicle of the address (More herself) have all been feminized. Just as Johnson has earlier been made a link between passive hosting and active poeticizing, so what the bluestockings experience as shared converse the men who share their circles must also experience.

The aim of More's *Epistle* is also different from Pope's. Whereas he wants to set up Arbuthnot as the model of manly generosity and intelligence, feeling and taste, More wants to present Boscawen as a complementary feminine model, focusing on sensibility, not as some kind of excessive sentiment, which we have already seen her criticize trenchantly, but rather as a kind of regulated sentiment. When "ill-directed," as in much of the literature of the time, sensibility unchecked becomes a danger in itself:

> While her fair triumphs swell the modish page,
> She drives the sterner virtues from the stage:
> While Feeling boasts her ever tearful eye,
> Fair Truth, firm Faith, and manly Justice fly:
> (1: 34)

More's aim is not to purge sentiment, but to show its just regulation by exploring its meaning in this occasional verse and by presenting an exemplary woman who herself becomes the image of genuine sensibility.

It is not a coincidence that she chooses a woman who, as a mother, has "deeply felt." Having lost a husband ("Britain's hero") and two sons, and having a son in combat in the American War, Boscawen represents the woman possessing those "sterner virtues" in unison with "Sweet Sensibility." Again, More alludes to Pope's chain of balanced antitheses and middle state of moderated happiness in the *Essay on Man:*

> Heav'n gives its counterpoise to every ill,
> Nor let us murmur at our stinted pow'rs.
> When kindness, love, and concord, may be ours.
> The gift of minist'ring to other's ease,
> To all her sons impartial she decrees;
> The gentle offices of patient love,
> Beyond all flattery, and all price above;
> The mild forbearance at a brother's fault,
> The angry word suppress'd the taunting thought;

Subduing and subu'd, the petty strife,
Which clouds the colour of domestic life;
The sober comfort, all the peace which springs,
From the large aggregate of little things;
On these small cares of daughter, wife, or friend,
The almost sacred joys of *home* depend:
There Sensibility, thou best may'st reign,
Home is thy true legitimate domain.
A solitary bliss thou ne'er could'st find,
Thy joys with those thou lov'st are intertwin'd. . . .
                          (1: 35, More's emphasis)

This passage, clearly directed toward *men* ("to all her *sons*"), domesticates
not only sensibility, which in any case would already have been seen as a
domestic virtue, but *all* morality. It is in the "large aggregate of little things"
that charity and love and courage and justice and truth are found. Sensibility
"exalts the whole," and makes life liveable in an otherwise discordant world.

The poem ends with ambivalence, an ambivalence which is implied
throughout by the tension between the taut Popian verse and the post-Augus-
tan emphasis on domesticating sensibility. If in order for men to be whole,
they must embrace domesticating sensibility, is it also true that women must
embrace the sternest virtues of manly enterprise? Once again, Boscawen, "you
[who] fondly melt, / In raptures none but mothers ever felt" (34), is the perfect image, a mother awaiting the news of her son gone to war:

Yet why those terrors? Why that anxious care?
Since your last hope the deathful war *will* dare?
Why dread that energy of soul which leads
To dang'rous glory by heroic deeds?
Why mourn to view his ardent soul aspire?
You fear the son because you knew the sire.
Hereditary valour you deplore,
And dread, yet wish to find one hero more.
                          (1: 36, More's emphasis)

This palpable tension between sensibility's intertwining bliss and solitary
"hereditary valour" is not resolved within the poem. It is left for More's feminine descendants to make sense of these seemingly contradictory connections
by fleshing out the philosophy of domestic affections. At first, this may seem
an odd way to close an epistolary poem on sensibility. But actually, it is perhaps the most effective way. More leaves Boscawen in that horrible moment
of suspense, not knowing whether she will have to mourn her son's valiant
death, or rejoice for his life spared, or if she will have to rejoice because his
death *is* valiant. Boscawen's domestic plight requires not only an appropriate
emotional response, but also that emotional response itself will imply a sociomoral response, which will signal her courage, justice, faith, and loyalty to
the state. Likewise, we readers, both male and female, are tested, as we are
called on to practice the kind of genuine sensibility in relation to Boscawen
which More has defined as the regulating tenor of her verse.

4

It is ironic that someone so obsessed with the conservation of ancient values should also be the one to usher in the new order of public feminine influence. Anna Barbauld, a republican in politics and dissenter in religion, might at first glance seem a more likely candidate, but perhaps it is Barbauld's more liberal politics that prevent her from becoming the crucial pivotal figure in an age of counterrevolutionary ferment. Despite the divergence in politics, the similarities between the two women are significant. Lucy Aikin, Barbauld's niece, explains how Barbauld's education was "entirely domestic." Her father, a schoolmaster like More's, "proud as he justly was of her uncommon capacity, long refused to gratify her earnest desire of being initiated into this kind of knowledge [Greek and Latin]. At length, however, she in some degree overcame his scruples; and with his assistance she enabled herself to read the Latin authors with pleasure and advantage" (*Works of Anna Laetitia Barbauld* 1: vii). In her childhood Barbauld is surrounded by "the ruder sex," which according to Aikin, endangers her proper upbringing, "[b]ut maternal vigilance effectually obviated this danger" (1: viii). Aikin, writing in the 1820s, when, as we have seen, the romantic conception of poetic genius has taken hold, constructs Barbauld's development partly in terms of romantic myth, but with significant differences:

Her recollections of childhood and early youth were, in fact, not associated with much of the pleasure and gaiety usually attendant upon that period of life: but it must be regarded as a circumstance favourable, rather than otherwise, to the un-folding of her genius, to have been thus left to find, or make in solitude her own objects of interest and pursuit. The love of rural nature sunk deep into her heart; her vivid fancy exerted itself to colour, to animate, and to diversify all the objects which surrounded her: the few but choice authors of her father's library, which she read and re-read, had leisure to make their full impression—to mould her sentiments and to form her taste; the spirit of devotion, early inculcated upon her as a duty, opened to her by degrees an exhaustless source of tender and sublime delight; and while yet a child, she was surprised to find herself a poet. (1: viii–ix)

Barbauld's recollections of early childhood are not the happy memories that would be expected; because the small village in which she lived "was unable to afford her a single suitable companion of her own sex" (1: vii), her education is prone to "strictness and seclusion" (1: viii). Influenced by romantic ideology, Aikin sees Barbauld's initial solitude as "favourable," but it is not so much this solitude as her "spirit of devotion, early inculcated upon her as a duty" which opens "the exhaustless source of . . . delight" indicative of poetic genius. "Just at the period when longer seclusion might have proved seriously injurious to her spirits" (1: ix), Barbauld's father takes a position in a dissenting academy at Warrington, Lancashire, where Barbauld can participate in a congenial, busy intellectual environment. Fortunately, according to Aikin, "[a] solitary education has not produced on her its most frequent ill effects, pride and self-importance: the reserve of her manners proceeded solely from bashfulness, for her temper inclined her strongly to friendship and to social pleasures" (1: x). As opposed to Moore's view of Byron's poetic development, Aikin sees it as essential for her aunt to be enveloped, sooner or later, by "social pleasures"; in fact, she suggests that it is Barbauld's "active imagination" which serves "as a charm against that disgust with common characters and daily incidents, which so frequently renders the conscious possessor of superior talents as once unamiable and unhappy" (1: x). The kind of feminine space created for More through the household of five spinster sisters, who live together for sixty years, Barbauld does not experience, but both her brother and husband encourage her poetry-writing. In fact, it is her brother who persuades her to bring out her first collection of poems in 1773 and a joint collection of prose pieces with him in the same year.

Despite her republican politics, Barbauld's attitude toward women and literature is similar to More's. When Elizabeth Montagu asks Barbauld to set up an academy for young ladies to rival male academies, Barbauld responds that this kind of systematic schooling "appears to me better calculated to form such characters as the 'Precieuses' or the 'Femmes sçavantes' of Moliere, than good wives or agreeable companions" (1: xvii). In her opinion, young women should

gain these accomplishments [a general tincture of knowledge] in a more quiet and unobserved manner [than young men]:—subject to a regulation like that of the ancient Spartans, the thefts of knowledge in our sex are only connived at while carefully concealed, and if displayed, punished with disgrace. The best way for women to acquire knowledge is from conversation with a father, a brother or friend, in the way of family intercourse and easy conversation, and by such a course of readings as they may recommend. (1: xviii)

Influenced by the educational philosophy of Rousseau, Barbauld's view of female education is even more conservative than that of More, who considers Rousseau's theories immoral. Barbauld has also been obviously influenced by her own mode of education, reliant on men mentors and taught to be grateful for every scrap of knowledge she is able to glean. Ironically, Barbauld herself is a famous teacher of *boys* in her husband's Palgrave boarding school, where she is responsible for English composition, geography, and dramatic productions. Conscious of the contradiction between her views on female education and her own status as a famous woman author, Barbauld attempts to justify her position to Montagu thus:

Perhaps you may think, that having myself stepped out of the bounds of female reserve in becoming an author, it is with an ill grace I offer these sentiments: but though this circumstance may destroy the grace, it does not the justice of the remark; and I am full well convinced that to have a too great fondness for books is little favourable to the happiness of a woman, especially one not in affluent circumstances. My situation has been peculiar, and would be no rule for others. (1: xviii–xix)

Like More, Barbauld does not recommend that others take her route, for she sees herself as a special case. In this way More and Barbauld are more timid than their bluestocking mothers, and yet it is this very timidity that enables them to make headway as famous authors in an age of reactionary retreat. The next generation of feminine poetesses will transform this self-castigating timidity into the outright virtue of poetic vulnerability, the capacity to *affect* and *be affected* by those for and to whom one writes, but they will begin to reject the idea that the female poet is a special case for a theory and practice which entail the overt propagation of feminine genius. For the later feminine poetesses come to recognize and embrace unapologetically the notion that "affluent circumstances" can be the result, rather than the cause, of poetic productivity, a notion anathema to poets like More and Barbauld, who still view poetry-making as merely an extension of the *conversation* of co-equal patrons.

The best explanation of Barbauld's conception of female poeticizing is found in her poem "On a Lady's Writing" (1: 59):

> Her even lines her steady temper show,
> Neat as her dress, and polished as her brow;
> Strong as her judgment, easy as her air;
> Correct though free, and regular though fair:
> And the same graces o'er her pen preside,
> That form her manners and her footsteps guide.

As we have seen with Tighe, feminine grace becomes indistinguishably a moral virtue and a poetic virtue. This little polished, regular poem practices what it preaches. If feminine temper must be even, steady, easy, correct, and fair, so must feminine poeticizing. And yet in the heart of the poem is an attribute not usually applied to femininity: strength. Although for a woman's judgment to be strong could mean that she knows how to remain chaste, it could, and must, also mean judgment in the larger sense entailing intelligent and just discernment in intellectual matters. The same kind of reading applies to the phrases "correct though free" and "regular though fair." A woman's correctness is usually enforced by a plethora of sociomoral restrictions and strictures, but through the writing of poetry the woman can experience a kind of freedom that is paradoxically still strict and restricted. Likewise, women are usually depicted as fair but fickle, like Lady Mary's tempestuous Chloris. Poetry allows them to remain within the empire of beauty while displaying their capacity for constancy, not merely as a kind of chastity, but as a valuable intellectual quality.

The limits of Barbauld's feminism are also the limits of her poetics. A woman who cannot grant women absolute equal rights with men also cannot grant them the right to write freely from the dictates of their own desire. Female poets, including the later feminine poetesses, are very hesitant to claim the kind of freedom to desire to write that Wordsworth claims for himself because this apotheosis of desire seems to unhinge the poetic self not only from customary social restrictions, but more importantly from the ideal of shared social desire. In her poem "The Rights of Women" (1: 185–187), Barbauld argues *against* women's rights because she thinks this political demand leads to misshared desire. As the poem appears to tell women to "rise, assert thy right," it actually ridicules this battle cry by assuming woman's rule to be merely over what Lady Mary calls the empire of beauty:

> Go, bid proud Man his boasted rule resign,
> And kiss the golden sceptre of thy reign.

> Go, gird thyself with grace; collect thy store
> Of bright artillery glancing from afar;
> Soft melting tones thy thundering cannon's roar,
> Blushes and fears thy magazine of war.

Lady Mary, because of her historical circumstances, represses her desire to write propagandistic poems about and for women's rights and yet beneath the subterfuge of her art, her feminist voice can still be heard. More and Barbauld, because of their historical circumstances, are able to write propagandistic poems about and for women, but only as long as they write against women's rights. Whereas Lady Mary suggests that if woman is to be free, she must conquer her obsession with love and chastity, and enter the larger world of social productivity, Barbauld suggests that it is love that makes the demand for women's rights and the entry into the larger world inappropriate and self-defeating:

> But hope not, courted idol of mankind,
> On this proud eminence secure to stay;
> Subduing and subdued, thou soon shalt find
> Thy coldness soften, and thy pride give way.

> Then, then, abandon each ambitious thought,
> Conquest or rule thy heart shall feebly move,
> In Nature's school, by her soft maxims taught,
> That separate rights are lost in mutual love.

Natural rights are subdued ironically by nature's school, which teaches women softness, rather than the kind of hardness which is required to rule empires. Separate rights would be the ruin of "mutual love," but since nature automatically disarms the woman, softening her demand, then separate rights will always give way to a woman's need to love and be loved.

Robert Burns's poem, "The Rights of Woman," serves as a good "masculine" contrast to Barbauld's "feminine" objection to the doctrine of women's rights—indicating how even when male and female poets express the same idea, their different cultural positions encourage them to approach that subject with a different sense of "propriety." Whereas Barbauld treats the women's rights doctrine seriously, even as she attempts to counter it, Burns trivializes the subject by treating it humorously. Putting the argument in the mouth of "Miss Fontenelle on her benefit night," Burns humors the woman who speaks as well as the cause that she is made to speak against. The doctrine is presented not only as a supplement to the rights of man, but also as an afterthought:

> While Europe's eye is fixed on mighty things,
> The fate of Empires, and the fall of Kings;

> While quacks of State must each produce his plan,
> And even children lisp The Rights of Man;
> Amid this mighty fuss, just let me mention,
> The Rights of Woman merit some attention.
>
> (*Poems and Songs* 527)

The humor in Burns's poem is found, not in an irony that dashes expectations, but instead that fulfills them all too well. Women are advocating their rights because, predictably, they want "some attention." They want to bring men's attention away from "mighty things" and back toward women's "empire of beauty." Burns's woman either cannot distinguish between the import of "mighty things" and the triviality of a "mighty fuss," which she is about to make herself, or she playfully refuses to accept a distinction that she understands, exploiting her feminine wiles in order to display her "merit" for attracting men's "attention." In either case, Burns is chuckling at her flaws, as Lady Mary points out male admirers tend to do, by being amused *with* her or, more precisely, bemused by her charms. It is not surprising, then, that the "rights" which Burns's woman claims through the "Sexes' intermixed connection" are those "excesses" of the male chivalric "imagination" that Hannah More warns women of: "Protection," "Decorum," and "Admiration."

> Smiles, glances, sighs, tears, fits, flirtations, airs;
> 'Gainst such an host, what flinty savage dares.—
> When aweful Beauty joins in all her charms,
> Who is so rash as rise in rebel arms?
>
> But truce with kings, and truce with Constitutions,
> With bloody armaments, and Revolutions;
> Let Majesty your first attention summon,
> Ah, ça ira! The Majesty of Woman!!!
>
> (*Poems and Songs* 528)

Burns has his lady interconnect the fate of the sexes, but in a wholly different way from Barbauld, or the affectional poetesses whom we shall examine later. Burns's lady pits the empire of beauty against the empire of power knowing full well that her plea is neither seriously given nor seriously taken, knowing that its effectiveness lies wholly in the pretty ineffectuality of the plea—how it is given with "[s]miles, glances, sighs, tears, fits, flirtations, airs." Thus Burns manages to diffuse not only the potential seriousness of a plea for woman's rights, but also, and perhaps more damningly, the reality of woman's actual influence in sociopolitical culture at this juncture in history. By returning women securely to that ornamental realm which Lady Mary, More, and Barbauld attempt to exit, Burns, blinded by his admiration for his own facetious gallantry, separates, at least in verbal terms, the masculine world of constitutions, bloody armaments, and revolutions from the proper feminine sphere of "aweful Beauty."

The contrast between Burns's flippant, flattering tone and Barbauld's wistful earnestness could not be more stark. And whereas conceptually Burns's humor depends on a sleight of the pen—intermixing the connection of the sexes only to separate them more securely, Barbauld's seriousness depends on the clarity or clearsightedness of its irony: "separate rights are lost in mutual love." There is, of course, potential humor lurking within Barbauld's irony, but the humor itself depends on the sharedness of men's and women's stakes. Burns induces laughter by renormalizing the cultural norm that is being threatened by a call to women's rights. The advocate of women's rights, whether male or female, is categorically excluded from the purview of the poem, and yet the humor of the poem is based on that exclusion. Unless we know what the true advocate of women's rights believes, the poem cannot have its humorous edge. The excluded other, the woman's rights advocate, defines the norm through her exclusion, while the included other, the female speaker, derives her meaning from an unexpressed juxtaposition. The female speaker fully fulfills normative expectations, ironically by taking on the suppressed position of the abnormal other (proclaiming woman's rights) while simultaneously abnegating that position through her sense of decorum as much as through the common sense of her words. On the other hand, Barbauld's irony and potential humor depend on the mutuality of the norm expressed by the poem: all parties (whether male or female, whether against or for women's rights) are taught in "Nature's school" (whether they realize it or not) and must succumb to nature's law. Rather than fulfilling our cultural expectations through normalizing acts of exclusion, Barbauld, even as she reaffirms the status quo, encourages all of her readers, regardless of gender-identification, to share (or be lost) in that mutual love in the very act of reading the poem itself. By interfusing the social obligation of the sexes, by naturalizing the triumph of love over women, Barbauld also implicitly questions the effectuality of man's empire of power and begins to domesticate that empire by scrutinizing it through the lens of nature's "soft maxims."

Like More, Barbauld is suspicious of that desire which leads men to "hereditary valour" and solitary conquest, and the cry for women's rights seems to her to take women down that rugged road. It is appropriate, then, that she, like More, should question that larger world of conquest which seems so much at odds with "mutual love." In "Written on a Marble" (1: 148), Barbauld offers a mordant critique of man's empire of power:

> The world's something bigger,
>   But just of this figure
> And speckled with mountains and seas;
> Your heroes are overgrown schoolboys
> Who scuffle for empires and toys,
>   And kick the poor ball as they please.
> Now Caesar, now Pompey, gives law;
>   And Pharsalia's plain,
>   Though heaped with the slain,
>   Was only a game at *taw*.

Has a more skillfully trenchant and concise indictment of the desire for conquest ever been written? Anticipating Percy Shelley's "Ozymandias," Barbauld shows how men have reduced the management of world affairs to a boy's game of marbles. She reminds them that the world is "something bigger" than the marble they take it for. Punning on the word "marble" (meaning both the small ball used in boy's games and the hard rock used to commemorate heroes), Barbauld condemns the kind of heroism that leads to heaps of slain bodies. Conquering heroes attempt to immortalize themselves, to write their names in marble. But as a Caesar is supplanted by a Pompey, and one emperor gives way to the next, it is slain bodies that result instead of the sensible rule of law. Ironically, Barbauld's little poem, itself written as though in marble, writes into the commemorative stone something altogether different from the glorification expected when heroes are discussed.

As guardians of sociomoral culture, More and Barbauld can write this kind of poetic propaganda without too much censure. Both writers, for instance, compose poems in honor of William Wilberforce, parliamentary champion of the movement to abolish the slave trade. The woman writer's special concern with the "Negroe's chain" (Barbauld's *Epistle to W. Wilberforce* 1: 173) goes back more than a century to Aphra Behn's *Oroonoko, or the History of the Royal Slave.* Barbauld connects Britain's failure to abolish the slave trade to a larger failure of conscience, a failure that portends inevitable ruin. Composing a kind of anti-pastoral, she implicitly indicts those poets who prefer to paint rosy pictures of pastoral ease instead of facing the reality of Britain's course:

> Nor, in their palmy walks and spicy groves,
> The form benign of rural Pleasure roves;
> No milk-maid's song, or hum of village talk,
> Soothes the lone poet in his evening walk:
>
> . . .
>
> No heart-expanding scenes their eyes must prove
> Of thriving industry and faithful love:
> But shrieks and yells disturb the balmy air,
> Dumb sullen looks of woe announce despair,
> And angry eyes through dusky features glare.
> Far from the sounding lash the Muses fly,
> And sensual riot drowns each finer joy.
>
> (177)

Influenced by George Crabbe's criticism of pastoral poets in *The Village* (see *Complete Poetical Works* 1: 157–167), Barbauld's epistle, like Crabbe's poem, offers a radically different view of poetry's productivity from what the romantic poets attempt to claim. Like Crabbe, Barbauld uses the pleasure of poetic decorativeness to undermine that pleasure by suggesting that the lies propagated and sustained by pastoral poetry contribute to tyranny over the slave as much as the actual policies and weapons that maintain the slave system. Any poet who finds in the English countryside "thriving industry and faithful love" has not looked far enough, for just beyond his sight are the "shrieks and yells," the "sounding lash," and the "sensual riot" that result from slavery. And it is not only in the actual savage encounter between slaveholder and slave that "sensual riot" occurs, but also at home, in the finest parlors, on the softest couches.

Crabbe depicts the interconnection between the leisured master and his peasant by literally bringing the master onto the peasant's turf, the way More brings Mr. Johnson into the Shepherd's "poor hovel," in order to educate the gentleman by forcing him to see reality through the peasant's eyes. But whereas More's portrait of the gentleman is optimistic, allowing him to learn exactly what he needs to know in order to sustain hierarchical values, Crabbe's poem directly addresses the master cynically in order to suggest the implausibility of the master's reform. Whereas More domesticates the gentleman in order to demonstrate the rightful power of his authority, when rightfully practiced, Crabbe feminizes the master to demonstrate the perverse ineffectuality of his authority:

> Say ye, opprest by some fantastic woes,
> Some jarring nerve that baffles your repose;
> Who press the downy couch, while slaves advance
> With timid eye, to read the distant glance;
> Who with sad prayers the weary doctor teaze
> To name the nameless ever-new disease;
> Who with mock patience dire complaints endure,
> Which real pain, and that alone can cure;
> How would ye bear in real pain to lie,
> Despis'd, neglected, left alone to die?
> How would ye bear to draw your latest breath,
> Where all that's wretched paves the way for death?
>   (*The Village,* Book 1, 250–261)

The master is so enmeshed in his narcissistic leisure, so bored by the luxury of profitable but unproductive ease, that he can afford to invent diseases to weary the village doctor, while the poor in the village lie in "real pain" and die from real disease. The "downy couch" of Pope's Belinda, according to Crabbe, is no laughing matter, and for reasons complementary to Lady Mary's. Crabbe here feminizes his reader, placing *him* in Belinda's lap of luxury, to make the stark contrast between the real productivity that results from painfully real labor and the idle profit accrued by the master's and the pastoral poet's exploitation of the peasant. As Crabbe suggests throughout the poem, the master/poet is a parasite, existing on the labor of slaves who "advance / With timid eye, to read the distant glance" of authority. Crabbe hopes to show how the master/poet must be seen in his true light: unproductive, dependent, pampered, hysterically hypochondriac—effeminized by his unnatural separation from his inferiors.

If Crabbe universalizes the feminine state of marginal luxury to show the relation between personal idleness and sociopolitical oppression, Barbauld inverts Crabbe's formula to make the same point. Instead of the powerful master ensconced upon his couch, she depicts the beautiful mistress ensconced "on sofas of voluptuous ease":

> Lo! where reclined, pale Beauty courts the breeze,
> Diffused on sofas of voluptuous ease;
> With anxious awe her menial train around
> Catch her faint whispers of half-uttered sound;
> See her, in monstrous fellowship, unite
> At once the Scythian and the Sybarite!
> Blending repugnant vices, misallied,
> Which frugal nature purposed to divide;
> See her, with indolence to fierceness joined,
> Of body delicate, infirm of mind,
> With languid tones imperious mandates urge;
> With arm recumbent wield the household scourge;
> And with unruffled mien, and placid sounds,
> Contriving torture, and inflicting wounds.
>
> (*Works* 1: 176–177)

Alluding to Crabbe's scene of enragement, Barbauld refigures the same image back to its Popian context, but with a significant difference. As in Crabbe, no longer is the lady's luxury a laughing matter. The empire of beauty is pale, not because it is the conventional sign of feminine attractiveness, but rather because it is ghastly, unnatural, deadly. Just as Crabbe pictures a powerful man effeminized by his luxury, Barbauld pictures an influential lady masculinized by her petty reign. Like the men who practice power by wielding the lash of slavery, this pale lady, "with unruffled mien, and placid sounds," spends her idle hours "contriving torture" to inflict metaphorical wounds on her "menial train." Through the allusion to Crabbe and Pope, Barbauld wants us to make all of those connections that pastoralizing poets tend to evade. The maids, who, catching their lady's "faint whispers" "with anxious awe," spend their time unproductively tending to her "imperious" commands, are equated with the slaves who advance in Crabbe's poem "with timid eye." Though the violence of "sensual riot" is hidden behind the "unruffled mien, and placid sounds" in the empire of beauty, that violence is no less real than the whip-lashing that occurs on the slave plantations far from the lady's parlor. In fact, according to the logic of Barbauld's poem, the lady's idle luxury "mandates" the slaver's whip, just as she "with recumbent arm" wields "the household scourge."

Protected by the idea that a woman's duty is to bring her finer sentiment to bear in order to restrain the ruder tendencies of man's conquesting desire, Barbauld thus brings the realm of politics into poetry's decorative bower. "[P]ale Beauty," "[d]iffused on sofas of voluptuous ease" (1: 176), is united in "monstrous fellowship" with the slavers, for Barbauld, following the logic of Lady Mary, argues that the woman who self-indulgently demands excessive finery at home contributes to slavery abroad. Her decorative poetry must redress the balance demanded by "frugal nature" by transplanting simple pastoral with "the household scourge."

Implicit in Barbauld's poetry is a critique not only of such social evils as empire and slavery, but also of the Augustan complacency celebrated in

Pope's *Windsor Forest.* In many of Barbauld's poems England is depicted as
falling to ruin *as a result* of its rise to empire. "Corruption follows with gi-
gantic stride, / And scarce vouchsafes his shameless front to hide," she writes
in the *Epistle to Wilberforce.*

> Stern Independence from his glebe retires,
> And anxious Freedom eyes her drooping fires;
> By foreign wealth are British morals changed,
> And Afric's sons, and India's, smile avenged.
>
>   (1: 178)

As she tells Wilberforce to "seek no more to break a nation's fall" (1: 179),
Barbauld prophesies, in the manner of Cassandra, a doom that counters the
future predicted for England by poets like Pope and Wordsworth. The poem
Eighteen Hundred and Eleven, one of her most riveting, is very controversial
when it is first published, exactly because to depict such doom during the
jingoistic war years could in itself be considered seditious. In this poem, Barbauld is committed to revealing all of England's social problems, but she does
not seem interested in spurring individuals to action. Instead, that doom is presented as a foregone conclusion. Once again, her poetry anticipates Shelley's
1819 political poems, but Barbauld's critique is explicitly and definitely from
the point of view of domesticating sensibility. This is the first stanza of the
poem:

> Still the loud death drum, thundering from afar,
> O'er the vext nations pours the storm of war:
> To the stern call still Britain bends her ear,
> Feeds the fierce strife, the'alternate hope and fear;
> Bravely, though vainly, dares to strive with Fate,
> And seeks by turns to prop each sinking state.
> Colossal power with overwhelming force
> Bears down each fort of Freedom in its course;
> Prostrate she lies beneath the Despot's sway,
> While the hushed nations curse him—and obey.
>
>   (1: 232)

By using trochees and spondees to create an intense falling rhythm, Barbauld
gives the sense of urgency, the sense of *bearing down* that is being described
in the poem. The poem prophesies Britain's fall to empire as a symptom of
man's ills in the longer course of history and in the contentious relation to
nature. "Bounteous in vain, with frantic man at strife, / Glad Nature pours
the means—the joys of life." Like Wordsworth, More equates "Glad Nature"
with the fecund matron, but for a very different reason. Like Nature, the
"matron" is "[f]ruitful in vain" as she "counts with pride / [t]he blooming
youths that grace her honoured side" (1: 233). Similar to More's depiction
of Boscawen fearing the need to mourn a son murdered in war, Barbauld's
natural matron is at strife with man's conquesting desire. "No son returns to
press her widowed hand, / Her fallen blossoms strew a foreign strand." Questioning the logic which claims that men must die for their country, Barbauld

pits the empire of power against the empire of beauty, the latter being in tune with nature's beauty, just as the fertile mother is in tune with nature's bounty:

> —Fruitful in vain, she boasts her virgin race,
> Whom cultured arts adorn and gentlest grace;
> Defrauded of its homage, Beauty mourns,
> And the rose withers on its virgin thorns.
>
> (1: 233)

Barbauld's vision is one of inescapably linked desire, so it is a mistake to think, as Pope and Wordsworth do, that England is protected by her island position:

> And think'st thou, Britain, still to sit at ease,
> An island queen amidst thy subject seas,
> While vext billows, in their distant roar,
> But soothe thy slumbers, and but kiss thy shore?
> To sport in wars, while danger keeps aloof,
> Thy grassy turf unbruised by hostile hoof?
> So sing thy flatterers;—but, Britain, know,
> Thou who hast shared the guilt must share the woe.
>
> (1: 234)

Just as all affections are linked within the domestic environment, so in the world, though "something bigger," every nation is linked to every other. At the heart of *Eighteen Hundred and Eleven* Barbauld reveals a Britain soon to be desecrated, a Britain to which curious tourists will come as the British now go to Rome to ponder an empire in ruins.

> Oft shall the strangers turn their eager feet
> The rich remains of ancient art to greet,
> The pictured walls with critic eye explore,
> And Reynolds be what Raphael was before.
>
> (1: 243–244)

Arguing against Adam Smith's idea of an ever-expanding empire based on the free-flowing circulation of capital, an idea that the romantic poets implicitly exploit in their appeal to the ever-expanding empire of mind, Barbauld presents instead a world in which profit in one sphere means loss, slavery, and ruin in another. Like the classical conception of fortune, Barbauld figures Britain's genius as a fickle lover:

> The Genius now forsakes the favoured shore,
> And hates, capricious, what he loved before;
> Then empires fall to dust, then arts decay,
> And wasted realms enfeebled despots sway;
>
> (1: 245–246)

Barbauld's view is much closer to the classical tendencies of the second generation, who believe that there is an internal flaw within power as it is presently conceived, which brings the powerful down as surely as it enables their rise. In the conclusion, Barbauld once again suggests the interconnection between the political empire of power and the natural sphere of beauty:

> But fairest flowers expand but to decay;
> The worm is in thy core, thy glories pass away;
> Art, arms and wealth destroy the fruits they bring;
> Commerce, like beauty, knows no second spring.
>   (1: 249)

In a sure, strong voice, Barbauld predicts England's fate as irreversible. How ironic that this *tour de force* should be executed by a woman who believes that women should not become authors and should refrain from entering the masculine world of politics and knowledge.

At one end of Barbauld's discourse is the kind of agitated polemics of poems like *Eighteen Hundred and Eleven, Epistle to W. Wilberforce,* "The Rights of Woman," "To the Poor," and "On the Expected General Rising of the French Revolution in 1792," poems which approximate More's *Cheap Repository Tracts* and treastises written for the upper-classes. At the other end are the refined and restricted overly self-consciously feminine poems like "On a Lady Writing," similar to much of More's poetry. What the later feminine poetesses do is to take the middle ground between these two extremes, creating connections between sweet sentiment and polemics, between beauty and power, between woman's little domestic world and the masculine world of imperial conquest.

Occasionally, Barbauld anticipates this transfusion, as she does in her remarkable poem "Washing-Day" (1: 202–206), a rewriting of Virgil's *Georgics* from the woman's point of view. Barbauld celebrates one of woman's lowliest chores, making her subject poetic without romanticizing it, depicting the tedium of household work without demeaning the work itself, and demanding that we take such work as seriously as men's work without failing to see the humor embedded in the comparison. She begins her poem by turning the Muses into gossips, just as we readers must be turned into housewives in order to enjoy and appreciate the poem:

> The Muses are turned gossips; they have lost
> The buskined step, and clear high-sounding phrase,
> Language of gods. Come then, domestic Muse,
> In slipshod measure loosely prattling on
> Of farm or orchard, pleasant curds and cream,
> Of drowning flies, or shoe lost in the mire
> By little whimpering boy, with rueful face;
> Come, Muse, and sing the dreaded Washing-Day.

As Barbauld mocks the way male poets have mythologized the Muses so that they can rise above the ordinary and tedious reality of women's domestic world, she brings the Muses down to earth, turning them into gossiping housewives who speak in "slipshod measure" rather than in the fanciful language made correct by male poets or the polished and even lines that Barbauld herself has given credence to. Barbauld here manages to banish the feminine correctness demanded by masculine desire in favor of womanly freedom spawned more from women's own needs.

The poem is explicitly addressed to those already in the know, or to those willing to embrace the sympathetic resonance of knowing:

> Ye who beneath the yoke of wedlock bend,
> With bowed soul, full well ye ken the day
> Which week, smooth sliding after week, brings on
> Too soon. . . .
>
> (1: 202–203)

As in *Eighteen Hundred and Eleven,* Barbauld is unsparing, but this time her tone is all homespun common sense and her style indulgently tolerant and goodhumored. The poem veers toward the mock-heroic, not, like Pope, to use the traditional standards of heroism in order to ridicule her subject, but rather to redefine the terms of heroism itself:

> From that last evil, O preserve us, heavens!
> For should the skies pour down, adieu to all
> Remains of quiet: then expect to hear
> Of sad disasters,—dirt and gravel stains
> Hard to efface, and loaded lines at once
> Snapped short,—and linen-horse by dog thrown down,
> And all the petty miseries of life.
>
> (1: 203)

Barbauld's language, freed temporarily from the constraints of masculine desire, revels in its own freedom. It becomes irresistibly particularized and graphic, portraying the rough-hewn miseries of life in all their squalid splendor.

> Saints have been calm while stretched upon the rack,
> And Guatimozin smiled on burning coals;
> But never yet did housewife notable
> Greet with a smile a rainy washing-day.
>
> (1: 203–204)

At first seeming to compare washwomen with stoic saints, Barbauld refuses even this glorifying analogy. Instead, she wants us to savor the irritation that this chore brings, and the forbearance that it demands, once again without losing sight of its humor. By swerving to an outside view of the activity in the latter part of the poem, Barbauld enables her male readers (and her upper-class women readers) to partake of the fun while also demanding their sympathetic understanding:

> Woe to the friend
> Whose evil stars have urged him forth to claim
> On such a day the hospitable rites!
> Looks, blank at best, and stinted courtesy,
> Shall he receive. Vainly he feeds his hopes
> With dinner of roast chicken, savoury pie,
> Or tart or pudding:—pudding he nor tart
> That day shall eat. . . .
>
> (1:204–205)

Finally, Barbauld shifts the focus to herself in childhood, awed and puzzled by this womanly ritual:

> I well remember, when a child, the awe
> This day struck into me; for then the maids,
> I scarce knew why, looked cross, and drove me from them:
> Nor soft caress could I obtain, nor hope
> Usual indulgencies. . . .
>
> (1: 205)

The high seriousness with which the maids take their work is only matched by "my mother's voice . . . [u]rging dispatch" (1: 206).

> [B]riskly the work went on,
> All hands employed to wash, to rinse, to wring
> To fold, and starch, and clap, and iron, and plait.
> Then would I sit me down, and ponder much
> Why washings were.
>
> (1: 206)

The disparity between the child's leisure, the capacity to sit and ponder, and the women's endless hard work (represented by that series of infinitive verbs) is akin to Wordsworth's sense that the hard work of building a nation is at odds with the idle pursuit of poetry. But whereas Wordsworth attempts to recuperate poeticizing as hard work, as the supreme form of labor, Barbauld is satisfied to let the disparity stand. In fact, she stresses that disparity, since the little girl's pondering is essentially rhetorical. There is no grand philosophical reason for the labor. It simply must be done by someone. And yet the little girl's pondering is certainly a mock mirror image of the poet's own pondering in the poem. Like the little girl, the mature poetess sits down to ponder in her verse why washings are. Is women's busy labor essentially at odds with the idleness of poeticizing? Barbauld does not stay to ponder out the question. Instead, she gives us another analogy:

> Sometimes through hollow bowl
> Of pipe amused we blew, and sent aloft
> The floating bubbles; little dreaming then
> To see, Mongolfier, thy silken ball
> Ride buoyant through the clouds—so near approach
> The sports of children and the toils of men.
> Earth, air, and sky, and ocean, hath its bubbles,
> And verse is one of them—this most of all.
>
> (1: 206)

This is as close as the poem comes to dreaming away the tedium of women's work reality. The children make a game of bubble-blowing from the women's work, just as men, "overgrown schoolboys," make a game of marbles from the serious work of building a nation—"so near approach / The sports of children and the toils of men." Once again, she identifies her verse with leisured children's play, but not with a sense of distress or dissonance. Capping the poem with the good humor that runs throughout, she, not surprisingly, interconnects the fairytale game of the children, the dreary work of the maids and the mother, and the work of writing verse. These activities are all natural in their own way, just as nature itself everywhere displays its own bubbles. This very poem, Barbauld suggests, is most of all a bubble: a silly game, a little dream, a silken ball riding the clouds, a world magically blown from her pen only to pop into nothingness. Tongue in cheek, Barbauld frees herself to question the seriousness of her poetrywork, and at the same time she is able to see the making of women's poetry in a light so naturally homespun that it has the look and feel of just another washing-day.

5

Even as female poets of More's and Barbauld's generation profit from the commodification of poetry, even as they begin to make their living from their poetic activity, they refuse to conceive of themselves as working within the parameters of a vocation. Whereas the male romantics are anxious to promote the vocational status of poetry-making, the women poets are anxious to suppress the emerging relation between poetic activity and vocation. Both male and female poets of this generation, however, want to disengage poetry from the ignobility of market entrepreneurship, the men in order to protect the myth of self-possessing desire untrammelled by the crude whims of a reading public, the women in order to protect their sense of feminine decorum. More's ideal of a co-gendered network of conversant friends is, of course, no more fully the reality than Pope's fraternal coterie or Wordsworth's solitary poet-priest. Although Vesey, to whom *Bas Bleu* is addressed, and Boscawen are patrons of a sort, they are not the kind of patron that is embedded within the history of the genre More exploits in her occasional verse. As More herself notes in the preface to her works, "Literary patronage is so much *shorn of its beams,* that it can no longer enlighten bodies which are in themselves opake; so much abridged of its power that it cannot force into notice a work which is not able to recommend itself" (1: vii). In *Bas Bleu* the conflict between More's desire for a universe of equally gentle and respected conversant friends and the reality of a heterogeneous market of buyers is repressed by using ironically the figure of commerce to represent the ideal of mutual patronage among a universe of equals:

> But 'tis thy commerce Conversation,
> Must give it use by circulation;
> That noblest commerce of mankind,
> Whose precious merchandise of Mind!
> (1: 17)

Insofar as the bluestocking circles constitute a sort of mental *laissez faire* enterprise, this metaphor holds true, but once we realize that bluestockings are not a universe of equal friends, but a small network of class-conscious cliques, the metaphor breaks down. More needs to influence the larger world outside these circles, and the only way to do so is to employ print, rather than conversation, and to risk profit or ruin on the literary market. The free-flow of conversation can occur only when those institutions which enable it for this tiny class are conserved. Once More is confronted with the need to address, not amiable patrons, but the disgruntled lower classes, she must shift from the politics of conversation to the politics of conversion, which are related, but not synonymous. That she is able to use conversation as a means of converting the masses indicates her power as a propagandist, but once she begins to converse outside her circles of leisured friends, the mode of converse itself radically changes. She must write in the convoluted mode that we have already noted, not as an equal friend, but as a superior guardian of culture who, because of her feminine sympathy, can teach as though she is one of those from whom she must also separate herself in order to be true to customary class relations.

The disruptive movement toward a new economic structure, then, provides a fissure through which women writers can enter. In fact, this movement makes it practically necessary for women to enter the publishing market. Upper-class and middle-class men have to be freed to serve productively (as producers of capital and commodities) in the new capitalist-industrial system. Because these men must be prepared for managerial roles in a mechanizing, utilitarian society, literary culture is opened to women. As the British ruling class is being transformed from one based on the stability of inherited wealth, privilege, and leisure to one based on the steady growth of commerce, capital, and labor, literary activity must be re-institutionalized so that literature itself becomes gradually feminized; as it becomes more marginal, it is redefined as women's "work," in order to discourage males from seeing it as influentially productive (men's) "work." By the Victorian period, the fear of poetry's unproductivity has become so palpable that Tennyson makes it a central theme within his poetry. By the end of the nineteenth century, it has become so trenchant that—despite the fact that literary men still dominate— literature has come to be seen as decorative and effeminate or as extraneously decadent and dandyish. As women's work, poetic activity becomes an extension of woman's domestic role. Following More's lead, middle-class women can engage in literary activity as an integral part of their social service; as social workers, they extend domestic caretaking outward to become guardians and nurturers of sociomoral culture, lovingly tending to society's more immaterial (meaning inconsequential and superrogatory, as well as intangible) needs of the spirit while men conquer the material wilderness of industry and trade. As the empire of spirit—classical learning, religion, *belles lettres,* and morality—becomes a handmaiden to the real work of science, technology, trade, and industry, women are allowed to take that empire as their own.

Due to their crisis-mentality, the upper classes during the French Revolutionary and Napoleonic era can see as fortuitous the advent of writers like More, Barbauld, Fanny Burney, and Maria Edgeworth. Such feminine writers are now *needed* in order to assure the proper functioning of a gendered society.[4] Rather than extraneous scribbling eccentrics, they become the nurturers of a threatened tradition while helping to smooth the way to a tumultuous future. These women exploit a potentially dangerous leveling medium—print—in order to educate young ladies and culture as a whole in the ways of tradition, so that female writing, already an irreversible phenomenon, is managed, accommodated, and conventionally institutionalized. Ironically, the very mechanism that nourishes social discord within Britain (discord that could easily be attributed to the external threat of France) is also the instrument providing the means for combatting social discord and the threat of revolution. If seditious principles are being spread to an ever-increasing market of lower-class readers, then the same market mechanism, the same publishing technology and strategies, can be used to spread conservative principles. And just as the only answer to the threat of print seems to be more print, the only answer to the threat of women writers seems to be more women writers. A radical female writer like Mary Wollstonecraft can only be countered with a proper lady writer like Hannah More. What More passes down to her feminine descendants, then, is both a blessing and a curse: she provides them with a protected horizon from which they can record women's own desire, but that horizon itself is an opportunity defined by its limits. In the next chapter, we'll examine how those limits are enforced and resisted by both men and women.

7

The Politics of Taste:
Writing Women and the Resistance
to Feminine Desire

Once a new breed of poets has begun to enter the literary market, the question and the problem for the literary establishment is how can these writers be judged critically without disturbing predefined standards of taste. Added to the trauma of this dilemma, of course, is the fear that this new breed of writers could embody more than just another literary movement; they could represent radical change imminent within culture as a whole. Will this new breed prove monstrous, like Frankenstein's creation, or will it be a harmlessly amusing addition to literary culture?

To many early nineteenth-century critics, literacy itself appears as a raging monster that has slipped through the firm hands of aristocratic patrons and protegées and into the rough hands of a mobbish reading public. Besides attempting to regain control by shutting down the actual machinery of print—which, of course, the Tory government proceeds to do with a vengeance through censorship and oppressive sedition laws—the only option is to use that machinery to supply the uncontrollable market with appropriate reading material. The reading public has become a beast that can be restrained only by keeping it well fed. Women writers, like women readers, are an integral part of this new beastly presence. Just as women cannot be stopped from reading whatever they can get their hands on, so women writers cannot be stopped from publishing their morsels, as long as the beast wants to consume them. From the woman writer's point of view, however, the process must not have appeared as so much out-of-control. The slightest misstep could damage or eliminate her chances of succeeding on the market, for her career is not only left to the whim of that fickle monster, the reading public; it is also left to the resolute discretion of fathers, brothers, male publishers, and male reviewers, who might censure and censor her the moment she appeared to them as monstrous, the moment she appeared to them as too palpable a manifestation of that monstrously capricious readership that has given birth to her. By examining how feminine poetesses could expect to be received by the literary establishment, we shall better understand the kinds of poetry that they are able to write. In examining the politics of taste, this chapter focuses on the reception of the poetess often considered to be the greatest woman writer of her time by her contemporaries, Felicia Hemans. What compels contemporaries to bestow this honor on Hemans? How does this appraisal of her affect traditional masculine predilections of taste? And why does her fame perish after it seems to have been immortalized?

1

In his introduction to the Garland Series's photo-facsimile of Hemans's poetry, Donald Reiman attempts to explain briefly the present oblivion of a poet whose "number of editions . . . must, I think, outstrip that of all such rival woman poets in the nineteenth century (and, therefore, for all time)" (Introduction v). Reiman claims that "[t]hough Felicia Dorothea Hemans was personally liked by the few literary contemporaries she met—notably Scott and Wordsworth—she was not taken seriously as a poet or dramatist." He goes on to claim, regarding Hemans's winning a couple of prize competitions for poetry: "The simple truth is, of course, that genuine poets who follow their own genius seldom, in maturity, compete for prizes by writing poems on a specified subject" (viii–ix). I would suggest that the truth here is more complicated than this. William Wordsworth may never have competed for a prize, but, as poet laureate (the prize for his whole poetic career), he certainly writes poems on "specified subjects" in his maturity. More important, however, Hemans's attempts to establish herself as a serious poet cannot be judged simply according to what a Wordsworth would or would not do. Although it would have been unlikely for Hemans to have ever become poet laureate, she certainly desires to hold such a position. Isn't it possible that Hemans enters those contests in order to bring attention to her potential as a voice of the state? And isn't it also possible that a talented woman—perhaps even a woman of "genius"—at a loss as to how to diminish the prejudice against the idea of a female laureate, might see the winning of smaller nationalist prizes as a means of achieving a larger, more elusive goal? Hemans's status as a woman, and her position as one of the first public female poets, places her career in a different context from a male poet of the upper class, for she has precious few foremothers either to point her way or to point her away from paths that may turn into dead-ends. Considering the circumstances, entering those contests may have, after all, been one of her most prudent decisions. Not only does she win, thus proving that a woman can write an impressive poem on a subject previously considered male terrain; she also bolsters her career by getting her name into the periodicals. Literary men may not take such contests seriously because they can afford not to. Aspiring literary women definitely have less leeway for such a cavalier attitude.

Reiman's statements help to clarify the need for making distinctions of gender when talking about the careers of these early women poets. They also help to indicate how the pervasiveness of romanticist assumptions influences the discussion of these poets. When we examine more closely what Reiman means by "genuine poets who follow their own genius," we discover that he means "romantic poets." Reiman concludes thus:

A final judgment of Felicia Hemans' poetry cannot, of course, be rendered now. But to readers of these seven volumes in *The Romantic Context: Poetry,* I suggest two elements to be included in that final evaluation: First, Hemans will be found, in spite of her admiration of Wordsworth, Byron, and other Romantic poets, to exhibit in her own themes and ideals a substantial case of cultural lag, drawing most of her inspiration from the Enlightenment and remaining closer to Pope and Cowper than to her greater contemporaries. Second, the very neatness and polish of versification and the clarity of the syntax and diction of Hemans' poetry will be seen as attributes of this cultural lag. Repeating the truisms of her upbringing, Hemans never evidences the struggle toward self-discovery that characterizes such poems of growth as *Religious Musings, Tintern Abbey, Childe Harold, Alastor,* or *Endymion.* For her, the thinking process and the moral conclusions are prior to, not inherent in, the poetic act. (x–xi)

These conclusions are riddled with romanticist assumptions. Hemans's early poetry, especially, does draw "inspiration from the Enlightenment," but whether this is "cultural lag" or not has to be much more closely examined. It just may be the case that Hemans's rejection of full-fledged romantic discourse is not an "in spite of" but rather a "because of." We always give the male romantics the benefit of self-consciousness about their poetic decisions; we should, at least, begin on such ground with the female poets, and, if necessary, revise the premise as we progress. To view Hemans solely in the context of Pope and Cowper is problematic. It would be more fruitful to consider her relation to her contemporary sister poets, for Hemans sees herself as part of a new sisterly endeavor, one that ultimately moves beyond both Wordsworth and Pope.

   Not only do Reiman's assumptions tend to denigrate Hemans by identifying her as an unself-consciously belated Augustan; they also seem to imply that to be a gifted Augustan is necessarily less than to be a gifted romantic. When Reiman speaks of Hemans's "neatness and polish," her "clarity of . . . syntax and diction," he seems to suggest that poetry containing these qualities is not as great as poetry that self-consciously records a "struggle toward self-discovery." What Reiman calls "self-discovery" I would suggest is the same self-possession I have argued is the primary motive of romantic poeticizing. Two questions are pertinent here. First, because Hemans rejects romantic struggle, does it necessarily mean that there is no struggle and growth "evidenced" in the poetry? The final statement of Reiman's paragraph implicitly makes such a claim. Second, must good poetry necessarily include struggle and growth? Poetry has not always been conceived in such terms. As we have seen in the contrast between Keats's self-conscious staging of a struggle for poetic development and Mary Tighe's nondevelopmental poetic constancy, the idea of poetic evolution is based on historically-situated cultural rituals of maturation, rituals that themselves are gender-determined. The same kind of distinction can be made in relation to "the thinking process" that Reiman seems to preclude from Hemans's poetry. Thinking and romantic thinking are two different things, though in our criticism we often tend to conflate them. Hemans does not engage in the latter in her poetry; she most certainly engages in the former.

The extent to which Hemans repeats "the truisms of her upbringing" is debatable, but as long as we associate her poetic upbringing primarily with masculine forms of poetry, whether Augustan or romantic, we shall always prevent ourselves from establishing a more catholic view of the conditions under which she conducts her poetic enterprise. Reiman's concern in the above passage seems to be the degree of originality of Hemans's work. We must remind ourselves that originality itself is a problematic standard by which to judge this woman's literary production, especially when it is the romantic conception of originality that is being applied. As we have seen that originality means something quite different for the Augustans than it does for the romantics, and that it has different implications even for poets within the romantic canon, it is more than likely that Hemans would also hold a view of originality disparate from both Augustan and romantic ideology. Indeed, since as a female poet she lacks the historical belatedness that Said identifies as the source for the drive toward originality, originality itself may be more or less a nonissue for her. Just as Shelley, influenced by the feminine others in his life, begins to question the impulse toward romantic originality, so it is feasible that Hemans, whose most significant influence is the feminine sphere of domesticity, might have rejected romantic originality out of various concerns and fears, including disagreement with romantic ideology itself.

My point here is not to single out Donald Reiman, who, like other major romanticist critical historians, has contributed immensely to our understanding of the romantic period. Rather, I want to stress two important inescapable factors that lurk always behind our criticism. First, our appraisals of poetry are synonymous with the history that has made those appraisals possible. Whether or not we view Hemans historically as a romantic poet will necessarily help determine how we tend to judge her as a poet in our romantic criticism. It is not surprising that Reiman, like Woolf, falls into the trap of romantic hypostatizing; it is a trap that is nearly impossible—if not absolutely so—to walk around. Second, romantic assumptions cannot be divorced from gender assumptions. That Hemans is not a canonized romantic poet is intimately tied to her cultural and historical situation as a woman. A critic does not have to be an ardent sexist to dismiss a poet like Hemans with or without a hearing. The point is that it is so difficult to give a poet like Hemans a hearing in the first place. Such a hearing would entail the development of an ideology and an aesthetics that is not based in romanticist assumptions. Critical taste is a political, historical creature. It is also a tautological process. We tend to judge poets based on the standards implicit in the work of already canonized poets, and yet those standards are in themselves based on the dehistoricized, hidden predilections which led to the canonization of those poets in the first place. To read a poet like Hemans not only means that we must examine as a historical-cultural phenomenon the taste which made her famous and then obliterated her; it also means that we must recognize how our own critical ideology operates within the same historical corrider that determined Hemans's fate as a poet.

I would question Reiman's claim that although Hemans "was personally liked by the few literary contemporaries she met—notably Scott and Wordsworth—she was not taken seriously as a poet or dramatist." As indicated in Chapter 1, writers of the time tended to conflate the character of the poet with the worth of the poetry, as Shelley does in his *Defence of Poetry* (see *Political Writings* 194). As erroneous as the idea appears to us (a difference in taste?), it is a commonplace one of the time. This idea is especially germane to a woman who has embarked upon the road to literary notoriety. How else can a woman justify putting pen to paper and paper to press? If the expressed objective of her enterprise is solely to edify, then her audience is more than willing to be edified by her. Even moreso than with the male poets, then, the quality of Hemans's work is repeatedly and consistently judged by the putative virtue and prudence that beam from the interior of her life through the words of her poetry. The reviewers of her time (and she was reviewed religiously) rank her highly—often as the best poetess of England—and because of her expressed objective, they take her seriously both as a woman and a poet.[1] When Wordsworth calls Hemans "that holy Spirit, / Sweet as spring, as ocean deep" in his "Extempore Effusion upon the Death of James Hogg," he is praising the holiness and depth of her poetry as much as the saintliness and profundity of her character.

It is true, however, that to Wordsworth, Scott, and their (male) colleagues, a poetess is not a poet, and an authoress must be taken seriously in a different manner from a male author. In order to reconstruct Hemans's position in her time, however, we must consider more fully the crucial relations she had with other poets, female and male, as well as her relation to the reading public that made her famous.

2

We have heard much of late regarding the rights and sphere of woman. The topic has become trite. One branch of the discussion, however is worthy of careful notice—the true theory of cultivated and liberal men on the subject. This has been greatly misunderstood. The idea has been often suggested that man is jealous of his alleged intellectual superiority, while little has been advanced in illustration of his genuine reverence for female character. Because the other sex cannot always find erudition so attractive as grace in woman, and strong mental traits so captivating as a beautiful disposition, it is absurdly urged that mind and learning are only honoured in masculine attire. The truth is, that men of feeling instinctively recognize something higher than intellect. They feel that a noble and true soul is greater and more delightful than mere reason, however powerful; and they know that to this, extensive knowledge and active logical powers are not essential. It is not the attainments, or the literary talent, that they would have women abjure. They only pray that through and above these may appear the woman.

Here we have a "cultivated and liberal" man offering us "the true theory," "greatly misunderstood," of "the rights and sphere of woman." This is not the beginning of an essay on women's rights, or more appropriately women's rightful domestic sphere, but rather the beginning of an essay re-introducing Felicia Hemans to an American reading public greedy for yet another collection of her works. (Hemans was as popular—if not more so—in the United States as in Britain throughout the nineteenth century.) The essay is worth examining in some detail for three reasons: 1) it is prototypical of the male response to Hemans's work during the nineteenth century; 2) it brings to the surface much of the anxiety that stays just beneath the surface in most earlier reviews of her work; 3) it represents the Victorian consolidation of an ideology that is merely nascent and more troubling to the men and women of the early nineteenth century. In writing this essay for Rufus W. Griswold's edition of the *Poems* (New York: Leavitt & Allen, 1853), H. T. Tuckerman, attempting to put Hemans into her proper sphere as a female poet, unwittingly puts the field of nineteenth-century ideology into proper perspective for us.

Tuckerman immediately associates the phenomenon of female publishing with the "trite" subject of women's rights. As much as he would prefer to avoid that "other" subject, he is compelled by his ostensible subject (the genius of Felicia Hemans) to address the "other." The other subject, of course, is his genuine concern, because it is his greatest distress. He cannot—with a settled conscience or an unsettled unconscious—discuss a poet who happens to be a woman unless he first discusses how a woman can be a poet without threatening a man. Tuckerman's strategy exemplifies the pattern of many reviews of Hemans's poetry. They begin with a digression that happens to be the true subject. These reviews are as much a form of psychic defense as a form of appraisal; they enable the critic to perform the crucial cultural endeavor of putting women poets in their natural and social place while ostensibly simply going about the mundane task of literary criticism. This is why Tuckerman must dismiss the issue of women's rights immediately and as quickly as he mentions it. A woman writing poetry has nothing to do with women's rights he wants to say, although he'd rather not have to say it, since raising the issue *raises* the issue.

In raising the issue, one must also bring up another issue that is even more distressing than women's rights—that is, a man's right to define women's sphere, to determine the borders of women's poetry. This issue induces so much anxiety in Tuckerman that he sublimates it. Tuckerman unconsciously confounds any potential distinctions that might (and should) be made between women and men, between who is charging and who is being charged. Who is the initial "we" of the essay, women or men? We may all be doing the hearing (the topic has become trite), but who is doing all the talking that has made the subject trite in the first place? Who has "misunderstood" "the true theory," women or men or both? It is not coincidental that this discourse on gender difference refuses to admit sexual distinctions into the rhetorical situation of the essay. By cloaking actual social differences—the issue of women's rights—behind a patronizing, paternalistic "we," Tuckerman's discourse pretends to speak not just for all men, but also for all women. It is only through this rhetorical ploy—a form of ingratiation—that one man can talk so freely about what all women must be and think and write.

Tuckerman wants to leave behind the true problem ("that man is jealous of his alleged intellectual superiority") for a specious assertion (that man has "genuine reverence for female character"), which once again cloaks the true distress: that women poets potentially disturb the set relations between the sexes. Tuckerman is so quick to grant women a higher, nobler purpose, a more virtuous and significant role, because by doing so he can more easily re-set the natural boundaries beyond which woman cannot and therefore should not travel. By doing so, he can allow women to write poetry—a kind of poetry that he genuinely feels he and his culture need and that he believes men are incapable of providing—while simultaneously (dis)solving the problem of sexual equality by dividing poetry into gendered spheres of influence. Because a woman's place is to nurture the soul—sentiment, the affections—and since the soul is higher than "mere" reason or intellect, "however powerful," any woman who attempts to write masculine poetry stoops to a level beneath her. When she seeks those masculine attributes of "extensive knowledge and active logical powers," which are inessential to her but essential to men, she lowers herself to the coarser level of men—no matter how powerful such a level may appear. I don't think Tuckerman intends a paradox, but, of course, this is what seals the seams of his logic. Women, who take care of the private sphere of unheroic domestic life, are actually the nobler creatures. Men, who are granted the capacity to write on grand, momentous topics in a powerful, commanding voice, are actually the more trivial creatures. Needless to say, the logic of the separate spheres, which undergirds all of Tuckerman's critical commentary, is rather messy itself. If women are naturally all the things Tuckerman wants to claim, then they would not be able to cross over into man's proper sphere. That which is naturally determined does not need a moral imperative to reinforce its enactment.

And yet, Tuckerman feels compelled both to describe a natural, immutable condition and to warn against women's changing that condition. Men "only pray" that woman, as she gains literary notoriety, "appear" as woman. "They [men] desire that the harmony of nature may not be disturbed; that the essential foundations of love may not be invaded; that the sensibility, delicacy, and quiet enthusiasm of the female heart may continue to awaken in man the tender reverence, which is the most elevating of his sentiments" (v). Here Tuckerman inscribes the genuine objective of the essay: the fulfillment of man's desire. In an essay that is supposed to serve merely as a prefatory appraisal of woman's voice, as only a prelude to woman's own grand symphony, Tuckerman guarantees that what we hear as we listen to Hemans is a feminine melody set to masculine time and moving toward masculine resolution.

In an attempt to provide exempla for how potential gender-confusion can result in the reaffirmation of natural gender difference, Tuckerman turns appropriately to a literary device, one as common in the romantic period—in

Scott, Byron, and Hemans herself, for instance—as in the plays of Shakespeare: "Portia is highly intellectual; but even while arrayed in male costume and enacting the public advocate, the essential and captivating characteristics of her true sex inspire her mien, and language" (vi). What Tuckerman is attempting to prove is that demeanor—or what Hannah More calls "propriety"—is what counts. Portia may dress in men's clothes, may even be smart and eloquent, but she knows that she is a woman, and her knowing can be sensed in her "mien" and her "language." This example sets up one of the crucial distinctions between masculine and feminine poetry: women and men may ostensibly write about the same themes, they may even seem to write about them with the same degree of eloquence and intellectual rigor (though the latter becomes extremely problematic); but they can *never* (or *should* never) write in the same way, with the same approach, attitude, or expression (mien), or with the same method, manner, or style (language).

There is an essential quality of sex, to be felt rather than described, and it is when this is marred, that a feeling of disappointment is the consequence. . . . The triumphs of mind always command respect, but their style and trophies have diverse complexions in the two sexes. . . . It matters not how erudite or mentally gifted a woman may be, so that she remains in manner and feeling a woman. (vi)

The "essential quality of sex" must be "felt" because Tuckerman cannot describe it, just as he must assert its existence exactly because he cannot prove or demonstrate it. As Tuckerman goes on to define this "sphere" as "undoubtedly the influence and power of the affections," he reveals the fissure that resides at the heart of his ideology. If feminine poetry is simply an extension of woman's role as domestic caretaker, moral guardian (man's "better angel" he calls her), and cultural refiner, why only at this juncture in history has she been allowed to claim this extended function? It is a question that Tuckerman must repress in order to dwell safely within the ideology that promises to fulfill his desire.

Tuckerman must also repress the question of the audience for female poets, for such a question would complicate his discourse to the point of disrupting its seemingly well-sewn seams. Rather, he must assume that women write primarily for men—an ironic situation, to say the least. "Man delights to meet woman in the field of letters as well as in the arena of social life [read here: he delights to meet women who occupy the same field in letters as in social life]. . . . With exquisite satisfaction he learns at her feet the lessons of mental refinement and moral sensibility. From her teachings he catches a grace and sentiment unwritten by his own sex. Especially in poetry, beams, with startling beauty, the light of her soul" (vii). What we discover is that women write poetry for the advancement of man (in the narrowest sense of that word), exactly. She writes poetry to teach him what he cannot otherwise know about her, and what he cannot otherwise learn from himself. "There he reads the records of a woman's heart" (vii). Punning on the title of Hemans's most celebrated volume of poems, *Records of Woman,* Tuckerman turns her attempt to create feminine history into yet another form of masculine fulfill-

ment. Even in writing she becomes the object of his gaze as the records of her
heart become the readable signs of his embracing desire. "He hears from her
own lips how the charms of nature and the mysteries of life have wrought in
her bosom" (vii). Just as Tuckerman has appealed to the beauty of her soul
as an indication of the merit of her poetry, he now laces his language with the
yearnings of sexual desire: her own lips reveal the charms and mysteries that
he desires to possess in possessing her. Even as he ostensibly discusses the
highness of her purpose and the nobility of her soul, he predictably resorts to
masculine images of feminine physicality. The sentence moves from lips and
charms to the bosom. In the meantime, we have lost not only the "records"
so lovingly recorded by this poeticizing woman, but also the women readers
for whom those records are primarily recorded. Hemans becomes both the
prototype of his argument—the ultimate representative—and the archetype
of his unconscious needs—the ultimate representation. No wonder she is so
cherished by the reviewers and readers of her time. She, better than any other
woman poet, manages to write poetry without disturbing the harmony between the sexes.

We could analyze the appraisals that Tuckerman makes and the passages
he chooses from her poetry to show how his "other" subject always determines his view of his ostensible subject, but we can be much more concise by
letting Tuckerman once again speak for himself: "It was the opinion of Dr.
Spurzheim, an accurate and benevolent observer of life, that suffering was essential to the rich developement of female character" (xiii). Woman suffering
is Hemans's forte, Tuckerman suggests. Unlike the male, who may have any
number of self-possessing motives for poeticizing, the female is relegated to
the sphere of suffering, self-sacrifice, salvation. She writes to save men from
themselves. He misses in her poetry what we shall examine later, woman conquering, woman defining her own heroics. Even a poetess as prototypical and
archetypical as Hemans, however, occasionally fails to fulfill masculine desire. Whenever she strays into masculine terrain, Tuckerman gently nudges
Hemans back into her own sphere, as he does in his appraisal of Hemans's
Byronic poem *The Restoration of the Works of Art to Italy*. "Knightly legends, tales of martial enterprise—the poetry of courage and devotion, fascinated her from the first. But when her deeper feeling [*sic*] were called into play,
and the latent sensibilities of her nature sprung to conscious action" (xv), it
is then that she excelled, according to Tuckerman. In this way, Tuckerman
appears not to be dictating to Hemans what her sphere is, and to all women
poets what their sphere must be. Such desire is "deeper," is "latent," within
the woman herself. "It is, indeed, irreverent to dictate to genius," he says as
he proceeds irreverently to do exactly that, "but the themes of female poetry
are written in the very structure of the soul" (viii). As long as Hemans sticks
to the themes written in the deep structure of her feminine soul, she is a
great—the greatest—poetess. "When [poetesses] overstep their appropriate
domain," however, "much of their mental influence is lost" (vii). "Lost"
here means wasted, in a contrapuntal way to the way Wordsworth uses it in
"Nutting" or Shelley in *Julian and Maddalo*. Females waste themselves—be-

come ruined or lost—when they fail to fulfill masculine expectations, not when they fail to fulfill their own promise, and masculine expectations turn out, unfortunately, to be societal expectations as well. "Lost" also means to be morally in error, lost to sin. The actual problem for Tuckerman is that such erring influence is never "lost," never really wasted, for such influence changes men and women and such influence always possesses the potential for bringing back in full view that specter haunting the whole essay: the rights of woman, the equality of the sexes.

There is ample evidence from contemporary reviews to confirm that both men and women of Hemans's time are trudging their way awkwardly toward the position Tuckerman is able to hold so well, despite its logical inconsistencies—or because of them. The two great arbiters of literary taste and public ethics, Francis Jeffrey of the *Edinburgh Review* and William Gifford of the *Quarterly*, both take time to give Hemans significant reviews in their respective journals, and both anticipate Tuckerman's pattern, albeit without the ideological smoothness enabled by historical belatedness. Jeffrey begins his review of *Records of Woman* and *The Forest Sanctuary* by trying to (re)-establish the lines of gender threatened so obviously by female poeticizing.

Women, we fear, cannot do every thing; nor even every thing they attempt. But what they can do, they do, for the most part, excellently—and much more frequently with an absolute and perfect success, than the aspirants of our rougher and more ambitious sex. They cannot, we think, represent naturally the fierce and sullen passions of men—nor their coarser vices—nor even scenes of actual business or contention—and the mixed motives, and strong and faulty characters, by which affairs of moment are usually conducted on the great theatre of the world. (*Edinburgh Review* 50 [Oct. 1829]: 32)

Like Tuckerman, Jeffrey initiates his discourse by attempting to repress the issue of woman's equality, and he does so by suggesting, again like Tuckerman, that what she can do, she does better—that is, more perfectly—than her male counterpart. This appears to be exorbitant praise for women poets at the expense of their brothers. What is submerged here, however, is the patronizing and paternalistic logic of the statement. Women do smaller things better than men; smaller things are more easily done perfectly than grander things; therefore, women do what they do best more perfectly than men do what they do best. This logic, of course, leaves intact the *a priori* premise that what women do is (or should be) lesser.

Jeffrey is ambivalent about the ultimate cause of gender difference, whether it is social training ("from their being seldom set on such tedious tasks") or, as the following passage seems to suggest, "natural training":

Their proper and natural business [their "sphere" in Tuckerman's language] is the practical regulation of private life, in all its bearings, affections, and concerns; and the questions with which they have to deal in that most important department, though often of the utmost difficulty and nicety, involve, for the most part, but few elements; and may generally be better described as delicate than intricate;—requiring for their solution rather a quick tact and fine perception than a patient or laborious examination. For the same reason, they rarely succeed in long works, even on subjects the best suited to their genius; their natural training rendering them equally averse to long doubt and long labour. (32)

Like Tuckerman, Jeffrey is basing his judgment implicitly on bodily difference. The opposition between delicacy and intricacy, between nicety and strength of duration, are mental qualities derived from physical attributes, and then applied to literary discourse. It is not surprising, then, when Jeffrey admonishes Hemans for attempting long poems and encourages her to produce more little ones (47). It is also not surprising when he delineates as the poetess's proper sphere "the deep and dangerous learning of feeling and emotion" that women are "instinctively schooled in" (33). Recognizing that "[i]t has been so little the fashion, at any time, to encourage women to write for publication," it is difficult for Jeffrey to "prove these truths by examples" (33). Finally, like Tuckerman, we get Hemans as prototype and archetype, though with a less enthusiastic appraisal of her work: "We think the poetry of Mrs. Hemans a fine exemplification of Female Poetry—and we think it has much of the perfection which we have ventured to ascribe to the happier productions of female genius" (34). After predetermining that Hemans must be what women are supposed to be, and therefore that her poetry cannot disturb "the harmony of nature" by disrupting the contours of his desire, Jeffrey proceeds to apply the predictable epithets of praise: "infinitely sweet, elegant, and tender—touching, perhaps, contemplative, rather than vehement and overpowering . . . informed with a purity and loftiness of feeling, and a certain sober and humble tone of indulgence and piety" (34).

Writing for the *Quarterly* (24 [Oct. 1820] 130–139), William Gifford offers a similar nervous assessment of Hemans, indicating how this issue cuts across superficial political lines from the more Whiggish *Edinburgh* to the Tory *Quarterly*. Gifford begins in a key similar to Tuckerman's and Jeffrey's:

This certainly is not the age in which those who speak slightingly of female talent should expect to be listened to with much attention. In almost every department of literature, and in many of art and science, some one or other of our own contemporaries and countrywomen will be found, in spite of all the disadvantages of an imperfect education, occupying a respectable, at least, if not a prominent situation. And this remark, if true any where, is undoubtedly so when applied to poetry. (130)

Like Tuckerman and Jeffrey, Gifford recognizes that "no judicious critic will [can] speak without respect" about such poets as Baillie, Tighe, and Hemans. Shifting away from the mode in which all male critics are entitled and obligated to belittle scribbling bluestockings and to trivialize their endeavors is no easy task for any critic. The mode shifted to, however, always contains both masculine defensiveness and insecurity as well as a stern fatherly warning, usually enunciated as a mere observation. Gifford's observation about Hemans is exemplary:

If we may judge too of her, in another point, from her writings, Mrs. Hemans is a woman in whom talent and learning have not produced the ill effects so often attributed to them; her faculties seem to sit meekly on her. . . . It is something at least to know, that whether the emotions she excites be always those of powerful delight or not, they will be at least harmless, and leave no sting behind: if our fancies are not always transported, our hearts at least will never be corrupted: we have not found a line which a delicate women [*sic*] might blush to have written. (130–131)

Gifford's sigh of relief is all but audible in his prose. Another female poet, but at least another one who confirms masculine expectations of femininity. Hemans's poetry evidences no "ill effects" attributable to "talent and learning" in women, ironically the same "talent and learning," as he acknowledges at the beginning, whose denial to women has disadvantaged them ("the disadvantages of an imperfect education"). Good feminine poetry is like the sin of omission: it does not overexcite (men?) to a state of corruption; it does not leave a sting behind; it does not embarrass other women's delicacy or the poetess's own; it does not offend men; in a word, it is harmless.

Hemans's poetry, Gifford is anxious to claim, does not disturb the predetermined status of the sexes. But like his male cohorts, Gifford is forced into a position of protesting too much:

[D]elicacy of feeling has long been, and long may it be, the fair and valued boast of our countrywomen; but we have had too frequent reason of late to lament, both in female readers and writers, the display of qualities very opposite in nature. . . . Certain we are, that the most dangerous writer of the present day finds his most numerous and most enthusiastic admirers among the fair sex; and we have many times seen very eloquent eyes kindle in vehement praise of the poems, which no woman should have read, and which it would have been far better for the world if the author had never written.

Of course, the scoundrel is Byron, whose ambivalent relation to "his most numerous and enthusiastic admirers" we have already discussed. The interesting issue here is the relation between women who read and those who write. Gifford acknowledges the influence, and is troubled by it. It is a short step from a woman reading and vehemently praising Byronic poetry to a woman attempting to write Byronic poetry.

3

Recognizing the effect on literary men of their newly acquired poetic aspirations, women are quick to attempt to placate and assure their brothers. Women reviewers, anxious to reassure their nervous brothers, appear to follow a pattern similar to that of men critics, but in their feminine voices is a new tone of self-confidence as well as the familiar one of self-effacement and capitulation to masculine expectation. Women critics were as anxious to praise Hemans, to present her as a shining example of feminine genius uncorrupted by men's perverse predictions, as men were to appraise her potential effects on their own desire. Also in the tone of female reviewers is the thrill of a new adventure, a grand venture never risked before, an experiment sure to prove fertile. Take, for example, Maria Jane Jewsbury's retrospective review of Hemans's work in *The Athenaeum* (172 [Feb. 12, 1831]: 104–

105).[2] Jewsbury (later Fletcher), herself an "authoress" of some renown and a friend and literary daughter-sister to Hemans, begins by relishing the prototypical status usually given to Hemans by male critics like Jeffrey and Gifford: "Were there to be a feminine literary house of commons, Felicia Hemans might very worthily be called to fill the chair as the speaker—a representative of the whole body, as distinguished from the other estates of the intellectual realm" (104). Jewsbury gladly grants Hemans a position as "representative of the whole body" of female poets. The metaphor she chooses, however, even as it refuses to draw attention to any contentiousness between male and female, derives from that sociopolitical sphere in which women are denied their civil rights. It is difficult to say whether Jewsbury is conscious of the implications of the metaphor—though she very well might be. Her unconsciousness, however, would only make the metaphor all the more significant for understanding the feminine response to aggressive masculine desire. It is almost as if Jewsbury is, unintentionally, answering and rebelling against her male colleagues even as she confirms their expectations.

What does she mean by "the other estates of the intellectual realm"? She could mean the other genres taken (over) by other women writers, and her following hypothesis tends to confirm such a conjecture: "If she [Hemans] wrote, or rather published prose, for write it we know she does very charmingly, it would be characterised by the same qualities that mark her poetry" (104). Or those "other estates" could mean other intellectual domains, like science and art, which as Gifford notes, women have newly entered. That is, Hemans is even more representative and more capable than male reviewers have indicated. The metaphor of speaker of the House of Commons communicates this well. One individual is chosen to represent her district—the realm of poetry or science or art—and then from these representatives, one is chosen to represent the whole body of representatives. What Jewsbury is implying is that Hemans represents all women of potential genius—those newly entering such fields as art and science, not just all female poets or even all writers. Hemans's genius is so ample and diverse that, if she had so chosen, she could have taken (over) other estates as her realm. This challenge to "other estates," however, is an infectious business, much like the process of female publication itself. Just as Hemans could have, if she had chosen, written great prose works, she could have, if she had chosen, written great masculine works—of poetry, of prose, or of anything else. Whether consciously or not, Jewsbury implicitly suggests this when she says: "If she . . . published prose, . . . it would be characterised . . . by some [qualities] that in poetry cannot well appear:—wit, for instance" (104). As we shall see, wit is a problematic attribute for women of Hemans's generation. Thus, when Jewsbury suggests that Hemans could have, if she had chosen, been a great wit, she is potentially suggesting that she could have invaded and conquered the supposedly masculine realms of intellect.

Intuitively realizing that she treads on dangerous ground, Jewsbury apparently withdraws in order to calm her readers and to assure continued feminine poeticizing, and she does so by following the example of her fathers.

Rather than denying the possession of wit to Hemans (and thus to women in general), she divides the terrain according to gender difference. If there can be "poetry" and "feminine poetry," why not "wit" and "female wit"? "The wit of society is sparkling repartee, intellectual snap-dragon; poetical wit is essentially imaginative—spiritual rather than satiric—and female wit differs as much from man's, as Coeur de Lion chopping the iron mace by a single blow of his straight ponderous sword, differed from Sultan Saladin severing the down pillow with his thin shining scimitar" (104). Jewsbury is able to stake a new claim—the realm of wit—for women while still appeasing masculine desire: feminine wit is as "harmless" as trying to assault a pillow with a scimitar.

In implicitly answering male critics of Hemans, Jewsbury is conscious of how gender categories can backfire against women. She cannot deny the existence of the categories—indeed she must affirm them fervently both for men's sake and for women's—but she can transform the effect and use of them. She can, as she has done with the idea of feminine wit, make a virtue of gender segregation, as we find her doing in the following passage:

It is ridiculous to compare poets who have no points in common—equally vain to settle their priority of rank: each has his own character and his own station without reference to others. There will always be a difference between the poetry of men and women—so let it be; we have two kinds of excellence instead of one; we have also the pleasure of contrast: we discover that power is the element of man's genius—beauty that of woman's;—and occasionally we reciprocate their respective influence, by discerning the beauty of power, and feeling the power of beauty. (104)

The schism that men have made in order to assure their own dominance over poeticizing, Jewsbury transforms into the richness of differentiation. If (masculine) poetry and feminine poetry are indeed different, then it is ridiculous to compare them, but not ridiculous to engage in the pleasure that results from the difference. But Jewsbury's logic is much more subversive than this. Not only is women's poetry different from men's, every poet, whether male or female, is different from every other: "each has his own character and his own station without reference to others." Each poet, then, must be judged according to her or his own objectives and motives and subjects—an astute critical principle that all of us too seldom consider. While seeming to re-affirm the masculine desire for separate spheres, Jewsbury has dissolved the arbitrary lines of gender by demonstrating their arbitrariness. If we are going to talk about difference, then let's talk about differences, she suggests. If women's genius consists in beauty and men's in power, then isn't there a beauty in power and a power in beauty? This question is crucial, for it underlines exactly the mode of Hemans's poetic practice, to transform the beauty of feminine suffering into the feminine power of affection, to controvert what the male views as beautiful into an act of female empowerment. This fact is not lost on Jewsbury: "Mrs. Hemans has written pieces that combine power and beauty in an equal degree" (104).

Jewsbury is not simply answering her male counterparts and reacting to the conflictual sociopolitical conditions that have spotlighted women poets—

putting them at the center only to bar them from moving beyond that sphere of light that encircles them. She is also recording woman's coming into her own space, woman's answering to her own voice. The essay is indeed an immortalization of Hemans, a eulogy of praise that claims recognition for women's space. She is as much talking to Hemans as talking about her, talking to other aspiring women writers as talking about them. She sees herself in Hemans, and hopes to see Hemans in herself; she sees potential Hemanses of the future taking root in the Hemans whose literary career she sketches. And this is a drastically different process from Coleridge's eulogy for his rival–brother Wordsworth in three ways. 1) The reflective relation that Jewsbury creates between herself and her sister–poet contains no trace of rivalry; every word of praise reflects back positively, rather than negatively, to Jewsbury, for Hemans's genius represents and proves the potential of her whole sex. 2) Because Hemans represents her sex, the reflection is multiple. Rather than a tug-of-war between two individual self-possessing geniuses, Jewsbury's eulogy becomes a celebration of potentially infinite influences among, she hopes, an ever-increasing number of actual women geniuses. 3) Finally, Jewsbury's aim is to expel any trace of elegy from her eulogy. She wants neither to prophesy her own death as a writer because of her sister's transfiguration into an eternal presence, nor to wish-fulfill her sister's death by reflecting it in her own. The longer Hemans lives as a literary genius, the longer Jewsbury and other women writers may also come to live.

As Jewsbury charts the development of Hemans's genius, she is outlining the map for future feminine poetic endeavor. Just as women's poetic notoriety has grown virtually from no (male) seed, so Hemans's genius has developed almost miraculously from no seed. "The oak is not in the acorn," Jewsbury writes, contradicting conventional (male) wisdom on poetic genius. "There is not a greater disparity between the text-hand of the child, and the formed, delicate, flowing autograph of the woman, than exists between their compositions" (104). This serves as hope to future women who show no promise, who suffer from imperfect education, lack of experience, lack of resources. If Hemans, the most celebrated poetess of her time, could write poems that "contain nothing of the promise that has since been so splendidly fulfilled," then others can accomplish the same feat. The path that Jewsbury charts is ambivalently presented: it is both one of flexible adjustment, as opposed to the paradigm of masculine growth that poets like Wordsworth and Keats have celebrated, and one of Wordsworthian ordained "progression."

That the childhood of our poetess was no common thing—that she had, from its dawn gleams and visitings of the imagination that has since won for her such high fame—that from very early years she walked in the light of her own spirit, is true; but she has yet manifested more *progression* than any one who has written as much, and whose course we can as faithfully follow. . . . Mrs. Hemans has differed as materially from herself as from any other writer; and not in minor points merely, but in very essential ones. (104, Jewsbury's emphasis)

Coexisting with the masculine paradigm of poetic development is another kind—more erratic and unteleological. It is as if Jewsbury feels compelled to include the masculine conception of poetic progression by alluding to Words-worth ("gleams and visitings of the imagination"), as a way of guaranteeing Hemans's poetic ordination to men (and women) who would question the possibility of genius not being predestined. The oak *is* in the acorn. At the same time, however, she speaks to women who very well may not feel or-dained, predestined, self-confident about their poetic calling. These readers need to know that a poetic career is a series of unpredictably erratic shifts, from one style to another, from total lack of promise to acclaimed genius, from anonymity to fame. These women need to know that the oak is not necessarily in the acorn.

Jewsbury also identifies the cause for such erratic shifts. At first, He-mans "fettered her mind with facts and authorities, and drew upon her mem-ory when she should have relied upon her imagination" (104). This is not a condemnatory criticism, but rather a sympathetic appraisal. Jewsbury surely knows that a woman, lacking the classical education most male poets take for granted, had to prove that she could master their language. It is a kind of overcompensation that perhaps future female poets will be able to avoid be-cause Hemans herself has experienced it for them. This is why Jewsbury qualifies the statement: "She did not possess too much knowledge"—which, of course, would be the male accusation here—"but she made too much use of it" (104). Jewsbury implicitly lets her aspiring sisters know that there is no such thing as too much knowledge for women, despite what men continue to assert. But one must be careful how she displays that knowledge (to men). Not only can such display of knowledge have negative consequences for a woman's career when men begin to tag her a bluestocking; it can also—and more importantly—burden the poetry and distance the woman from her own "warmth," from her own experience and affections. Jewsbury proceeds to ex-plain that this was exactly Hemans's difficulty: "She was diffident of herself, and, to quote her own admission, 'loved to repose under the shadow of mighty names.' Since then she has acquired the courage which leads to simplicity" (104). Because women are taught to trust "the shadow of mighty [male] names," rather than the authority of their own experience, they can easily fall into the trap of writing poetry that fails because it is not their own, but belongs instead to the name of the father. Hemans succeeds despite this in-auspicious beginning exactly because she is willing to experiment, to change the whole character of her poetic personality, even though it goes against the grain of masculine practice. Shifting from writing in the "classic" style to com-posing translations, from composing translations to writing in the "romantic" mode, Hemans finally comes into her own: "Those were the days when she translated, and when her own poetry had somewhat the air of translation. . . . But now this is no longer the case. The sun of feeling has risen upon her song—noon has followed morning—the Promethean touch has been given to the statue—the Memnon yields its music. She writes from and to the heart, putting her memory to its fitting use—that of supplying materials for imagina-tion to fashion and build with" (104). And as the sun of Hemans's feeling spreads itself, casting a long shadow over masculine "superiority," Jewsbury and her other reading and writing sisters share in that sunlight and partake of Hemans's noon. There is more than enough room, for there are so few. The more female poets there are, the more there can be. Thus, Jewsbury's concluding image celebrates the beauty and power of Hemans's works—the beauty that men can view with diminished rancor, the power that women can experience with heightened pride and determination. She appropriately chooses an image that represents the union of opposites, the dissolution of boundaries, and the crossing over into unmapped territory: "The superb creeping-plants of America often fling themselves across the arms of mighty rivers, uniting the opposite banks by a blooming arch: so should every poet do to truth and goodness—so has Felicia Hemans often done, and been, poetically speaking, a Bridge of Flowers" (105). As a bridge (power) of flowers (beauty), Hemans binds masculine strength to feminine affection. She represents the bridge to that space toward which "every poet" must move. In this conclusion, Jewsbury cleverly and subtly claims universality for a woman poeticizing; she claims that Hemans is a bridge (a single genderless standard of truth and goodness) to a new space not only for unknown poetesses but also for male poets who are yet to come.

Jewsbury's conclusion may be read as prophecy or wish-fulfillment, depending on the optimism of the reader. The real situation for women poets was much different. Men do not see them (yet) as a bridge, but rather as a new bud on the vine of feminine variety. The women poets all too often see themselves in the same light. Or worse, they are seen, and see themselves, as unintentional monsters—not a new bud, but a mutation. Coexisting with the glowingly fresh self-confidence of Jewsbury's discourse is a familiar defensiveness, as she attempts to circumvent the accusations that men are sure to consider, if not to make, and that women are certain to feel, if not to express. At the heart of the essay, we discover also the core of feminine anxiety, not an anxiety of influence, but an anxiety of perception. How will men view us; how will they view our efforts; and how will they determine how we view ourselves?

To deal with this anxiety of perception, Jewsbury, rather than returning to the image of light that she uses toward the beginning of the essay, selects a softer, more liquid image in order to reassure her readers of Hemans's naturalness: "Her matronly delicacy of thought, her chastened style of expression, her hallowed ideas of happiness as connected with home, and home-enjoyments;—to condense all in one emphatic word, her *womanliness* is to her intellectual qualities as the morning mist to the landscape, or the evening dew to the flower—that which enhances loveliness without diminishing lustre" (105, Jewsbury's emphasis). The lustre, the light, is still there. It cannot be dimmed even by the cultural demands and pressures placed on women who aspire to write. This analogy—womanliness is to intellect as dew is to flower—manages to reaffirm woman's conventional role as nurturer of private, domestic life while still insisting that the female poet must build on intellect as much as the male poet. Her poetry is the natural effect of both her "matronly" attributes and her intellect. In fact, her maternal qualities (dew and mist) merely enhance the lustre (intellect) that is bestowed by the sunlight (her poetry).

In case her readers are still insecure about female intellect not disturbing the "natural" harmony of the sexes, Jewsbury offers a mental exercise. She moves temporarily from the realm of actual perception and judgment, which it turns out is no better here than the realm of *pre*ception and *pre*judgment—to a hypothetical realm divorced from actuality:

> We appeal to any one who is imaginative. If, after sighing away your soul over some poetic effusion of female genius, a personal introduction took place, and you found the fair author a dashing dragoon-kind of woman—one who could with ease rid her house of a couple of robbers—would you not be startled? Or, if she called upon you to listen to a discussion on Petrarch's love in a voice that brayed upon your sense of hearing, would you not feel that nature had made a mistake? Without a doubt you would. Your understanding might in time be converted; you might bow at the very feet, and solicit the very hand, the proportions of which at first inspired terror, but your Imagination, a recreant to the last, would die maintaining that a poetess ought to be feminine. All that we know are so; and Mrs. Hemans especially. (104)

What if your favorite poetess really did turn out to be a monster? A manly woman capable of protecting her own house? Eventually, you might come to realize the foolishness of your preconception, and worship at the feet of the monster who once terrified you. Your imagination, however, as opposed to your understanding, would remain a "recreant" to the very end, demanding that a poetess be "feminine." By making the palpable fear of a monster-poetess seem like foolish fantasy, a game that we play to reassure ourselves, Jewsbury resubmerges the fear of the manly woman while retaining the force of her argument. A female genius who happens to be masculine would merit our attention as much as a female genius who happens to be conventionally feminine. Of course, Jewsbury must immediately reassert that there are no masculine poetesses, and that it is especially ludicrous to raise the issue in the context of Hemans.

4

But there are "masculine" poetesses, and Jewsbury herself could easily be perceived as one. The epithets that come to mind as we read Jewsbury's essay are exactly those that Tuckerman, Jeffrey, and Gifford reserve and preserve for male geniuses. I have already used the adjective "intricate," which, of course, Jeffrey opposes to delicate as an unlikely female attribute. The essay is "laborious" in the positive sense that Jeffrey uses it, patiently weaving through the logical complexities of a problem. The essay even begins with a metaphor taken from that realm of "serious affairs" that Jeffrey claims women are averse to. Jewsbury is rigorously analytical, bringing the soft and liquid evening dew to her discourse only at touchingly climactic moments.

Both Harriet Browne Owen, Hemans's sister, who set many of Hemans's lyrics to music, and Henry Chorley, Hemans's friend and first biographer, characterize the relationship between Hemans and Jewsbury as the attraction of opposites. Chorley says that Hemans "would enrich and mellow the quick and naturally somewhat harsher mind of" Jewsbury, while the latter "would sometimes playfully exercise her great natural powers of reasoning which had been strengthened by the responsibilities and difficulties of her youth, to call back her fanciful friend." Chorley pictures them as two poles, each restraining the other, each excited by the dramatic contrast in character, each natural in her own way. Like Jewsbury herself, Chorley is anxious to show that neither poet was in any way unnatural. Hemans, he says, came "through Poetry to Thought," while Jewsbury came "through Thought to Poetry" (*Memorials of Mrs. Hemans* 1: 172). Regardless of the direction, Jewsbury strengthening Hemans or Hemans refining Jewsbury, both are natural manifestations of female genius, Chorley implies.

Owen, who is concerned to revise the picture Chorley had painted of her sister, is more willing to exploit the adjectives "feminine" and "masculine" in making the contrast. It is a contrast that can only serve to reclaim her sister's naturalness (conventional femininity) as a female genius by using Jewsbury's genius as masculine foil:

[I]t was scarcely possible to imagine two individual natures more strikingly contrasted—the one so intensely feminine, so susceptible and imaginative, so devoted to the tender and the beautiful; the other endowed with masculine energies, with a spirit that seemed born for ascendency, with strong powers of reasoning, fathomless profundity of thought, and feelings, like those of her own Julia [in *The Three Histories*]. (*Works* 1: 142)

Even Owen, however, is clearly fascinated by the foil as much, if not more, than by the standard. The passage on Jewsbury's intellect continues, working itself almost to the point of rapture. Again and again, these women writers attempt to purge the monster only to discover that attempting to purge it further identifies it as a real force that exists within themselves.

According to Chorley, Jewsbury describes her impression of Hemans through her character Egeria in *The Three Histories:* "She did not dazzle— she subdued me. Other women might be more commanding, more versatile, more acute; but I never saw one so exquisitely feminine" (quoted by Chorley, *Memorials* 1: 187). It is not the "commanding" or "acute" woman who subdues the "harsher" masculine one, but the "feminine" woman who subdues the masculine one. There is a kind of innocent desire—which might inappropriately be called envy but might be more appropriately identified as homoeroticism—that Jewsbury has for her sister writer. She understands that part of Hemans's strength as a successful poet derives from her conventional vulnerability as a woman; Hemans turns that vulnerability of affection into a kind of empowerment of her whole sex. Jewsbury continues her description of Egeria–Hemans:

Her nature was at once simple and profound; there was no room in her mind for philosophy, or in her heart for ambition,—one was filled by imagination, the other engrossed by tenderness. Her strength and her weakness alike lay in her affections: these would sometimes make her weep at a word,—at others imbue her with courage. . . . I might describe, and describe for ever, but I should never succeed in portraying Egeria; she was a muse, a grace, a variable child, a dependent woman—the Italy of human beings. (Quoted by Chorley, *Memorials* 1: 188–189)

Egeria's dependency, her weakness, cannot oust her strength; in fact, it becomes a source of strength, but it is a strength to be admired and shared, rather than envied and vied for. It is a strength that mirrors, self-deceptively, Jewsbury's own potential for being a genius while still being feminine, for being strong while not being a monster. The reflective relationship between these two literary women is typical for women authors of the period, or at least for all of those in Hemans's wide circle of authoress friends.

Hemans herself is troubled by the threat of being perceived as a monster, and her sister Harriet Owen is prompted to write her memoir clearly because there is a slight chance that Chorley's account of the representative poetess might be perceived monstrously. Owen initiates her memoir by protesting the indecorousness of writing a memoir of a woman who wished her life to remain private. "Perhaps there never was an individual who would have shrunk more sensitively from the idea of being made the subject of a biographical memoir, than she whom, by a strange fatality, so many imperfect notices have been given to the world" (*Works* 1: 1). Owen realizes, however, that "it is now too late to deprecate or to deplore." In publishing excerpts from Hemans's correspondence, "a very inadequate estimate of her character" has been created, an estimate "which was, doubtless, little contemplated by the kindly-intentioned editor," Chorley. As Owen's language indicates, her task is to rectify the image of her sister, reclaiming "a portion with which her admirers will best sympathize." (Owen is quoting a review of Chorley's *Memorials* from the *Dublin University Magazine* of August 1837.) What Owen restores is the icon of the chaste virgin mother, devoted to her children and her God. What she has to repress is the threat of the female wit, who gleefully ridicules her admirers in her private correspondence, who complains about the oppressive duties of managing a household, who becomes deeply depressed at the death of her own mother. In other words, Owen must oust the dragon-lady and reclaim the prototypical/archetypical feminine poetess.

But this task is not an easy one, for once the veil is lifted, one can attempt to lower it again only by lifting it more, by printing more letters, by talking more about the poet, by bringing more attention to her private life. A proper lady is not supposed to be talked about—even in the most rapturous terms. Talking about Hemans only brings more attention to the fact that she was a famous lady; that she was famous only makes it more difficult to assert her absolute feminine demeanor. "The spell having thus been broken, and the veil of the sanctuary lifted," Owen writes, "it seems now to have become the duty of those with whose feelings the strict fulfilment of her own wishes would have been so far more accordant, to raise that veil a little further, though with a reluctant and trembling hand" (2).

One instance of Owen's subtle retouching of Chorley's picture will suffice. In 1818, Hemans's husband left for Italy, for reasons of health, and they never saw each other again. Explaining why Hemans did not follow her husband to Italy, Chorley states: "Mrs. Hemans, whose literary pursuits rendered it advisable for her not to leave England, remained with her family" (1: 42). Such an offhand comment, which is really not so offhand since Chorley is thoroughly devoted to the poetess as a poet, encourages readers to question Hemans's dutifulness as a wife. Her literary career is more important than her husband? Owen has some difficulty explaining away Hemans's priorities without bringing too much attention to them: "It has been alleged, and with perfect truth, that the literary pursuits of Mrs. Hemans, and the education of her children, made it more eligible for her to remain under the maternal roof, than to accompany her husband to Italy. . . . [N]othing like a permanent separation was contemplated at the time, nor did it ever amount to more than a tacit convenient arrangment" (29–30). Owen, in an effort to deflect blame, resorts to the passive voice. She significantly adds the phrase about "the education of her children." And she implies that Hemans was staying with her mother, stressing her filial duties, rather than deserting her husband. In fact, Hemans was much closer to her mother than to any one else. In both biographies, her father's death is overlooked; however, her mother's death is repeatedly referred to as a turning point in Hemans's life. Even so, Owen spends much more time relating Hemans's concern for five children (all sons, much to Hemans's regret). At one point, Owen states, "[W]ith that endearing predominance of the mother over the author, which formed one of the loveliest features of her character, she would turn to some nursery topic" (76–77). It is not that Chorley in any way suggests that Hemans neglected her children. The point is that he did not have to suggest it for it to become a central issue. Because he prints letters in which Hemans discusses the conflict between her societal duties and her writing, he puts a crack in the icon, an icon that was already very fragile. As Owen comes to the rescue of her sister's feminine image, she must return her sister to domesticity as a priority in the poetess's life, and do so without denigrating her sister's poetry.

Chorley also prints extensive correspondence in which Hemans describes encounters with her common readers, whom she frequently ridicules for their expectations and fears of a female poet. Her readers idolize her. They make trips across the Atlantic to meet her. They see her as the sort of sage that George Eliot is to become for the Victorians. Owen tells an anecdote about a man who, having "been first awakened from the miserable delusions of infidelity" by Hemans's poem *The Sceptic,* insists on seeing the poet in order to express his eternal gratitude for her salvational role (255–256). Owen is much less prone to discuss the less idealized attitudes of "admirers," whom Hemans refers to constantly in her letters. As Chorley points out, after Hemans has settled in provincial Wavertree, her neighbors feel that her space is theirs and have no qualms about showing up to gawk at the famous female writer. "Some came merely to stare at the strange poetess; others to pay proper neighborly morning calls, and discuss household matters. Great was their surprise at finding that she was not ready with an answer on these important topics" (1: 216). There is more than a little bit of sarcasm in Chorley's attitude toward these visitors, an attitude he inherits from Hemans herself.

That her neighbors expect her to have advice on household management—when actually, as she says, she has very little knowledge of such matters—indicates not only how little they understand what was important to her, but also how much their expectations have been shaped by a culture that makes feminine poetry an extension of woman's domestic function. It seems not to occur to them that their constant invasion of her privacy contradicts their ideology about the detrimental effects of fame and publicity on woman's naturally reticent character.

Hemans, however, is painfully conscious of the contradiction, especially since her goal is to synthesize the rights of a poetic career with all the rites of a feminine course of life. Her painful self-consciousness manifests itself through her playful wit, which Jewsbury hints at. In the following invaluable letter, Hemans takes jabs at her admirers even as she reveals the internalized fear of being perceived as a monster:

I appear to be regarded as rather a "curious thing;" the gentlemen treat me as I suppose they would the muse Calliope, were she to descend amongst them; that is, with much *solemn* reverence, and constant allusions to poetry; the ladies, every time I happen to speak, look as if they expected sparks of fire, or some other marvellous thing, would proceed from my lips, as from those of the Sea-Princess in Arabian fiction. If I were in higher spirits, I should be strongly tempted to do something *very* strange amongst them, in order to fulfill the ideas I imagine they entertain of that altogether foreign monster, a *Poetess*, but I feel too much subdued for such *capricci* at present. (Chorley, *Memorials* 2: 279–280, Hemans's emphases)

Interestingly, it is the gentlemen who idolize her, the ladies who view her as monstrous (or so she "imagines"). Like the miserable infidel who is saved by her poetry, these men relate to her in the same way they would to the (feminine) muse in their own poetry. Their solemnity is a form of sublimation, a way of avoiding the full force of woman's genius by making her a muse incarnate, a way of shielding themselves from the gender-confounding monster by turning her into a thoroughly feminine goddess. The lady admirers, on the other hand, might be more prone to express their fear as wonder. Is there something monstrous lurking in this lady poetess that can infect me as well? Is she the kind of creature we have been warned of so often? Needless to say, their fear is interweaved with fascination and the delight of wonder. Hemans's use of the word "marvellous," of course, indicates the combination of miraculous, unnatural, and wonderful. Just as the men's curiosity is terror sublimated into wonder (the romantic sublime), the women's is wonder sublimated into fear.[3] Finally, Hemans's own anxiety reveals itself. Does she imagine these responses to her strangeness? Her urge is to confirm their worst fears, to estrange herself, to embrace the monster she fears to be. But, as we shall see, this is not a likely or viable option for Hemans. She chooses, rather, to reverse the charge by making a monster of the reading public. "That monster known by the name of the *People* is tormenting me" (Chorley, *Memorials* 2: 187), she says. It is they who have burst the bounds of gender decorum by assaulting her feminine privacy. Through her wit, she chastises them, and yet that wit itself is problematic, for even as she exploits it to reclaim her natural femininity, she crosses the line of proper feminine decorum.

5

The limits set on women's poetry through the fear of monstrosity are also the basis from which critics can eventually attack them and deny them a place in the canon. Using a subspecies of the criteria employed to judge normative male poets, critics can appraise and praise the new breed of women poets while retaining the fundamental standards of taste that have evolved within the literary tradition. While fulfilling the larger requisites applied to "poets," "poetesses" must also display the subgeneric attributes of delicacy, regularity, simplicity, piety, sentimentality, and modesty. All of these subgeneric attributes are *sociomoral* values interpolated as *literary* criteria, and the same may be said of the overarching standards applied within the masculine tradition. For instance, one of the traditional standards for (male) poetry employed constantly in the periodicals of the 1820s is naturalness of diction, a quality evolved from the classical standard of plain language, and heavily influenced, of course, by Wordsworth's poetic philosophy. The subgeneric quality for female poetry is simplicity, meaning not just direct and unembellished diction, but also ingenuousness and unassuming innocence. Likewise, male poetry of the time is required to avoid scurrilousness, since one of the major traditional objectives of poetry is nobility of purpose, yet for women's poetry this means the more stringent scrupulosity entailed in the social virtue of feminine chastity. A female poet as racy as Byron would, of course, not have made it into print, much less into the canon. This subspecies of criteria enables the literary establishment to accommodate women poets, but temporarily with implied reservations which can later be used to revoke critical assent by claiming that these women were popular *because* of special local, historical conditions, rather than because of some supposedly intrinsic merit evidenced in (male) poets who fulfill the larger requisites of taste, which are assumed to be universal and transhistorical.

We can see this kind of accommodation in the praise that John Wilson and his cohorts in the *Noctes Ambrosianae* endow on the most prominent female poets of their time. "I do not know whether my gallantry blinds me, but I prefer much of the female to the male poetry of the day," Tickler says, as he goes on to praise Baillie, Hemans, L.E.L., and Tighe (1: 35–36). Gallantry does not so much blind these men as it frames their capacity to see. They can rate these four very popular women poets above Wordsworth and his followers exactly because their assessment is framed by a redefined sense of what poetic standards must be if women are to be included. In fact, Tickler's praise of the women poets is a reaction to the exorbitant praise that North (Wilson) and other writers bestow on the Lake poets in their largely successful attempt in *Blackwood's Magazine* to canonize these poets. The subspecial criteria are evident in Tickler's assessments, especially of Hemans, Tighe, and Landon. Tickler lowers Hemans's rating a bit because she is "[t]oo fond . . . of prattling about Greece and Rome," a case of those bluestockings peeping out. But Tickler is able to contain this threat of monstrosity by moving on to her appropriately feminine versification.

Because in the dialectic of historical change every action must have a co-equal adverse reaction, the subspecies of feminine criteria cannot be enunciated in the critical establishment without those larger standards being affected. Although the fundamental process of affirming taste and judging poets does not change, the parameters of poetic experience do change as a result of female poeticizing. The standards of taste must be altered, if only temporarily, in order to assimilate these women as great poets, but not so much that the established process of rating poets or the whole critical apparatus within which this process operates has to be questioned. Remembering that poetry itself is experiencing a sea-change in that it is becoming marginalized to play an immaterial role within an industrializing, production-oriented culture, the accommodation of women's poetry enables the literary establishment to adjust itself to altered expectations for (male) poetry. What we begin to see is a conflict between the romantic desire to view poetry as an influential kind of work that shapes material life through its immaterial power and the utilitarian desire to view poetry as a pleasing, but essentially superfluous activity that distracts men from the real work of technological advancement, economic growth, and sociopolitical progress. These altered and conflicting expectations can be seen in Tickler's attitude toward Wordsworth: "And what the devil, then, would you be at with your great bawling He-Poets from the Lakes, who go round and round about, strutting upon nothing, like so many turkey-cocks gobbling with a long red pendant at their noses, and frightening away the fair and lovely swans as they glide down the water of immortality?" (1: 36). The problem with those "bawling He-Poets from the Lakes," we discover, is that they are too self-important. "Wordsworth is a poet," Tickler suggests, "but unluckily is a weak man. His imagination shows him fine sights, but his intellect knows not how to deal with them" (1: 36). North agrees: "[A]nd then how ludicrously he overrates his own powers. This we all do; but Wordsworth's pride is like that of a straw-crowned king in Bedlam" (1: 36). The basis for their praise of the women is the obverse of their disparagement of the male poets: women poets can be seen as great because the role of poetry is being diminished, but can men be great if they are merely poets? Wordsworth's mistake is to think that he can become a great man through poeticizing, *despite* the fact that poetry itself has become domesticated and feminized. After ridiculing Wordsworth's "Address to the Sparrow," North asks, "Can that be a great man?" Hardly, Tickler suggests, and "[h]ad that man in youth become the member of any profession (which all poor men are bound to do), he would soon have learned in the tussle to rate his powers more truly" (1: 36). Once poetry has been marginalized and allowed to subsume feminine limits, those limits begin to "contaminate" the taste for male

poetry as well. Once critics begin to assess male poets in relation to other productive professions, their greatness will become as suspect and limited as poetry's role in a production-oriented culture.

Hazlitt begins the section of *Lectures on the English Poets* devoted to
living poets by confessing that he is "a great admirer of the female writers of
the present day; they appear to me like so many modern Muses. I could be in
love with Mrs. Inchbald, romantic with Mrs. Radcliffe, and sarcastic with
Madame D'Arblay: but they are novel-writers, and, like Audrey, may 'thank
the Gods for not having made them poetical' " (289–290). Like John Wilson's in *Blackwood's,* Hazlitt's objective in his *Lectures* is to consolidate and
extend (by updating) the canon of national literature, but because Hazlitt's
influence within and over the literary tradition has been more pronounced
and substantial than Wilson's, what we find is an assessment of female writing
much more in line with the predilections of the current critical establishment.
Hazlitt prefers female novelists over female poets, just as the modern critical
establishment has obliterated the early nineteenth-century poets in favor of
the novelists. Hazlitt's attitude toward the women poets tends toward the paternalistic and condescending.

The first poetess I can recollect is Mrs. Barbauld, with whose works I became acquainted before those of any other author, male or female, when I was learning to
spell words of one syllable in her story-books for children. I became acquainted
with her poetical works long after in Enfield's Speaker; and remember being much
divided in my opinion at that time, between her Ode to Spring and Collins's Ode
to Evening. I wish I could repay my childish debt of gratitude in terms of appropriate praise. (290)

By limiting Barbauld's poetry to a phase of childhood, he subordinates her
influence upon him and upon the literary tradition as a whole. She becomes a
poet to be read by children, *not* by adults. Clearly, he has not returned to her
work to reassess it in preparing these comments. His opinion of her is everywhere shaped and distorted by the nostalgic glow of his simple childhood,
rather than by the maturity that he brings to his comments on poets like Gray
and Collins, poets whom he knows well and returns to in manhood. He was
divided in his opinion "at that time" of childhood as to whether her "Ode to
Spring" rivals Collins's "Ode to Evening." It is interesting to note Hazlitt's
general assessment of Collins, who is given much more space than Barbauld
and examined in much more specific detail (see 230–234). Fortunately for
Collins, the oak is in the acorn; his genius is salvaged by its own inevitable
brilliance. One of the "proofs of [Collins's] capacity" is his "Ode to Evening," Hazlitt suggests, and he concludes his comments on the minor poet by
quoting it. Obviously, he does not consider it worth his time to return to Barbauld's ode to settle his opinion on its merits in relation to Collins's ode.
When he implies that he cannot "repay" his "childish debt of gratitude in
terms of appropriate praise," he could mean either that she was so important
to him *then* that he does not have enough praise to repay her for that early
influence, or that her importance *then* in his childish period must not interfere with his mature assessment *now*. I think the second reading is more in

line with his succeeding comments: "She is a very pretty poetess; and, to my fancy, strews the flowers of poetry most agreeably round the borders of religious controversy. She is a neat and pointed prose-writer" (290). He clearly values her prose over her poetry, though his judgment of both is determined by the same "gallantry" that characterizes Tickler's praise. There is no sense here of the range, variety, complexity, strength, imaginativeness of Barbauld's work in the way he provides for a poet like Collins, whom he ranks as "minor."

At least, he has read, long ago, some of Barbauld's poetry. "Mrs. Hannah More is another celebrated modern poetess," Hazlitt writes, "and I believe still living. She has written a great deal which I have never read" (291). Evidently, enough has been said.

The third woman to make up his "trio of female poets" is Joanna Baillie. He singles out *De Monfort,* which was her most popular play: "There is in the chief character of that play a nerve, a continued unity of interest, a setness of purpose and precision of outline which John Kemble alone was capable of giving; and there is all the grace which women have in writing" (291). Is it Kemble the actor who gives the play the aforementioned qualities, or Baillie the author? Most reviewers, even as they laud *De Monfort,* stress the play as a vehicle for the talent of the celebrated actor. Fortunately, the play has "all the grace" expected of women's writing. The irony here is that when Baillie's plays are first published anonymously in 1798, everyone assumes that they are written by a man, especially because of the elaborate theoretical treatise that prefaces the plays. It is only after Hester Piozzi and Mary Berry note the playwright's unprecedented emphasis on older heroines and unusual sensitivity toward intelligent women characters that speculation changes about the sex of the author. Even after Baillie is identified as the sole writer of *Plays on the Passions* in 1800, some critics refuse to accept that the "Introductory Discourse" could have been written by a woman, suggesting instead that Baillie's brother has written the preface, without any proof whatsoever of the brother's participation or even of his interest in dramatic writing or theory. The revelation of Baillie's authorship of the plays creates a sensation in Britain, and she is immediately dubbed the female Shakespeare, with reviewers predicting her immortality and her capacity to save the British stage from torpor. Once again, Hazlitt's assessment is much more consonant with the historical outcome of Baillie's literary fate.

Having thus expressed my sense of the merits of this authoress, I must add, that her comedy of the Election, performed last summer at the Lyceum with indifferent success, appears to me the perfection of baby-house theatricals. Every thing in it has such a *do-me-good* air, is so insipid and amiable. Virtue seems such a pretty playing at make-believe, and vice is such a naughty word. It is a theory of some French author, that little girls ought not to be suffered to have dolls to play with, to call them *pretty dears,* to admire their black eyes and cherry cheeks, to lament and bewail over them if they fall down and hurt their faces, to praise them when they are good, and scold them when they are naughty. It is a school of affectation: Miss Baillie has profited of it. She treats her grown men and women as little girls treat their dolls—makes moral puppets of them, pulls the wires, and they talk virtue and act vice, according to their cue and the title prefixed to each comedy or tragedy, not from any real passions of their own, or love either of virtue or vice. (292)

In adhering to the criteria of piety and feminine chastity, Baillie opens herself to the charge of being a "baby-house" playwright. The femininity which is supposed to protect her authorial project becomes the basis for denying Baillie a place in the canon of great writers. The irony, once again, is that Baillie's *Plays on the Passions* is perhaps the most ambitious poetic project taken on by a woman in the early nineteenth century. The plays themselves, especially *Ethwald,* Parts 1 and 2, clearly aspire to the larger standards for great drama usually identified in Shakespeare. Just as Hazlitt is perhaps the critic most responsible for Shakespeare's domination of the canon since the early nineteenth century, it is not surprising that his opinion of Baillie has also been adopted by the literary establishment.

What has happened to all the other female poets writing between 1780 and 1818 when the first edition of Hazlitt's *Lectures* is published? Tighe, who dies in 1810, Hemans, who is beginning her career, are especially notable omissions, since their work is in vogue during the decade of Hazlitt's *Lectures*. Women poets are mentioned only under the section "On the Living Poets"; evidently, all dead poets are male. Hazlitt's omissions tell us as much about the national canon he is interested in forming as about the ideology that informs his taste. When Hazlitt makes his "transition" from the female trio to the plethora of male poets, the role that gender plays in his critical judgment becomes even more obvious. He chooses Samuel Rogers, "a very lady-like poet," as his transition, since Rogers's *Pleasures of Memory* is "not far" from the women's poetry. "He is an elegant, but feeble writer," and Rogers's language, according to Hazlitt, "is a tortuous, tottering, wriggling, fidgetty translation of every thing from the vulgar tongue, into all the tantalizing, teasing, tripping, lisping *mimminee-pimminee* of the highest brilliancy and fashion of poetical diction" (293).

I am *not* suggesting that Hazlitt's single critical voice, regardless of how influential that voice has been, is responsible for the course of canonization in British literature. Instead, I would stress the ideological consonance between Hazlitt and romanticism itself. Hazlitt is the critic who does the most to formulate and promote romantic ideology just at the juncture when the battle over the future of British literary taste, which we examined in Chapter 1, is being waged in the periodicals. His career, spanning between 1807 and 1828, coincides exactly with the years when the canonicity of the first generation of romantic poets is being hotly debated. More accessible than Coleridge, more apparently *British* in his rhetoric, and more pragmatic and openly concerned with working out the family tree of great British writers, Hazlitt takes on the voice of authority in his many popular lectures, periodical essays, and books. In post-Johnsonian phrases, but displaying Johnsonian self-confidence and common sense, he establishes himself as the legitimate heir of Johnson's critical estate while smoothing out potential contradictions in romantic ideology and establishing the legitimate descent of the romantic poets from the line of

Chaucer, Spenser, Shakespeare, Milton, Dryden, Pope, Swift, Thomson, and Gray. Writing for the influential *Edinburgh Review,* for Leigh Hunt's *Examiner,* and for Hunt's and Byron's *The Liberal,* Hazlitt provides a critical link between the Lake school and the "Cockney" school of poetry, becoming the champion of a unified romantic ideology even before romantic taste is identifiable as such. Like Hunt and Keats, he is attacked by Lockhart in *Blackwood's Magazine* for associating himself with the "Cockney" school, but what Lockhart and others in "Maga" and in the *Quarterly Review* fail to see is that the Cockney school, which they disparage, are the prominent literary beneficiaries of the "bawling He-Poets from the Lakes." On one hand, Hazlitt's voice is heard so loudly even today partly because it is a strong, self-possessing voice, purging the influence of other critics as it seeks to propagate its own immortal line of descent, in the tradition of romantic masculine desire; on the other hand, the growing influence of romantic ideology throughout the Victorian period and into the modern era has helped to assure that Hazlitt's voice would have a sympathetic hearing. As he becomes the heir apparent of the critical terrain of the masculine literary inheritance, he passes on the traditional standards of taste that have helped to determine his primacy while reformulating national taste in the shape of romantic desire. Since romantic ideology diminishes women's role in the literary process, it is not surprising that Hazlitt, the supreme romantic apologist, engages in the characteristic romantic maneuver: purging feminine desire by limiting its influence to a stage of childhood, which must be outgrown by the truly great poet-critic. Reading Hazlitt, then, is like hearing our own voices, for in it resonates the tones which we as critics have been taught to echo, as we have learned to make our literary history according to the contours of romantic masculine desire.

6

As we have seen, both male and female writers, like Jewsbury, Owen, and Chorley, wanting to promote women's poetry, are forced to resist the full potential of feminine desire by internalizing the limits set by masculine critics like Jeffrey, Gifford, Wilson, and Hazlitt. Despite these limitations, however, women writers are learning not only how to explore the power of their desire within those cultural limits, but also how to analyze with rigor, subtlety, and "grace" the kind of politics engendered by the segregation of the sexes in literary taste. While the aforementioned writers pursue their agendas by attempting to repress and cover the reality of gender dissension, Anna Jameson (1794–1860) employs the strategy of Wilson's *Noctes Ambrosianae* to unveil exactly how sexual politics operates in the literary discourse of the mid-nineteenth century. Beginning her career as a governess, Jameson also demonstrates the dialectic of historical change, by showing how some women of her generation have begun to move beyond the more timid stance of More and Barbauld, ironically returning to the more militant stance of the first generation bluestockings, who take seriously the need for equal education for women.

Like Baillie, Jewsbury, Aikin, and Hemans, Jameson is devoted to establishing a history about and for women, and like them, she begins to move more boldly and self-confidently into areas usually preserved for men, including art and literary criticism, history, theology, and social polemics. In 1832 she publishes the first edition of her successful book *Shakespeare's Heroines: Characteristics of Women, Moral, Poetical, and Historical,* as a result of which she becomes one of the most respected Shakespeare critics of the century. Influenced by Hazlitt, and the whole masculine tradition of Shakespeare criticism, Jameson is nevertheless more interested in Shakespeare's women than in Shakespeare. Her book explores the relation between fictional characterization and "character," the mental, moral, emotional personality of an individual or social group. How could a man have come to create the best women characters in literature? Are these fictional characters drawn from the actual character of women in ordinary life? How have these fictional characters influenced presuppositions and expectations of women's real character? Grateful for the sensitive attention that Shakespeare gives to women characters and women's character in a tradition where records of women are scarce, Jameson celebrates Shakespeare's heroines and through her own book begins to trace the characteristics of real women from the artistic sketches of fictional characters.

Alda.   You will not listen to me?
Medon. I do, with all the deference which befits a gentleman when a lady holds
            forth on the virtues of her own sex.

This exchange initiates Jameson's *Characteristics of Women,* which begins with a dialogue between a man and a woman in a library, perhaps hers, a dialogue that sounds like something between Platonic dialectics and the male-female sparring matches so common in Shakespeare's comedies. Jameson feels compelled to justify writing her book, and she chooses to do so cleverly through a Shakespearean-Platonic conversation rather than through a defensive prefatory disquisition. Appropriately, the dialogue begins with Alda asking Medon, her male counterpart, a question: "You will not listen to me?" The difference between interrogative here and declarative, and between plea and command, is practically nonexistent. Alda is as much observing that Medon will not really listen as she is requesting him to hear; she is both stating that he will not hear and demanding that he at least listen. Medon's response confirms the need for her question. She is not begging for his "deference"; she is demanding his attention. She is not about to "hold forth on the virtues of her own sex"; rather, she is simply trying to record the characteristics of women. Alda knows that in the charged environment of her own newly acquired library, however, her words will be misunderstood, distorted, ridiculed. After noting his gentlemanly deference, Medon recites a quotation about wronging "the praise of women" from "some old poet that has fixed itself" in his memory. Alda listens patiently to Medon's recitation, but she is anxious to speak for herself, rather than to hear once again what "some old poet" has to say about "a parricide of his mother's name." So she demands yet again, "but now will you listen to me?" And yet again Medon refuses to hear. "With most profound humility," he says. Finally frustrated by his inability to respond to her voice rather than to his preconception of her voice, Alda says in an irritated but firm tone: "Nay, then! I have done, unless you will lay aside these mock airs of gallantry, and listen to me for a moment!" Okay, he will listen, but first he must ask a question, if she promises, "as a reasonable woman," that she will "not be affronted with the question." "[D]o you really expect that any one will read this little book of yours?" he asks.

I can imagine Hemans and all her sister writers, at this point, chuckling along with Jameson, for not only has Jameson captured perfectly sexual repartee—the friction that occurs whenever feminine desire confronts the recalcitrance of masculine ideology—but also she has captured perfectly the plight of the woman writer at the beginning of the nineteenth century. Medon's question could be translated as, why are you writing this little book? Or, why are you women publishing these little books anyway? Remembering the questions Pope asks himself in the *Epistle to Dr. Arbuthnot* and that Wordsworth implicitly asks himself in *The Prelude,* Alda's response seems rather timid. It is worth citing in full, both because it accords so well with Hemans's own ideology and because it generalizes for us the situation of women writers in the romantic period.

Accident first made me an authoress: and not now, nor ever, have I written to flatter any prevailing fashion of the day for the sake of profit, though this is done, I know, by many who have less excuse for thus coining their brains. This little book was undertaken without a thought of fame or money: out of the fulness of my own heart and soul have I written it. In the pleasure it has given me, in the new and various views of human nature it has opened to me, in the beautiful and soothing images it has placed before me, in the exercise and improvement of my own faculties, I have already been repaid: if praise or profit come beside, they come as a surplus. I should be gratified and grateful, but I have not sought for them, nor worked for them. Do you believe this? (2)

Perhaps Medon is so quick to respond "I do" to Alda's apology because the apology fits his own ideology so neatly. Alda is not trying to compete with men for money and fame. She is writing out of feminine self-sacrifice, out of the fullness of her feminine heart and the illumination of her feminine soul. But if we listen carefully to what she is saying, this is not quite it. Alda points to the "many who have less excuse for thus coining their brains" for lucre and fame, and though Medon no doubt reads this as the many scribbling females who have recently entered the market, Alda no doubt is thinking of the many men who have written for far less noble reason than she and escaped such damning scrutiny. If we attend carefully, we hear a distinctive voice here. How unlike the justification of both Pope and Wordsworth is her first sentence. She does not say, that from childhood she lisped in numbers and the numbers came. She does not rehearse an autobiography that returns us to the mythical origin of ordained desire, asking, was it for this that nature nurtured me. Rather, she says that "accident first made" her an author.

This should remind us of Jewsbury's sketch of Hemans's poetic career. The origin for a woman author is an arbitrary beginning, but this does not mean that the objective as well, that the poetic end, is arbitrary. In fact, what Alda gives us are all final causes, ends in themselves. Alda's book is an exercise in self-exploration. By self-exploration, I do not mean the kind of search for a self that Wordsworth is obsessed with. I mean a search to discover and record the variety of the social self, the variety of human nature, by uncovering women's experience as a distinctive form of useable knowledge not just for women, but for all human beings. In effect, she is, like Hemans, constructing a bridge of flowers. Alda wants to open her mind to the "various views of human nature" and to be pleased by that variety. She wants to exercise the improvement of her faculties. Like Jewsbury writing her eulogy to Hemans, Jameson in writing this book on Shakespeare's heroines is actually writing a handbook on womanly genius—how to acquire it, how to detect it, how to use it. Jameson is not writing primarily for profit or notoriety (although such desires cannot be as quickly discounted as Alda and Medon assume); she is writing so that women may continue to write, and so that their numbers may increase. Like Lady Mary, Jameson seems to feel that until women have arrived at a more intellectually and emotionally satisfying conception of themselves, until they have explored together the common nature that they share, they cannot prosper as writers, nor can they enjoy the variety of human nature.

When Medon so quickly agrees with Alda's explanation of why she writes and publishes, we might suspect that he really does not understand, and true to habit, he does not. "I presume you have written a book to maintain the superiority of your sex over ours;" he says, "for so I judge by the names at the heads of some of your chapters; women, fit indeed to inlay heaven with stars, but, pardon me, very unlike those who at present walk upon this earth" (3). Since his Keatsian idealization of the feminine aesthetic is by now familiar to us, we shall pass over it, as Alda does. But there are two genuine issues presented by Medon's comment, the first issue Alda would like to ignore or forget, the second is next to her heart. The first, of course, is the issue of sexual equality. With the mere suggestion of that issue, she imagines herself in the form of a monstrous dragon-lady roughly throwing male thieves from her house. "[A]s to maintaining the superiority, or speculating on the rights of women—nonsense!" she cries. "[W]hy should you suspect me of such folly?—it is quite out of date. Why should there be competition or comparison?" Here we are again on that "trite" subject of women's rights, that subject which has been talked to death and talked out of fashion, but that no one seems ever to want to talk about. But we find Alda, in talking about something else, returning despite herself to that trite and out-of-date subject. At one point she even begins to sound like the monstrous Mary Wollstonecraft: "It appears to me that the condition of women in society, as at present constituted, is false in itself, and injurious to them,—that the education of women, as at present conducted, is founded in mistaken principles, and tends to increase fearfully the sum of misery and error in both sexes" (4). The aim of Jameson's study is explicitly the re-education of woman, an aim that naturally overspills from the fullness of her heart and soul. But she feels compelled to try to disentangle that aim from the web of sexual equality and women's rights, an impossible task.

The second issue, the one next to Alda's heart, is the distinction between women portrayed in literature and actual women, and this issue as well is intimately connected to her aim of feminine re-education, and also to her suppressed desire for some form of sexual equality. Medon asks her why she has not "given us an epitome of [her] experience, instead of dreaming over Shakespeare" (4). Alda's answer to that question is rather complex, and we cannot do it justice here. But we must note the duplicity of her response. The first answer, it seems to me, has as much to do with masculine desire as with feminine re-education. She says that she might have given an epitome of her own experience, "if [she] had chosen to become a female satirist, which [she] will never be" (4). Satire, she suggests, "turns life into a jest, and a very dull one" at that. "It makes us indifferent to beauty, and incredulous of goodness; it teaches us to consider *self* as the centre on which all actions turn, and to which all motives are to be referred." It is a form of (masculine) "arrogance" (4–6).

As we shall see, Jameson's view of satire is closely allied with Hemans's. Both are distrustful of masculine self-possession, and feel that women must avoid the appearance and the reality of such "arrogance" at all costs. Such an attitude, however, fits snugly with the masculine ideology that had discouraged women from writing for so long. Medon is happy to hear that Alda finds satire so distasteful. "I have the pleasure in reminding you that a female satirist by profession is yet an anomaly in the history of our literature, as a female schismatic is yet unknown in the history of our religion. But to what do you attribute the number of satirical women we meet in society?" (7). In this sentence Medon has, of course, managed to erase from literary history the influence of Eliza Haywood and Lady Mary Wortley Montagu, women who fought their way into male Augustan cliques by exploiting the dominant mode of literary discourse of their time, satire, by making their breed anomalous.

Women should not engage in satire because, like religious factionalism, it is a contentious and divisive kind of behavior unbecoming for the nurturers of the affections, the keepers of domesticity, and the refiners of social sympathy. Jewsbury wants to claim the potential for feminine wit, but she is quick to make it harmless, spiritual, poetic. Likewise, Chorley wants to praise Hemans's wit, but has to redefine that wit so that it does not raise the specter of monstrosity:

[T]o conceive the true grotesque, indeed, without trenching upon the farcical, the mind must have a power over the springs of tears as well as of laughter. But the world in its short-sightedness too often refuses to acknowledge the existence of this twofold possession, particularly in a woman; and Mrs. Hemans was wisely unwilling to risk the chance of being confounded with the heartless and satirical, whose laughter comes of disappointment and bitterness, not elasticity of temper: for a similar cause, she rarely gave her spirits way in general society. (Chorley, *Memorials* 1: 243–244)

Chorley astutely suggests that to be able to nurture the affections—to have power over the springs of tears—is also to possess wit—to have the power to induce laughter. But when a woman uses her wit to ridicule, she immediately becomes heartless, as though ridicule cannot be a sign of fondness, love, and compassion. Just as Hemans is careful to avoid wittiness in her public demeanor, so Jameson rejects it outright in her book. Or does she? Isn't the introductory dialogue itself an instance of what Jewsbury would call female wit and Chorley would call the "elasticity of temper"—the ridicule that comes from largeness of heart rather than "disappointment and bitterness"? Medon is most definitely the butt of Jameson's ridicule, though it is a gentle, fond sort of teasing. There must be some bitterness and disappointment in Jameson's psyche, but she sublimates it. Rather than lashing out in the fury of her anger, she stays, as much as possible, within the boundaries of proper feminine behavior, the same way that Hemans restrains the great force of her anger by venting it in gentle ridicule. But, as we have seen, even this gentle ridicule was enough to crack an icon of feminine propriety.

Jameson's attitude toward satire, then, is necessarily duplicitous. She must appear to reject it outright, even as she practices it. She answers Medon's question regarding the "number of satirical women . . . in society" by attributing such bad manners not to their nature, but to

a state of society in which the levelling spirit of *persiflage* has been long a fashion; to the perverse education which fosters it; to affections disappointed or unemployed, which embitter the temper; to faculties misdirected or wasted, which oppress and irritate the mind; to an utter ignorance of ourselves and the common lot of humanity. (7)

In addition to the qualities of disappointment and bitterness that Chorley identifies, Jameson adds that crucial element, "an utter ignorance of ourselves and the common lot of humanity." In recording the nature and natures of women, her book will help to rectify this flaw. Her book will direct the faculties and prevent them from being "wasted," where "wasted" is used in a different sense from Tuckerman's adjective "lost." Jameson is not so much thinking here about the potential erring from conventional feminine behavior or about the effect of women's erring on men—as Tuckerman is. Rather, I think she is considering all the womanly genius lost in the past, exactly because women were ridiculed by men for attempting to use it. Later in the speech Alda says that satirical women in society result from "frivolous habits, which make serious thought a burden, and serious feeling a bane, if suppressed, if betrayed, a ridicule" (7). Perhaps Hemans, Owen, and Jameson are so hesitant to endorse satire because they have suffered so deeply from its effects. Women are "by nature too much subjected to suffering," Alda continues, "in many forms—have too much of fancy and sensibility, and too much of that faculty which some philosophers call *veneration,* to be naturally satirical" (7).

Immediately following this interchange between Alda and Medon, in which they seem to agree about the inappropriateness of satire for women, Medon again reveals how masculine desire has impaired his ability to hear Alda's voice. Opposing her own method to satire, Alda waxes eloquent on the poetry of the affections:

But to soften the heart by images and examples of the kindly and generous affections—to show how the human soul is disciplined and perfected by suffering—to prove how much of possible good may exist in things evil and perverted—how much hope there is for those who despair—how much comfort for those whom a heartless world has taught to contemn both others and themselves, and so put barriers to the hard, cold, selfish, mocking, and levelling spirit of the day—Oh would I could do this.

Medon.   On the same principle, I suppose, that they have changed the treatment of lunatics; and whereas they used to condemn poor distempered wretches to straw and darkness, stripes and a strait waistcoat, they now send them to sunshine and green fields, to wander in gardens among birds and flowers, and soothe them with soft music and kind, flattering speech.

Alda.   You laugh at me! perhaps I deserve it. (8)

Alda pours out her soul to Medon, and Medon returns her outpouring with ridicule. The wit that enables him to reduce her method to absurdity is the satire that enables him to reduce her confident, bold voice to a whimpering "perhaps I deserve it." Here we see Alda "subjected to" one of the many forms of "suffering" she has just been attempting to explain to Medon. Here we see him practicing the very ridicule that she has just condemned. If Medon had listened, he would know that Alda is not talking about the treatment of lunatics and "distempered wretches" when she speaks of those whom "a heartless world has taught to contemn both others and themselves"; she is talking, instead, about ordinary women and men, about Medon and herself. She is talking about the re-education of women from a state of ignorance about themselves to a state of knowledge about common humanity, and also the re-education of men who have for so long denied the variety of human nature, and the pleasure derived therefrom. Perhaps Medon's satirical response is defensive, a way of deflecting the monstrously bold voice he has just encountered, a way of coping with the desiring other who has just enunciated her passion, a way of defending against the earnestness itself of her generous affections. When he says in a penitential tone, "No, in truth; I am a little amused, but most honestly attentive: and perhaps wish I could think more like you," then we perhaps optimistically hope, along with Alda and Jameson, that he can begin genuinely to listen, and to hear the voices she records so lovingly in her book.

The same masculine ridicule that temporarily silences Alda has prevented women from knowing themselves and from recording their own experience, the characteristics of their nature. This is why Jameson, when she searches for subjects to record, must turn to the fictional characters of Shakespeare rather than to women of actual life. "Women are illustrious in history, not for what they have been in themselves, but generally in proportion to the mischief they have done or caused," Alda explains. "Those characters best fitted to my purpose are precisely those of which history never heard, or disdains to speak" (9). Relying on the idea that poetry is truer than history, Alda reasons that history has recorded only the extremes of feminine behavior. "[W]hereas in history we see, in one case, a fury of discord, a woman without modesty or pity; and in the other, an angel of benevolence and a worshipper of goodness; and nothing to connect the two extremes in our fancy," in poetry a more accurate assessment can be garnered (10).

Ironically having to reconstruct women's experience out of men's fictions, Jameson in her book parallels poets like Hemans, Lucy Aikin, Letitia Landon, and Joanna Baillie, who set out to retell familiar stories by filling in the silences within and with their own voices. This means having to redefine feminine heroics, not by starting afresh, but by starting in the muddle of past myth and the confusion of the historical present. Their heroines, then, are self-consciously feminine, refusing to let the monster peep out, but at the same time they are not their brothers' mythologizing visions of women. These women writers begin to make subtle distinctions between masculine courage and feminine, in the same way that Jewsbury has attempted to distinguish between masculine and feminine wit. Alda, for instance, offers an explanation of feminine patriotism when Medon blurts out that he hates "political women"—"a woman run mad with politics" (22–23). She argues: "Believe me, when we do feel it, our patriotism, like our courage and our love, has a purer source than with you; for a man's patriotism has always some tinge of egotism, while a woman's patriotism is generally a sentiment, and of the noblest kind" (23). This may at first sound exactly like the kind of idealization that men are prone to make about women's virtue—and no doubt Medon will gladly take it as such. I would suggest, however, that, though it is an idealization, it is not the same kind of idealization that Wordsworth, Coleridge, Byron, Shelley, Keats, Tuckerman, Gifford, Jeffrey, Medon make. When Alda says that women are courageous "through our affections and mental energies, not through our vanity or our strength" (27), she is attempting to transform masculine myth into feminine history, masculine desire into feminine experience. The affections give her both a theme and a method, and ones that it is difficult for men to accuse of monstrosity. "A woman's heroism is always the excess of sensibility," Alda says (27). While Jameson was theorizing thus toward a feminine nature from fictional Shakespearean heroines, female poets were making the same kinds of generalizations through their own depictions of fictional heroines. As we shall see, though their records necessarily contain significant traces of masculine influence, women poets were beginning to record self-consciously tracings marked in their own hearts from influences shared among themselves. The final chapter focuses on the poetry of Felicia Hemans, with brief glances at the work of Baillie and Landon, in order to understand, in Jewsbury's words, how the oak can be and not be in the acorn, how feminine desire can give birth to itself while recording its own growth out of the fathers' vision.

8

Records of Women:
Inscribing Feminine Desire
in the Poetics of Affection

Hemans begins her career at the age of fifteen with the publication of *Poems*
and proceeds to become one of the most respected and popular poets in
nineteenth-century Britain and America. A prolific poet, unlike many of the
other female writers we have examined, Hemans devoted herself almost exclusively to the production of poetry, original and translations, continuing to
write until her death in 1835 and continuing to be read until the end of the
nineteenth century.

1

Owen identifies the "two strains dearest" to Hemans's nature as "the
chivalrous and the tender" (*Works* 1: 56). These two strains—chivalric romance and romantic sentiment—in turn help to identify the factors that bring
success to women like Hemans. In one of her most crucial works, an essay
on the "Scenes and Passages from the 'Tasso' of Goethe," published the year
before her death (*New Monthly Magazine and Literary Journal* ns 3 [1834]:
1–5), Hemans reveals her conception of poetry. It is not coincidental that she
should choose to write on Goethe writing on Tasso, for in Goethe we find the
romantic interest (the "tender" strain) and in Tasso the romance interest
(the "chivalrous" strain). Analyzing and translating Goethe's poetry, and
Tasso's life, Hemans argues that there is an inescapable conflict between the
inner serenity of the poet (the realm of the romantic, of sentiment and affection) and the outer struggle for worldly quest and conquest (masculine romance). Hemans reads Goethe's "Tasso" as "a picture of the struggle between
elements which never can assimilate—powers whose dominion is over spheres
essentially adverse; between the spirit of poetry and the spirit of the world."
And she asks, "why is it that this collision is almost invariably fatal to the

gentler and the holier nature?" (1). Reading Goethe's "Tasso," and not the historical Tasso, as a man who is too "tender" for the necessary adversities of chivalrous quest in the world, she charts his life to its tragic resolution through Goethe's drama. According to Goethe's portrait, Tasso is set on capturing in poetry the worldly exploits of the warrior knight: "Not steel to steel / Is bound more closely by the magnet's power / Than the same striving after lofty things / Doth bind the Bard and Warrior" (Hemans's translation of Goethe, 2). But as Antonio, the warrior Tasso befriends, describes the world of knightly quest, combat, and competition to Tasso, the effect on Tasso's inner poetic life is devastating:

> With eagerness,
> Yea, with a strange delight, my soul drank in
> The strong words of th'experienced; but, alas!
> The more I listen'd still the more I sank
> In mine own eyes;—I seem'd to die away
> As into some faint echo of the rocks,—
> A shadowy sound—a nothing!

"Antipathy" develops between the warrior and the poet, as the "cold, keen irony" of Antonio "has irritated" Tasso "almost to frenzy," and eventually leads to a duel between them (3). As a crucial sign of chivalric competence and manly performance, it is appropriate that this duel should cause Tasso's imprisonment and his exile both from his own dreams of Homeric grandeur and from his lady-love. His solitary confinement and exile represent his imprisonment within his own sensitive poetic mind and his exile from the outer world that he cannot enter, "the catastrophe being that of the spiritual wreck within, unmingled with the terrors drawn from outward circumstances and change" (5). Tasso is "thus borne down by the cold triumphant worldliness of the courtier Antonio" (2). Hemans's only disappointment with the drama is that it "fails to excite a more reverential interest, a more tender admiration." Goethe's Tasso is "wanting in dignity, in the sustaining consciousness of his own high mission; he has no city of refuge within himself" (2). Hemans is compelled to offer Byron's Tasso as a "fine contrast and relief to the music of despair with which Goethe's work is closed" (5).

Hemans's intertextual analysis (interjecting also Wordsworth, Coleridge, Dante, and Tasso himself, as well as Byron) unconsciously rehearses and comments on the historical transformation of poetry from a manly calling to a feminine market enterprise, even as it provides a key for reforming poeticizing so that men can feel comfortable engaging in it. If we take Tasso to be the male romantic poet—Goethe, Wordsworth, or Byron—we see that he mirrors the fear of disempowerment and feminization. In the final confrontation between Antonio and Tasso, the poet cries, "Can I then image no high-hearted man / Whose pangs and conflicts have surpass'd mine own?" (5). He cannot. And so as he sinks, he reaches for Antonio in the same way that his lady Princess Leonora "clings" to him earlier: "[T]o thee I cling— / I grasp thee with mine arms. In wild despair / So doth the struggling sailor clasp the rock / Whereon he perishes!" (5). The romantic poet, caught in the circle of his own "self-communion," trapped by his own poetic desire, cannot reach out to the world beyond his dreams. As he internalizes his quest, he also tends to exile himself from visibly masculine forms of conquest. The only hope of the romantic poet is to re-envision his inner struggle as the equivalent of external conquest, to controvert apparent vulnerability of affection into the power of suffering, as we have seen Wordsworth attempt to do, and as we shall see Hemans praising him for doing. Hemans chastises Goethe for not having taken that step in his drama, and she offers Wordsworth's vision and ironically Byron's Tasso as alternatives.

Tasso is so powerful an embodiment of the romantic dilemma not just because he represents how the male romantics cling to a vision of manliness that seems to forsake them, but also because he attempts to relive a past mythic glory by recording the exploits of Antonio. Before his downfall, Tasso's "visionary rapture" enables him to view himself as a "Bard," glorious as the "Warrior" he is to commemorate. "Then will I dream that on the enchanted wave / I see Elysium pictured!" Nostalgically, he seeks to cast the glow of a mythic romance past over the confused reality of present life in Ferrara.

> Might I but see the minstrels and the chiefs
> Of the old time on that pure fountain-side
> For evermore inseparably link'd
> As they were link'd in life!
>
> . . .
>
> . . . Homer's life
> Was self-forgetfulness: he pour'd it forth,
> One rich libation to another's fame;
> And Alexander through th'Elysian grove
> To seek Achilles and his poet flies.
> Might I behold their meeting!
>
> (2)

Hemans's translation of Goethe's reading of Tasso's life reminds us of Wordsworth's first poets who turned blows into words and words into blows through language that dared to imitate manly adventure, reminds us of Peacock's satirical equation between warriors and poets in the infancy of primitive society. Hemans's Goethe's Tasso wants to link Homer to Achilles, Alexander to himself in one chain of manly conquest. He assumes, Byronically and ironically, that Homer's life is as glorious as the warriors whose lives he memorializes in his epic poems. Unlike the romantic poet, Homer, in pouring forth his rich libation to another's fame, is able to forget himself. Like Byron, it is "self-forgetfulness" that Tasso desires, but cannot possess, that Goethe writes about because it is so ineluctable to him. That very self-consciousness, however, is also the engine of his poetic desire and eloquence. It is self-consciousness, the acid that eats away his capacity for manly action, that is also the potion that burns into his soul and pains him into poetic utterance: "To me a God / Hath given strong utterance for mine agony, / When others in their deep despair, are mute" (5).

The romantics, too, look back nostalgically to a glorious past and attempt to coat their feminized present with its glow. They, too, turn to chivalrous romance as a way of repressing their unchivalric present. The irony is that the poetic form that they turn to—quest romance—in order to circumvent feminization is the very form that first invites women into the poetic arena. Walter Scott makes high poetry accessible to the middle classes, including women, by bringing poetry closer to the familiar prose romances that these readers are already consuming. This fact is often mentioned by the writers of the time. For instance, in a review of Hemans's *Modern Greece,* the critic devotes almost half the essay to discussing the recent democratization of poetry and its negative effects:

"The Lay" converted thousands, and "Marmion" tens of thousands, and the *whole* world read poetry. Had Mr Scott given out the same quantity of poetical thoughts and images, in poems constructed like "The Task," or "The Pleasures of Hope," his readers would not have numbered one for a hundred. . . . The whole secret is, that Mr Scott gave to the world a series of brilliant romances, and turned into this new-made channel all who ever in their lives read and relished fictitious compositions. All the poets, good and bad, forthwith wrote metrical romances. . . . (reviewer's emphasis, *Blackwood's Magazine* 1 [August 1817]: 516)

The reviewer goes on to note that there is "no want of excitability in the multitude," and that "these readers have tired even of romances in a metrical form" (516). After bemoaning the fickleness of the multitude and the fact that "profit will also fail," returning poetry "to its ancient proverbially unprofitable level," the reviewer praises Hemans, "who has had no higher aim than to regale the imagination with imagery, warm the heart with sentiment and feeling, and delight the ear with music, without the foreign aid of tale or fable." Because Hemans "has hitherto written to a select few," she has "passed almost unnoticed by the multitude" (517). This reviewer is right about Scott's influence, about the expanded readership due to the "aid of tale or fable," but he is a bit hasty in celebrating Hemans's more purely poetic interests, as later volumes of her poetry will make clear. Like the other women poets of her time, her sense of poetry is inextricably bound to her passion for romance narrative, and it is this passion, along with Scott's reconceptualization of the poetic, that helps to make poeticizing a congenial activity for her.[1]

The nostalgia for romance, then, is duplicitous, affecting the male romantics and the new female writers in some significantly different ways. Whereas the aura of romance allows men to recapture the masculinity of their poetic project just at the point when they fear its loss most, the same form allows women to experiment with poetry as a familiar structure of feminine experience. Just as the prose romance has been quickly and easily appropriated and feminized by women writers, so with poetic romance.[2] Men and women poets, therefore, tend to value different aspects of the romance aura. There are two groups of male writers: those who value the external quest or narrative aspect, such as Scott, Landor, and Southey; and those who value the internalized quest, the "major" male romantics. Whereas the former group views chivalric romance as a reclamation of history, as a reclamation of their heroic past, the second group views it likewise as a reclamation of the poet's visionary power over the external world. Female writers, on the other hand, tend to be fascinated by the immanent conflict between masculine and feminine desire embedded within the form, and as Leslie Rabine has argued about feminine prose romance, women romancers "seek to rediscover the already existing but invisible *interconnections* between domestic and sociopolitical, public and private, sexual and historical spheres" (*Reading the Romantic Heroine* 13). Poetic romance is a safe habitat for women writers both to experiment with high poetry and to examine the friction between feminine and masculine desire without overtly placing men and women in adversarial positions.

We can sense resistant feminine desire confronting the history of masculine ideology even in Hemans's review of Goethe's "Tasso." Hemans gives over a good portion of her essay to Tasso's lady-love, Princess Leonora d'Este, and to a translation of a conversation between the Princess and her confidante, Leonora de Sanvitale. The Princess intuitively recognizes that Tasso is headed toward tragedy, but she is powerless to prevent his self-doom, exactly because it is *self*-doom. Princess Leonora is the means through which Tasso could reach out beyond his self-communion to a larger world of feeling combined to action, but, trapped by his own desire to masculinize his calling, he is unable to see her in this light. This is, however, the light that Hemans sees her in as she paints Princess Leonora as a manifestation of the Madonna:

The spirit of Leonora has been at once elevated and subdued by early trial: high thoughts, like messengers from heaven, have been its visitants in the solitude of the sick chamber; and, looking upon life and creation, as it were, through the softening veil of remembered suffering, it has settled into such majestic loveliness as the Italian painters delight to shadow forth on the calm brow of their Madonna. (3)

Later, we shall see Leonora herself taking Tasso to task for not being able to look through "the softening veil of remembered suffering." Hemans, however, can comfortably oppose Leonora's state of mind to Tasso's because on the surface the Princess meets all the demands of femininity. Leonora has been purified from all visible traces of questionable independence. Princess Leonora is *not* like Shakespearean heroines, Hemans suggests, "females . . . in whom, even under the pressure of heaviest calamity, it is easy to discern the existence of the sunny and gladsome nature which would spring up with fawn-like buoyancy, were but the crushing weight withdrawn" (3). Hemans sees the Princess as an object-lesson in self-sacrifice. Her character "has all the deep devotedness of a woman's heart, with the still purity of a seraphic guardian, taking no part in the passionate dreams of earthly happiness" (3). It at first appears that Hemans celebrates the weight of centuries of masculine desire on the female temperament. It appears that Hemans is writing entirely from within masculine desire, accepting its contours as her own, that she, once she begins to write poetry, writes it from within the romantic poetry that is written about her as a woman. Does Hemans's poetry simply enunciate the words that Wordsworth would have Margaret and Lucy speak, if they were to be his feminine poets, rather than just the objects of his own will to possess himself?

I think not. Hemans's Princess Leonora is an answer to Tasso's desire, as much as its potential fulfillment or its potential salvation. Like Jewsbury or Jameson's Alda, Hemans's Princess Leonora swerves away from masculine desire even as she seems fully to exist within it. The subtlety of this difference is necessary both for the woman poet's sake, so that she may not trip across the monster she fears to be, and for the man's sake, so that he may feel secure in his masculine enterprise even as that enterprise is questioned by her. Lurking behind Hemans's portrait of the Princess are those nagging issues, sexual equality and women's rights, but Hemans keeps them at bay, consciously stressing instead what woman has to offer man, what man has neglected in woman, leading to his own self-tragedy. We can hear these issues clamoring behind Hemans's description of Leonora's character: "A deep feeling of woman's lot on earth,—the lot of endurance and of sacrifice,—seems ever present to her soul, and speaks characteristically in these lines, with which she replies to a wish of Tasso's for the return of the golden age" (3). The phrase "woman's lot on earth" speaks volumes. Endurance and sacrifice may be "woman's lot," but unless men respond responsibly to these feminine virtues, rather than responding only to their own dreams of themselves, they cannot help but falter. This is what the Princess tells Tasso, after he has announced his "wish . . . for the return of the golden age":

> When earth has men to reverence female *hearts,*
> To know the treasure of rich Truth and Love,
> Set deep within a high-soul'd woman's breast;—
> When the remembrance of our summer prime
> Keeps brightly in man's heart a holy place;—
> When the keen glance that pierces through so much
> Looks also tenderly through that dim veil
> By Time or Sickness hung 'round drooping forms;
> When the possession, stilling every wish,
> Draws not Desire away to other wealth;—
> A brighter day-spring then for *us* may dawn;
> Then may *we* solemnize our golden age.
>
> (Hemans's emphases, 3)

The Princess suggests—ever so gently—that Tasso has misread his own problem. The problematic relation is not so much between him and his male rival, or between a glorified past and the confounded present, but between him and her, between male and female. She opposes to his "high-hearted man" a "high-soul'd woman," whose *heart* he needs to learn to read and reverence if he is ever "to know the treasure of rich Truth and Love." As Jameson subtly suggests, man's knowledge is half knowledge and therefore distorted knowledge. Until he begins to listen to woman and to hear her voice, he will never be pleased by the variety of human nature. His "keen glance" must also learn to look "tenderly through that dim veil" that has become women's lot in life.

In fact, Tasso possesses this tender knowledge because he is a poet, though he has suppressed it out of his fear of being feminized by it. "When the possession, stilling every wish;— / Draws not Desire away to other wealth," then Tasso will be able to embrace women's desire fully and thus able to accept fully the tenderness within himself. Once men learn to accept the shared wealth of common desire, their wish for "other wealth"—for conquest—will be stilled. Notably, Hemans's Princess stresses the first person plural, transforming Tasso's self-possessing desire for a past that will link him to manly men into the desire for a future day when desire itself is shared by women and men. Hemans gently chastises Goethe from outside the text for having failed "to excite a more reverential interest, a more tender admiration," for having failed fully to accept the transformative power of feminine affection. Accordingly, through the Princess she chastises him from within the text for having failed to "reverence female *hearts*," for having failed to look "tenderly" as well as keenly "with the glance that pierces through so much."

Furthermore, Hemans stresses the relation between two women, underscoring what Virginia Woolf is later to point out, that the ties that bind woman to woman are neglected in the history of literature. Princess Leonora and her best friend Leonora (fortunately, for Hemans, reflecting each other even in their names) are living images of the link—the shared desire—that Tasso disables himself from achieving. As Leonora attempts to solace her Princess, she reminds her that at least the Princess has "gather'd into the full soul / Inalienable wealth" (4), exactly what the Princess has just admonished Tasso to do. And Hemans ends her translated extract with these words from Princess Leonora: "A treasure may be ours, / Only we know it not, or know, perchance, / Unconscious of its worth!" (4). Needless to say, these words apply to Tasso and to Goethe, and it is only a Leonora or a Princess Leonora, wrestled from Goethe's own masculine vision and re-imaged through the influence of Hemans's feminine desire, who can utter them.

Leonora becomes a suppressed hero, rather than just the heroine of Goethe's tale. She becomes the one who must make the ultimate sacrifice when she decides to give up Tasso in order to avoid the ruin that he eventually makes of himself. She "reproaches herself for not having listened to the monitory whispers of her soul," for not having advised Tasso sooner to beware Antonio, to beware his own miscalculating desire (3). In Hemans's reading, the tragedy transpires as much as a result of Leonora's oversight, as a result of Tasso's blindness. Momentarily overshadowed by Tasso's desire, she forgets to listen to "the secret signs and omens of the breast," to the "oracle" that "speaks low within our [women's] hearts" (3). Momentarily overwhelmed by Tasso's vision of himself, she forgets, like him, to reverence the knowledge hidden within "female hearts." Tasso's quest misfires, then, because both the hero and the heroine neglect the potential power of feminine affection.

I would go so far as to say that the plot of masculine quest romance itself depends upon that neglect.[3] What enables the knight's quest—whether destined for success or failure—is the repression of what the damsel desires, that she may need a quest of her own. The quest can proceed only if the ever-threatening tension between masculine and feminine desire is held at bay or repressed. As long as the romance heroine does not question her role as purely desired object, the male hero can externalize his desire through conquest of "other wealth." As long as the romance heroine does not question the male's tacit equation between her and "other wealth," the hero will be self-justified in seeing the conquest of territory and people as metonymic for obtaining the heroine herself and the spiritual values that she always represents. Not only does she become the justification and reward for his outward movement into conquest; also she becomes desire itself, always representing what the questing male needs rather than what the female is or can be, always representing his desire, never recording her own. Hemans's poetic romances revise this pattern, not by altering the movement of masculine desire, nor by changing what the heroine represents. Rather, what Hemans does is to overlay feminine desire onto this pattern, or to place a subterranean current of feminine desire beneath the visible pattern, a current that can be heard only when we listen very closely. This subterranean current, even as it moves through the preset channels of masculine myth, clashes with that myth and enables us to focus on the tension that occurs when a rare feminine voice speaks simultaneously with a blustering male choir.

2

Hemans's recording of feminine desire is even more obvious in her poetic romances than in the essay on Goethe. Any one of her longer narrative or dramatic poems—*The Abencerrage, The Widow of Crescentius, The Tale of the Secret Tribunal, The Siege of Valencia, The Forest Sanctuary, De Chatillon, The Vespers of Palermo*—could be used to demonstrate this point. All of these poems pit the masculine world of external quest and conquest against the feminine world of internal sentiment and affection, and, as in her reading of Goethe's "Tasso," gender difference crosses sexual lines. In the same way that Leonora exchanges earthly quest for unearthly suffering and self-sacrifice and that Tasso fights off his intrinsically tender poetic nature for a vision of manly external quest, the male and female characters in her romances possess the potential for both masculine quest and feminine affection. All these characters must learn to assimilate the two competing urges within them. There is no doubt that Hemans privileges the feminine world of powerful affection, but her internal world is drastically different from the romantics' internalization of quest romance.

At the end of her poem *The Restoration of the Works of Art to Italy*, Hemans expresses the function of art thus:

> Gaze on that scene, and own the might of Art,
> By truth inspired, to elevate the heart!

To bid the soul exultingly possess,
Of all her powers, a heighten'd consciousness.

(Works 2: 166)

The reader is instructed to gaze on "Raphael's pure and perfect line" through Hemans's poetic evocation of that line. The function of both the visual and the verbal arts is "to elevate the heart," to raise consciousness (the mind) to the heightened state of the heart. It would be erroneous here to read consciousness as *self*-consciousness, as self-possessing consciousness. Indeed, Hemans seems to mean something almost opposite. Hemans's heightened consciousness is the capacity to know one's own heart, to know how it is linked to others' feelings, and to know the limits and powers, the tensions and extensions that derive from reverencing the heart. Hemans's consciousness never moves outside of *human* bonds, and in this way, she differs from both Susan Levin's and Margaret Homans's portraits of Dorothy Wordsworth, who celebrates the alterity of the alien natural object.[4] Upon finishing one of Hemans's romances—or lyrics, for that matter—the reader discovers the deepness and broadness of her own heart in the guise of another's suffering or joy (though usually it is suffering). In this way, Hemans teaches the power of beauty, to men as well as to women, and she teaches the beauty of power, to women as well as to men. But the difference between knowing powers and limits is so subtle that we could almost say that it is basically the same lesson, a lesson that tends to dissolve the rationale for gender difference as it demonstrates the similar effect of heart-knowledge on men and women.[5] What women must learn is that heart-knowledge cannot protect them from the demands of public life, from the political strife of the state. What men must learn is that heart-knowledge is the basis for all their public actions, for all of the motivations and aims that make them the more visible agents of state guardianship.

Take for example *The Siege of Valencia (Works* 3: 284–385), first published in 1823. The plot of the poem is minimal and unobtrusive, although it is more complex than most of her plots. Gonzalez, the governor of Valencia, is forced to sacrifice his two young sons, who have been captured by the Moors, rather than give up the blockaded city. Against the urging of her husband and her daughter Ximena, Elmina secretly risks her own life to make a deal with the Moors, the return of her sons for the surrender of the city. Otherwise, she reasons, the city will be captured eventually anyway—since the soldiers are collapsing from starvation and no help is in sight. After arranging to get the Moors into the city, she is double-crossed by Abdullah, the leader of the Moors, who beheads her sons. The king's soldiers arrive, but not in time to save the boys, their father, or Ximena, who have all given up their lives for the state. Bereft of all her familial bonds, deprived of her domestic security, Elmira at last realizes the larger significance of affectional sacrifice. She realizes that her heroic attempt to save her children, though empowered by the right affection, has been misplaced. Her affection is then transferred to the state, as she comes to realize the continuity between political freedom and domestic happiness. Finally, she heroically accepts her fate as a state widow.

This narrative situation is typical of Hemans's tales. Unlike Scott, Southey, Landor, or any of the other externalizing romancers, Hemans eschews
the kinds of complicated Spenserian plots that have become associated with
quest romance since as far back as Tasso. In most of her situations warriors
are prevented from enacting their conquests by external circumstances beyond
their control. The siege of Valencia is also a siege on masculine quest. Rather
than plot, Hemans gives us a sequence of incidents, each incident being a
crisis designed to present the emotional turmoil of the characters and to provoke sympathetic turmoil in the readers. These emotional crises are invariably
domestic in nature, even when their cause is some form of public conflict. Or
more accurately, Hemans repeatedly explores the complex relation between
the state and the hearth. Her tales articulate the idea that rarely, if ever, can
the heart be at home in the hearth, where its greatest security lies. Always, the
heart is called to a nobler purpose that seems to contradict the security of
home and its familial and familiar affections, and only in the end is it revealed
that the demands of the state and the demands of the heart derive from the
same affections and drive toward the same end. More than learning how to
act in the world, her characters learn how to feel in a world where most actions are futile. In other words, rather than internalizing the quest, Hemans
leaves it external, but she problematizes its power to resolve either the plot's
crisis or the moral dilemma of the characters and readers. Accordingly, she
presents the continuity of affection as the only means through which resolution (both incidental denouement and moral resoluteness) can be achieved.
Because affection has the power to transfer love of family to love of state and
the power to induce "emulative zeal" in the reader, it can link all the elements
within and outside the text that at first appear disconnected and alien.

On the surface, the *Siege* seems to follow the pattern expected of a tragic
quest romance. The hero, Gonzalez, achieves his goal at the moment of his
death. His values of honor, courage, loyalty are reaffirmed, and he is re-
warded for his resolution, although the glory comes in death rather than in a
long life and longer fame. But Gonzalez is able to remain true to his values
only by not acting. His honor is tested when he must refuse to regain his sons
by some underhanded method. His courage is tested when he must refuse to
attack the Moors as Abdullah beheads his elder son before his father's eyes.
His loyalty is tested when he must refuse to act at any point in the immediate
interest of himself or his family. With each assault on his obligation to do
battle and conquer, he must replace that desire to act with deepened feeling
for the significance of his position and his relations. Each assault encourages
him to feel more deeply for his state, his king, his religion; each assault forces
him to feel more deeply the invisible tie between his domestic bonds and his
public obligations.

We can see how Hemans substitutes the value of physical strength and
manly action for the value of affection in three incidents that focus on Gonzalez's crises. His first crisis occurs when he learns of the capture of his children and is helpless to act. Rather than supporting her husband's desire to be
steadfast to the state, Elmira intensifies his desire to assert his affection for

his children. Torn between what seems to be a battle between duty and affection, Gonzalez says, "I must not pause / To give my heart one moment's mastery thus" (304). When Ximena offers to "bring the lute / Whose sounds thou lovest," Gonzalez instructs her thus:

> If there be strains of power
> To rouse a spirit, which in triumphant scorn
> May cast off nature's feebleness, and hold
> Its proud career unshackled, dashing down
> Tears and fond thoughts to earth; give voice to those!
> I have need of such, Ximena!—we must hear
> No melting music now!
>
> (291)

Gonzalez is unable to restrain the power of his affection. It is impossible to root out "nature's feebleness"; the best he can hope for is a transference of that powerfully natural affection to his steadfastness for the state. As his daughter facilitates that transference, his wife attempts to impede it. When she begins to criticize his inaction, he reminds her to maintain the position that she has held in his life thus far:

> Urge me not,
> Thou that through all sharp conflicts hast been found
> Worthy a brave man's love!—oh, urge me not
> To guilt, which through the midst of blinding tears,
> In its own hues thou seest not!
>
> (299)

Believing that affection is a form of feminine blinding, he must warn his wife not to use it as a weapon, not to vacate her supportive role.

His second crisis occurs when he discovers that Elmira has surrendered the city for the safety of their sons. The woman who is supposed to be the guardian and reward for his steadfastness is suddenly the cause for his disillusionment. When Elmira begins to question her role as mere symbol for her husband's values, he necessarily begins to question his role as quester for those values. Like Tasso, he begins to feel that his whole life has lost its meaning.

> Now my life
> Is struck to worthless ashes!—In my soul
> Suspicion hath ta'en root. The nobleness
> Henceforth is blotted from all human brows;
> And fearful power, a dark and troublous gift,
> Almost like prophecy, is pour'd upon me,
> To read the guilty secrets in each eye
> That once look'd bright with truth!
> —Why, then, I have gain'd
> What men call wisdom!—A new sense, to which
> All tales that speak of high fidelity,
> And holy courage, and proud honour, tried,
> Search'd, and found steadfast, even to martyrdom,

> Are food for mockery!—Why should I not cast
> From my thinn'd locks the wearing helm at once,
> And in the heavy sickness of my soul
> Throw the sword down for ever?—Is there aught
> In all this world of gilded hollowness,
> Now the bright hues drop off its loveliest things,
> Worth striving for again?
>
> (344)

In his moment of nihilistic anxiety, not even his faithful daughter can solace or inspire him. She attempts to replace her mother as the symbol of chivalric values: "Father! look up! / Turn unto me, thy child!" But he must regain his balance before he can accept the substitution:

> Thy face is fair;
> And hath been unto me, in other days,
> As morning to the journeyer of the deep;
> But now—'tis too like hers!
>
> (345)

Gonzalez's final trial of affection is when he must witness the beheading of his first son. Garcias, his trustworthy knight, pleads with him to leave, but Gonzalez refuses, having promised his son that he will watch the boy bravely meet his fate. "Who hath told *thee* how much man's heart can bear?" he asks Garcias (360). As Gonzalez gradually learns to bear the kind of domestic suffering usually reserved for women in their roles as mothers and wives, he grows stronger, able to wait and watch in the midst of deepening affection while suppressing the urge to move out and take physical action against a sea of troubles.

The true focus of the drama is Elmira, for it is she who is transformed most fundamentally, and ironically it is she who catapults the plot from a lethargic state of siege into energetic motion. To do so, however, she must cross and then recross the gender barrier, gaining the knowledge of masculine quest only to resign herself to the deeper knowledge of the feminine heart. Elmira crosses the gender line by disobeying the three authorities whose absolute rule she is supposed to represent through her feminine virtues. First, she betrays her husband by disobeying him and by refusing to represent his worth. He warns her that the person who attempts to save the boys must be seen as a traitor (296). But when he refuses to act, she herself acts, not only going against his command but also stepping out of her proper sphere of feminine waiting. The second authority she betrays is religion by refusing to take the advice of the priest Hernandez when she reveals her scheme to him. Hernandez tells her:

> This must not be. Enough of woe is laid
> E'en now upon thy lord's heroic soul,
> For man to bear, unsinking. Press thou not
> Too heavily th'o'erburthen'd heart.—Away!

> Bow down the knee, and send thy prayers for strength
> Up to Heaven's gate.
>
> (320)

But not even religion can sway Elmira from her course of action. She tells
the priest, as she has previously told her husband, that he obviously cannot
know what lies in a mother's heart. It is her heart that is overburdened, not
her husband's, and so she must act even though her action pulls her out of
the sphere of domesticity into the sphere of political strife. The final authority
she betrays is, of course, the state, and as she later realizes, in betraying the
state, she also betrays her own domestic obligations, her own wifely and maternal affections.

Elmira is quick to dismiss both Hernandez and Gonzalez because she is
so confident of the affection she has been taught to nurture in others. When
her husband warns her against becoming a traitor, she immediately lashes out
at him by uncovering the gendered basis of his priorities:

> Oh, cold and hard of heart!
> Thou shouldst be born for empire, since thy soul
> Thus lightly from all human bonds can free
> Its haughty flight!—Men! men! too much is yours
> Of vantage; ye that with a sound, a breath,
> A shadow, thus can fill the desolate space
> Of rooted up affections, o'er whose void
> Our yearning hearts must wither!—So it is,
> Dominion must be won!—Nay, leave me not—
> My heart is bursting, and I *must* be heard!
> Heaven hath given power to mortal agony,
> As to the elements in their hour of might
> And mastery o'er creation!—Who shall dare
> To mock that fearful strength!
>
> (296–297)

Mistakenly, Elmira thinks that her husband's obsession with conquest pre-
cludes his capacity to feel the rootedness of affection that is her agony and
her strength of rebellion. She simultaneously condemns and envies the man's
lot. It is appropriate, she suggests, that men are "born for empire" because
their affections can be uprooted with "a sound, a breath, a shadow." The same
affection, however, that makes her weak with tears and puts her at a disadvantage in relation to men also is the source of her strength. The bursting of her
heart becomes the might of a tempest, a turbulent wind that masters the very
creation which it is supposed to nurture with its mild, life-sustaining breath.

Later, Elmira delves deeper into masculine values and deeper into her
husband's already overburdened heart:

> There is none,
> In all this cold and hollow world, no fount
> Of deep, strong, deathless love, save that within
> A mother's heart.—It is but pride, wherewith

> To his fair son the father's eye doth turn,
> Watching his growth. Ay, on the boy he looks,
> The bright glad creature springing in his path,
> But as the heir of his great name, the young
> And stately tree, whose rising strength erelong
> Shall bear his trophies well.—And this is love!
> This is *man's* love!
>
> (302, Hemans's emphasis)

She goes on to serialize for twenty lines the countless acts of domestic affection that characterize *"woman's tasks"* (302–303, Hemans's emphasis). Like Jameson pointing out the difference between masculine and feminine courage, patriotism, and virtue, Elmira sees her husband's love as simply an extension of his desire for self-possessing fame. Having identified this as his true concern (and it is not entirely off the mark), she damns him to a hell of what Hemans calls "self-communion" in her essay on Goethe: "May you live / To be alone, when loneliness doth seem / Most heavy to sustain" (303). Of course, her curse comes back to haunt her in the end, but here it is a powerful indictment—even if an erroneous one in the moral design of the drama—of man's self-obsession. "But an hour comes to tame the mighty man / Unto the infant's weakness," Elmira warns her husband, for he shall find that the loyalties he now values above the life of his children are all self-deluding phantoms:

> Ay, then call up
> Shadows—dim phantoms from ancestral tombs,
> But all all—*glorious*—conquerors, chieftains, kings,
> To people that cold void!—And when the strength
> From your right arm hath melted, when the blast
> Of the shrill clarion gives your heart no more
> A fiery wakening; if at last you pine
> For the glad voices, and the bounding steps,
> Once through your home re-echoing. . .
>
> . . .
>
> . . . —when those days are come,
> Then, in your utter desolation, turn
> To the cold world, the smiling, faithless world,
> Which hath swept past you long, and bid it quench
> Your soul's deep thirst with *fame!* immortal *fame!*
> Fame to the sick of heart!—a gorgeous robe,
> A crown of victory, unto him that dies
> I'th'burning waste, for water!
>
> (303–304, Hemans's emphases)

Elmira's prophecy comes to pass, but it is she who must endure it, not her husband. She is only able to bear her fate through the same source that empowers and encourages her to go against the will of her husband for the first time in her life, the power of affection.

Thinking that the masculine institutions that enable the power to act have not the feeling to act, Elmira takes it upon herself to save her children. At first, her task is ambiguous. Her plan seems to be simply to plead for mercy at Abdullah's feet, an act that in itself the priest and her elder son Alphonso consider treacherous and unchristian. Hernandez also brings to her attention the danger of her mission. A man willing to take the lives of two innocent boys will not flinch at taking the life of their mother as well. But blinded by the power of affection, not recognizing its limits, she proceeds with her plan.

It is appropriate that Elmira must crossdress in order to fulfill her disobedient task. As Tuckerman points out, "even while arrayed in male costume and enacting the public advocate, the essential and captivating characteristics of [Portia's] true sex inspire her mien, and language." This is because Shakespeare's crossdressing heroines put on male costume in order ultimately to restore the harmony of a well-defined gendered world. It is a form of overcompensation, tilting the scales in order to rebalance them. We can sail through Shakespeare's crossdressing comedies securely knowing that on the opposite shore the old familiar order will prevail. When Scott reinvigorates the theme and strategy of crossdressing in *Marmion* (to be picked up by Byron later), he uses it as a form of purgation. Blinded by her love for the villain of the romance, Constance, a lapsed nun, crossdresses in order to perpetrate evil; she is accordingly expunged from the text through her death. Just as her crossdressing is a sign of deluded and pitiable weakness that perverts her sense of morality, so her extremely violent demise indicates the re-establishment of the old order, in which the dictates of masculine chivalric romance hold sway over sexual roles. Hemans, who would certainly be familiar with both Shakespeare's and Scott's crossdressing heroines, opts to emulate Shakespeare, but not without a tinge of significant influence from Scott. Like Portia, Elmira sets out to redress an injustice, but like Constance, she is misguided by her feminine affection. Elmira's crossdressing is not so much the perversity of wickedness as the perversity of well-intentioned shortsightedness. Appropriately, then, her crossdressing does not restore balance, but instead complicates the crisis.

When Elmira throws off her mantle and helmet, Abdullah is amazed: "How hast thou dared / To front the mighty thus amidst his hosts?" (327). Elmira is nonplussed, as she offers the Moorish chief a lesson not that different from the one she has given to her husband:

> Think'st thou there dwells no courage but in breasts
> That set their mail against the ringing spears,
> When helmets are struck down? Thou little know'st
> Of nature's marvels. Chief, my heart is nerved
> To make its way through things which warrior men,
> Ay, they that master death by field or flood,
> Would look on, ere they braved!—I have no thought,
> No sense of fear! Thou'rt mighty! but a soul
> Wound up like mine is mightier, in the power

> Of that one feeling pour'd through all its depths,
> Than monarchs with their hosts! Am I not come
> To die with these my children?
>
> (328)

Unable to comprehend her feminine courage, Abdullah immediately asks, "Doth thy faith / Bid thee do this, fond Christian?" not realizing that in fact her faith countermands it. But we the readers realize it, and we cannot help but admire her courage despite or perhaps because of its rebelliousness. I sense very strongly that Hemans, too, despite her moral designs here, has a great deal of fondness and respect for her romance hero(ine). In effect, Elmira has, as she herself suggests, done what all the knights of Valencia have not been "nerved" to do. As her action loosens the siege and retriggers activity so that the drama can move relentlessly toward its catastrophe, she displaces the conventional male hero and disrupts the pattern of nondevelopment expected of a romance heroine. Even as Elmira is "chastened" (to use her own word, 378), we realize that she had to tilt the scales in order to restore balance within herself. Just as Gonzalez has been brought to the outer limit of action and forced to discover power in longsuffering emotions, so in order to understand the limits of heart-knowledge, Elmira has been forced to exercise its power to its outer limit. Pressed to enact the power of affection in the realm of worldly forces and political strife, Elmira can return to domesticity now cognizant of the continuity between the hearth and the state, between the state and the heart.

This is a lesson that Ximena, the hero*ine* of the romance, does not need to learn. And because Ximena has nothing to learn, because she accepts her status as symbol with less overt resistance, she fits the conventional mold of romance heroine perfectly—almost. The play opens with Ximena singing the kind of national ballad that Hemans herself is to become famous for. Ximena's song is a premonition of the role she will choose as patriotic martyr—a sort of Joan of Arc; it is a prophecy of her own death as heroic self-sacrifice. Elmira, disturbed that her daughter's song has lost its "young / And buoyant spirit of the morn" (288), is unaware of the larger significance of the political events surrounding them, but Ximena is fully aware from the beginning. "[T]his / Is not the free air of our mountain-wilds," she tells her mother (288), and when her mother tells her that she should "move, / As a light breeze of heaven, through summer bowers" (a very Shelleyan image), Ximena attempts to explain the inescapable effect of the siege:

> Ay, days, that wake
> All to their tasks!—Youth may not loiter now
> In the green walks of spring; and womanhood
> Is summon'd unto conflicts, heretofore
> The lot of warrior-souls. Strength is born
> In the deep silence of long-suffering hearts;
> Not amidst joy.
>
> (289)

From the beginning Ximena is a contrast to her mother. The daughter understands how the power of feminine affection must be transferred from the limited sphere of domesticity to the other limited sphere of the state. When Elmira offers their daughter to Gonzalez as the embodiment of the "shadows" his inactivity has caused, he sees instead "a change / Far nobler on her brow" (299). His praise of his daughter serves implicitly as a condemnation of his wife:

> She hath put on
> Courage, and faith, and generous constancy,
> Even as a breastplate.—Ay, men look on her,
> As she goes forth, serenely to her tasks,
> Binding the warrior's wounds, and bearing fresh
> Cool draughts to fever'd lips; they look on her,
> Thus moving in her beautiful array
> Of gentle fortitude, and bless the fair
> Majestic vision, and unmurmuring turn
> Unto their heavy toils.
>
> (300)

Both Gonzalez's and Ximena's use of soldierly language to describe Ximena's demeanor is not arbitrary. She becomes literally a soldier through a process of metonymic shifts. At first, she is associated with soldiering because she tends to wounded soldiers, a thoroughly feminine activity, though one most commonly performed by men on the battlefield of manly conquest. Then she moves closer to soldiering when she takes it on herself to revitalize the morale of the soldiers by reminding them of their glorious past, of anticipated fame and patriotic death on the battlefield. This, too, is within the feminine sphere, although more ambiguously so, because it is more commonly performed by male minstrels and by the soldiers of highest rank on the battlefield. She has moved from being a nurse to being a historian and an indirect agent encouraging direct agents into action. She lets her father know that she is prepared for a larger role when he suggests that "melting music" is inappropriate in the midst of political strife and combat:

> I know all high
> Heroic ditties of the elder-time,
> Sung by the mountain-Christians, in the holds
> Of th'everlasting hills, whose snows yet bear
> The print of Freedom's step.
>
> (291–292)

Elmira's role here cannot help but remind us of how Hannah More, in transferring woman's domestic concern to social welfare as a whole, was able to enlarge the role of women during the crisis of the French Revolution, suggesting that "influence" is woman's best "talent."

As Elmira sets in motion the action, Ximena sets in motion the counter-action of the play. After discovering what her mother has done, she determines to rouse the citizens, who have given up all hope. Carrying the banner of her ancestors, she, reminiscent of Cythna, calls the men to battle:

> I've that within me, kindling through the dust
> Which from all time hath made high deeds its voice
> And token to the nations;—Look on me!
> Why hath Heaven pour'd forth courage, as a flame
> Wasting the womanish heart, which must be still'd
> Yet sooner for its swift consuming brightness,
> If not to shame your doubt, and your despair,
> And your soul's torpor?—Yet, arise and arm!
>
> (352)

Just at the point that Gonzalez is enraged beyond his control and decides to attempt to save his second son, Ximena arrives leading the citizen-soldiers and carrying the banner. Appropriating the French Revolutionary image later captured in Delacroix's famous painting of Liberty as a woman carrying the banner and leading the rebels to victory, Ximena becomes the symbolic figure of liberation.[6]

Unlike her mother, even as she subtly invades the territory of manly conquest, Ximena does so through the conventional representations reserved for the feminine in masculinist ideology. After her venture onto the edge of the battlefield, she returns home to pray and die. Like Moses who is given an image of the promised land only because he cannot enter it, she is allowed to glimpse masculine quest only because she is fatally bound to feminine vulnerability. Her uncommon valor can only be matched with uncommon feebleness, and accordingly she dies, as it were, from no real physical cause, but literally from a heart throbbing too violently in her tender frame. From the beginning she has seen her domestic fate as intertwined with the life of public conquest. Even as she rejoices in her fate—unable to fight but able to lead the forces to the edge of battle—we sense her regret: her courage, unlike the men's, is a "flame / Wasting the womanish heart." She is always cognizant that the source of her power is the heart, which binds the hearth and the state, the past and the present, passivity and activity, suffering and passion, life and death.

As Chorley points out, Ximena's voice represents Hemans's own (*Memorials* 2: 324). More precisely, Ximena is the character within the drama with whom Hemans could most comfortably identify without visions of monstrosity. Elmira, too, is her voice, though it is one that needs chastening in order to fit neatly into the pattern of masculine myth and into the sphere of feminine poeticizing. What Ximena does within the poem, Hemans is attempting to do with the poem itself. The drama is one of those "heroic ditties of the elder-time," designed to connect "religious feeling with . . . patriotism and high-minded loyalty" (Advertisement to the *Siege, Works* 3: 285). One of Hemans's earliest poetic attempts is concerned with the peninsular war, where her brother is fighting. And despite strictures against women writing on such topics, she self-consciously justifies her interest, based on reasoning similar to More's and to Jameson's in the introduction to the *Characteristics*. In a letter of 1808, she writes: "[T]hough females are forbidden to interfere in politics, yet as I have a dear, dear brother, at present on the scene of action, I may be allowed to feel some ardour on the occasion" (*Memorials* 1: 31). Like Ximena, whose concern for her brothers' and father's welfare carries her closer to soldiering, so Hemans herself saw the domestic relation as a justification for a patriotic outpouring. Owen describes Hemans's response to the peninsular war thus:

[H]er young mind [she was fourteen] was filled with glorious visions of British valour and Spanish patriotism. In her ardent view, the days of chivalry seemed to be restored, and the very names which were of daily occurence in the despatches, were involuntarily associated with the deeds of Roland and his Paladins, or of her own especial hero, "The Cid Ruy Diaz," the campeador. (*Works* 1: 11)

Like Scott and Wordsworth, Hemans romanticizes the Spanish campaign, seeing it through the eyes of a chivalric past even as she understands that what is at stake is the strength of modern nationalism and the future of British imperialism. Unlike Scott and Wordsworth, she must protect herself from being viewed as a "woman run mad with politics" (in Medon's words), and she does so by placing her political interest behind the veil of domesticity and writing political poems that take as their immediate concern the trials of feminine affection. In this sense her chivalric romances are not that different from the political tracts Hannah More is writing a decade earlier. In her own way, even like Elmira, she has stolen the garb of a soldier and invaded the enemy camp.

3

In *The Siege of Valencia* Hemans is carrying forth a tradition established by Joanna Baillie, whom Hemans admires greatly and whose influence is everywhere felt in the younger poet's works. In the introduction to the first volume of her series *The Plays on the Passions* (published between 1798 and 1836), Baillie offers a complex theory of dramatic art based on the concept of "sympathetic curiosity," which probably influences Hemans's idea of "emulative zeal." Baillie defines sympathetic curiosity thus: "It is our best and most powerful instructor. From it we are taught the proprieties and decencies of ordinary life, and are prepared for distressing and difficult situations. In examining others we know ourselves" (*Dramatic and Poetical Works of Joanna Baillie* 4). Baillie's "Introductory Discourse" comes out the same year as Wordsworth's *Lyrical Ballads* and, as Stuart Curran suggests, has many similarities with Wordsworth's preface, which it predates by two years ("Romantic Poetry: The I Altered" 185–186). Baillie's idea of sympathetic curiosity can also be traced to the eighteenth-century cult of sentiment. Her interest, however, is as thoroughly rationalist as it is sentimental. Like Wordsworth, she wants to rescue British literature from the trend toward what she sees as the unrealistic and unnatural impulses displayed in Gothic fiction, even though, again like Wordsworth, her work is influenced by the Gothic. Whereas Wordsworth returns to the "primitive" ballads of Britain's daring past, Baillie returns to the drama of Renaissance England, especially Shakespeare, in an attempt to revitalize national literature and bring nobility of purpose to the English stage. Baillie's objective is to interfuse feeling with thought, passion with contemplation, by encouraging the reader to consider not only the apparent effects of the most obvious emotional outbursts on individual behavior but also how the more hidden, subterranean mental states function within the larger realm of social conduct.

Universal, however, as this disposition undoubtedly is, with the generality of mankind it occupies itself in a passing and superficial way. Though a native trait of character or of passion is obvious to them as well as to the sage, yet to their mind it is but the visitor of a moment; they look upon it singly and unconnected: and though this disposition, even so exercised, brings instruction as well as amusement, it is chiefly by storing up in their minds those ideas to which the instructions of others refer, that it can be eminently useful. Those who reflect and reason upon what human nature holds out to their observation, are comparatively but few. No stroke of nature which engages their attention stands insulated and alone. Each presents itself to them with many varied connections; and they comprehend not merely the immediate feeling which gave rise to it, but the relation of that feeling to others which are concealed. (4)

Baillie wants to explore the profound origin and natural consequence of passion, rather than simply presenting the superficial social feeling usually represented in novels, romances, plays, and lyrics, for she believes that in this way her audience will be taught to reflect upon the complex interconnections between passion and behavior, between individual action and social interaction. Having contemplated these complexities, the audience is encouraged to "store" these "ideas" in their minds, enlarging their capacity for sympathetic curiosity and thus making possible a profounder sort of responsive passion, a more binding sense of social interconnectedness, and a more deepened sense of moral responsibility. Both Baillie and Wordsworth, then, are concerned with constructing a literary-moral poetics which will enable their readers to experience emotion as a primordial and spontaneous event, a transitory moment of feeling in itself, and simultaneously to contemplate its origins and effects as a sustained phenomenon.

This approach to literature dictates to Baillie the need for "real and natural characters" represented under the influence of "strong and fixed passions" (10). She seeks in the language of her plays to represent real social intercourse, and she pares the plot to an unswerving, unified, inevitable course of action characteristic of classical drama. It is not the bold and diverse actions, she reasons, that instructs the audience, but rather the ordinary, recognizable, but subtle patterns of behavior stemming from the "varieties of the human mind" (4).

The fair field of what is properly called poetry, is enriched with so many beauties, that in it we are often tempted to forget what we really are, and what kind of beings we belong to. Who, in the enchanted regions of simile, metaphor, allegory, and description, can remember the plain order of things in this every-day world?

. . . I will venture, however, to say, that amidst all this decoration and ornament, all this loftiness and refinement, let one simple trait of the human heart, one expression of passion, genuine and true to nature, be introduced, and it will stand forth alone in the boldness of reality, whilst the false and unnatural around it fade away upon every side, like the rising exhalations of the morning. With admiration, and often with enthusiasm, we proceed on our way through the grand and beautiful images raised to our imagination by the lofty epic muse: but what, even here, are those things that strike upon the heart; that we feel and remember? Neither the descriptions of war, the sound of the trumpet, the clanging of arms, the combat of heroes, nor the death of the mighty, will interest our minds like the fall of the feeble stranger, who simply expresses the anguish of his soul, at the thoughts of that far distant home which he must never return to again. . . . (6)

Though it would be interesting to flesh out here the many ways in which Wordsworth's preface is similar to Baillie's "Introductory Discourse," I am more interested in Baillie's influence on Hemans. Even though both Baillie and Hemans want to explore the "epic" masculine world of combat and conquest, they always domesticate that interest by showing its limitations, how it is limited by its relation to the supposedly smaller and more trivial world of the domestic affections. So, unlike Wordsworth and the other romantics, sympathy for these women is not a matter of internalizing the "epic" in order to experience self-possession and visionary conquest; instead it is a matter of sustaining the validity of the internal by reminding their readers of the unseverable bonds between internal feeling and external social conduct. What remains internal and uncommunicated becomes a threat to the sustainability of the wider community with which one is intimately interconnected even when one is a "feeble stranger . . . far distant" from home. This is what Hemans learns from Baillie's *Plays on the Passions,* as Baillie very well may have learned it from second-generation bluestockings and sentimental poetesses like More and Barbauld.

Hemans also learns from Baillie to stress plot as *suffering action* rather than plot as a burst of grand, varied activity. And although action is more psychologized in Baillie, Hemans follows her mentor in demonstrating how the most apparently virile, daring acts can lead to catastrophe and inaction, rather than to heroism, while barely noticeable, seemingly trifling activity of the mind and heart can reverse the fate of empires. Hemans would have encountered this idea in practically every tragedy and in many of the comedies that Baillie wrote. The plays often focus on women and men thrown together into the same dilemma of having to decide between the political demands of the state and the affectional dictates of domestic community, exactly the situation of both Elmira and her husband in Hemans's *Siege of Valencia.*

In her first play, *Basil,* for instance, the heroine Victoria, bored with her constricted and tedious life in the castle, begins to flirt with the visiting general of the emperor's army, Basil. Victoria's confidante and governess, Countess Albini, warns her of the potential danger of her behavior in a conversation that focuses on the conflict between individual desire and social duty:

> *Victoria.* O, love will master all the power of art!
> Ay, all! and she who never has beheld

> The polish'd courtier, or the tuneful sage,
> Before the glances of her conquering eye
> A very native simple swain become. . . .
> . . . Did nought but flatt'ring words and tuneful praise,
> Sighs, tender glances, and obsequious service,
> Attend her presence, it were nothing worth:
> I'd put a white coif o'er my braided locks,
> And be a plain, good, simple, fire-side dame.
> *Albini* (raising her head from her book).
> And is, indeed, a plain domestic dame,
> Who fills the duties of an useful state,
> A being of less dignity than she,
> Who vainly on her transient beauty builds,
> A little poor ideal tyranny?
> *Isabella. Ideal too!*
> *Albini.*   Yes, most unreal pow'r:
> For she who only finds her self-esteem
> In others' admiration, begs an alms;
> Depends on others for her daily food,
> And is the very servant of her slaves;
> Though oftentimes, in fantastic hour,
> O'er men she may a childish pow'r exert,
> Which not ennobles, but degrades her state.
> *Victoria.* You are severe, Albini, most severe:
> Were human passions plac'd within the breast
> But to be curb'd, subdu'd, pluck'd by the roots?
> All heaven's gifts to some good end were giv'n.
> *Albini.* Yes, for a noble, for a generous end.
>
>   (27, Baillie's emphasis)

But Victoria, enamored by her power over Basil, does not listen to Albini's warning that it is not worth the "pleasure of a little pow'r" to "fetter Basil with a foolish tie, / Against his will, perhaps against his duty" (27). Albini's prophetic Cassandra voice, of course, proves right. Victoria tyrannizes over Basil to the doom of both. Furthermore, her "artless power" is no different from her father's cunning artful power as he betrays Basil and the emperor. For the Duke and Victoria both distort and abuse the natural passions, the Duke the passion of loyalty and his daughter the passion of love. Baillie's point is indeed the same as Wollstonecraft's: as long as women are trained to gain power over men by abusing the natural passions, both women and men will remain locked in a deadly embrace, women the slaves of their little unreal empires and both male and female the slaves of men's real empires. In Act 4 of the play, Rosinberg, the friend who attempts to advise Basil in the same way that Albini advises Victoria, and to the same effect, argues with Isabella, Victoria's lady-in-waiting. When Isabella refers to what Rosinberg calls women's "artful snares" as an "empire," Rosinberg responds: "A short-liv'd tyranny, / That ends at last in hatred and contempt." "[B]ut some women do so wisely rule," Isabella suggests, and Rosinberg counters, "[B]ut they are rarely found" (41). Blinded by his love, Basil lingers at the Duke's castle longer than he should have, resulting in the mutiny of his soldiers, his disgrace in the eyes of the emperor, and eventually suicide. Victoria then realizes the extent of her little actions and uncurbed passions on the larger world of the state. Feeling remorse, she heroically sentences herself to a cloistered existence.

In perhaps her most remarkable play, *Ethwald,* Part 1, Baillie explores the opposite side of the mirror by showing what happens when men place political ambitions above domestic community. Although the play focuses on Ethwald's rise to power, it also charts the contrasted fall of two very different women, Bertha and Elburga. Bertha, Ethwald's childhood sweetheart and fiancée, attempts to curb her lover's obsession with war and conquest. Ignoring Bertha's warnings, his father's pleas, and a prophecy which has predicted that he should stay off the field of battle, Ethwald goes to war for his king and saves the day. Driven by his own success, Ethwald wins the favor of the king and attracts the attention of Elburga, who is betrothed to Edward, the king's son and heir to the crown. Rather than experiencing envy or hatred, as would be expected, Edward admires and even loves Ethwald, but to Ethwald and Elburga Edward's affection signals weakness and incompetence. After Ethwald gains the crown by murdering the king and emprisoning Edward, Elburga agrees to marry him, thinking that through him she will be able to exert her own power within the kingdom. But she discovers, instead, that her power is limited to her feminine influence over her husband; she waffles between one extreme of haughty defiance and blackmail and the other extreme of wifely attention and seduction, but to little avail. Finally, she realizes that in the ruthless realpolitik of the state, her (masculine) ambition is as vulnerable as Bertha's or Edward's (feminine) affection. And Ethwald himself comes to realize that ironically the prophecy of his youth is not defeat on the battlefield but success in the struggle for empire, for that success ruins him and cuts him off from his family, his friends, and eventually his subjects, who are beaten down by constant warfare. In various scenes Baillie is especially effective in showing the erroneous logic of Ethwald's desire for an ever-widening empire. She portrays the effects of battles on the domiciles of those who must fight them, as maidens seek their lovers on bloody fields, matrons seek to protect their helpless children, fields go untended, and confusion and lawlessness rule. In another scene, Baillie forces Ethwald to confront the consequences of his desire when he sees Bertha, the only woman he has loved, transformed into a homeless, lost, and wandering naif, driven to insanity, like Ophelia, by the ceaseless machinations of power.

4

Women poets are so sensitive to the potential conflict between domesticity and the wider world of public fame because the conflict is so palpable in their private lives and in their poetic careers. For Hemans, each major poem becomes a reworking of this troublesome conflict, each time resolving the conflict with a persistence that demonstrates how unsettling the conflict itself is to her psyche. Nevertheless, this conflict is minimized for Hemans because her domestic life is relatively free from the kinds of pressures many other women are certainly feeling from relatives and friends.

In a way, Hemans's early domestic conditions are most congenial to the making of the most successful female poet of England. While her sister stresses the Wordsworthian context of a country life, Chorley tends to stress the familial context, which Hemans herself also stresses. Hemans exists in an unusually feminine environment, nurtured by her mother, supported by her sister, and distant from potentially overbearing masculine influences. The influence and presence of Hemans's father seem to have been so minimal that both Owen and Chorley overlook him and his death in their biographies. Without a doubt, the focal figure of Hemans's life is her mother, moreso than either her siblings or her sons, and definitely moreso than her husband, whom she never sees after their early separation. "Mrs. Hemans always spoke, and it will be seen, *wrote* with enthusiastic affection of her parent:" Chorley says, "it was to her that her earliest attempts at composition were confided" (*Memorials* 1: 13).

It is clear that Hemans writes for her mother and sister, keeping at bay the more general audience that might discourage her spirit. But, more importantly, she writes for them because they *are* her audience. They embody for her the very qualities that she seeks to attain and that she hopes to instill in her readers. Her mother and sister become both the anticipation and the fulfillment of her poetic designs. They respond to her work because they already intuitively possess the powers of affection that she seeks to stir up in her readers. This mirror relation between her and her mother and sister, between her mother and sister and her audience, and between her audience and herself is nicely captured in one of Chorley's anecdotes: "Mrs. Hemans considered [*The Forest Sanctuary*] as almost, if not altogether, the best of her works. . . . When she read it, while in progress, to her mother and sister, they were surprised to tears at the increased power displayed in it" (1: 123–124). There are two significant ambiguities in this statement. Is the poem one of her favorites because of the response it elicits or does it elicit that response because it best embodies her poetic aims? Are her mother and sister "surprised to tears" because Hemans has displayed such feminine genius in creating this poem or does the poem's sentimental content overpower them and force their tears? I suspect that all of these things are true at once. Hemans gauges the success of her poem by the number of tears evoked from her feminine confidantes, and she writes the poem anticipating their judgment of her success according to the poem's immediate effect on their affection. Their affection for her—their devotion to her—should ideally be directly proportional to the affection inspired by the poem. If Hemans can get them to feel as strongly in reading the poem as they feel in their personal relation to her, then she is genuinely a great writer. There is, then, absolutely no distinction between the rhetoric of poetic effect and the realm of domestic affection, for the domestic is also the rhetoric of effect and the poetic the realm of affection.

The affecting poem itself becomes the terrain of effect intimately linked with affection, for it is a poem self-consciously about the effect of the domestic affections. *The Forest Sanctuary,* for instance, is an extremely sentimental poem about a man forced to travel to the new world with his son and wife in order to escape the merciless oppression of the Catholic Inquisition. The poem is a series of critical incidents told retrospectively by a man who has witnessed the burning of his best friend and his friend's two sisters at the hands of the Inquisition. Presenting in graphic detail the emotional turmoil of the family unit heroically meeting their fate, the poem celebrates the unity of that unit even under the greatest imaginable duress. Like the *Siege of Valencia* the poem eschews conventional male plot for feminine incidentalism. It is *The Forest Sanctuary* that provokes Jeffrey to warn her against "becoming too voluminous." No doubt it is the lack of "intricate" conventional plotting that motivates this criticism. But, like Wordsworth, though much more in Baillie's radical manner, Hemans wants to make the sentiment give significance to the incident, rather than vice versa. In order to accomplish this rhetorical end, Hemans purges her language of all metaphorical and allegorical intent, focusing the language totally on the profusion of mimetic effect: the emotional state portrayed in the poem is replicated in the reader. Unlike male romancers like Scott, who want to entertain and instruct their readers through the suspense of a polished tale, Hemans's sole concern is the effect that each incident—indeed, each word—will have on the emotional state of her reader. Unlike the male romantics, who in each poem attempt to create a symbolic system that will usurp the quotidian world, which will image a transcendent reality by creating a language that transforms all of reality into the symbolic real, Hemans's sole concern is the power of mimetic description to affect the reader's feeling. Whether language is intrinsically metaphorical or allegorical is irrelevant to her, whether philosophically it can mirror either the quotidian world or some transcendent reality has little bearing on her poetics, for the purpose of language in her poetics is purely rhetorical. And the adequacy of her language can be measured practically through the direct emotional response of her immediate audience.[7]

The Forest Sanctuary is exactly the kind of feminine poem that occasionally baffles her contemporary male critics and universally embarrasses later critics. Perhaps, before proceeding, we need to remind ourselves that the critical standards that relegate tearful literature to an intrinsically minor category are themselves based on masculinist assumptions about gender and literature. We now read a male writer like Dickens *despite* his sentimentalism for the same reason we no longer read a woman writer like Hemans at all. But to dismiss the sentimentalism in Dickens is not only a way of covering over the pervasive influence of women writers on nineteenth-century literature; it is more fundamentally a way of purging the feminine from literary discourse in general. It is a form of blindness that continues to drive the critical process, even despite the contemporary influence of feminist criticism. It is a way of fighting off the feminization of literature which is so integral and influential an aspect of the literary process since the mid-eighteenth century. By reclaiming Hemans's affectional poetics, then, we are representatively also reclaiming the power of the "feminine" within literature and within ourselves.[8]

There is no doubt that Hemans sees her goal as the feminization of culture at large. Bringing her readers to tears is not simply a way of sensitizing them individually; it is more importantly a way of transforming them collectively into a community of shared desire. And unlike Shelley's similar project, Hemans has no qualms about the femininity implied in her methods and ends, even though her project is intertwined with a Tory ideology of state nationalism, British imperialism, religious conservatism, and feminine conventionalism. *The Forest Sanctuary* must be viewed in this larger macrocosm, as well as in the mirroring microcosm of Hemans's reflective mother-sister audience. The task of such a poem is to reach as deeply as possible into the visceral depths of its reader's heart and to direct that depth of feeling toward an alien subject who becomes as familiar as the self. To accomplish this end, Hemans constructs a series of incidents that intensify the crisis of feeling and increasingly redirect the reader away from her own readerly solitude.

One such incident is the depiction of the procession to the scene of sacrifice. Hemans describes the demeanor of the two sisters, who are almost interchangeable, like Princess Leonora and Leonora de Sanvitale in her translation of Goethe's *Tasso*. As we witness the experience through the narrator's eyes, we are encouraged not only to feel, as the narrator feels, the sisters' experience, but also to understand intellectually and psychologically the power and significance of our feelings. In other words, the incident presents us with a mediating discourse on heart-knowledge as it invites us to feel the immediacy of heart-experience. Repeatedly, this double process of knowing through feeling and feeling by knowing is enacted in scenes that portray feminine suffering, either through women who suffer, or through men who are learning to suffer with women, or both. In the following passage, the narrator is gaining heart-knowledge through a retrospective experience of woman's suffering:

> And yet, alas! to see the strength which clings
> Round women in such hours!—a mournful sight,
> Though lovely!—an o'erflowing of the springs,
> The full springs of affection, deep as bright!
> And she, because her life is ever twined
> With other lives, and by no stormy wind
> May thence be shaken, and because the light
> Of tenderness is round her, and her eye
> Doth weep such passionate tears—therefore she thus can die.
>
> (*Works* 4: 15)

Theresa, the object of the male narrator's visionary gaze here, transforms the male's experience from an initially alien perspective. She cannot be held at a conventional reverential distance, even though she is reverenced by him in a conventional manner. Her passionate tears are also his, in that he is forced to re-create them for us and for himself and in that he is forced to relive them in his own experience of suffering. He is able to endure his exile only because of the heart-knowledge he gains from such women as Theresa, her sister Inez, and his own wife. Hemans complicates her task by deciding on a male narrator, but she also intensifies it by demonstrating the universality of affection's transformative power.

Hemans further complicates her task by bringing the reader vicariously into the scene. In the stanza directly following the one quoted above, the narrator invokes Theresa, an invocation that also serves to address the reader directly:

> Therefore didst *thou*, through that heart-shaking scene,
> As through a triumph move; and cast aside
> Thine own sweet thoughtfulness for victory's mien,
> O faithful sister! cheering thus the guide,
> And friend, and brother of thy sainted youth,
> Whose hand had led thee to the source of truth,
> Where thy glad soul from earth was purified;
> Nor wouldst thou, following him through all the past,
> That he should see thy step grow tremulous at last.
>
> (16)

As Theresa is moved again through that heart-shaking scene, the reader is also moved visually and emotionally. Theresa cheers the brother whose hand has led her to truth, but implicitly she is also leading her symbolic brother, the narrator, to that truth to which she has been led by her blood brother—a chain of affection that covertly begins to dissolve the gendered dichotomy in which it is imaged.

In another incident a knight snatches Inez, his fiancée, from the procession, and attempts to take her away, but she refuses to be separated from her siblings and from religious self-sacrifice. In fact, the siblings' devotion to one another is as much sanctified as their devotion to their God. Just as this martyred family's devotion represents the capacity of domestic affection to rise above social condemnation and death itself, so the experience of the narrator's family replicates that power through sanctified devotion in exile. The poem returns to Hemans's favorite theme concerning the relations among the heart, the hearth, and the state. Again and again, Hemans suggests that freedom can only be found in exile because the native home is the scene of state oppression. On the surface it may sound as though she has republican sympathies, but she does not. Her point tends to be that both men and women must nurture in the heart the freedom that cannot be found at home. This is a Spartan lesson. The narrator and his son, uprooted from all that they love, uprooted from the scene where the domestic affections first took root, must learn to re-incorporate those affections in an alien and hostile habitat. Significantly it is father and son, after the wife's/mother's death, who must begin again, and they can only succeed if they incorporate the feminine affection of which they are physically bereft in having left the native hearth and in having experienced the death of their female guide. This is another way to universalize the power of affection. Men cannot merely rely on women to nurture in them this emotional resolve; they must learn to nurture it themselves. And they must learn to nurture it away from the hearth, in the realm of the state, where its power is most needed. Countermanding Elmira's angry words, Hemans is here saying that man need not, because he is born for empire, be deprived of bearing heart-knowledge in the midst of imperial tyranny.

The reading experience itself becomes a community experience, an experience that gives priority to common (meaning both familiar and shared) affection over solitary vision. Instead of exploiting the power of affection to make her readers vulnerable to her own individuated vision, like Byron or Wordsworth, instead of making the reading public into an empire that must be conquered by the poet's strong self-possessing voice, Hemans tends to create a sense of other-identified selfhood, in which the writer's feeling reflects the reader's experience, and vice versa, in which each reader's heart-experience becomes the sharing of common heart-knowledge. In *The Forest Sanctuary,* the "solitude" which ends the poem is not really solitude, but shared affection. "I look forth, and learn the might / Of solitude, while thou art breathing soft, / And low, my loved one," the narrator says to his son and to us as readers (67). The narrator has been able to reach this point of resolution only because he has been feminized by the women we have encountered in the poem. He can endure exile and aloneness only because he has incorporated the social affections.

This community even in the midst of solitude is indicated in three ways in the text. First, the feminine everywhere haunts the hero's savage new land. The son in a moment of gladness suddenly asks for his mother, and the father responds: "That was but a gleam / Of memory, fleeting fast" (64–65). The mother's influence and that of the others who have died, however, remains with them. "All, save the image and the thought of those / Before us gone; our loved of early years, / Gone where affection's cup hath lost the taste of tears" (65). They hear the Oronoco stream, which sounds

> So like a spirit's voice! a harping tone,
> Lovely, yet ominous to mortal ear,
> Such as might reach us from a world unknown,
> Troubling man's heart with thrills of joy and fear!
> 'Twas sweet!—yet those deep southern shades oppress'd
> My soul with stillness, like the calms that rest
> On melancholy waves: I sigh'd to hear
> Once more earth's breezy sounds, her foliage fann'd,
> And turn'd to seek the wilds of the red hunter's land.
>
>   (65)

And as the river gives forth its sweet tone and earth fans her foliage, the father hears his son's soft breathing "on the breast of night" (67). Earth and its elements become feminine presences, a chorus of sounds mixing with their own. Second, the father and the son begin self-consciously to create their own community of feminine affection. And finally, the reader is invited to participate in this community through the insistent second-person address of the poem. Just as the narrator establishes a link with sympathetic presences—past and present, human and natural, familiar and alien, masculine and feminine—within the poem, he also establishes a link with the reader, allowing the reader to experience the linking power of affection even in the midst of readerly solitude. Thus the poem re-creates the scene of domestic affection that Hemans anticipates and actually experiences with her mother and sister.

Hemans enjoys a rare feminine space in her household setting that encourages her poeticizing activity because that activity is itself an extension of feminine space. Perhaps even more important than the absence of interfering men in this environment is Hemans's own freedom from common domestic concerns. Chorley repeatedly points out how crucial to Hemans's poetic development this freedom within domesticity is:

[T]he peculiar circumstances of Mrs. Hemans' position, . . . in a household, as a member and not as its head, excused her from many of those small cares of domestic life, which might have either fretted away her day-dreams, and, by interruption, have made of less avail the search for knowledge to which she bent herself with such eagerness; or, more probably still, might have imparted to her poetry more of masculine health and stamen [sic], at the expense of some of its romance and music. (1: 43)

In other words, her peculiar feminine space—being taken care of by an intensely supportive mother while not having herself to take care of authoritarian men—allows her more easily to write poetry and it allows her to write in a manner that will not be deemed monstrous.

We can understand how crucial this feminine space is to Hemans by considering Letitia Landon's less congenial lot. Landon's parents indulge her precocious poeticizing, just as Hemans's do; however, the similarities stop there. After the death of Landon's father, she becomes increasingly responsible for her mother and brothers, who are at best indulgent of her work because it brings money into the household. But they are very critical of her unmarried state. And after Landon moves into a London boardinghouse, her life and career become even more difficult. Her life is plagued with scandal, so much so that repeatedly she has to halt literary relations with men whom she views as mentors. The stress and strain of a woman's public life show in her poetry. Always in need of money, she writes hastily, changing to novels when poetry becomes unprofitable, and making literary decisions solely on the advice given her about the market.[9]

In her letters, Hemans constantly expresses gratitude that she is never subjected to such a fate. She may even have Landon in mind when she makes the following comment: "Of all things, never may I become that despicable thing, a woman living upon admiration! The village matron, *tidying up* for her husband and children at evening, is far, far more enviable and respectable" (*Works* 1: 175). Fortunately, Hemans is spared both fates, but she is extremely conscious of other women who are not. When news reaches her of Jewsbury's sudden death, her response is characteristic:

I would rather a thousand times that she should have perished thus, in the path of her chosen duties, than have seen her become the merely brilliant creature of London literary life, at once the queen and slave of some heartless coterie, living upon those poor *succès de société,* which I think utterly ruinous to all that is lofty, and holy, and delicate, in the nature of a highly endowed woman. (*Works* 1: 276)

Better that Jewsbury (now Mrs. Fletcher) should die before she becomes a "merely brilliant creature" like Landon or Lady Blessington. Jewsbury's "chosen duties," in fact, do cause her death, for they require her to follow her husband to India, where she contracts the disease that kills her. Landon's life ends similarly when she follows her husband—who is willing to marry her despite her scandal-plagued history—to Africa, where London scandal carries little weight. We have to remind ourselves that Hemans has chosen not to follow "the path of her chosen duties" when she lets her husband go to Italy alone.

Death, or even inhibiting household drudgery, is better than facing society alone, outside of the domestic setting, as a monstrous lady of notoriety. Though spared the scandal that is so treacherous for an unmarried literary woman like Landon, Hemans is not entirely protected from the adversities of "chosen duties" in the household. She writes to Baillie in 1827, just before her mother's death: "I have none but boys; a circumstance I often am inclined to regret; for I married so young that they are even now beginning to spring from childhood into youth themselves" (Chorley *Memorials* 1: 143). Boys are more prone to leave home in order to make their own homes, more prone to leave home sooner. Boys need a different kind of education from girls, a kind that Hemans's own poeticizing knowledge would be less equipped to provide; they require longer and more costly education, and they must be supplied with vocations—all of which Hemans acknowledges as burdensome. Hemans's greatest regret, however, is the absence of feminine community that results from having all male children. She prides herself on being able to educate her boys as she sees fit, yet this is not the same as educating girls. Like Wordsworth growing beyond his Mother Nature by moving through her, Hemans's sons must necessarily move beyond her. "I must expect that they will long for, and be launched into, another world than the green fields in which they are now contented to play around me" (Chorley 1: 143).

The biggest crisis of Hemans's life—the one that seems to have weakened her health and shortened her life—is her mother's death. Intensifying this "irreparable loss" (Chorley 1: 130) is the break-up of her household "on the marriage of one of her family [her sister], and the removal of another [her brother] into Ireland," a break-up that "threw her exclusively upon her own resources, and compelled her to make acquaintance with an 'eating, drinking, buying, bargaining' world, with which, from her disposition and habits, she was ill fitted to cope" (Chorley 1: 131). Many of Hemans's letters after 1828—and much of her poetry—is coated with world-weariness. Her sister's marriage is almost as devastating as her mother's death, and, in fact, it becomes synonymous with death, as she explains in a letter to Baillie: "I am to lose this, my only sister,—indeed I may almost say, my only companion,—very shortly: she is about to change her name and home, and remove very far from me. O how many deaths there are in the world for the affections"

(Chorley 1: 151). She recognizes that the very affections that are the source of her power are also necessarily the source of intense vulnerability. In a letter to Mary Russell Mitford, she identifies the break-up of her family as the reason for her psychic and physical illness: "[M]y spirits were . . . overshadowed by constant depression. My health also had been much affected by mental struggles" (Chorley 1: 238). Like one of her own characters—Ximena or De Chatillon, for instance—the domestic affection that empowers her also brings her an early death. The dispersal of her feminine space threatens not only her personal well-being, but also her capacity to write poetry, since her poetry is an extension of that space. Fortunately, however, Hemans is able to exploit her emotional turmoil in her poeticizing, rather than merely being victimized by it.

Hemans repeatedly says that she is only able to enjoy (to bear or tolerate) fame because of the protection of her feminine space. In another letter to Mitford, she associates positive fame, as opposed to the kind of monstrous fame Landon experiences, entirely in terms of a *reflective* relation in a domestic context:

I have been a drooping creature for months,—ill, and suffering much from the dispersion of a little band of brothers and sisters, among whom I had lived, and who are now all scattered; and, strange as it may seem to say, I am now, for the first time in my life, holding the reins of government, independent, managing a household myself; and I never like anything less than *'ce triste empire de soi-même.'* . . . Your mother, I believe, is always an invalid, but I hope she is able fully to enjoy the success of her daughter, as only a mother can enjoy it. How hollow sounds the voice of Fame to an orphan. Farewell, my dear Miss Mitford— long may you have the delight of gladdening a father and mother! (*Works* 1: 155– 157)

Fame is improper and destructive unless it is reflected glory, the fame that increases the bond between mother and daughter or sister and sister. We see this idea repeated with manic force in Hemans's letters, with both Owen and Chorley pointing it out as a crucial aspect of her personality. " 'Fame can only afford *reflected* delight to a woman,' was a sentiment she increasingly felt and expressed," according to her sister (*Works* 1: 49, Owen's emphasis). In another letter, she writes: "I have been all my life a creature of hearth and home, and now that the 'mother that looked on my childhood' is gone, and that my brothers and sisters are scattered far and wide, I have no wish, but to gather around the few *friends* who will love me and enter into my pursuits. I wish I could give you the least idea of what *kindness* is to me—how much more, how far dearer than *fame*" (Chorley 1: 212–213, emphases in original; see also *Works* 1: 154). Hemans attempts to replace her family with her friends—especially other literary women—in sustaining the support of feminine space. Her letters become Pauline missives of appraisal and praise to genial women like her sister, Mitford, Jewsbury, Baillie, and Howitt as she self-consciously creates a devoted community of kind and tender poets, whose spiritual lives must be nurtured for survival in an unfeeling, contentious world.

The potentially negative effect of fame on woman's domestic happiness becomes a crucial theme in early nineteenth-century feminine poetry. It is almost as if fame, along with death, is the sole threat to the power of feminine affection—an irony, since the creative genius that makes these women famous resides in that power. When Hemans comes across a statue of Sappho, "representing her at the moment she receives the tidings of Phaon's desertion," she immediately allegorizes it: "There is a sort of willowy drooping in the figure, which seems to express a weight of unutterable sadness, and one sinking arm holds the lyre so carelessly, that you almost fancy it will drop while you gaze. Altogether, it seems to speak piercingly and sorrowfully of the nothingness of Fame, at least to woman" (*Works* 1: 226; also see Chorley 2: 172). The idea of Sappho's "utter desolation of heart" (*Works* 1: 248) so impresses her that she returns to it later in her poem "The Last Song of Sappho." For Hemans, Sappho becomes the ultimate symbol of the conflict between woman's domestic happiness and worldly fame. Sappho sits on a rock facing the sea with her lyre at her feet. Like Byron's Harold, she addresses the ocean in the nadir of her solitude, but the solitude is a sort of damnation, brought on by fame itself, rather than the reclaiming of self that it is for the romantic poet. "My spirit finds response in thee, / To its own ceaseless cry—'Alone, alone!'" (*Works* 7: 10). Unlike Wordsworth in the *Prelude,* Sappho needs to be listened to *and* responded to. Her poetic desire is not the drive for self-ordination, the drive for a self-echoing voice that glorifies the solitude of self-possessing vision; rather such solitude is the perversion of the poetic process for her. The peace that it is impossible for her to find in the human community, she seeks in the sea:

> Away! my weary soul hath sought
>   In vain one echoing sigh,
>   One answer to consuming thought
> In human hearts—and will the *wave* reply?
>
> Sound on, thou dark unslumbering sea!
>   Sound in thy scorn and pride!
>   I ask not, alien world, from thee,
> What my own kindred earth hath still denied.
>
> And yet I loved that earth so well,
>   With all its lovely things!
>   —Was it for this the death-wind fell
> On my rich lyre, and quench'd its living strings?
>
> —Let them lie silent at my feet!
>   Since broken even as they,
>   The heart whose music made them sweet,
> Hath pour'd on desert-sands its wealth away.
>   (10–11)

The broken lyre is an external sign of the broken heart, each dependent on the other, and because it is senseless to pour her heart's sweet music on desert sands, rather than into other human hearts, she sits imploring the sea for an answer she knows it cannot give and contemplating suicide as the only answer. Even the sea-bird has love and home, she says, sounding like Shelley's *Alastor* poet: "They wait thee in the quiet nest, / And I, th'unsought, un-watch'd-for—I too come!" Like Byron, she is "with this winged nature fraught, / These visions wildly free," but unlike Byron, her problem is not that fame is too ephemeral and uncertain. It is that fame has placed barriers between herself and humankind. If solitude must accompany fame for a woman, then Sappho will reject them both. She does so by giving to the sea her "laurel-wreath," with "a lone heart, a weary frame." This poem, with its tortured elisions and irregular, syncopated rhythms, is one of Hemans's most successful, I think, for it transforms Sappho's lament into the heart-experience that fosters heart-knowledge, increasing the human bond between us and this lone female poet even as it gives voice to the deathly weariness of solitude.

In the lyric "Woman and Fame" Hemans addresses Fame itself, con-fronting directly the ambivalence that it breeds. And again, she pits fame against community, success in the world against failure in private affection:

> A hollow sound is in thy song,
>   A mockery in thine eye,
> To the sick heart that doth but long
>   For aid, for sympathy—
> For kindly looks to cheer it on,
> For tender accents that are gone.
>   (*Works* 6: 182)

Not surprisingly, Landon is even more obsessed with the treacherous path that fame constructs for women. In poems like *The Improvisatrice* (heavily influenced by Madame de Staël's *Corinne*), *A History of the Lyre*, "The Sum-mer Evening's Tale," "Lines of Life," "Stanzas to the Author of 'Mont Blanc,' 'Ada,' etc.," "Sappho," and her elegy for Felicia Hemans, she returns again and again to this theme with a despair that Hemans herself never matches. In "Felicia Hemans," she asks the dead poetess:

> Was not this purchased all too dearly?—never
>   Can fame atone for all that fame hath cost.
> We see the goal, but know not the endeavour,
>   Nor what fond hopes have on the way been lost.
> What do we know of the unquiet pillow,
>   By the worn cheek and tearful eyelid prest,
> When thoughts chase thoughts, like the tumultuous billow,
>   Whose very light and foam reveals unrest?
>   (*Poetical Works* 334)

Using imagery, syntax, and rhythms that are reminiscent both of Mary Tighe and Hemans herself, Landon addresses this poem to one who can truly under-stand, another poetess. The first line break makes it appear that Landon will reject the idea that fame has been purchased too dearly, but that rejection it-self is firmly rejected for a series of doubts and further questions. Pressed to bear her soul and pour out her heart to Hemans much as Hemans's Sappho pours out her heart to the unlistening sea, it is not surprising that Landon writes one of her most affecting and effective poems ironically in a poem that questions the worth of her own poeticizing. If Hemans could hear her from the grave, she would no doubt sympathize, but she would also applaud without a tinge of anxiety or rivalry Landon's achievement, an achievement all the more crucial because it rejoices in the power of feminine affection even as it records the vulnerability of "woman's lot on earth."

5

In her career Hemans too experiences the unkindness that the world is more than willing to expend on the woman who dares to venture too far from home, and conversely she experiences the healing available to her from her heartful coterie of supportive sister and brother writers. The first and only London production of her romance tragedy *The Vespers of Palermo* is hooted and ridiculed, so much so that the actors are barely able to complete the play. How much of this is due to Hemans's gender is debatable, though Kemble, who is the driving force behind the staging of the play, attributes "the failure, without the slightest hesitation, to what he delicately calls 'a singularity of intonation in one of the actresses'" (*Works* 1: 71). Significantly, however, Hemans herself stresses the role of her gender in the response to the play. In a letter to H. H. Milman, one of the many friends who writes to console her, she writes:

As a female, I cannot help feeling rather depressed by the extreme severity with which I have been treated in the morning papers. I know not why this should be; for I am sure I should not have attached the slightest value to their praise; but I suppose it is only a proper chastisement for my temerity; for a female who shrinks from such things, has certainly no business to write tragedies. (*Works* 1: 72–73)

The "extreme severity" of the critics is an affront both because it seems ungentlemanly to handle a lady in such a manner and because it reminds her of how difficult it is to be taken seriously as a writer when one is female. Of course, she does attach more than the slightest value to their praise, and so her depression does not phase us. She is as much chastising herself for being so vulnerable to their criticism as they are chastising her for her "temerity." Hemans's depression, however, is not simply personal; it is *reflected* disappointment, because just as she sees her fame reflected in the whole of her sex, she perceives her failure as a failure for all aspiring women writers. She feels— and not incorrectly—that she carries on her shoulders the burden of the woman poet's future. In letters to her female friends her dismay is more apparent:

If ever I should try the fortune of the theatre again, I must endeavour to ensure the strictest secrecy as to my name till my fate shall be decided: there is a prejudice, I am satisfied, against a female dramatist, which it would be hardly possible to surmount. (Chorley 1: 102)

Hemans does not display the least bit of uncertainty about the quality of her drama; rather she is "satisfied" that the problem lies entirely with prejudice against her sex. And she is no doubt justified in her assessment, for when the play is performed only two months later in Edinburgh, it meets with tremendous applause. Even so, Hemans is prepared for "something violent to sober us. I dare say I must expect some sharp criticism from Edinburgh ere all this is over" (*Works* 1: 76). Hemans has probably profited here from Baillie's experience with the theatre. Though Baillie is much more successful than Hemans, with plays being staged in Britain and America, the stage success of Baillie's plays does not match the praise given her dramas in the periodicals, nor does it match the efforts of influential literary figures like Scott, Byron, John Kemble, and Edmund Kean, all of whom try to keep Baillie's plays before the public. Baillie, too, could expect "sharp criticism from Edinburgh," for Jeffrey was one of the few dissenting voices, along with Hazlitt's, against her plays. But unlike Thomas Moore, who is in the habit of challenging his critics to duels, Jeffrey and Byron being two of the men he challenges, Baillie and Hemans can only suffer in self-restraint. At first Baillie refuses to meet Jeffrey, suggesting that it might intrude on his critical distance and thus soften his criticism, but in time her only literary foe becomes one of her best friends.

Hemans, too, has a way of transforming adverse criticism into a moment for sympathetic curiosity. Owen suggests about Hemans that "[f]ew would, perhaps, have borne" the "unexpected" initial failure "with feelings so completely untinged with bitterness, or with greater readiness to turn for consolation to the kindness and sympathy which poured in upon her from every side" (*Works* 1: 71–72). Not only does the heartful coterie protect her from the trials of fame by deflecting some of the reflected light away from her and by assuring she will not end in dreaded solitude; that coterie also ensures that the onus of failure is lightened by shared affection. Unlike the "heartless coteries" of Augustan poets or the self-possessing individualism of the romantics, her literary network thrives on the affection that enables genuinely reflected fame.

Guided by the dictates of feminine affection and reflected fame, and extremely sensitive to the need for more female writers, these first poetesses are something more than literary correspondents and something less than rivals, as we have defined that term in relation to the male romantics. Appropriately, it is the great female dramatist of the north who, in corresponding with Hemans, first gives her the news of an impending Edinburgh production of the *Vespers*. Rather than Baillie viewing her English "rival" as a rival, she seems delighted to have another woman's voice in the sparsely populated female choir. Milman writes to Hemans about a play by Mitford on a similar theme and expresses concern that Mitford's play will overshadow Hemans's. Refusing to accept Milman's masculinist interpretation of the situation, she does not see Mitford's drama as a threat:

I had been somewhat surprised, but not in the least uneasy on seeing Miss Mitford's play announced, as I felt satisfied that had anything occurred to prevent the ultimate representation of mine, I might depend on you giving me information. With regard to the point of precedence, it is one to which I am wholly indifferent; my only anxiety is to be relieved from the long suspense which circumstances have unavoidably occasioned. (Chorley 1: 73–74)

Like Milman, critics were quick to imply rivalry among female writers, insinuating that there was room for only one woman to represent each realm—Tighe for Ireland, Baillie for Scotland, Hemans for England—as if one poetess is more than enough for any nation. (A sort of limited triumvirate is also implied in Hazlitt's "trio of female poets.") But the women themselves see their enterprise in a rather different light. They recognize that if they fail, it will not be because another woman has succeeded in their place, but rather because no woman at all has been allowed to succeed. Understandably, Hemans's "only anxiety" relates to what she knows could be a prejudicial response to her play; she does not have the luxury of concerning herself with the anxiety of influence and the poetics of rivalry.

In this sense, the female poet's historical situation is drastically different from the male romantic's, and her will to poeticize must be considered in this different light. The women's desire to poeticize is genuinely a shared enterprise, and influence among them assures that they can more readily go forward together, rather than each being singled out and roughly handled by "Fame." Hemans delights in the network of influence that binds her to Jameson, to Tighe, and to Baillie, just as Landon gladly accepts Hemans's influence as a sign of her own poetic development. If they are to succeed in recording women's experience, they must be willing to listen to one another's voices and to hear the similarities and differences with pleasure. In fact, under such circumstances the similarities among them become even more delightful than the differences, since such similarities indicate that they are recording accurately the experience of their sex.

We can hear the delight of influence in Hemans's voice whenever she speaks of her "archrival" Baillie. For instance, in this letter to one of her many sister writers, as Hemans praises Baillie, she is as much appraising herself:

[N]othing in all her writings delights me so much as her general idea of what is beautiful in the female character. There is so much gentle fortitude, and deep-devoting affection in the women whom she portrays, and they are so perfectly different from the pretty '*un-idea'd* girls,' who seem to form the *beau ideal* of our whole sex in the works of some modern poets. The latter remind me of a foolish saying, I think of Diderot's, that in order to describe a woman, you should write with a pen made of a peacock's feather, and dry the writing with the dust from butterflies' wings. (Chorley 1: 96–97)

Hemans's description of Baillie's recording of woman could be a description of her own later *Records of Woman*. (The letter was written in 1823 and *Records* was published in 1828.) The influence that she must avoid is one that would lead her to record woman inaccurately or unjustly—the influence of "some modern writers," the influence of the foolish fathers, the Diderots, who have misrecorded woman for so long.

It is more than fitting, then, that when Hemans comes to publish *Records,* she writes to Baillie requesting "another favor." "[I]t is the permission to dedicate to you, of whose name my whole sex may be proud, a work which I shall probably publish in the course of this present year. . . . I hope you will allow me to offer you . . . this little token of unfeigned respect" (Chorley 1: 146). Desiring to return the favor, to reflect her influence back to the one whose influence is reflected in her and whose influence has enabled reflected fame to both poets and to their whole sex, Hemans gladly and openly records the influence that has enabled her to write these records of women. Owen aptly calls this attitude "sisterly disinterestedness":

It is pleasing to dwell upon the generous appreciation with which she was regarded by the gifted of her own sex, and the frank, confiding spirit which always marked her intercourse with them. She would rejoice in their success with true sisterly disinterestedness; and the versatility of her tastes, to which every thing really good in its kind was sure to be acceptable (always excepting science and statistics, from which she stood aloof in silent awe), gave her a capacity for enjoying with equal zest, the noble simplicity of Mrs. Joanna Baillie, the graphic reality of Miss Mitford, the true-hearted originality of Mary Howitt, or the exquisite tenderness of Miss Bowles. (*Works* 1: 120–121: see Chorley 1: 235–237)

Hemans's attitude toward influence and rivalry, however, goes beyond sisterly disinterestedness, beyond a commitment to the way women writers should relate to one another, to a critique of how men writers relate among themselves. Owen notes that Hemans's love of German literature is intimately connected to "the cordial feeling of brotherhood, so conspicuous amongst its most eminent authors, and their freedom from all the petty rivalries and manoeuvers, on which she herself looked down with as much wonder, as of contempt" (*Works* 1: 58). And in one letter Hemans herself writes of "my great distaste for reviews in general," connecting this distaste with "their perpetual bitterness, and jealousy, and strife, from which I turn with so much dislike. . . . How different seems the spirit of the literary men in Germany!" (Chorley 1: 274–275). Accordingly, how different is her own spirit. She captures it perfectly in *The Works of Art to Italy* when she instructs the "Young Genius" to practice "emulative zeal." In her own poetry, precursors and contemporaries—both male and female—are viewed as models or exemplars, rather than as threats to be exploited or overcome. Because her task is to prove that women can be poets, not that she can outdo other poets, she is grateful for anyone—especially any female—who can help show her the way.

6

We have seen how different are the motives, aims, and practices of female poets from their male counterparts in early nineteenth-century Britain, but we should not overlook the common historical circumstances that ground these significant differences. It would be erroneous to call Hemans or one of her sister poets a romantic poet, in the way that term has been employed in over one hundred years of literary history. This does not mean, however, that these poets' ideology of feminine affection must be totally divorced from romantic ideology. We find, in fact, that there is mutual influence between the male romantics and the female affectional poets, an influence that the women usually gratefully acknowledge, but that the men, as we have seen, tend to repress for various complex reasons. I would go so far as to say that the trend of romanticism itself—from the early sentimental poets of the late eighteenth century to the high romantics—is one of the most important factors enabling women to view themselves as poets, just as the inscription of feminizing sentiment itself is an integral, though suppressed, part of masculine romantic ideology. By simultaneously popularizing and legitimating the idea that poetry is the realm of private experience, is the realm of personal affection, the romantics, early and late, unintentionally authorize women to view themselves as legitimate poeticizers of their own experience. After all, if women's sphere is the realm of private experience, the realm of domestic affection, who better can express and inspire a discourse about that realm than women themselves. If it is not classical education or some other abstruse form of training that makes poets, if it is the poet's own experience of himself that makes the poet, then she can make herself a poet as readily as he can.

This is why when Owen seeks a beginning for her sister's biography, she immediately turns to Wordsworth, much as Jewsbury does in her essay on Hemans. "The recollection of what she was at that time," Owen writes, "irresistibly suggests a quotation from Wordsworth's graceful poetic picture," and Owen proceeds by quoting from "She was a phantom of delight" (*Works* 1: 12). Wordsworth's picture of a "perfect Woman," however, is problematic when applied to Hemans, for nowhere in the poem is it suggested that this "lovely Apparition" can or should or will record her own vision of herself and her sex. All of the virtues mentioned in the final stanza of the lyric most certainly apply to Hemans, but even so they omit her supreme virtue, her capacity to inscribe the power of affections in "tender" romances and lyrics. Owen perhaps comes closer to moving Hemans outside of Wordsworth's myth of the feminine when she describes the young poetess as leading a life parallel to Wordsworth's. "In the calm seclusion of this romantic region [Denbighshire, Wales]," Owen writes, "with ample range through the treasures of an extensive library, the young poetess passed a happy childhood, to which she would often fondly revert amidst the vicissitudes of her after life. Here she imbibed that intense love of Nature which ever afterwards 'haunted her like a passion' " (*Works* 1: 4–5). Here, Hemans looks like a carbon copy of Wordsworth, wandering both through the past literary treasures of books and the present treasures of nature. At least she has been identified as a literary subject rather than merely as an object of someone else's literary vision. Nonetheless, when Owen suggests that Hemans in "[s]ome of the happiest days the young poetess ever passed . . . would worship Nature at so fitting a shrine" as the countryside of Conway (*Works* 1: 16), we must be careful not to confuse Hemans's happy days and her "worship" of Nature for Wordsworth's. Both Owen and Chorley stress the Wordsworthian influence. Chorley goes so far as to suggest that Wordsworth has a "beneficial and calming effect" on her as "his great and noble powers grew upon her with every year of her life. . . . Mrs. Hemans' copy of Mr. Wordsworth's works might be called her poetical breviary: there was scarcely a page that had not its mark of admiration or its marginal comment or illustration" (Chorley 2: 107–108). Fortunately, the greater portions of these biographies are more discriminating when it comes to clarifying Hemans's relations to other poets, including Wordsworth. They provide a wealth of information that contradicts this view of Hemans as a female Wordsworth.

Perhaps it is best, however, to turn to Hemans's own assessment of the romantic influence, since she writes willingly and amply about it in correspondence and poetry. What we quickly begin to see is that Hemans emulates from the romantics that which is most congenial to her own poetics and the rest she either ignores or criticizes. As she moves from a fascination with romance narrative to a greater interest in lyric during her later volumes, she changes her loyalties from Byron to Wordsworth, but this change is not merely structural. First of all, we must remind ourselves that even when she writes narrative romance it is not the kind of romance written either by Scott or Byron, though it borrows from both. As opposed to Scott's devotion to extremely conventional, intricate plots, Hemans concentrates on character, meaning both characterization and moral disposition, and, as we have already seen, she creates an incidentalism that stresses the impact of emotional crises on the reader. Whereas Byron seems to be ever seeking new narrative forms to express his obsession with the exotic, the inexpressible, and the forbidden, whereas he seems to need to burst all narrative conventions in an attempt to express his distrust of strictures and systems, Hemans's rejection of conventional romance plots has much more to do with her desire to extend feminine space into the literary terrain. Because she sees her realm as the domestic, she is much more concerned with the inexpressible that resides just within our reach. Nevertheless, in both Byron and Wordsworth she recognizes kindred spirits who value the overflowing of passion and who understand its powers, if not its essentially, humanly binding limits. Hemans's change in emphasis is actually not much of a change because even when she writes romances she stresses what we think of as the lyrical aspect.

Her change from Byron to Wordsworth is also not a true alteration because she simply comes to believe that Wordsworth represents more closely than Byron what she desires a male poet to be. According to the "chief companion" of her last years, Hemans is torn between Shelley and Wordsworth:

[D]uring the four last years of her life, she never, except when prevented by illness, passed a single day without reading something of [Wordsworth's]. I have heard her say, that Wordsworth and Shelley were once the spirits contending to obtain the mastery over her's: that the former soon gained the ascendency, is not, I think, to be wondered at; for much as she delighted in Shelley, she pitied him still more. In defining the distinction between the genius of Wordsworth and that of Byron, I remember her saying, that it required a higher power to still a tempest than to raise one, and that she considered it the part of the former to calm, and of the latter to disturb the mind. (Chorley 2: 263)

Whether it is Byron or Shelley who is combating Wordsworth for her spirit makes little difference, for her metaphor explains exactly why she would even-

tually have to temper her passion for either of the former. For the same reason that she criticizes Goethe's *Tasso,* she criticizes the younger romantics.
They are unchastened Elmiras; they have not learned the balancing between
heart-knowledge and heart-experience that women have been forced to achieve
in their lives. The turning point for Hemans's loyalty comes when she reads
Tom Moore's memoirs of Byron that are extracted for the periodicals in
1829. "[H]er disappointment at the extracts which appeared in the periodicals" was "so great as to prevent her reading the work when published."
After 1829 she relinquishes the relic—a small lock of Byron's hair—that
she has worn before then (Chorley 2: 21–22). In the summer of 1830 she
meets Wordsworth for the first time and is able to substitute him for Byron as
the male poet of her affections. Chorley fortunately prints ample correspondence from her when she was in residence near Dove Cottage, and all of it
demonstrates how high is her regard for Wordsworth.

What Wordsworth does is to restore her faith in the compatibility between the domestic affections and poetic genius, not so much by what he
writes as by how he presents himself in his home environment. She writes
from "Dove Nest" in June of 1830:

[W]hen the subject calls forth any thing like enthusiasm, the poet [Wordsworth]
breaks out frequently and delightfully, and his gentle and affectionate playfulness
in the intercourse with all the members of his family, would of itself sufficiently
refute Moore's theory in the Life of Byron, with regard to the unfitness of genius
for domestic happiness. (Chorley 2: 115; see also *Works* 1: 211)

Rather than revising her commitment to affectional poetics when Byron and
Shelley fail to live up to that notion of poetry, she reads Wordsworth as the
perfect instance of her poetics. Her dislike (one might even say fear) of
Moore's "shallow theory" so distresses her that she discusses it with Wordsworth and reports back to her sister how delighted she is with his response.
" 'It is not because they possess genius that they make unhappy homes, but
because they do not possess genius enough; a higher order of mind would enable them to see and feel all the beauty of domestic ties,' " Wordsworth tells
her with his characteristic smugness (*Works* 1: 209–210). Of course, Wordsworth must defend domestic happiness as a sign of greater poetic genius,
since not to do so would cast doubt on his own claim to both.

What probably never crosses Wordsworth's mind is why the issue is so
important to Hemans. It is not so much that she needs a male poet who can
be both great and domestically stable. It is rather that Moore's theory calls
into question the possibility of feminine poetic genius even existing. If the female poet is an extension of feminine domestic space and is the prophet of
affection, as Hemans definitely believes, and if poetic genius is intrinsically
antithetical to such domesticity, as Moore believes, then no woman can be a
poetic genius—no woman can be a poet. I would suggest that this is the true
anxiety behind Hemans's concern for Shelley's, Byron's, Wordsworth's domestic bliss, or lack thereof. Moore's theory about poetic genius, which ex-

plicitly assumes that poeticizing is a male activity, is actually also a theory that makes women poets into non sequiturs.

What Hemans desires to see in Wordsworth is what Wordsworth desires her to see, and so they become fast friends (not unusual for Hemans but uncharacteristic for Wordsworth). She calls him "a sort of paternal friend" and talks about his "almost patriarchal simplicity" (*Works* 1: 207–209). She is soon dedicating poems to him and entitling one of her volumes *Songs of the Affections*. Beyond their convergences in politics, religion, and the value of "domestic ties," however, there is a rift between them that does not appear in her correspondence, but glares out from the poetry. Not surprisingly, considering what we have seen is her attitude toward fame, solitude, rivalry, influence, and recording woman's experience, her poetry answers Wordsworth's with such firmness and cogency that it is difficult not to think that she is responding specifically to Wordsworth's errors. The most important poem in this context is "The World in the Open Air" (*Works* 4: 150–152). The poem is almost a parody of the romantic nature/solitude poem. It invites the reader to "Leave ye man's home, and forget his care," and "Come to the woods, in whose mossy dells / A light all made for the poet dwells." After four stanzas of conventional invitation and praise of the natural life away from "man's dwellings with all their woe," the poem responds, "Yes! we will come," and for four parallel stanzas, "we" enjoy the promises that the naturalist poet has claimed for a pastoral life. *But* the poem pivots in a stanza beginning "But if." If, in the midst of nature, we come across "A line like the pathway of former feet," or "the grey ruins of tower or cot," or the cross of a hermit's cell, or some "token sad of a mortal grave"—if we meet any of these things:

> Doubt not but *there* will our steps be stay'd,
> There our quick spirits awhile delay'd;
> There will thought fix our impatient eyes,
> And win back our hearts to their sympathies.
>
> (Hemans's emphasis)

What Hemans has done is first to load every natural sign with a human signal, so that it is no longer possible to see nature without also seeing human "sympathies." Any line in nature becomes the pathway of former feet; every nook becomes a potential grave. It is these human signals that will halt us, not the sublimity or beauty of nature itself.

> For what, though the mountains and skies be fair,
> Steep'd in soft hues of the Summer-air,—
> 'Tis the soul of man, by its hopes and dreams,
> That lights up all nature with living gleams.
>
> Where it hath suffer'd and nobly striven,
> Where it hath pour'd forth its vows to heaven;
> Where to repose it hath brightly pass'd,
> O'er this green earth there is glory cast.

Revising Wordsworth's "glory" so that it is "cast" in a human, rather than a natural, hue, the poem shifts the focus of noble strife from Wordsworth's tug-of-war between maturing poet and maternal nature, to the struggles within human communities. It is humanity that gives meaning to nature's signs, and therefore only humanity is worthy of such attention. We may trek into the woods to attempt to forget human woes, but those woes must follow us there, for we cannot leave our humanity behind. Nothing in nature is alien to us because we view all of nature through all-too-human eyes. This is not to be bemoaned, however. For Hemans sees it as the glorious gift of human affection, a capacity that we cannot escape even when we think we have left domesticity far behind. *"We,* only *we,* may be linked to God!" the final line asserts (Hemans's emphasis). And implicit in the poem is another assertion: *we,* only *we,* may be linked to each other.

In "The Traveller at the Source of the Nile" (4: 154–156), which follows "The World in the Open Air," Hemans returns to this theme. The poem records the emotional turmoil of a conquesting discoverer who, in finding the source of the Nile, discovers within himself a power he cannot vanquish:

> The rapture of a conqueror's mood
>   Rush'd burning through his frame,—
> The depths of that green solitude
>   Its torrents could not tame;
> Though stillness lay, with eve's last smile—
> Round those far fountains of the Nile.

As the "wild, sweet voices" of his home call him back to "[h]is childhood's haunt of play," the victory of conquest becomes the heart-knowledge of defeat.

> Where was the glow of power and pride?
>   The spirit born to roam?
> His alter'd heart within him died
>   With yearnings for his home!
> All vainly struggling to repress
> That gush of painful tenderness.

As the conqueror weeps, his attempt to repress the tenderness that is a part of his nature is foiled. In this poem Hemans reminds us that it is not women alone who must face the treachery of fame. Despite what men tell themselves, they too are under the spell of the domestic affections. The attempt to quell "tenderness" will not lead to more power, but to self-deluding solitude, moral error, and a weakness more devastating than affectionate vulnerability. In learning this lesson of the heart, the would-be conqueror has been feminized, but his feminization comes perhaps too late, just as we have seen in Mary Shelley's *Frankenstein.* "With all that lay between" him and his home, him and his natural humanity, he may die with the knowledge in his heart, but like Sappho, with no one to share it with. In poems like "The Boon of Memory," "Dartmoor," "The Chamois Hunter's Love," "The Return," "The Two Homes," and many more, Hemans answers the romantics and creates her own distinct vision of the relation between nature and humanity. As opposed to Wordsworth's visionary conquest over nature and over his reader, Hemans points out how men seek to conquer nature only to end up victimizing themselves and others. She points out how the relation to nature is actually a deceptive relation between the human and humanity. And in place of the romantic's self-possessing control of the reader's vision, she offers consciously and repeatedly the shared experience of an italicized "we." She offers the potential of shared desire for a humanity that can never escape the power and vulnerability of their shared affection, even in midst of a savage solitude.

7

By making himself the pathetic object, Wordsworth collapses the distance between the pitying observer and the suffering he contemplates. The source of emotion and the emotion itself are both located in the self. Wordsworth's, like all sentimentalism, is liable to turn into self-pity; the basically inward concerns, the focus upon one's own response, make the sentimentalist particularly vulnerable to a kind of solipsistic pathos.

James Averill locates here (*Wordsworth and the Poetry of Human Suffering* 51) exactly the ethos of Wordsworth's concern with sentiment and affection. I would revise his generalization, however, to stress that what Wordsworth represents is a particular masculine response to sentiment that is bred by and within male poets during late eighteenth-century and early nineteenth-century Britain. Coleridge claims that Wordsworth is "unrivalled among the writers of the present day in manly sentiment."[10] His "manly sentiment," however, is best described in terms of what Averill calls "solipsistic pathos." For even when the poet takes others as the objects of his pity, such as Simon Lee or Margaret, they become vehicles for establishing a powerful discourse upon his own powerful response to human suffering. This is why the objects of suffering are so often either lower-class, downtrodden men, children, or women: he wants to accentuate the difference between their pitiable condition of inarticulate inactivity and his own situation as a discursive subject who must consider their pain and contemplate ways of dissolving that pain into the aesthetics of self-possessing poetry. Even though Margaret is the object-lesson of suffering humanity, the subject-lesson of active suffering is the poet himself, whose projections are split into wise old man and eager young poet. The objectified sufferer, the woman who experiences the real pain, becomes excluded from the subjectivity of the poem's painful self-understanding. It is not *all* sentimentalism that leads to this impasse of "solipsistic pathos," however; it is more accurately the masculine sentimentalism of poets like Wordsworth where this impasse becomes itself a celebration of self-individuation.

The crucial factors that determine the romantic interest in the domestic affections are self-empowerment and self-possession. Possession enables power and power signals possession. Wordsworth's troping of the domestic scene, therefore, has a different emphasis from Hemans's troping of it. In his early poem *An Evening Walk,* we get an exemplary image of Wordsworthian domesticity:

> Sweetly ferocious, round his native walks,
> Pride of his sister-wives, the monarch stalks;
> Spur-clad his nervous feet, and firm his tread;
> A crest of purple tops the warrior's head.
> Bright sparks his black and rolling eyeball hurls
> Afar, his tail he closes and unfurls;
> On tiptoe reared, he strains his clarion throat,
> Threatened by faintly-answering farms remote:
> Again with his shrill voice the mountain rings
> While, flapped with conscious pride, resound his wings!
>   (*Poetical Works,* lines 146–155)

This portrait of the rooster captures every element of Wordsworthian domesticity with uncanny inclusiveness. As Jean Hagstrum points out, this portrait can be seen as a "foreshadowing" of the poet's own relation to Dorothy, Mary, and Sara, his "sister-wives" (see *The Romantic Body* 77–78). The tenderness of the domestic scene that Hemans emphasizes is here rejected for a sweet ferociousness, with the feminine quality of sweetness merely modifying the more essential masculine quality of ferociousness. This domestic scene is not a community of shared desire, but a hierarchy of emotion with all attention focused on the "monarch." The "sister-wives" may be seen as equal not only in their sharing of a common space, but also in their equal adoration of the male monarch. Wordsworth has here transformed the feminine space of domesticity and potentially shared desire into an image of the masculine sociopolitical sphere. Once the male invades that space, he coopts its features for his own dominion. The sphere of masculine quest and conquest is troped self-consciously in the portrait, as the rooster becomes a warrior-king, firmly treading the limits of his claimed territory and stalking the grounds with feet that are both nervous (of losing his territory) and spur-clad (willing to fight off any rivals). The final lines stressing the rooster's voice sound like Wordsworth's descriptions of his own poetic voice within nature's expanse. Just as the poet must prophesy amidst the claims of rival poets, the rooster must "strain" his "clarion throat" (the clarion being an instrument of prophets) amidst the threat of rival roosters from "faintly-answering farms remote." The faintness and remoteness of those other roosters assure him that his territory is safe. It is not so much the other roosters, however, which confirm his status as monarch-king, but nature's echo. As the rooster flaps his wings with "conscious pride" within his "native" (naturally possessed) realm, he accepts nature's voice as an echo of his own. His place is naturally determined, ordained, and cannot be usurped, even by nature, which ordains him in the first place.

Hagstrum points to another passage in Wordsworth's corpus that is crucial for understanding the poet's view of the domestic affections (see *The Romantic Body* 100). In the first version of *Home at Grasmere,* he summarizes the objective of his domestic life, which is but a mirror reflection of his poetic ambition. Wordsworth marks his progression from masculine wandering to domesticity:

> I seemed to feel such liberty was mine,
> Such power and joy; but only for this end:
> To flit from field to rock, from rock to field,
> From shore to island, and from isle to shore,
> From open place to covert, from a bed
> Of meadow-flowers into a tuft of wood,
> From high to low, from low to high, yet still
> Within the bounds of this huge Concave; here
> Should be my home, this Valley be my World.
>
> (35–43)

What we have here is a set of paradoxes. He is at liberty even though he is constrained by domestic walls and duties. He still manages the spirit of masculine wandering, even though he is limited to one valley home. And even though he is hemmed in by the boundaries of a single plot of earth, he possesses in that plot the whole world. Somehow, the poet's little domestic setting, transcending its feminine limitations, becomes conquest of the whole world:

> And did it cost so much, and did it ask
> Such length of discipline, and could it seem
> An act of courage, and the thing itself
> A conquest?
>
> (64–67)

Settling down is transformed into a form of questing conquest, requiring an act of courage. What Wordsworth emphatically wants to deny is that it has cost him anything, and even more emphatically, that it has cost him his masculinity. And so the potentially emasculating realm of feminine space becomes miraculously for him a safe haven of masculine self-possession:

> But I am safe; yes, one at least is safe;
> What once was deemed so difficult is now
> Smooth, easy, without obstacle; what once
> Did to my blindness seem a sacrifice,
> The same is now a choice of the whole heart.
> If e'er the acceptance of such dower was deemed
> A condescension or a weak indulgence
> To a sick fancy, it is now an act
> Of reason that exultingly aspires.
> This solitude is mine; the distant thought
> Is fetched out of the heaven in which it was.
> The unappropriated bliss hath found
> An owner, and that owner I am he.
> The Lord of this enjoyment is on Earth
> And in my breast. What wonder if I speak
> With fervour, am exalted with the thought
> Of my possessions, of my genuine wealth

> Inward and outward? What I keep have gained,
> Shall gain, must gain, if sound be my belief
> From past and present rightly understood
> That in my day of childhood I was less
> The mind of Nature, less, take all in all,
> Whatever may be lost, than I am now.
> For proof behold this Valley and behold
> Yon Cottage, where with me my Emma dwells.
>   (74–98)

As his possessions, including Emma, become the proof of his compensation, of his conquest, he becomes a solitary Lord, who must forever gain and never lose, who can rule his world with a "choice of the whole heart." Perhaps the greatest miracle is that he can gain the world without sacrificing his soul, that he can possess all he desires without sacrificing his own self-possession.

Coleridge, too, is enamored with this idea that the security of feminine space, of a supportive home environment, holds the secret to unrivaled worldly conquest. Even before he begins to envy and resent Wordsworth's domestic peace, reading that peace as a signal of his rival's winning of the poetic war, he figures secure domesticity as the precondition of masculine conquest. In "Reflections on Having Left a Place of Retirement," there seems at first to be a conflict between domestic happiness and manly conquest, but like Wordsworth, Coleridge is able to resolve the conflict so that domesticity itself becomes conquest. This is why at the core of the poem is a mountain prophecy. As he climbs "with perilous toil and reach'd the top" of the mountain (*Poetical Works* 28), he also transcends the domestic below by incorporating it into his vision:

> It seem'd like Omnipresence! God, methought,
> Had built him there a Temple: the whole World
> Seem'd *imag'd* in its vast circumference:
> No *wish* profan'd my overwhelmèd heart.
> Blest hour! It was a luxury,—to be!
>   (38–42, Coleridge's emphases)

Just as Wordsworth transforms his little plot of earth into conquest of the whole world, so Coleridge by climbing above the domestic scene and taking it in with his prophetic eye remakes it in the image of omnipresent divinity. As he must go "to fight the bloodless fight / Of Science, Freedom, and the Truth in Christ" (61–62), he takes that domesticity with him as a sign of his capacity to possess the world by possessing himself within his own space. The "slothful loves and dainty sympathies" of domestic affection may be trivial in comparison to the grand fight on which he is about to embark; they may even be a threat to his courage, "pampering the coward heart / With feelings all too delicate for use" (47–48). Nevertheless, they are necessary possessions, for they remind him, in "some delicious solitude" (58), of his power to possess without being possessed in turn.

Despite apparent similarities, this kind of self-possessing domesticity is totally opposed to Hemans's affectional poetics. Again and again, it is not possession that defines genuine domesticity, but the bonds that link sister to sister, brother to sister, wife to husband, etc., bonds that make each vulnerable to the other and all strong enough to withstand exile from the hearth and homeland. For Hemans, the true test of affectional power is *loss* of ownership, whether it is loss of loved ones or loss of property itself or both. *The Forest Sanctuary* is perhaps the most lucid statement of this idea, but there are many other poems that express it. "The Chamois Hunter's Love" inscribes many of the ironies of the relation between the power of feminine space and the masculine desire for self-possessing solitariness. The hunter's "love," the subject of the poem, contains the irony of the poem, for his love is both the woman who has left her "native" home behind in order to bind herself to the hunter and it is the feeling of devotion that he should have for his wife. The question of the poem is whether his "love" can be called genuine affection, the kind of love that gives his wife the courage to leave the safety of her parents' home for the danger of a mountainous, lonely hut. The poem begins with the disparity between her devotion and his wandering:

> Thy heart is in the upper world, where fleet the chamois bounds,
> Thy heart is where the mountain-fir shakes to the torrent-sounds;
> And where the snow-peaks gleam like stars, through the stillness
>   of the air,
> And where the Lauwine's peal is heard—Hunter! thy heart
>   is there.
>
> (see *Works* 6: 24–26)

The hunter's heart is amidst nature, where he wanders. Her heart, however, is with him, and she affirms her devotion even as she knows that he loves his solitary questing more than he loves her: "I know thou lov'st me well, dear friend! but better, better far, / Thou lov'st that high and haughty life, with rocks and storms at war." The politics of possession in the poem indicate the difficulty of "woman's lot on earth." She must leave "my blessed home, my father's joyous hearth, / With all the voices meeting there in tenderness and mirth" in order "to sit forsaken in thy hut." Hemans's repetition of possessive pronouns is crucial for understanding the poem. It is the hunter's hut that is isolated and forsaken. All that she owns has been given up: her father's home, which ironically is her father's rather than her own, and her own heart.

> It is my youth, it is my bloom, it is my glad free heart,
> That I cast away for thee—for thee, all reckless as thou art!

The line break accentuates her rare ownership of something only to snatch that possession from her. Her refrain ("And yet I will be thine") reveals the only compensation that she gains for having given up her only possession. What she gains is his ownership of her, and he gains her without having to lose anything himself. He has not even given her his heart, which she would gladly take. The wife's sacrifice records the conventional feminine heroics of longsuffering, but with a difference. By emphasizing the politics of possession, Hemans subtly demonstrates the desolating reality of the woman's plight. "Thy path is not as mine," she says, as she refuses "to woo thee down from

those thy native heights." It is difficult not to read the poem at least in part
with the duplicity of dramatic irony. We as readers and the wife know something that the hunter does not. We know what it means "[t]o wake in doubt
and loneliness," and yet to hold on to a firm commitment. We know what it
means to lose all possessions except the power of affection, which cannot be
given away even when the heart itself has been sacrificed on the altar of masculine wandering.

Hemans records woman in "The Chamois Hunter's Love," but she also records man through his absence, through his omission. In many other poems,
the weakness of masculine solitary wandering is even more pronounced. For
instance, in "Nature's Farewell" Hemans portrays a young man leaving "his
childhood's home" (see *Works* 6: 114–116). As he feels compelled to leave,
Nature mocks him gently, calling him back:

> "Knew'st thou with what thou art parting here,
> Long would'st thou linger in doubt and fear;
> Thy heart's light laughter, thy sunny hours,
> Thou hast left in our shades with the spring's wild flowers."

The "dreamer" youth thinks that he is going to conquer the world, but "Nature" knows better. It is only in losing what he already possesses that he will
come to understand the value of heart-knowledge:

> "Thou wilt visit the scenes of thy childhood's glee,
> With the breath of the world on thy spirit free;
> Passion and sorrow its depth will have stirr'd,
> And the singing of waters be vainly heard.
>
> "Thou wilt bear in our gladsome laugh no part—
> What should it do for a burning heart?
> Thou wilt bring to the banks of our freshest rill,
> Thirst which no fountain on earth may still."

Perhaps Hemans is envisioning the leave-taking of her own sons and forewarning them; perhaps she is thinking specifically of Wordsworth returning to
the banks of the Wye and recollecting his childhood with a heavy heart. The
world can give heart-experience ("passion and sorrow"), but only in the context of *human* bonds can heart-knowledge be gleaned. As the "burning heart"
comes home again—for so it must—it comes home in the guise of manly sentiment, no longer able to share the common desire of domestic space. As is
often the case for Hemans's adventurous male wanderers, what little he comes
to understand, he comes to understand too late: "But he knew not, till many
a bright spell broke, / How deep were the oracles Nature spoke!"

Hemans has here inverted the romantic formula of progression from
emasculating dreaminess to masculine worldliness that we see in such poems as Byron's "To Romance," Coleridge's "Reflections on Having Left a
Place of Retirement," Book 5 of Wordsworth's *Prelude,* and Keats's *Fall of
Hyperion.* For Hemans, the male is a dreamer not when he resides within
feminine space but once he begins to consider himself beyond the power of

domestic affection, beyond the impact of human bonds. Mistakenly, he thinks that solitary questing in the world will fulfill him, only to realize too late that his quest is a pipe dream that will bring him back home unable to share productively the affection that fortunately binds all human beings to one another and to God. Ironically, Hemans puts these "oracles" in the mouth of nature. It is nature, ironically, that ordains the domestic scene as the true site of human activity; it is nature that constrains human desire within the bonds of purely human affection.

8

The ideology of romanticism fails to explain Hemans's perspective on nature and human nature. So does Augustan ideology. Hemans may have returned to some aspects of Augustan ideology, such as the positive nature of literary influence and the empowering support of the literary coterie. Her acceptance of influence and coterie, however, is drastically different from the Augustans. She clearly understands that her adversary is not some other coterie, or some group of scribbling poets. If anything, she identifies herself with the otherness of an always potentially ousted scribbler, for the fear of her own monstrosity is always near. Her adversary, instead, is desire ever-reshaped by masculine ideology—not the men who embody and enact that ideological desire. In fact, she can gladly turn to such men—Byron and Wordsworth, for instance—when she needs precursors. Her heartful coterie entails literary partisanship only in the sense that it speaks for and with women. It is not designed to exclude others (like the Augustan coterie), but rather to support all of those women who share a desire to record, for the first time, woman's shared desire.

Women poets of the early nineteenth century cannot afford to ignore their literary fathers, nor do they desire to. They can begin to write only in the midst of historicized desire. The men who have recorded their own desire are needed, even when they have misrecorded women's desire. They refuse to attempt to forget the father's influence, the way both Augustans and romantics attempt to evade the mother. Instead, even as they mother themselves, having precious few literary mothers, they refuse to claim self-generating motherhood the way their literary fathers have claimed self-fathering. Their belated fame becomes always a reflected kind of emulative zeal. They embrace all influence that is congenial to their project and lovingly criticize and correct those with whom they cannot agree.

The contours of feminine desire are necessarily different from masculine desire in early nineteenth-century poetry. What we learn from examining these first successfully publishing women poets is how impoverished our notion of literary history is and how drastically that notion must change if we are to gain a more incisive critical awareness of our own assumptions, not just of gender, but of other factors as well. Reclaiming these first women poets does not simply mean that we should attach them to the house of romantic poetry for the sake of liberal inclusiveness. That would be a distortion of male romanticism and a disservice to the female affectional poets. It means more fundamentally that we must re-examine romanticism itself, and enriched with the knowledge garnered from these recovered sources, that we must re-write their history and in so doing rewrite our own. It means that we must re-consider the way we think about, research, teach, and write about the poetic traditions we have inherited. It means that we must reconstruct our critical vocabulary and the theoretical bases on which that vocabulary has been grounded. We must transform our critical practices to enable us to be more conscious of our blindness, always aware, however, of the impossibility of to-tal vision. In taking on these endeavors, we may find, like Jameson's Alda, exercise and improvement of our critical faculties and newly recordable plea-sures in the various views of human nature opened to us.

Notes

Introduction

1. An excellent discussion of the sociopolitical and educational status of women in the romantic period and how this status affects their capacity to write poetry can be found in Irene Tayler and Gina Luria, "Gender and Genre: Women in British Romantic Poetry," in *What Manner of Woman* (98–123).

2. This is the kind of question that Margaret Homans asks about Dorothy Wordsworth in Chapter 2 of her study *Women Writers and Poetic Identity*. Homans compares Dorothy's poetics with William's, explaining how their differences can be attributed to gender socialization. It's interesting to contrast Homans's discussion of the differences between Dorothy and William with the explanations of Jonathan Wordsworth, John F. Danby, and William Heath. Both of the latter depict William's poetic development as influenced by, but growing beyond Dorothy's sensibility. Heath writes: "Wordsworth's subordination—if that is the word for it—to his sister's sensibility was short-lived. The act of freeing himself from this dependence, whether deliberately or unconsciously, was the composition of his finest short poem [*Resolution and Independence*], which seems to bring together all that Wordsworth had known and wanted to be since they came to Grasmere." See *Wordsworth and Coleridge: A Study of Their Literary Relations in 1801–1802* (108–120); Danby's *The Simple Wordsworth* (98); and J. Wordsworth's *The Borders of Vision* (158).

3. In her study *The Proper Lady and the Woman Writer: Ideology as Style in the Works of Mary Wollstonecraft, Mary Shelley, and Jane Austen*, Mary Poovey analyzes Mary Shelley's "characteristic ambivalence with regard to female self-assertion" (115) and reads her work as a critique of romanticism (see especially Chapter 4).

4. In *The Romantic Ideology: A Critical Investigation* Jerome McGann presents a theoretical justification for literary historicism that is genuinely critical and distanced, using the present to ground a critique of the past and the past to critique the present. Clifford Siskin has also taken up this question, using what he calls "my new generic literary history" (11), based on Foucault's discourse analysis, to examine the historical and discursive logic of romantic writing (see *The Historicity of Romantic Discourse*).

5. Dominick LaCapra has explained the necessities and difficulties of such a project in *Historicism and Criticism*. He uses the term "transference" to denote the tendency of projecting our present concerns onto the past, but, as he argues, such transference also indicates "a notion of time not as simple continuity or discontinuity but as repetition with variation or change. . . . Transference implies that the considerations at issue in the object of study are always repeated with variations—or find their displaced analogues—in one's account of it, and transference is as much denied by an assertion of the total difference of the past as by its total identification with one's own 'self' or 'culture'" (72). Jerome McGann has also written instructively about this problem in *The Romantic Ideology* and more recently in *Social Values and Poetic Acts*, where he argues: "The poetic lays out its materials as representative things: it is an act of re-presenting. Furthermore, we are not to imagine that the poetic involves simple acts of imitation or

"reference"—representations *of* a given reality or human world. Being an event of language, the poetic 'makes representations,' as one might say of persons that they 'represent themselves' in certain ways. This quality of the poetic is important to keep in mind because it calls attention to poetry's mediated character—that in a crucial sense poetry's representations are self-representations" (82). Although I'm not sure why McGann needs to single out "poetry" here (perhaps the influence of romantic ideology, which tends to give priority to poetry), I do think it is useful to think of literary work in general as a form of "mediation" between past and present, enabling continuity through the discontinuities that it re-presents, as a representation of the culture that spawns it.

6. This is why I tend to question some of the tendencies of McGann and Julia Kristeva, both of whom, in quite different ways, claim for poetic discourse some kind of intrinsic revolutionary value (see, for instance, *Revolution in Poetic Language* 57). Because Kristeva tends to assume the historical continuity of grammatical rules and poetic practices, she also assumes the inherent antigrammatical structure of poetic discourse. As I try to make clear throughout this study, I believe that the ideology of a given literary work depends as much on the cultural practices of reading and writing which the reader, as a historical agent, brings to that literary work, as on the structures that take their meaning from the cultural context.

7. In *Sensational Designs,* Jane Tompkins offers an exemplary model for such a study. She presents a compelling rationale for examining how contemporary canons are informed and formed by cultural politics and history, and she shows why canonical "literature" itself must be reconnected to the historical contingencies of taste (see especially "Introduction: The Cultural Work of American Fiction").

Chapter 1

1. Letter 268 (1 May 1805) in *Letters of William and Dorothy Wordsworth* (1: 586–587).

2. Wordsworth himself uses the word "self-possession" in the 1805 version of *The Prelude* when he speaks of a "happy state" in which "harmonious imagery" comes along "like dreams" and mingles with "a consciousness of animal delight, / A self-possession felt in every pause / And every gentle movement of [his] frame" (Book 4, lines 392–399). Jonathan Wordsworth speaks of this self-possession as "a mind wholly sufficient, a body whose movements give delight even when suspended" (*Borders of Vision* 12).

3. For an enlightening study of the relation between the romantic values of solitude and landscape and the population debates of the early nineteenth century, see Frances Ferguson's essay "Malthus, Godwin, Wordsworth, and the Spirit of Solitude."

4. For a good discussion of the romantics' conflicting attitudes toward science, see Hans Eichner, "The Rise of Modern Science and the Genesis of Romanticism."

5. In *The Economics of Imagination* Kurt Heinzelman offers a fascinating study of the historical and conceptual relation between political economy and literature, with much of the study focusing on nineteenth-century discourse. See also Siskin's argument in Chapter 7 of *The Historicity of Romantic Discourse,* "High Wages and High Arguments" (151–163).

6. In "Romanticism and the Colonization of the Feminine," Alan Richardson rightfully cautions against viewing the literary tradition as "simply 'masculine,' " as he points out how "in moving from an 'Age of Reason' to an 'Age of Feeling,' male writers drew on memories and fantasies of identification with the mother in order to colonize the conventionally feminine domain of sensibility" (13). Although I fully agree with Richardson that "a strict duality of male writer as subject and woman (usually conflated with nature) as object" must be questioned, I think that we must also clarify how romantic writers, fearing that they are losing control of the literary tradition, do attempt to enforce "a strict duality." In other words, two interrelated phenomena occur simultaneously: the male writers' colonization of the feminine and their attempt to separate their

own self-possessing poetic endeavors from the very feminine which they appropriate. For an analysis of how romantic poets, especially Byron and Keats, attempt to master the domain of the feminine, which threatens them exactly because it serves as the basis for their sense of literary productivity and power, see Sonia Hofkosh's essay "The Writer's Ravishment."

7. For further discussion of Dorothy's gendered role in William's poetry (and especially in "Tintern Abbey"), see Homans, "Eliot, Wordsworth, and the Scenes of the Sisters' Instruction," reprinted in *Bearing the Word*. See also Susan Levin's *Dorthy Wordsworth and Romanticism.*

8. In a letter to William Harness, Byron writes: "The latter part of my life has been a perpetual struggle against affections which embittered the earliest portion; and though I flatter myself I have in a great measure conquered them, yet there are moments (and this was one) when I am as foolish as formerly." See Moore's *Life* in the *Works of Lord Byron* (2: 101).

9. In *Wordsworth and the Vocabulary of Emotion,* Josephine Miles estimates that there are 9000 statements naming "emotion and its signs" out of 53,000 lines of poetry, an average of once in every six lines (22). For historical discussions of the sources of romantic interest in the emotions, see Chapter 3 of Peter Thorslev's *The Byronic Hero* (35–50) and Chapter 1 of James Averill's *Wordsworth and the Poetry of Human Suffering* (21–54).

10. See Manning's *Byron and His Fictions* (65).

11. In *The Romantic Mother,* Barbara Schapiro analyzes the mother–son relations in romantic poetry, concluding that "Wordsworth's ecstatic moments express either conquest, or a harmonious, integrated relationship with the environment, as in *Tintern Abbey*. His moments of exultation display a true liberation, a real resolution of his ambivalent parental ties" (99). I would end the preceding sentence with the word "conquest," omitting the "either." Considering Schapiro's heavy reliance on traditional Freudian and objects-relations psychoanalysis, I can understand how she reaches such a conclusion. I think, however, that she reads Wordsworth as he desires to be read, rather than from a more critically distanced stance. I take a view much more similar to Gayatri Chakravorty Spivak, who uses revisionary psychoanalysis in her essay "Sex and History in *The Prelude*": "Wordsworth projects the possibility of being son *and* lover, father *and* mother of poems, male *and* female at once" (47). In " 'Behold the Parent Hen:' Pedagogy and *The Prelude*," Mary Jacobus explains this phenomenon in relation to Wordsworth's and Rousseau's educational systems: *"The Prelude* is not, as it represents itself, an account of Wordsworth's education at the hands of Nature. Rather, it's an educational treatise directed at the missing mother. . . . *The Prelude* repeats the self-constituting trope which makes *Emile* an account of how the child becomes father to the man without the help of his mother" (paper delivered at the English Institute, Cambridge, Mass., September 1986). See also James A. W. Heffernan's "The Presence of the Absent Mother in Wordsworth's *Prelude.*"

12. The now standard reading of Wordsworth, and I think a valid one, is to downplay nature's *controlling* role and to stress how the aim of his development is to grow beyond nature. However, it is still easy to overestimate Wordsworth's ready acceptance of nature's importance to him. For instance, Michael Cooke tends to do so in his study *Acts of Inclusion: Studies Bearing on an Elementary Theory of Romanticism,* in which he argues that the romantics incorporate and empower the feminine and dispose a change in the masculine, using the crucial role of Wordsworth's feminine nature as a primary case (see Chapter 3, "The Feminine as the Crux of Value"). Although this argument seems truer for Percy Shelley and Blake, it is extremely problematic for all of the male romantics. Cooke bases his claims on the premise of the "complementary wholeness" of the sexes sought by the romantics, but it is exactly this idea of complementariness that encourages the disempowerment of women, especially during the nineteenth century. As Kate Millett has shown in *Sexual Politics,* one of the most effective ways of subverting women's demands for equality during the nineteenth century was for

men to point to the way the sexes complement each other and then grant the equal
value of each sex's virtues (see especially pp. 106–111 and 179–201). And as Gilbert and
Gubar point out, no matter how potentially sympathetic romantic radicalism and rebelliousness might potentially make these poets to women, they were "after all fundamentally 'masculinist' with Milton" (211).

13. See *The Romantics Reviewed,* Part A, 1: 13–21, ed. Donald H. Reiman.

Chapter 2

1. In *The World of Pope's Satires,* Peter Dixon explains the import of conversation
to the Augustans. See especially Chapter 2 (14–39). Also see Jon P. Klancher's *The
Making of English Reading Audiences,* which traces the complicated relations among
the rise of market publishing, the increasing import of literary journals during the eighteenth and nineteenth centuries, and the changing attitude toward an enlarged reading
public. Klancher demonstrates how the journals tended to encourage the dialogic aspect
of writing and reading.

2. Maynard Mack states that "up to a point, the Romantic critics are right about
Pope. He *is* a city poet, not simply in the obvious ways they saw, but in deeper ways
they failed to see. . . . And always in Pope the thing that is being lost, or lost and
recovered, and lost again, is a vision of the civilized community, the City" (*The Garden
and the City* 4–5).

3. The paradox of Pope's situation is that he presents the guise of patronage although he has essentially begun to move away from the economic structure of patronage.
He wants the psychic and sociopolitical spirit of the institution without its monetary dependence. By selling his publications, he frees himself economically from a single patron,
but he binds himself to those who buy his works. Not surprisingly, the subscribers to his
works turn out to be such men and women who would serve as his patrons in the first
place. I am indebted to two books for the history of patronage: Brean S. Hammond's
Pope (especially 86 ff.) and A. S. Collins's *The Profession of Letters.*

4. In *This Dark Estate* Thomas R. Edwards points out how *The Epistle to Dr.
Arbuthnot* vacillates between control and outrage (104), and he claims that these outbursts humanize the speaker and allow us to sympathize with him (108). Morris also
points out how these outbursts are "a deliberate strategy," but he argues that such anger
allows Pope to balance Horatian and Juvenalian satire. "[I]ndignation is not his permanent state of mind or an uncontrollable passion, as it sometimes seems in Juvenal" (see
Genius of Sense 234–235).

5. For a discussion of Pope's use of Sporus's homosexuality, see also Eve Kosofsky
Sedgwick's *Between Men* (173–175).

Chapter 3

1. Not long after Coleridge becomes acquainted with Wordsworth, he writes a letter
to Cottle, which states: "I speak with heart-felt sincerity & (I think) unblinded judgement, when I tell you, that I feel myself a *little man by his side;* & yet do not think
myself the less man, than I formerly thought myself" (*Letters* 1: 325, Coleridge's emphasis). The latter part of this statement is problematic, and it becomes more difficult
for Coleridge to assert it as their relationship progresses. Several entries in Coleridge's
Notebooks make his intense gender anxiety palpable, especially his fear of lacking the
"manliness" that Wordsworth possesses. "[A]nd must I not be beloved *near* him except
as a Satellite?" he asks himself. "But O mercy mercy! is he not better, greater, more
manly, & altogether more attractive to any the purest Woman?" See the *Notebooks* 2:
3148 and 2998. Like Coleridge, many modern critics have tended to use gendered
locutions as a way of appraising romantic poetry. John Danby, for example, states

"Wordsworth . . . was the last great representative in English Poetry of the renaissance tradition. . . . They wrote for their capacities, they addressed themselves to the active capacities of their audience. . . . [T]he tradition might be called masculine in its aims and performance" (*The Simple Wordsworth* 146). Then he proceeds to describe the qualities of this "masculine" tradition, qualities that he obviously values himself: "Its values are those of order, control, discipline, decision, the wakeful mind that must weigh alternatives and decide between them. Keats was [on the other hand], as they said, effeminate" (149).

2. McFarland offers an excellent examination of Coleridge's psycho-literary development, tracing the significance of his artistic self-doubt within the context of social and familial relations. For a reading more empathetic with Coleridge (a Coleridgean reading) than mine, see Kelvin Everest's *Coleridge's Secret Ministry,* especially 11–44.

3. Christensen's Chapter 4 is especially helpful for understanding the way Coleridge uses Wordsworth's genius to claim his own poetic genius (118–185).

4. Of course, the poem that eventually becomes "Dejection" is originally a verse letter to Sara Hutchinson. The movement is from a specific woman addressee, with whom Coleridge is in love, to other male friends, to William specifically, to a generalized male ("Edmund"), back to a woman addressee now robbed of all specificity. It is almost as if Coleridge is attempting to strengthen his own poetic confidence by experimenting with these various influential listeners. To whom the poem is addressed is as important as the speaker's persona, for it helps to determine that persona.

Chapter 4

1. Poovey writes: "For the young Mary Shelley, the collision between what we now call the 'Romantic' model of originality and the 'Victorian' model of feminine domesticity was particularly dramatic. Not only did the public backlash against Mary Wollstonecraft provoke in her daughter an intense combination of pride and shame, anger and fear, but the social conservatism her father embraced after Wollstonecraft's death became as much a part of the young Mary Godwin's situation as her mother's ambiguous legacy." Poovey also points out how it is easier for Percy, being a male aristocrat, "to assert those principles [of independence and self-confidence] and act upon them even more flamboyantly than Wollstonecraft had done" (*The Proper Lady* 116).

2. See Chapters 2 and 3 of *The Proper Lady* (48–113).

3. In *Bearing the Word,* Homans, following Irigaray, argues that it is the cutting of the umbilical cord "[l]ike the primordial murder of the mother that makes possible the symbolic order" (24).

4. Since the story of Shelley's contorted relationships with women has been told and analyzed many times already, I will forego such a discussion here. See Richard Holmes's *Shelley: The Pursuit* and Nathaniel Brown's *Sexuality and Feminism in Shelley* (especially 36, 105–109, 138).

5. The outstanding studies of Shelley's utopianism include Ross Woodman's *The Apocalyptic Vision in the Poetry of Shelley,* which analyzes the conflict between Shelley's desire for transcendence of social reality and his desire for sociopolitical action; Michael Scrivener's *The Radical Shelley;* Richard Cronin's *Shelley's Poetic Thoughts;* P. M. S. Dawson's *The Unacknowledged Legislator: Shelley and Politics;* and Marilyn Butler's *Romantics, Rebels, and Reactionaries.* Each of these books has helped to shape my own understanding of Shelley's politics.

6. Nathaniel Brown discusses how Shelley reinvests the poetic commonplace that makes the eyes the window to the soul (*Sexuality and Feminism* 14–18).

7. In "Elective Affinity in the *Revolt of Islam,*" E. B. Murray argues that Shelley, influenced by the popular notion of "elective affinity," intends the child to be psychically born to Laon because Cythna wills it so, even as the tyrant impregnates her in his act of rape. This argument makes sense especially in light of Shelley's tendency to give priority to the mind or to spirit.

8. The definitive reading of *Prometheus Unbound* in these terms can be found in Earl Wasserman's *Shelley: A Critical Reading* (255–374).

9. The idea of *Prometheus Unbound* as a reader's allegory was first proposed by Newman I. White in "Shelley's *Prometheus Unbound,* or Every Man His Own Allegorist." In "Deconstruction or Reconstruction: Reading Shelley's *Prometheus Unbound,*" Tilottama Rajan offers a more refined and complicated version of this approach to the poem showing how questions of identity and difference in the self, in the reader (both implicit and explicit), in the work, and in the optional processes of reading (deconstructive, hermeneutical, performative) all converge within the lyrical drama. "It is limiting to see a text of this kind as a decentered void, because the mode of political allegory assumes some affective and referential power for literature, even as the choice of allegory rather than documentary problematizes this power. Of course there is a price to be paid for this power. As a text which continues to claim some relationship between literature and history, *Prometheus Unbound* recognizes its own historicity, its own vulnerability to having its significance constituted differently by different readers" (338). Shelley's poem self-consciously calls attention to the limits of its readers' histories not only to stress the limitations of desire potentially isolated by the act of reading, but also to enact the potential of what Jean Hall calls "the socialized imagination, the fusion of public and private concerns in a dance of world-creating harmony" (see "The Socialized Imagination" 348).

10. In John C. Bean's "The Poet Borne Darkly," for instance, in order to argue for the unity of the poem Bean switches the "unifying theme" from "the poet's quest for love" to "his quest for spiritual knowledge." Bean is able to solve structural and thematic problems by doing this, but what I see as the crucial problem still remains, and in fact is replicated within Bean's critical method. In "unifying" the poem, Bean further represses the role of the feminine "other" within the poem. For me, the real question of *Alastor* is how to reach out to the (feminine) other, whether that other embodies the potential for other-directed love or communally shareable "spiritual knowledge." In order to answer this question, we have to reincorporate the feminine into the poem and into our critical methods.

11. The apparent disparity between the narrator's comments in the preface and the poem's exemplum is considered the biggest critical problem of *Alastor*. Bean resolves the problem by unifying the poem around a single theme. Lisa Steinman, on the other hand, follows and elaborates on Wasserman's reading by stressing the role of skepticism. "The narrator too has failed to find a likeness of his ideal self," she writes, "and has produced a tale about the visionary's failure. And yet he has created his song, and this song, in following the footprints of the visionary and in showing us the narrator's desire, transforms the world" ("Shelley's Skepticism" 268). I would say rather that the narrator's song shows us how his self-possessing male desire *fails* to transform the world. For other attempts to clarify the relations among the poem, the preface, and Shelley's precursors, see Gerald Enscoe's *Eros and the Romantics* (70), Earl Leslie Griggs and Paul Mueschke's "Wordsworth as Prototype of the Poet," Joseph Raben's "Coleridge as Prototype of the Poet," Raymond Havens's "Shelley's *Alastor,*" and Bryan Cooper's "Shelley's *Alastor*: The Quest for a Vision." Like Steinman and unlike most other critics, I think the disparity between preface and poem should not be unified or explained away, but accentuated.

12. I am borrowing from Frederick Garber's language here. Garber writes: Wordsworth's "protection of the discreteness of the objects he experiences, his refusal . . . to overwhelm them with his own urgent, impelling being, is in part a protection of his own individuality, which he does not want to lose by blending it with another or by being swamped" (*Wordsworth and the Poetry of Encounter* 29).

13. As Homans points out, the romantic quest is always doomed from the beginning, because the poet needs his desire to be unfulfilled in order for the quest that gives meaning to his poetic project to remain unterminated (see *Bearing the Word* 160–107).

Chapter 5

1. For a good Wordsworthian rhetorical analysis of Wordsworth's poetry, see Don Bialostosky's *Making Tales*, especially 28–36. For a more detailed discussion of how Wordsworth exploits gender in order to turn his readers into ideological disciplines, see my article "Naturalizing Gender: "Woman's Place in Wordsworth's Ideological Landscape."

2. The question of Madeline's state of mind is crucial for interpreting the poem. Hagstrum identifies three categories of readers as following: 1) "modern metaphysical critics" who read Madeline's dream as imaginative vision and Porphyro's entering that dream as visionary transcendence of reality; 2) "realistic critics" like Jack Stillinger who see Madeline as a victim of Porphyro's seduction; and 3) ironists who accept both readings, arguing that the poem "leaves us with openminded undecidability." (See *The Romantic Body* 52.) In an impressive reading of the poem—but one I cannot fully accept—Stuart M. Sperry attempts to moderate and synthesize the transcendentalist and realist readings of the poem ("Romance as Wish-Fulfillment"). I suppose I fit most with the ironists, for I see Keats as encouraging both readings, indicating the conflict within his own desire, within us as readers, and within the ritual of romance itself. Also see Jack Stillinger's "The Hoodwinking of Madeline: Skepticism in *The Eve of St. Agnes*" (67–93).

Chapter 6

1. As Averill points out, "poetesses were in vogue in the eighties as readers demanded multiple editions of Anna Seward, Hannah More, Charlotte Smith, Ann Yearsley (the Poetical Milkwoman)" and as Maria Williams's first volumes of poetry appear during this time (*Wordsworth and the Poetry of Human Suffering* 30). See also Stuart Curran's essay "Romantic Poetry: The I Altered."

2. The paradox of More's strict submission to traditional social values despite her active engagement in social reform perhaps derives from her strong religious evangelism. Indeed, that paradox is even richer, for even though More's strong evangelical beliefs question or go beyond the authority of the established Anglican Church, she refuses to leave the established church, submitting herself, at least for all apparent purposes, to the authority of the Church of England even as she continues to practice her faith in a thoroughly evangelical manner, taking orders directly, so to speak, from the more pious and unmediated God of the evangelicals rather than from a God cloistered and mediated by centuries of accumulated ritual and authoritarian theology. Just as belief in total submission to a personal God ironically gives evangelical Prostestants more freedom of will, more literal freedom to determine their response to God's will, so More's total submission to the authority of established gender roles ironically gives her the assurance that her apparently free acts of the will are actually prescribed by that submission. In *The Industrial Reformation of English Fiction*, Catherine Gallagher has explained how this paradox manifests itself in More's fiction: "Hannah More's stories thus contain a consistent form of providential causality, but in these tracts the issue of freedom and determinism is complicated by the Evangelicals' simultaneous belief in both an all-determining Providence and human free will. For although the resigned, submissive characters seem passive in their relationship to the plot, their submission is maintained only by the utmost exertion of their wills" (38). As Gallagher has shown (see Chapters 1–3, pp. 3–87), the mixture of providential necessity and free will eventually encourages "these pious people" to espouse "certain social causes . . . on the basis of religious arguments" (41). Thus, we have the syndrome of otherworldly religious fervor leading to worldly sociopolitical activism and reform, a syndrome that becomes common during

the nineteenth and twentieth centuries, and that I think More helps to establish and legitimate, especially for women.

3. See *Wordsworth's Second Nature,* especially 143–155.

4. In *The Feminine Irony* Lynee Agress discusses the rise of feminine education as a theme in female fiction and nonfiction of early nineteenth-century Britain (see especially 47–96).

Chapter 7

1. A common contemporary criticism of Hemans is that her poetry is too sentimental and too pious. I'm not sure that her work is any more pious or sentimental than Wordsworth's, but romanticist critics tend to subordinate this aspect of Wordsworthian poetics in favor of the psychological and visionary aspects in order to make him more palatable to contemporary literary sensibilities. What Hemans values in Wordsworth is exactly the piety and sentiment which contribute to her own critical demise at the end of the Victorian period.

2. The *Athenaeum* was founded in 1828 by James Buckingham in an attempt to establish an independent, fair, progressive periodical that would treat all the serious issues of society, ranging from social problems, to scientific discoveries, to literary reviews. In his history of the *Athenaeum* Leslie Marchand writes: "There was no noticeable change in the policy and scope of the journal or its general appeal to readers after Buckingham gave it up, partly because its policies were directed from the beginning mainly by 'Apostles,' a group of earnest young Cambridge men who hoped to reform the world, both in and out of the church, not by revolution or change in institutions but by moral or spiritual regeneration. . . . The editors were romanticists in their views on literature and art. Their literary opinions were mild and liberal, except when they were aroused by attacks on the school of Coleridge, or by what they considered Utilitarian cant. The tone was youthful and enthusiastic, dominated by the hopefulness and optimism of the reformer" (*The Athenaeum: A Mirror of Victorian Culture* 11). Jewsbury's article appears under the editorship of Charles Wentworth Dilke, Keats's friend, and one of Dilke's most important contributors was Henry Chorley, Hemans's close friend and first biographer.

3. Byron's attitude toward Hemans represents the underside of masculine desire. Whereas Hemans's admiring male readers transmute their fear of her potential monstrosity into the sublime of encountering a thoroughly feminine muse-goddess, Byron's fear of Hemans's feminine influence is transmuted into condescending disdain. He calls her "Mrs. Hewoman" and a "feminine He-man," quipping, "I do not despise Mrs. Heman[s] but if [she] knit blue stockings instead of wearing them it would be better" (*Letters* 7: 158 and 182). Omission of the "s" in Hemans's name must be intentional, for four years earlier (1816), not only is he getting the name straight, he is also complimenting Hemans's poetry, notably *The Restoration of the Works of Art to Italy,* which is influenced, of course, by Byron's own poetry. "It is a good poem," he says, "—very" (*Letters* 5: 108). When he later reads *Modern Greece,* published anonymously, he correctly states that obviously the person has never visited Greece (*Letters* 5: 262–263). No doubt, Hemans is as disappointed by the limits on her travel experience as Byron. In one letter (of 1820) he gives her qualified praise and again spells her name right: "Mrs. Hemans is a poet also—but too stiltified, & apostrophic" (*Letters* 7: 113). Perhaps what Byron sees in Hemans, and in "any female or male Tadpole of Poet Turdsworth's" (7: 158), is the mirror image of his own potential feminization. She reminds him of his own "tender" poetic nature and perhaps his own unconventional sexuality; in her he sees a reflection of his own potential monstrosity as a sheman or a hewoman, and the most convenient way to distance himself from that monstrous image is to respond to Hemans aggressively, belittling her by using the negative epithets provided by a gender-conscious society.

Chapter 8

1. For a more detailed discussion of the relation between Scott's poetic romances and the sociopolitical climate of early nineteenth-century Britain, see my article "Scott's Chivalric Pose: The Function of Metrical Romance in the Romantic Period."

2. For an analysis of the way women revise prose romance for their own purposes, see Frances L. Restuccia's "Female Gothic Writing: 'Under Cover to Alice' " and Leslie W. Rabine's *Reading the Romantic Heroine.*

3. Rabine writes: "Yet an autonomous feminine voice remains in the romantic text, in the form of a fragmented excluded other. She is just as much a part of romanticism as the unified masculine romantic subject although in a form that differs greatly from his explicitly realistic presence. She can be found in aspects of the heroine that have been excluded from explicit representation of the text, in aspects of other female characters, or in other elements of the text. Her silenced voice gives evidence of itself not in overt utterances, but in the conflicts between levels and elements of the text that disrupt the dominant narrative voice" (8).

4. See Homans's *Women Writers and Poetic Identity* (56 and 90) and *Bearing the Word* (65), and Levin's *Dorothy Wordsworth and Romanticism.* In her final chapter "Dorothy Wordsworth and the Women of Romanticism," Levin tends to do what I argue against here, since she argues that "women created a romantic literature of their own," developing "a woman's version of that tradition, to explore certain 'feminine' possibilities within the general phenomenon of romanticism" (157). Although she offers brief readings of Mary Shelley's *Frankenstein* and *The Last Man,* Levin does not discuss any of the women's poetry; therefore it is difficult to know what is the basis of her labeling it romantic.

5. William Wordsworth uses the term "heart-experience" in the final paragraph of Book 5 of *The Prelude:*

> Here we must pause: this only let me add,
> From heart-experience, and in humblest sense
> Of modesty, that he, who in his youth
> A daily wanderer among woods and fields
> With living Nature hath been intimate,
> Not only in that raw unpractised time
> Is stirred to ecstasy, as others are,
> By glittering verse; but further, doth receive,
> In measure only dealt out to himself,
> Knowledge and increase of enduring joy
> From the great Nature that exists in works
> Of mighty Poets. (584–595)

Predictably, his heart-experience and knowledge are ultimately related back to his originary myth of nature's ordination, rather than to the affectional praxis of human communities. This is especially ironic since Book 5 is supposedly devoted to explaining the influence of books on the poet's development. By displacing the thoroughly human knowledge of "mighty Poets" with the "great Nature" that fosters that knowledge, Wordsworth once again is able to distance himself from the threat of human influences.

6. Of course, in Delacroix's painting Liberty raises the tricolor in her right hand and bears a musket in her left. In his *Critical Catalogue* of Delacroix's paintings, Lee Johnson explains one of the potentially accurate legends that has become identified with the painter's source for Liberty. During the 1830 Revolution, a laundry girl, searching for her brother, found his naked corpse. "Counting ten bullets in his chest, she swore to kill as many Swiss. She shot nine, but as she tore her tenth cartridge a Captain of lancers killed her with a blow of his sabre" (1: 147). Such a legend suggests the reality of women's more active role during the revolutions in France as well as the way such a

reality could be allegorized into a more idealistic image of the feminine. Delacroix is so impressed by the image of feminine Liberty leading the proletarians that he is able to capture perfectly the spirit of revolution even despite his ambivalent politics (see Johnson 1: 146). Interestingly, something similar could be said of Hemans's portrayal of Ximena. Despite the poet's Tory leanings, she is compelled to record the spirit of women's revolutionary strength.

7. This is why romanticist theory and criticism does not apply to Hemans's work without substantial distortion of her own aims and methods. Such criticism tends to focus on one of the following critical traditions: 1) developing a mythological system in the tradition of Northrop Frye; 2) describing a naturalist symbolic system in the tradition of M. H. Abrams; 3) employing a structuralist approach to figurative language in the style of Paul de Man; 4) inventing a genealogy of influences in the manner of Harold Bloom; 5) exploring a hermeneutics that attempts to resolve the conflict between modern self-consciousness and transcendental art in the tradition of Geoffrey Hartman. None of these critical approaches, which have dominated romantic studies for the last thirty years, sheds much light on feminine poets like Hemans, at least partly because they are based on those very romantic assumptions which repressed feminine influence in the first place. For an insightful analysis of the theoretical and literary historical relations between romantic writers and contemporary critics, see Jonathan Arac's *Critical Genealogies: Historical Situations for Postmodern Literary Studies* (especially Part 1, pp. 1–113).

8. In Chapter 5 of *Sensational Designs,* "Sentimental Power: *Uncle Tom's Cabin* and the Politics of Literary History" (122–146), Tompkins makes a similar argument concerning nineteenth-century sentimental American novels by women: "The very grounds on which sentimental fiction has been dismissed by its detractors, grounds which have come to seem universal standards of aesthetic judgment, were established in a struggle to supplant the tradition of evangelical piety and moral commitment these novelists represent. In reaction against their world view, and perhaps even more against their success, twentieth-century critics have taught generations of students to equate popularity with debasement, emotionality with ineffectiveness, religiosity with fakery, domesticity with triviality, and all of these, implicitly, with womanly inferiority" (123). Exactly the same statement applies to the popular women poets of nineteenth-century Britain and twentieth-century critics of this period, except, as we have seen, the process of detraction and dismissal begins during the very decades (the 1790s through the 1830s) in which their popularity is greatest, so later modern romanticists could more easily ignore these once popular but now obscure "poetesses" than perhaps Americanists could ignore the popularity of nineteenth-century women's fiction.

9. See Helen Ashton's *Letty Landon* and Laman Blanchard's *Life and Literary Remains of L.E.L.* Even though Ashton's biography of Landon is an imaginative re-creation based on the limited sources available, it captures well the historical conditions and the probable psychological state of a feminine poet living in early nineteenth-century Britain.

10. Quoted by Lucy Newlyn in *Coleridge, Wordsworth, and the Language of Allusion* (18).

Bibliography

Abrams, M. H. *Natural Supernaturalism: Tradition and Revolution in Romantic Literature.* New York: W. W. Norton, 1971.

Agress, Lynne. *The Feminine Irony: Women on Women in Early-Nineteenth-Century English Literature.* Rutherford, New Jersey: Fairleigh Dickinson University Press, 1978.

Altick, Richard D. *The English Common Reader: A Social History of the Mass Reading Public, 1800–1900.* Chicago: University of Chicago Press, 1957.

Arac, Jonathan. *Critical Genealogies: Historical Situations for Postmodern Literary Studies.* New York: Columbia University Press, 1987.

Ashton, Helen. *Letty Landon.* New York: Dodd, Mead, 1951.

Averill, James H. *Wordsworth and the Poetry of Human Suffering.* Ithaca: Cornell University Press, 1980.

Baillie, Joanna. *The Dramatic and Poetical Works.* 2nd ed. London: Longman, Brown, Green, & Longmans, 1851.

Baker, Jeffrey. *Time and Mind in Wordsworth's Poetry.* Detroit: Wayne State University Press, 1980.

Barbauld, Anna Laetitia. *The Works with a Memoir by Lucy Aikin.* 2 vols. London: Longman, Hurst, Rees, Orme, Brown, & Green, 1825.

Bateson, F. W. *Wordsworth: A Re-Interpretation.* London: Longmans, Green & Co., 1954.

Bean, John C. "The Poet Borne Darkly: The Dream-Voyage Allegory in Shelley's *Alastor.*" *Keats-Shelley Journal* 23 (1974): 60–76.

Bialostosky, Don H. *Making Tales: The Poetics of Wordsworth's Narrative Experiments.* Chicago: University of Chicago Press, 1984.

Blanchard, Laman. *Life and Literary Remains of L.E.L.* 2 vols. Philadelphia: Lea & Blanchard, 1841.

Bloom, Harold. *The Anxiety of Influence: A Theory of Poetry.* London: Oxford University Press, 1973.

———. "The Internalization of Quest-Romance." In *Romanticism and Consciousness.* 3–24.

———. *Poetry and Repression: Revisionism from Blake to Stevens.* New Haven: Yale University Press, 1976.

———, ed. *Romanticism and Consciousness: Essays in Criticism.* New York: W. W. Norton, 1970.

———. *The Visionary Company: A Reading of English Romanticism.* 1961; Ithaca: Cornell University Press, 1971.

Bogel, Fredric V. *Acts of Knowledge: Pope's Later Poems.* Lewisburg, New Jersey: Bucknell University Press, 1981.

Bostetter, Edward. *The Romantic Ventriloquists.* 1963; Seattle: University of Washington Press, 1975.

Brisman, Susan Hawk. "Unsaying His High Language: The Problem of Voice in *Prometheus Unbound.*" *Studies in Romanticism* 16 (1977): 51–86.

Brown, Laura. *Alexander Pope.* New York: Basil Blackwell, 1985.

Brown, Nathaniel. *Sexuality and Feminism in Shelley.* Cambridge: Harvard University Press, 1979.

Burke, Edmund. *Reflections on the Revolution in France.* Ed. Conor Cruise O'Brien. 1790; New York: Penguin Books, 1979.

Burns, Robert. *Poems and Songs*. Ed. James Kinsley. Oxford: Oxford University Press, 1978.

Butler, Marilyn. *Romantics, Rebels, and Reactionaries: English Literature and Its Background, 1760–1830*. New York: Oxford University Press, 1981.

Byron. *Childe Harold's Pilgrimage and Other Poems*. Ed. John D. Jump. London: J. M. Dent & Sons, 1975.

———. *Don Juan*. Ed. T. G. Steffan, E. Steffan, and W. W. Pratt. New Haven: Yale University Press, 1973.

———. *Byron's Letters and Journals*. 12 vols. Ed. Leslie Marchand. Cambridge: Harvard University Press, 1973–1982.

———. *Poetical Works*. Ed. Frederick Page. New ed. John Jump. Oxford: Oxford University Press, 1970.

Carhart, Margaret S. *The Life and Work of Joanna Baillie*. Yale Studies in English 64. Albert S. Cook, ed. New Haven: Yale University Press, 1923.

Carswell, Donald. *Sir Walter: A Four-Part Study in Biography*. London: John Murray, 1930.

Chandler, James K. *Wordsworth's Second Nature: A Study of the Poetry and Politics*. Chicago: University of Chicago Press, 1984.

Chodorow, Nancy. "Family Structure and Feminine Personality." In *Women, Culture, and Society*. 43–66.

———. *The Reproduction of Mothering: Psychoanalysis and the Sociology of Gender*. Berkeley: University of California Press, 1978.

Chorley, H. F. "Original Papers." *The Athenaeum*. 395 (1835): 391–392.

———. *Memorials of Mrs. Hemans with Illustrations of Her Literary Character from Her Private Correspondence*. 2 vols. London: Saunders & Ortley, 1836.

Christensen, Jerome. *Coleridge's Blessed Machine of Language*. Ithaca: Cornell University Press, 1981.

Coleridge, S. T. *Collected Letters*. 6 vols. Ed. Leslie Griggs. Oxford: Clarendon Press, 1956.

———. *The Notebooks*. Ed. Kathleen Coburn. Vols. 1 and 2. New York: Pantheon Books, 1957 and 1961; Vol. 3. Princeton: Princeton University Press, 1973.

———. *Poetical Works*. Ed. Ernest Hartley Coleridge. Oxford: Oxford University Press, 1978.

Collins, A. S. *The Profession of Letters: A Study of the Relation of Author to Patron, Publisher, and Public, 1780–1832*. London: Routledge & Sons, 1928.

Cooke, Michael G. *Acts of Inclusion: Studies Bearing on an Elementary Theory of Romanticism*. New Haven: Yale University Press, 1979.

Cooper, Bryan. "Shelley's *Alastor:* The Quest for a Vision." *Keats-Shelley Journal* 19 (1970): 63–76.

Crabbe, George. *The Complete Poetical Works*. 3 vols. Ed. Norma Dalrymple-Champneys and Arthur Pollard. Oxford: Clarendon Press, 1988.

Cronin, Richard. *Shelley's Poetic Thoughts*. New York: St. Martin's Press, 1981.

Curran, Stuart. "Romantic Poetry: The I Altered." In *Romanticism and Feminism*. 185–207.

Danby, John F. *The Simple Wordsworth: Studies in the Poems, 1797–1807*. New York: Barnes & Noble, 1961.

Dawson, P. M. S. *The Unacknowledged Legislator: Shelley and Politics*. Oxford: Oxford University Press, 1980.

de Beauvoir, Simone. *The Second Sex*. Tr. and ed. H. M. Parshley. New York: Vintage Books, 1952.

Dekker, George. *Coleridge and the Literature of Sensibility*. New York: Barnes and Noble, 1978.

Deleuze, Gilles and Félix Guattari. *Anti-Oedipus: Capitalism and Schizophrenia*. Minneapolis: University of Minnesota Press, 1983.

de Man, Paul. *Blindness and Insight: Essays in the Rhetoric of Contemporary Criticism*. 2nd ed. Rev. Wlad Godzich. 1971; Minneapolis: University of Minnesota Press, 1983.

———. *The Resistance to Theory*. Theory and History of Literature 33. Minneapolis: University of Minnesota Press, 1986.

Dixon, Peter. *The World of Pope's Satires: An Introduction to the Epistles and Imitations of Horace.* London: Methuen, 1968.

Eagleton, Terry. *The Function of Criticism: From "The Spectator" to Post-Structuralism.* London: Verso, 1984.

Edwards, Thomas R. *This Dark Estate: A Reading of Pope.* Berkeley: University of California Press, 1963.

Eichner, Hans. "The Rise of Modern Science and the Genesis of Romanticism." *PMLA* 97 (1982): 8–30.

Eliot, T. S. *The Use of Poetry and the Use of Criticism.* Cambridge: Harvard University Press, 1933.

Enscoe, Gerald. *Eros and the Romantics: Sexual Love as a Theme in Coleridge, Shelley, and Keats.* Paris: Mouton, 1967.

Everest, Kelvin. *Coleridge's Secret Ministry: The Context of the Conversation Poems, 1795–98.* New York: Barnes & Noble, 1979.

Fabricant, Carole. "Binding and Dressing Nature's Loose Tresses: The Ideology of Augustan Landscape Design." *Studies in Eighteenth-Century Culture.* 8 (1979): 109–135.

Ferguson, Frances. "Malthus, Godwin, Wordsworth, and the Spirit of Solitude." In *Literature and the Body: Essays on Populations and Persons.* Ed. Elaine Scarry. Baltimore: Johns Hopkins University Press, 1988.

———. *Wordsworth: Language as Counter-Spirit.* New Haven: Yale University Press, 1977.

Ferry, David. *The Limits of Mortality: An Essay on Wordsworth's Major Poems.* Middletown, Connecticut: Wesleyan University Press, 1959.

Frye, Northrop. *The Anatomy of Criticism: Four Essays.* Princeton: Princeton University Press, 1957.

———. *Fables of Identity: Studies in Poetic Mythology.* New York: Harcourt, Brace, Jovanovich, 1963.

———. *The Secular Scripture: A Study of the Structure of Romance.* Cambridge: Harvard University Press, 1976.

———. *A Study of English Romanticism.* Chicago: University of Chicago Press, 1968.

Gallagher, Catherine. *The Industrial Reformation of English Fiction, 1832–1867.* Chicago: University of Chicago Press, 1985.

Garber, Frederick. *Wordsworth and the Poetry of Encounter.* Urbana: University of Illinois Press, 1971.

Gifford, William. *Quarterly Review* 24 (1820): 130–139.

Gilbert, Sandra M. and Susan Gubar. *The Madwoman in the Attic: The Women Writer and the Nineteenth-Century Literary Imagination.* New Haven: Yale University Press, 1979.

Gilligan, Carol. *In a Different Voice: Psychological Theory and Women's Development.* Cambridge: Harvard University Press, 1982.

Greenburg, Martin. *The Hamlet Vocation of Coleridge and Wordsworth.* Iowa City: University of Iowa Press, 1986.

Griffin, Dustin H. *Alexander Pope: The Poet in the Poems.* Princeton: Princeton University Press, 1978.

Griggs, Earl Leslie and Paul Mueschke. "Wordsworth as Prototype of the Poet in Shelley's *Alastor.*" *PMLA* 49 (1934): 229–245.

Hagstrum, Jean H. *The Romantic Body: Love and Sexuality in Keats, Wordsworth, and Blake.* Knoxville: University of Tennessee Press, 1985.

Hall, Jean. "The Socialized Imagination: Shelley's *The Cenci* and *Prometheus Unbound.*" *Studies in Romanticism.* 23 (1984): 339–350.

Hall, Spencer. "Wordsworth's 'Lucy' Poems: Context and Meaning." *Stuides in Romanticism* 10 (1971): 159–175.

Hammond, Brean S. *Pope.* Brighton: Harvester Press, 1986.

Hartman, Geoffrey. *Wordsworth's Poetry, 1787–1814.* New Haven: Yale University Press, 1971.

Havens, Raymond. "Shelley's *Alastor.*" *PMLA* 15 (1930): 1098–1116.

Hazlitt, William. *Lectures on the English Poets.* 2nd ed. London: Taylor and Hessey, 1819.

Heath, William, *Wordsworth and Coleridge: A Study of their Literary Relations in 1801–1802*. Oxford: Clarendon Press, 1970.

Heffernan, James A. W. "The Presence of the Absent Mother in Wordsworth's *Prelude*." *Studies in Romanticism*. 27 (1988): 253–272.

Heinzelman, Kurt. *The Economics of the Imagination*. Amherst: University of Massachusetts Press, 1980.

Hemans, Felicia Dorothea. *The Poetical Works*. Philadelphia: J. B. Lippincott, 1859.

———. *The Works of Mrs. Hemans, with a Memoir by her Sister*. 6 vols. Edinburgh: William Blackwood & Sons, 1839.

———. "German Studies No. 1." *New Monthly Magazine and Literary Journal* ns 3 (1834): 1–5.

Hofkosh, Sonia. "The Writer's Ravishment: Women and the Romantic Author—the Example of Byron." In *Romanticism and Feminism*. 93–114.

Holmes, Richard. *Shelley: The Pursuit*. New York: E. P. Dutton, 1975.

Homans, Margaret. *Bearing the Word: Language and Female Experience in Nineteenth-Century Women's Writing*. Chicago: University of Chicago Press, 1986.

———. "Eliot, Wordsworth, and the Scenes of the Sisters' Instruction." *Critical Inquiry* 8 (1981): 223–241.

———. *Women Writers and Poetic Identity: Dorothy Wordsworth, Emily Brontë and Emily Dickinson*. Princeton: Princeton University Press, 1980.

Jackson, Wallace. *Vision and Re-Vision in Alexander Pope*. Detroit: Wayne State University Press, 1983.

Jacobus, Mary. " 'Behold the Parent Hen:' Pedagogy and *The Prelude*." Paper. English Institute. Cambridge. Sept. 1986.

Jameson, Anna. *Shakespeare's Heroines: Characteristics of Women, Moral, Poetical, and Historical*. 2nd ed. 1833; London: G. Bell & Sons, 1911.

Jeffrey, Francis. *Edinburgh Review* 50 (1829): 32–47.

Jewsbury, Maria Jane. *The Anthenaeum* 172 (1831): 104–105.

Johnson, Lee. *The Paintings of Eugène Delacroix: A Critical Catalogue 1816–1831*. 2 vols. Oxford: Oxford University Press, 1981.

Johnson, Samuel. *Samuel Johnson's Literary Criticism*. Ed. R. D. Stock. Lincoln: University of Nebraska Press, 1974.

Jones, M. G. *Hannah More*. Cambridge: Cambridge University Press, 1952.

Keats, John. *The Letters*. 2 vols. Ed. Hyder Edward Rollins. Cambridge: Harvard University Press, 1958.

———. *The Poems of John Keats*. Ed. Jack Stillinger. Cambridge: Harvard University Press, 1978.

Klancher, Jon P. *The Making of English Reading Audiences, 1790–1832*. Madison: University of Wisconsin Press, 1987.

Kristeva, Julia. *Desire in Language: A Semiotic Approach to Literature and Art*. Ed. Leon S. Roudiez. Tr. by Thomas Gora, et al. New York: Columbia University Press, 1980.

———. *Revolution in Poetic Language*. Tr. Margaret Waller, with introduction by Leon S. Roudiez. 1974; New York: Columbia University Press, 1984.

LaCapra, Dominick. *History and Criticism*. Ithaca: Cornell University Press, 1985.

Landon, L. E. *The Poetical Works*. Boston: Phillips, Sampson, & Co., 1853.

Levin, Susan M. *Dorothy Wordsworth and Romanticism*. New Brunswick: Rutgers University Press, 1987.

Levinson, Marjorie. *Wordsworth's Great Period Poems: Four Essays*. New York: Cambridge University Press, 1986.

Mack, Maynard. *The Garden and the City: Retirement and Politics in the Later Poetry of Pope 1731–1743*. Toronto: University of Toronto Press, 1969.

Manning, Peter J. *Byron and His Fictions*. Detroit: Wayne State University Press, 1978.

Marchand, Leslie. *The Athenaeum: A Mirror of Victorian Culture*. New York: Octagon Books, 1971.

McFarland, Thomas. *Romanticism and the Forms of Ruin: Wordsworth, Coleridge, and Modalities of Fragmentation*. Princeton: Princeton University Press, 1981.

McGann, Jerome J. *Fiery Dust: Byron's Poetic Development*. Chicago: University of Chicago Press, 1968.

———. *The Romantic Ideology: A Critical Investigation.* Chicago: University of Chicago Press, 1983.

———. *Social Values and Poetic Acts: The Historical Judgment of Literary Work.* Cambridge: Harvard University Press, 1988.

Mellor, Anne K. *English Romantic Irony.* Cambridge: Harvard University Press, 1980.

———. "*Frankenstein:* A Feminist Critique of Science." In *One Culture: Essays in Science and Literature.* Ed. George Levine. Madison: University of Wisconsin Press, 1987. 287–312.

———. *Mary Shelley: Her Life, Her Fiction, Her Monsters.* New York: Methuen, 1988.

———. "Possessing Nature: The Female in *Frankenstein.*" In *Romanticism and Feminism.* 220–231.

———, ed. *Romanticism and Feminism.* Bloomington: Indiana University Press, 1988.

Miles, Josephine. *Wordsworth and the Vocabulary of Emotion.* New York: Octagon Books, 1965.

Mileur, Jean-Pierre. *Vision and Revision: Coleridge's Art of Immanence.* Berkeley: University of California Press, 1982.

Millett, Kate. *Sexual Politics.* New York: Ballantine Books, 1969.

Montagu, Mary Wortley. *Essays and Poems, and Simplicity, a Comedy.* Ed. Robert Halsband and Isobel Grundy. Oxford: Clarendon Press, 1977.

Moore, Thomas. *Complete Poetical Works.* 2 vols. New York: Thomas Y. Crowell & Co., 1895.

———. *Memoirs, Journal and Correspondence.* 8 vols. Ed. John Russell. London: Longman, Brown, Green, & Longmans, 1856.

———. *The Works of Lord Byron, with his Letters and Journals, and his Life.* 17 vols. London: John Murray, 1833.

More, Hannah. *The Complete Works.* 2 vols. New York: Harper & Brothers, 1835.

Morris, David B. *Alexander Pope: The Genius of Sense.* Cambridge: Harvard University Press, 1984.

Murray, E. B. " 'Elective Affinity' in *The Revolt of Islam.*" *JEGP* 67 (1968): 570–585.

Newlyn, Lucy. *Coleridge, Wordsworth, and the Language of Allusion.* New York: Oxford University Press, 1986.

Norton, Andrews. *The North American Review* 24 (1827): 443–463.

———. "Review of Mrs. Hemans's *Forest Sanctuary.*" *The Christian Examiner.* Rpt. Boston: Isaac R. Butts & Co., 1826.

Ortner, Sherry B. "Is Female to Male as Nature Is to Culture?" In *Women, Culture, and Society.* Ed. Michelle Zimbalist Rosaldo and Louise Lamphere. 67–87.

Owen, Harriet Mary Browne. *Memoir of Mrs. Hemens* in *Works.* Vol. 1.

Peacock, Thomas Love. "The Four Ages of Poetry." Rpt. in *Shelley's Critical Prose.* Ed. Bruce R. McElderry, Jr. Lincoln: University of Nebraska Press, 1967. 158–172.

Perkins, David. *Wordsworth and the Poetry of Sincerity.* Cambridge: Harvard University Press, 1964.

Poovey, Mary. *The Proper Lady and the Woman Writer: Ideology as Style in the Works of Mary Wollstonecraft, Mary Shelley, and Jane Austen.* Chicago: University of Chicago Press, 1984.

Pope, Alexander. *The Poems.* Ed. John Butt. New Haven: Yale University Press, 1963.

Raben, Joseph. "Coleridge as Prototype of the Poet in Shelley's *Alastor.*" *Review of English Studies* 17 (1966): 278–292.

Rabine, Leslie W. *Reading the Romantic Heroine: Text, History, Ideology.* Ann Arbor: University of Michigan Press, 1985.

Ragussis, Michael. *The Subterfuge of Art: Language and the Romantic Tradition.* Baltimore: Johns Hopkins University Press, 1978.

Rajan, Tilottama. "Deconstruction or Reconstruction: Reading Shelley's *Prometheus Unbound.*" *Studies in Romanticism* 23 (1984): 317–338.

Reiman, Donald H. Introduction. *Records of Woman.* By Felicia Hemans. New York: Garland, 1979.

———, ed. *The Romantics Reviewed: Contemporary Reviews of British Romantic Writers.* New York: Garland, 1972.

Restuccia, Frances L. "Female Gothic Writing: 'Under Cover to Alice.' " *Genre* 19 (1986): 245–266.

Review of *Modern Greece, A Poem. Blackwood's Edinburgh Magazine.* 1 (1817): 515–518.

Richardson, Alan. "Romanticism and the Colonization of the Feminine." In *Romanticism and Feminism.* 13–25.

Robinson, Charles E. *Shelley and Byron: The Snake and Eagle Wreathed in Fight.* Johns Hopkins University Press, 1976.

Rosaldo, Michelle Zimbalist and Louise Lamphere, eds. *Woman, Culture, and Society.* Stanford: Stanford University Press, 1974.

Ross, Marlon B. "Naturalizing Gender: Woman's Place in Wordsworth's Ideological Landscape." *ELH* 53 (1986): 391–410.

––––––. "Scott's Chivalric Pose: The Function of Metrical Romance in the Romantic Period." *Genre* 19 (1986): 267–297.

Russo, John Paul. *Alexander Pope: Tradition and Identity.* Cambridge: Harvard University Press, 1972.

Rzepka, Charles J. *The Self as Mind: Vision and Identity in Wordsworth, Coleridge, and Keats.* Cambridge: Harvard University Press, 1986.

Said, Edward. *The World, the Text, and the Critic.* Cambridge: Harvard University Press, 1983.

Schapiro, Barbara A. *The Romantic Mother: Narcissistic Patterns in Romantic Poetry.* Baltimore: Johns Hopkins University Press, 1983.

Scott, Walter. *The Complete Political Works.* Ed. Horace E. Scudder, Boston: Houghton, Mifflin, 1900.

Scrivener, Michael Henry. *Radical Shelley: The Philosophical Anarchism and Utopian Thought of Percy Bysshe Shelley.* Princeton: Princeton University Press, 1982.

Sedgwick, Eve Kosofsky. *Between Men: English Literature and Male Homosocial Desire.* New York: Columbia University Press, 1985.

Shelley, Mary. *Frankenstein: or, the Modern Prometheus.* Ed. James Rieger. Chicago: University of Chicago Press, 1974.

Shelley, Percy. *Poetical Works.* Ed. Thomas Hutchinson and G. M. Matthews. London: Oxford University Press, 1970.

––––––. *Shelley: Political Writings.* Ed. Roland A. Duerksen. New York: Appleton-Century-Crofts, 1970.

Simpson, David. *Wordsworth and the Figurings of the Real.* Atlantic Highlands, New Jersey: Humanities Press, 1982.

Siskin, Clifford. *The Historicity of Romantic Discourse.* New York: Oxford University Press, 1988.

Sperry, Stuart M., Jr. "Romance as Wish-Fulfillment: Keats' *The Eve of St. Agnes.*" *Studies in Romanticism* 10 (1971): 27–43.

Spivak, Gayatri Chakravorty. *In Other Worlds: Essays in Cultural Politics.* New York: Methuen, 1987.

Steinman, Lisa. "Shelley's Skepticism: Allegory and *Alastor.*" *ELH* 45 (1978): 255–269.

Stillinger, Jack. *The Hoodwinking of Madeline and Other Essays on Keats's Poems.* Urbana: University of Illinois Press, 1971.

Storey, Mark. *Byron and the Eye of Appetite.* New York: St. Martin's Press, 1986.

Tayler, Irene and Gina Luria. "Gender and Genre: Women in British Romantic Poetry." In *What Manner of Woman: Essays in English and American Life and Literature.* Ed. Marlene Springer. New York: New York University Press, 1977. 98–123.

Thorslev, Peter L., Jr. *The Byronic Hero: Types and Prototypes.* Minneapolis: University of Minnesota Press, 1962.

Tighe, Mary. *Psyche, with Other Poems.* 4th ed. London: Longman, Hurst, Rees, Orme, and Brown, 1812.

Todd, F. M. *Politics and the Poet: A Study of Wordsworth.* London: Methuen & Co., 1957.

Tompkins, Jane. *Sensational Designs: The Cultural Work of American Fiction, 1790–1860.* New York: Oxford University Press, 1985.

Tuckerman, H. T. "An Essay on Her Genius." Introduction to *Poems of Felicia Hemans.* Ed. Rufus W. Griswold. New York: Leavitt & Allen, 1853.

Wasserman, Earl R. *Shelley: A Critical Reading.* Baltimore: Johns Hopkins University Press, 1971.

Weinbrot, Howard D. *Alexander Pope and the Tradition of Formal Verse Satire*. Princeton: Princeton University Press, 1982.

Weiskel, Thomas. *The Romantic Sublime: Studies in the Structure and Psychology of Transcendence*. Baltimore: Johns Hopkins University Press, 1976.

Weller, Earle V. *Keats and Mary Tighe: The Poems of Mary Tighe with parallel passages from the work of John Keats*. 1928; New York: Modern Language Association, 1966.

White, Newman I. "Shelley's *Prometheus Unbound*, or Every Man His Own Allegorist." *PMLA* 40 (1925): 172–184.

Wilson, John. *Noctes Ambrosianae*. 4 vols. Ed. J. F. Ferrier. Edinburgh: Blackwood & Sons, 1876.

Wolfson, Susan J. *The Questioning Presence: Wordsworth, Keats, and the Interrogative Mode in Romantic Poetry*. Ithaca: Cornell University Press, 1986.

Wollstonecraft, Mary. *A Vindication of the Rights of Woman*. New York: Penguin, 1975.

Woodman, Ross Greig. *The Apocalyptic Vision in the Poetry of Shelley*. Toronto: University of Toronto Press, 1964.

Woolf, Virginia. *A Room of One's Own*. New York: Harcourt, Brace & World, 1929.

Wordsworth, Jonathan. *The Music of Humanity: A Critical Study of Wordsworth's "Ruined Cottage" Incorporating Texts from a Manuscript of 1799–1800*. London: Nelson, 1969.

———. *William Wordsworth: The Borders of Vision*. Oxford: Clarendon Press, 1982.

Wordsworth, William. *Home at Grasmere*. Ed. Beth Darlington. Ithaca: Cornell University Press, 1977.

———. *The Letters of Dorothy and William Wordsworth*. Vol. 1. 2nd ed. Arranged & ed. Ernest de Selincourt and rev. Chester L. Shaver. Oxford: Oxford University Press, 1967.

———. *Poetical Works* (in one volume). Ed. Thomas Hutchinson and Ernest de Selincourt. 1904; New York: Oxford University Press, 1985.

———. *The Prelude or Growth of a Poet's Mind (Text of 1805)*. Ed. with introduction by Ernest de Selincourt. London: Oxford University Press, 1960.

———. *The Ruined Cottage and the Pedlar*. Ed. James Butler. Ithaca: Cornell University Press, 1979.

———. *Selected Prose*. Ed. John O. Hayden. New York: Penguin Books, 1988.

Index